LEGAL EDUCATION
and Public Policy

Library of Congress Catalog Number: 2011028473
ISBN: 978-1-4128-4287-7
Printed in the United States of America

Library of Congress Cataloging-in-Publication Data

Lasswell, Harold D. (Harold Dwight), 1902-1978.
  [Analysis of political behaviour]
  Legal education and public policy / Harold D. Lasswell ; with a new introduction by Irving Louis Horowitz.
        p. cm.
  Originally published under title: The analysis of political behaviour. New York : Oxford University Press, 1947.
  ISBN 978-1-4128-4287-7
    1. Political science. 2. Policy sciences. 3. Law--Political aspects. 4. Political leadership--Psychological aspects. I. Title.

JA38.L4 2012
320.01--dc23

                                                              2011028473

LEGAL
EDUCATIO
and Public Policy

HAROLD D. LASSWELL
With a new introduction by Irving Louis Horowitz

Transaction Publishers
New Brunswick (U.S.A.) and London (U.K.)

CONTENTS

ACKNOWLEDGMENTS

The author desires to acknowledge the courteous permission received from responsible publishers and editors to reproduce, in whole or in part, articles appearing in the following journals and symposia : *American Journal of Sociology ; American Political Science Review ; American Scholar ; Chinese Social and Political Science Review ; Ethics ; Personnel Journal ; Political Quarterly* (London) *; Psychiatry : Journal of the Biology and the Pathology of Interpersonal Relations ; Public Opinion Quarterly ; Studies in Philosophy and Social Science ; Yale Law Journal ; The Future of Government in the United States, Essays in Honor of Charles E. Merriam,* edited by Leonard D. White.

The following colleagues have kindly allowed me to make use of joint papers : Myres S. McDougal, Professor of Law, Yale Law School ; Gabriel Almond, Assistant Professor of Political Science, Brooklyn College ; Dr. Renzo Sereno, University of Chicago. Aid in exploring some of the newer avenues to knowledge has been received from many sources. In particular, my acknowledgments go to the Social Science Research Committee of the University of Chicago ; the Rockefeller Foundation, New York City ; and the Library of Congress, Washington, D.C. Dr. Nathan C. Leites, of the Department of Political Science, University of Chicago, has been a productive collaborator and keen critic.

H. D. L.

INTRODUCTION TO THE TRANSACTION EDITION

[Harold Lasswell's *Legal Education and Public Policy*]

There is such a cascade of criticism launched against the social sciences—from the clerical right, which takes issue with its secular examinations as the end point rather than start point in studies of science and society, to the ideological left, which so often stands or falls (more often the latter) with teleological explanations of events—that anything short of moral judgment of the good society becomes an object of ridicule. As a consequence there is a tendency on the edges of social commentary to overlook or minimize the qualitative improvement social science has brought about in the study of human beings and human relations from the intimate sphere to the global framework. In the process of developing foundations of social research that have now become commonplace guides to every decent society, I would argue that few individuals have exercised a greater or more positive role in combating such emotive responses to social science and its public policy consequences than Harold D. Lasswell, who was born in 1902 and died in 1978.

It was my privilege to know Lasswell in several connections: as a member of an executive committee on publications for the *American Political Science Association*, and even more, as publisher of Transaction, which counts six of his book publications on its lists. This will be the seventh. Perhaps the most troublesome of our interactions occurred around the high moments of the Reverend Sun Myung Moon, founder of the Unification Church. Although he continues to live into his nineties, his religious, moral, and political movement had its high watermark in the 1970s. It was during this period that a collection of essays and articles that I edited on this ostensible religious movement, *Science, Sin, and Scholarship: The Politics of Reverend Moon*, was issued by MIT Press.

In one brief encounter, I dared question my very senior and esteemed colleague, Harold D. Lasswell, of whom I was then and still remain very much in awe. At a gathering of the executive committee of the APSA publications committee in the mid 1970s, I asked why he participated in the global conferences of the Unification Church. It all seemed so bizarre, so remote from Lasswell's history and center of intellectual gravity. I suggested in subdued terms that such involvement lowered his prestige among colleagues and devotees alike. To say the least, he was displeased with the question and its grave implications; especially since I raised the issue in the context of the offices of the American Political Science Association, which could be called a semi-public setting and not at all restricted to personal dialogue. But he was a gentleman, and after turning red as a beet, he regained his composure, and offered a series of explanations for his decision that still haunts and disturbs me. It went something like what follows; needless to add he cannot be held accountable for this paraphrase.

To start with, Irving, the Unification Church does not censor or instruct me on what I was to say, or whom I was to criticize. These trips to far away places were either to places I had known in earlier life or wanted to see—in this instance, without charge. As for the nature of the movement Moon led, it was certainly no worse than that of academics who participated in the Communist Party gatherings, and with far greater controls at the top than any I have witnessed elsewhere—much in which I have participated. Finally, I would ask of those critics to read what I write, and make judgments on such grounds, not presumed organizational goals of Reverend Moon, or for that matter, his attitudes toward the United States.

This is neither the time nor place to argue such rationalizations; although I confess to having done just that with Harold at the same luncheon table chaired by the then executive director of the APSA, Evron Kirkpatrick. In retrospect, what comes to mind is the frailty of leadership, of ways in which older "retirees" of academic professions are cast aside and forgotten in American society. Ours is a society that celebrates the young, and not one in which the elderly are honored. In brief, the history of ideas is not especially well-regarded as the "hot field" of the age. In that desperate effort not to end up on the ashcan of professional memories, the decision Lasswell made (and hardly his alone) to actively participate in Reverend Moon's unity of sciences program should be understood as a cry to be heard, not an embrace of a religious credo. The world belongs to the present, even as it must impact the past as its tries to interpret the future.

This brief segue of a personal sort, is what I would like to emphasize in the need, and not just right, to reproduce Lasswell's professional papers on political behavior. It is easily forgotten that this great figure in the development of public policy was first and foremost a student of behavior. For it was that aspect of human existence that provides for intelligence, for the machinery of discovery of the world as it is, in order to make it just a tad bit better. For that is what Harold was about, making the world a bit better by calling forth the tools of social and political analysis to help us in that task.

This volume of astonishing essays has been properly titled *Legal Education and Public Policy*; first because, *prima facie*, it occupies nearly half the volume as such, second it is a way to acknowledge his growing anxieties about a world of revolution, violence, and terror, and the mechanism of law as such in addressing such matters. That he did so without taking recourse in vague and fatuous appeals to world law and world order is an indication of how close to the marrow Harold remained. Third, this is a way to acknowledge the place of Myres S. McDougal in relation to his work, not to mention the many students of McDougal who shared with Lasswell the effort to fuse the legal and moral in the conduct of public policy. It was McDougal who coined, somewhat cynically, "the international law of war." This did not deter either of these Yale figures to argue the case and the ultimate benefits of democratic values as a ground for legal thought. What makes the use of the word *astonishing* appropriate however is not simply the subject matter that remains so vital to our political discourse, but the unusual accuracy of a variety of statements about the proximate future, tossed about with an ease that only someone who took seriously the task of social and political research as both a predictor of events, and even more the ethical consequences on which such predictions are grounded could achieve.

The major statement, at least in length, of the opening essay in this volume was one of many associations Lasswell had with McDougal. Together they went on to write *Law and Public Order in Space* (1963) and *Human Rights and World Public Order: The Basic Policies of an International Law of Human Dignity* (1980). This linkage was more than collegial. It was rooted in their shared belief that if law in an increasingly lawless world "is adequately to serve the needs of a free and productive commonwealth, it must be conscious, efficient, and systematic training for policy making." The linkage of legal training and policy making is not simply a theoretical mandate, but one that finds reflection in the actual conduct of government. This is what gives credence to the idea of "the empirical" to such long range goals. The problem that Lasswell had, and not an inconsequential one, is how the laws of a nation-state are to be elevated to the laws of international society. He desired to avoid the appellation of being a "realist," legal and otherwise, like Hans Morgenthau and Hans Kohn. For that meant a retreat from the pledge to democratization. But like so many others, he was unable to square this circle by a national law that carried military and police functions behind its scaffold, and an international law that bypassed the function and source of power.

Several of the smaller essays, like Lasswell's paper on "The Psychology of Hitlerism," written in 1933 and published in the *Political Quarterly* of Great Britain, provide a profound insight into what became the killing fields of Europe in the 1940s. Indeed, it is the point in Lasswell's career when he came closest to a Marxist view of European events. It is a curious, ironic twist that it was the Stalinist and the Soviet Party apparatus that rejected this class analysis. He chose instead to see the rise of National Socialism in Germany, as did R. Palme Dutt, Harold Laski, and other moguls of official party lines, as some collusion of the German bourgeoisie with the Nazi statist apparatus to oppress and destroy the socialist proletariat and assorted factory workers' unions. The strange fusion of virtue and ideology that the socialist ideologues of the pre-war days put forth is not a position that Lasswell could abide with much less wear with any comfort.

Lasswell saw early on that the class formations were complex, and that throttling the trade union movement was not the same as demobilizing the working classes, especially the lower strata of the lower middle classes, while lowering the operational costs of the upper bourgeoisie. The older parties of the right, aligned as they were with the aristocracy and plutocracy, could not suffice for such mass mobilization. He also recognized that some older portions of the upper bourgeoisie were quite early on willing to finance the march to power of Hitlerism. The

division of the Left, with socialist and social democratic leaders denouncing communists to Nazi Party officials, served to
further strengthen the participation of National Socialism in
building its economic base. For the communist party of Germany it was far simpler to surrender reality and retain illusions,
than the empirical way about, and here they had the benefit of
the German Protestant peasant tradition, in which the whole
class formation could unite in the excoriation of the Jew, who
was seen as a source of class misery cloaked behind economic
prominence and culture formations alike. He also introduced
an option that had been forgotten in post mortem analysis of
the regime: "Germans have assumed the yoke of Hitlerism in
the name of freedom, socialism and nationalism."

The brief essay on the rise of the propagandist harkens to
one of Lasswell's dominant career interests: the place of manufactured public opinion in shaping the symbols of the national
interest. In this, Lasswell sees the United States as the veritable
apotheosis of propaganda information and the politics of dissemination (at that time mostly via radio). But the intriguing
element here is the role of propaganda, or public opinion
management in shifting public values from the conduct of economic chaos and collapse engendered by the Great Depression
of 1929-1939 into a fundamental shift toward government as
the repository of good things, or if not the good themselves,
then at least a repository of equity of treatment. Government,
the state, that is to say The New Deal, made individuals in
both the working classes and lower bourgeoisie aware of an
alternative source of political energy and economic stability.
Through its legal and taxing powers the government became
not simply a regulatory mechanism but a public policy institution that could provide what the class system operating in
laissez-faire terms was unable to accomplish.

An intriguing exercise would be to examine how these cross-
cutting tendencies reflect themselves in the present structure of
economic authority in the United States. It is evident that the
public demands for increased goods and services, fueled by the
propaganda machine, has as its price corresponding demands
that government provide precisely what is being advertised. If
this made the poor people content, it would then matter little
that the bourgeoisie would approach electoral politics about its
own selfish ends in view. The theme of putting in places the

special interests and good tidings pledged by government has long been understood as the payoff to the business classes. In that sense, Lasswell appreciated that public policy in the new era would result in more government than ever. That would remind all operative classes that they are getting precisely what they have asked for—a larger slice of the economic pie. The government does just that in exchange for what it wants: greater social tranquility through respect for old laws, support for new laws, and increased taxes. It is not difficult to discern the broad outlines of the present welfare arrangements in the United States, Asia, and Europe.

An element in this volume of essays too readily ignored is the huge impact Lasswell had on bringing Freudian psychiatry and psychoanalysis into the study of political behavior. It is not that personal data is an invention of psychoanalysis or psychiatry. The political science community was never quite at home with such connections. But at the time of these essays, it was Freudian techniques that linked personality distortion into political decision-making that was most in evidence and most troubling. Lasswell singles out the interviewing technique of the psychiatrist, what he calls "the insight interview," as a criti-cal pivot to the study of political behavior. The development of intensive techniques predicated on universal norms rather than local customs and traditions permit analysis without the usual hostilities of the native leaders and influential elites to the social sciences. The Freudian world opened up self-analysis to political scientists who otherwise would see neuroses in the leaders they study but without self-referential points to measure their own biases. Lasswell saw the Freudian dimen-sion as the accelerating rapid advancement of the nature of social science research. Indeed, it permitted the development of political psychology that has catapulted the field to a major aspect of political science studies such as decision making among leaders, neurotic patterns of behavior encouraged by dictatorial unchecked norms of rule, and the behavior of specific actions by mass movements.

Looking at this aspect of Lasswell three quarters of a century after the publication of these essays, a certain exaggerated en-thusiasm for this line of research is in evidence. Then again, that was true of all branches of the culture and ideology. Christopher Caldwell, in his own work on the sources of poetry, *Illusion and*

Reality, made the same large claims for Freudian analysis as the unique twentieth century dimension of Marxian thought. It might be noted that Caldwell too was subject to criticism and discomfort by this presumed supplement to Marxism-Leninism. Psychiatry not only helped define the age, but served as an instrument in its very definition. Neurosis was seen as the collective malady of an epoch that made political prediction difficult if not impossible. The "taste" for psychology that Lasswell exhibited as a feature of mass technologies like radio are, of course, equally apparent in the more recent studies of television and electronic transmissions as such. There is a tendency, incorrect in my estimation, of looking past those studies of mass communication in the radio age. These obscure papers in fact, along with those of Paul Lazarsfeld and Robert Merton contained in their 1950 volume on *Continuities in Social Research*, served as foundation stones for quantitative shifts in a technologically informed view of communication studies. But Lasswell went beyond empirical studies, and drew conclusions in the fundamental alterations in mores and manners of the political culture that such technologies brought about.

The great essay on "The Garrison State," what Lasswell termed was "not a 'dogmatic forecast'. Rather it is a picture of the possible," had its first appearance in a small Asian journal of political affairs, but its impact was greatest when it first appeared in the January 1941 issue of *The American Journal of Sociology*. I suspect that this republication in a sociological journal had more to do with his connections to the University of Chicago than to a particular belief that the master sociological journal of its era was necessarily its best venue. But whatever the reason, the essay takes its place as one of the great statements on the emergence of the military-industrial state. What made it so unique is precisely the linkage of the needs of the military regime to the sentiments of the masses. He captured the Orwellian moment then in progress, by a configuration of social forces that make the breakdown of democratic norms not only palatable, but downright enviable.

The Garrison State fused the masses and the elites; it did this by addressing the morale factor in the modern economic order. It created work in the place of unemployment, it abolished the distinction between the battlefield and the home front, it placed society at the service of the unifying factor such as collective

responsibly in place of industrial initiative, government by
plebiscite in place of elections as the source of public opinion,
and the ideology of governance in lieu of the need for eccentric
opinions or outdated theologies. And for those who still did
not get the point of totalitarian rule, the choice was simple and
stark: obey or die. This notion bears a superficial similarity to
C. Wright Mills' "military-industrial complex." However, Mills
either did not see, or did not want to draw the conclusions that
Lasswell held: the diabolical bargain that huge and amorphous
social classes tacitly view themselves as partners in a new post-
industrial "social contract." For Mills it was ultimately capitalism as a social class rather than elitism as a political system that
defined the military government axis. The problem is that the
same set of forces was at work in the organization of National
Socialism in Germany and international communism in Russia.
The fact of a garrison state complex could hardly be explained
by the economic sub-system as such. Lasswell understood as
much, and hence the shortcomings of a pure economic interpretation of history or politics.

The key to this essay's well-regarded approach and I daresay
to Lasswell's work as such, is the unitary character of totali-
tarianism in stark and uncompromising terms. Those who saw
the problem of the twentieth century as one entirely grounded
in Italian fascism, German Nazism, or Russian communism,
missed the point of his linkage of these mighty European powers to the scenarios very much on display in the United States
of America as well. Lasswell could be a hard and even crusty
analyst of events, but his thought was rooted in the democratic
tradition pure and simple. That his concluding notes should be
references to the work of Hans Speier and Robert S. Lynd—a
pairing of an anti-Nazi refugee and an American sociologist
rooted in the American soil—was not so much an endorsement
of their specific approaches, as a recognition of new forms of
alliance that emerged in the depths of a pluralist culture. The
new era of the garrison state was a global force unto itself, not
a footnote to the history of any single economic doctrine.

Ultimately the task of a democratic culture is to embrace
social policy and genuine public opinion. The new face of to-
talitarianism went beyond its masks to search for options, and
the key option is public policy. For therein is the best hope for
clear statements of what the world could become by the best

efforts of free people, in contrast to what it was becoming at the dawn of the Second World War. Lasswell was not given to optimistic slogans or vapid pleasantries about a future world united in peace-loving endeavors. He had a strong aversion to tendentious formulations that promised much only to end in a swamp of confusion and contradiction. Democracy is a work in progress; but dictatorship is a system that does not fade in the night at its sight. These somewhat eclectic essays by a great scholar display just how far we have come, and painfully, how much we have yet to travel.

Irving Louis Horowitz
June 2011

I

HOW TO INTEGRATE SCIENCE, MORALS AND POLITICS

CHAPTER I

THE DEVELOPING SCIENCE OF DEMOCRACY *

The developing science of democracy is an arsenal of implements for the achievement of democratic ideals. We know enough to know that democracies do not know how to live ; they perish through ignorance—ignorance of how to sustain the will to live and of how to discover the means of life. Without knowledge, democracy will surely fall. With knowledge, democracy may succeed.

The significant advances of our time have not been in the discovery of new definitions of moral values or even in the skilful derivation of old definitions from more universal propositions. Our inheritance of brief definitions has been adequate. The advances of our time have been in the technique of relating them to reality.

In the process science has clarified morals. This, indeed, is the distinctive contribution of science to morality. Science can ascertain the means appropriate to the completion of moral impulse—means at once consistent with general definitions of morality and compatible with the fulfilment of moral purpose. The traditional sentences that define and justify morals, in common with all such sentences, use words of ambiguous reference. Each sentence is itself part of reality but refers to a larger reality. Standing alone, however, such a sentence is cryptic and fragmentary. The function of science is to complete it.

General sentences must be made part of a special language composed of postulates, definitions, and operational rules. The

* From *The Future of Government in the United States, Essays in Honour of Charles E. Merriam* [edited by Leonard D. White] (Chicago, 1942).

1

rules must specify how the key terms are to be used by observers who may take up various standpoints for the observation of reality. For artistic and propaganda purposes we may tolerate dangling sentences of ambiguous reference. But as students of politics we are seriously concerned with connecting them with the realities of Cabinet meetings, Congressional inquiries, trade association conventions, and general staff conferences ; hence it is necessary to participate in a long process of disciplined clarification.

Consider any one-sentence definition of the value that distinguishes democratic societies from other forms of human association. We may affirm that the democratic value is regard for the dignity of man. Hence society is democratic when it puts this value into practice ; it is then a commonwealth of mutual deference. Just what do these words mean ? How can the observer of political events decide when to use the term " democratic " in a sense consistent with the definition ?

Are we to determine the truth about a given community by limiting our attention to the government or by examining the structure of business corporations, ecclesiastical organizations, and fraternal orders as well ? Are we to instruct observers to rely upon the clauses of written constitutions or upon official election returns ? Are we to instruct them to look beyond the official figures to determine to what extent those who vote feel themselves free of intimidation ? Must they go beyond these questions to explore deeper attitudes, such as the degree to which the members of the community have a lively sense of genuine participation in the determination of democracy ? Without such accompanying specifications, no definition of democracy that purports to relate to reality can be other than word-mongering.

The friends of democracy who have turned to science have been acutely dissatisfied with the ambiguity of inherited political, social, and philosophical literature. To speak of the movement toward science as a revolt against philosophy is to fall into error. It was not impatience with democratic morals that led to the de-emphasizing of general definitions ; it was discontent with the chronic incompleteness of formulation in the traditional literature. The turning to the specific is more properly understood as a stampede to complete philosophy, to reconsider every generality for the purpose of relating it to observable reality.

The mood of impatience was directed as much against speculative science as against philosophy, whenever speculative science was cultivated far beyond the limits of available data. This attitude is exemplified in what Wesley Mitchell wrote about his student impressions of philosophy and economic theory : " Give me premises and I could spin speculations by the yard. Also I knew my ' deductions ' were futile . . . [Veblen] could do no more than make certain conclusions plausible—like the rest." [1]

Mitchell, and his American fellow-exponents of the scientific study of society, lived near the end of a long epoch of cultural optimism, in which democratic values had moved triumphantly toward universal acceptance. Democratic doctrine was affirmed by both the rulers of society and the most powerful exponents of revolutionary change. The Marxists did not reject democracy ; on the contrary, they declared that the only path to democracy was the overthrow of capitalism. They acknowledged the historical connection between free enterprise and free society ; but they denied that the capitalistic method of organizing the productive forces was any longer widening the area of human freedom. On the contrary, the Marxists suggested that the inexorable march of monopoly spelled the doom of freedom until the inevitable triumph of the revolutionary proletariat.

There were two replies to the Marxist indictment—to ignore the facts or to restudy them. In America the " individualistic " attitude was to deny the facts, to affirm the substantial identity between democratic values and the existing state of affairs. To liberals, and particularly to middle-western liberals, certain facts were all too conspicuous. By assembling them, they hoped to bring reality into closer conformity with doctrine. In intellectual circles hope of reform, not certainty of revolution, was the dominant view of the future.[2] In such a setting democratic values were not in question.

The Enlarging Focus of Attention

The urge for relevance has enormously enlarged the permissible focus of attention among professional students of government in America. Most of those who completed their graduate work during the 'nineties were equipped to study political doctrine, public law, and comparative government (with special reference

[1] *Methods in Social Science; A Case Book* [edited by Stuart A. Rice] (Chicago, 1931), pp. 676-7.
[2] Academic figures like Daniel De Leon, Columbia University, were most exceptional.

to Great Britain and the United States).   During subsequent decades the leading members of the profession steadily enlarged the scope of their studies to include political parties, pressure groups, and administrative agencies.   As they moved from the letter of the law to the significant features of the total context of socio-personal relations, they dealt with progressively more subtle themes connected with public opinion and political leadership, and they enlarged the geographical range of their minds to include the whole panorama of world events.

The expanding focus of scholarly attention is aptly exemplified in the publications of Charles E. Merriam, who began his career with *History of the Theory of Sovereignty Since Rousseau* (New York, 1900)—a conventional study of political doctrine.   Subsequent books contributed to the discovery of the larger environment ; there were studies of parties, public opinion, administration, leadership, world politics (the last being the " Civic Training Series ").   Meanwhile, other colleagues were following similar lines of development.   Charles A. Beard began with a study in English institutional history, *The Office of Justice of the Peace* (New York, 1904), and went ahead to explore the total economic and cultural setting of American institutions.   He studied administrative processes not only in the United States but in Yugoslavia and Tokyo and in recent years dealt with national policy in the light of world movements.

NEW PROCEDURES OF OBSERVATION

The expanding focus of attention brought with it the use of new procedures for the observation of reality.   By tradition students of government were chiefly collectors, making use of records of events they did not directly see.   They depended upon historical documents and court reports.   In the new search for the total relevant context, they relied in greater degree on more direct methods of observation, like the interview or direct participation.   Vigorous personalities, like James Bryce and A. Lawrence Lowell, had always kept alive the more active elements of the tradition that made such men as De Tocqueville possible.   There has, of course, always been a struggle within the breast of the scholar between to " wait and read " and to " go and see ".   When the scholar has a lecture-room the temptation is to narrow his orbit between the library and the podium, resisting the centrifugal lure of the great beyond.   In recent times the quest of reality has somewhat neutralized the centripetal forces of desk and rostrum, so that procedures of observation have been more widely utilized.

The repertory of procedures has itself expanded to meet new demands. Random personal contact has been supplemented by the use of carefully prepared questionnaires or polls given to representative groups. Time has been devoted to the preparation of forms for entering and tabulating the primary data of observation. In this connection the methods of the social anthropologist have been particularly stimulating ; the observer of non-literate societies has learned to discipline his casual impressions by candid records.[3]

COLLECTIVE FACT-GATHERING

Significantly enough, fact-gathering operations have become more collective as they became more abundant. Many of the facts contributed to political science have been observed by professors who had the aid of students or research assistants. This is the provenience of most of the material collected under the auspices of the Social Science Research Committee of the University of Chicago, or the Institute of Human Relations at Yale. But special research bureaux, often unconnected with universities, have contributed extensively to recent science. These agencies are more free than teaching departments to adopt strict standards with regard to research personnel and to develop a corps of helots to perform routine operations. Teaching departments are more tolerant of " time out " for courses and seminars, less careful of deadlines and somewhat more impatient with the deserving " mediocrity " than the more professionalized bureau of investigation. Conspicuous among the private bureaux are the National Bureau of Economic Research and the Brookings Institution. However, the government itself is playing a more prominent rôle in reporting on reality, notably through such executive agencies as the National Resources Planning Board and such congressional channels as the Temporary National Economic Committee.

It is significant that when Charles E. Merriam surveyed the state of political research at the end of World War I he emphasized the under-equipment of the college professors of government, who were supposed to contribute to their subject but who were often driven to thresh over old straw through sheer lack of

[3] Bronislav Malinowski wrote forcefully of method in *Argonauts of the Western Pacific* (London, 1922).

facilities for harvesting new facts.[4] The idea of a permanent corps of research assistants comparable with the laboratory technicians of the physical scientist was all too new. Handicapped by lack of funds for travel and for advanced study, each successive crop of students was thrown back upon its parochial frame of reference, destitute of opportunity to explore the larger world about which they were nominally qualified to speak. Hence the heavy stress by the fact-gatherers upon the need of ample funds for large-scale training programmes and upon the advantages of continuous collaboration in the prosecution of research. Hence, too, the institutional form of the Social Science Research Council, the university social science research council, and the National Resources Planning Board of the federal government.

New Ideas of the Scope of Politics

Sweeping changes in the focus of scholarly effort do not fail to bring about a revision of basic concepts, especially with regard to the scope of political science itself. Many American students had identified their field of investigation with government, but they had failed to distinguish between the meaning of government as a local institution and government as a function of society. As a function of society, government is the making of important decisions. What is locally called government often has very little to do with this function. We know that what is called government in a mill town may have but a modicum of influence on important decisions ; they may be made by the board of directors of the mill. If the function of government is the subject of research, the mill directors are the ones to be investigated, not the shadow-men locally called government officials.

As the scope of scholarly attention widened, more students of government became conscious of the difference between government as a social function and government as a locally named institution. They reached out after definitions of political science that would clarify their new feeling for relevance.[5]

It would be idle to assert that a conceptual or a terminological consensus has developed concerning the scope of political science. In terms congenial to the present writer, the function of government is power. (For the moment we will speak of the function of government or politics interchangeably.) Power

[4] *New Aspects of Politics* (Chicago, 1925).
[5] See Merriam, Charles E., *Political Power ; Its Composition and Incidence* (New York, 1934) ; Catlin, G. E. G., *The Science and Methods of Politics* (New York, 1927).

means the making of important decisions, and the importance of decisions is measured by their effect on the distribution of values. Values are such objects of desire as deference, safety, income. The power of individuals and groups is measured by the degree of their participation in the making of important decisions.

The definition of government and politics varies according to the nature and variety of values taken into consideration. For certain purposes it is convenient to circumscribe the scope of political science to the study of power. For more comprehensive comparisons the scope may be enlarged to include the study of other forms of deference, such as respect and insight. For certain broad problems of comparative politics it is expedient to conceive of the scope of political science as embracing the distribution of safety and income as well as deference. At this point the subject-matter of political science approaches that of the social sciences as a whole and merges with it. The most inclusive definition of political science thus speaks of it as the study of influence and the influential.[6]

The enlarged view of the scope of political science just referred to is not confined to the limits of the United States. On the contrary, parallel processes of generalization have gone forward throughout Western European social science. Never officially recognized as a separate university discipline in Europe, none the less the " sociology of politics " has been cultivated by specialists who sought an inclusive frame of reference for their study of changing distributions of value.[7]

THE SCIENCE OF DEMOCRACY

With the more inclusive science of politics many special sciences are possible. A special science is concerned with the fulfilment and preservation of specific forms of state and society. The science of democracy—one of these special sciences—bears much the same relation to general political science that medicine has to biology. Medicine is a branch of the total field of biology, limiting itself to a single frame of reference, the disease process. Democratic science is restricted to the understanding and possible control of the factors upon which democracy depends.

Suppose we explore in more detail the structure of this

[6] Lasswell, Harold D., *Politics : Who Gets What, When, How* (New York, 1936).
[7] Distinguished European names include Gaetano Mosca, Vilfredo Pareto, Max Weber, Robert Michels.

developing science of democracy.   A democratic government can be defined in terms of shared power, a democratic society in terms of shared deference (power, respect, insight) or shared influence (deference, safety, income).   What are the limits within which sharing may vary in a government or in a society that is entitled to be called " democracy " ?   With respect to power, we may stipulate that a democratic government authorizes majority participation in the making of important decisions.   The majority may express itself directly (direct legislation) or indirectly (elected officials).   The majority must participate actively (a large majority—let us specify a two-thirds majority—must qualify to vote and take part in elections).   The overwhelming majority must be free of intimidation.   Moreover, they must have confidence in their capacity to exert effective control over decisions, whether or not they vote on any given occasion. Communities are democratic if they conform to these specifications, and they are democratic in the degree to which they conform to them.

DEMOCRACY : A PATTERN OF SYMBOL AND PRACTICE

The foregoing definition of democracy refers both to symbol and to practice.   The prescription that the majority must be eligible to take part in elections is a reference to symbols—to words combined in sentences accepted as authoritative.   A statement is authoritative when it is agreed that it formulates what ought to be done.   Whom shall we ask in order to ascertain the state of expectation in a given community ?   In our society we have authorities, persons who are supposed to know about accepted doctrine.   There are lifelong students of constitutional law, and we would not hesitate to include them among our authorities on the state of expectation with regard to " government ".   They are not authorities, however, upon all of the decision-making rules in our society.   We do not expect them to be informed about the rules of trade associations, trade unions, churches, fraternities, producers' or consumers' co-operatives, or monopolistic private business.   Hence we must enlarge our jury.

In whatever way we constitute our panel of knowledgeable persons, we must specify the degree of agreement that is necessary to establish a given statement as doctrine.   For convenience, let us lay down the rule that eight in ten of our authorities must agree.

What is the degree of conformity between doctrine and

practice that is needed before the term "democracy" can be applied? Many clauses in statute books have quietly been allowed to lapse; they are not "law" even though they are in the code. Even if our authorities agree that a given statement is legal doctrine, investigation may reveal that it is largely inoperative. We need to specify a minimum critical frequency of conformity that must be realized before a given doctrine is a "rule". Thus the term "rule" is defined as "doctrine in practice" (within stipulated limits).

How are data-gatherers to proceed in determining the state of practice in a given situation? Official records may show whether elections are held at the time prescribed in the Constitution, and they may report the number of eligible voters who go to the polls. But even if these statements are accepted at face value, they do not reveal the state of intimidation or the degree of public confidence in the genuineness of democratic processes.[8]

The needed facts can be obtained only by observers who possess skills appropriate to the observation of reality. Such observers must be equipped to establish themselves where they find out what is said and done. They must make reliable and consistent records of what they see. These records must be properly analysed. The observations can aim at completeness (census) or at representativeness (sampling).

Mankind has thrown away most of its experience for lack of competent record-making, and successive generations are left with a more meagre social inheritance than need be. If mankind is to adapt civilization to the ideal of human dignity, each generation must be in a position to profit from past errors and to improve upon past achievement.

Men have tried to govern themselves and one another for many generations. In the literatures of ancient China, of East India, of the Mediterranean world, there is no dearth of general principles. But general statements of principle do not suffice. By themselves they do not communicate. We need detailed records of how men tried to put principles into practice—and what came of it. We need the bricks of data no less than the blueprints of precept, if we are to build successfully. To improve the social inheritance of the future, we must transmit generalization plus data.

Every friend of democracy can specify some records that he

[8] See Lasswell, "General Framework: Person, Personality, Group, Culture", in the present volume, Part II.

wishes had been left by preceding generations.   There have been great moments when men have detached themselves to some degree from the polemics of their age and have contributed to the reconstruction of knowledge and the redirection of education and public policy.   They have withdrawn a step from active combat, yet they have not frozen into the mould of ritualistic scholarship.   We need to know how such things can be.   A few of the facts we know—how the universities of Leyden (1575), Edinburgh (1583), and Strasbourg (1566 and 1621) emancipated themselves from the religious turmoil of their day and cultivated the sciences and the humanities.[9]   But we do not know the process in helpful detail ; adequate records were not made.

There have been great programmes of training for civic life. The system of training for public service that was instituted in China had its effect upon the level of skill and integrity available to the state.   Yet the level fluctuated enormously from time to time.   At one period the clash of personal, family, fraternal, and regional ambition spelled demoralization.   At other times the mills of central administration ground exceeding fine.   Proper records would unquestionably enable us to account for many of the astonishing variations in the course of Chinese history—a history that is only changeless in the eye of the uninformed.

Great collections of invaluable data have perished for lack of appreciation of their cumulative significance.   For generations the secret agents of the East Indian princes sedulously collected the most intimate obtainable details of the lives of officials and private subjects.   These details were not falsified by the needs of literary style.   The intellectuals of India left us no compendium of collected data.   They relied on the communicative value of the shrewd remark divorced from data.

We are told by the classical writers that men of honesty should be recruited to perform certain functions of government.   We know that spies were used to report upon the conduct of officials, often testing them with bribes.   What is lost is the description of who responded how.   What were the words or gestures that enabled the skilful observer to predict who would succumb to which appeal ?

In our own time the observation of human response has advanced by leaps and bounds.   Although we are still in the embryonic stage, it is no exaggeration to assert that more advances

[9] On the history of universities, see d'Irsay, Stephen, *Histoire des universités* (Paris, 1933-4).

have been made in the last forty years than at any time in the history of mankind.

The discovery of ways of studying human response has opened up new potentialities for the removal of obstacles upon the growth of democratic character and practice. Many of these obstacles have hitherto been unrecognized ; one instance is the distortion of human personality during adolescence. We have popularly thought of adolescent " storm and stress " as a necessary phase of growth. However, disciplined observation has shown that our civilization itself imposes suicide, schizophrenia, and malformation of personality upon so many of its adolescents. Not human nature, but specific features of our civilization are responsible— certain ways of rearing children, of incorporating the young into the patterns of a rivalrous civilization. How do we know this to be true ? The most convincing demonstration is the discovery of societies that do not sentence their youth to varying degrees of destructiveness.[10]

We need skilful observers of the total reality of personal and cultural development if we are to know the facts about the prevalence of democracy and to uncover the factors that condition the survival of free societies.

One long step toward reality is to accept no general sentence as a complete communication until we know how it is related to definite observational standpoints.

Exact Observation Yields Results Now

Many students of politics, confronted by the ambiguity of existing language, grow pessimistic about the possibility of science. Perhaps, therefore, it is worth emphasizing the point that exact methods of observation yield certain advantages now, quite apart from the contribution they may ultimately make to a highly systematic science of democracy.[11]

The democratic ideal includes a decent regard for the opinions

[10] Note especially the ethnological work of Margaret Mead, beginning with *Coming of Age in Samoa* (London, 1943). Among psychiatrists, consult Sullivan, Harry Stack, " Conceptions of Modern Psychiatry ", *Psychiatry*, vol. 3 (1940).

[11] Important advances have been made toward a statement of scientific procedure that brings the data of the social sciences and of the physical sciences into a common universe of events. We may speak of the manifold of events, and classify events into " movements " and " symbols ". A symbol refers ; a movement does not. For a long time physicalistic survivals limited the utility of Rudolf Carnap's logical positivism, but recent formulations have dropped these objectionable features. Even those who accepted a unified-field theory were reluctant to admit " words about words " as data of the same standing as " words about movements ". Hence the shipwreck of many efforts to apply correct general formulations to socio-personal events, where most of the data sentences are " words about words ".

and sensibilities of our fellows.   The moralists who have championed this ideal in the past have made no progress toward the discovery of methods appropriate to the understanding of the thoughts and feelings of others.   The instrumentation of morals has had to await reliable methods of observation.

With the best will in the world, we cannot take the attitudes of our fellows into consideration unless we know what they are, and this depends upon an adequate staff of skilful observers. Lacking these instruments, good intentions cannot possibly be fulfilled in practice.   Knowledge of any kind can be abused by men of ill will, and men of good will must always choose between their present impotence through lack of knowledge and their possible weakness through lack of power.   In the present state of the organization of knowledge, the members of the great society cannot live up to democratic morals ; with better organization of knowledge, they may achieve power without losing their good intentions in the process.

This much, at least, is clear :   Whether or not the methods of scientific observation contribute to the eventual completion of a systematic science of democracy, they are certain to contribute, here and now, to the practice of democratic morals.   Without science, democracy is blind and weak.   With science, democracy will not be blind and may be strong.

CHAPTER II

PSYCHOLOGY LOOKS AT MORALS AND POLITICS *

In common with any branch of social and political science psychology bears an instrumental relationship to morals and politics. Our moral values are *acquired* from the interplay of original nature with the culture into which we are born ; our values are *derived* from that part of culture that includes the basic postulates of metaphysics and theology ; our values are *implemented* by the part of culture called science and practice (including psychology and politics).

If there is any universal human experience it is this one : Moral intentions are often frustrated by weaknesses of which the individual is aware, yet feels incapable of removing. The relationship of psychological knowledge to many such cases of moral frustration is benign, for by the timely application of this knowledge the moral intention may be properly implemented. Soldiers who want to fight for their country are often prevented from doing so by sudden seizures of panic, by sudden attacks of blindness, by partial paralysis of arms and legs. Patient psychological observation has disclosed many of the causes that contribute to these traumatic seizures and has devised methods of relief. Often the sufferer has struggled to keep out of his mind both the fear of death and the feeling of self-contempt for experiencing fear. By his struggle against these disrupting and embarrassing thoughts and feelings, the soldier intensified his level of anxiety to an unbearable degree, and found partial relief in self-crippling reactions—the symptoms of shell shock—panic, blindness, paralysis. His personality was divided against itself. Such personalities can be assisted by appropriate psychological methods to achieve integration, hence to free themselves from the dominance of impulses that frustrate moral purpose.

The spectacle of frustrated moral intention is familiar in the ordinary experiences of civilian life. One is reminded in this connection of the history of a successful young lawyer who became inspired with the determination to rid his city of graft and corruption. He put his dynamic energy and professional skill at the

* From *Ethics*, April, 1941. Paper read before the American Political Science Association, Chicago, Illinois, December 29, 1940.

services of a citizens' organization that began to make a genuine
impression on local politics.   But there was a serious flaw in the
programme ; the intentions of the young lawyer were continually
running into difficulties because of his alcoholic excesses.   From
time to time he was seized by an insatiable thirst and went on
a debauch that lasted several days.   He was no silent, morose,
retiring drinker ; he belonged, rather, to the irritable variety
whose sensitiveness to insult becomes progressively more acute as
his perceptions of reality grow dim.   He frequently held doormen,
waiters, and even casual pedestrians responsible for alleged
indignities heaped upon him.   Hence the crusader for civic virtue
occasionally figured in a public brawl, casting himself and his
cause into disrepute.   Fortunately something is known about a
few of the many varieties of excessive alcoholism.   This civic
leader belonged to one of the more benign and better understood
varieties, the proper psychological measures relieved him of his
illness, thus removing an almost fatal barrier to his good intentions.

Less spectacular are the problems of those administrators who
struggle against a conspicuous defect in their handling of others.
One administrator, otherwise impeccable, was continually subject to angry outbursts against colleagues and subordinates.   He
struggled manfully against his " failing ", this internal check on
the achievement of his intention to set a praiseworthy pattern
of administrative conduct.   For a while he tried to gain self-
control by will power.   He tried all the standard remedies of
folklore—he " counted to ten ", but even when he counted to
ten times ten, he still took the hide off his subordinates when the
arithmetic was over.   Often such rudimentary expedients work ;
but the personality structure of this man contained so many
incompatible tendencies that he had need of less ritualistic and
more insightful methods.

All these men frustrated their best intentions.   Psychological
study showed that they defeated themselves by turning destructive
impulses against themselves.   More than that, the root of their
destructiveness was found in some lack of respect for themselves.
The " terrible tempered Mr. Bang ", the administrator with the
irascible temper, was a man who was struggling against certain
tendencies to treat himself with contempt.   It was found that
his eruptions were connected with situations in which he was
thrown with persons of more commanding physique than his
own.   By patient self-observation, he obtained insight into the
degree to which his adjustments to life had been determined by

his feelings of helplessness, and of compensating rage, at his diminutive body build. Such negative valuations of the self were not part of his conscious waking life. On the contrary, he automatically deflected his attention from his slightness of stature and failed to see the full intensity of his self-contempt, and to free himself from its destructive results.

There is no doubt that the young lawyer and civic crusader who disgraced himself and his cause was acting destructively. Here again, the significant source of his destructive impulses was severe anxiety about the status of the self. His drunken orgies came just after crises in which he was excessively tense, excessively intent upon the persuasion of others. The moment the ordeal was over, he relapsed into a state of weak self-indulgence. Through it all he was screening from himself the contempt that he felt for himself as one who was so excessively dependent upon the favourable emotional responses of other people. His concern about being unmanly was one of the most embarrassing threats to his self-respect.

The disciplined study of human personality has confirmed the ancient saying that the enemy of man is man, is man's own destructiveness. And more : the causes of destructive impulses have been painstakingly explored, and the upshot is to emphasize anew the pathogenic importance of insufficient self-respect. We can recognize these basic relations the most readily in the lives of children. We are familiar with the child who bullies weaker playmates, and we know how often this is connected with deep concern about the status of the self and represents an over-compensation against ridicule for a weak and flabby appearance. We know, too, the timid and " beaten " child, wholly withdrawn into itself, hopeless of affection. Destructive impulses spring in no slight degree from deficient self-respect ; these impulses may be discharged, in part, against other persons, as with the bully, or against the self, as with the " beaten " child.

These basic relations, so easy to grasp with reference to children, we often fail to extend to the whole of life, where they apply with equal truth. Part of the difficulty here is the complex interrelationship of destructive impulses and destructive practices. Even though we are in control of our own destructive tendencies, we may act destructively upon others. Despite our good intentions, even when we have been emancipated from self-crippling reactions, we may still have destructive effects upon other people. A great barrier to moral achievement, in addition to insufficient self-knowledge, is insufficient knowledge of the institutional routines of society and their effect upon others.

A typical problem of this kind confronts the administrator who sincerely desires to contribute to the welfare of others, yet finds it difficult to obtain the needed facts about the lives of other people and the way they are affected by official acts. The head of a huge department of government may earnestly seek to contribute to the realization of a democratic society. Assume that this administrator is put in charge of a resettlement administration. How is he to find out the facts about the impact of his administrative decisions upon the quality of living in these local communities ?

Moral intentions, we repeat, call for more than self-knowledge. They must be implemented by reliable knowledge of the attitudes of other people through time and of the factors that affect them. This is a realm to which modern psychological observation has made steady contribution. It is no longer necessary for the administrator to rely exclusively upon the hasty impressions of a busy field trip, or upon occasional petitions and protests. Competent participating observers can record their experience with fidelity and make it available to decision-makers. Sometimes the results show that democratic processes lack vitality because the local manager of the community has failed to maintain genuine consultation. It is obvious that democracy requires that people shall participate in the decisions that most concern them ; but many community managers grow slack and the frequency of democratic consultation dwindles toward zero. The observer can assemble the facts that are needed to portray the fluctuating volume of democratic processes of consultation. Fewer and fewer citizens may take part in community meetings. More and more citizens, when interviewed under conditions that encourage candour, may express scepticism about " what good it does " to take a hand in collective activities. The complaint may be that the local manager has no real influence and that the central administration does what it pleases. Washington seems far away and capricious in its decisions. A check-up over a period of several months may reveal that the central administrators have taken many decisions without clarifying—much less consulting—the local community. Busy administrators, in spite of all their sincerity, often fail to clarify—and one way to defer to the personality of another is to make clear to him what is going on. A check-up may also show that the government appears most often in a deprivational rôle—as a tax collector, a rent collector, an evictor, and the like.   Seldom if ever does the government express appreciation for a job well done.   And expressions of appreciation are among the most rudimentary, yet important, ways of contributing to the self-respect of deserving people.

In a democratic society, then, we are concerned about the flow of appreciation, of clarification, of consultation—for these are the specifics of deference.   When men and woman are deferred to, they are appreciated, clarified, consulted.   Whatever practices interfere with the flow of mutual respect, and arouse destructive impulses, endanger the fulfilment of a democratic order.

Manifestly the enemy of a democratic society is human destructiveness in all its forms—destructive impulses, destructive practices.   If our moral intention is to realize a democratic society, we need a science of democracy to implement the goal.   Such a science will draw heavily upon the findings and the observational methods of psychology, especially since psychological methods are the means especially appropriate to the discovery of the human consequences of living under any social order.   Some of the methods of psychology are appropriate to the cultivation of self-knowledge by candid self-observation, in this way reducing the frustration of moral intentions by incompatible tendencies within the personality itself.[1]   And by the proper correlation of psychological methods with other scientific procedures we may gain the knowledge needed to identify and to control destructive practices no less than destructive impulses.

Institutional practices are destructive when they arouse great concentrations of destructive impulse.   It is evident that profound crises of destructiveness are fostered by irregularity in the tempo of social change and by lack of balance in social structure.   Whatever contributes to such irregularities and unbalance is dangerously destructive.

Irregularity of social change places too great a burden upon the capacity of men to adjust to their environment.   Those who increase abruptly in influence are prone to act destructively—to behave with arrogant lack of consideration toward their fellows.   Those who are made suddenly weak are also provoked to destructiveness—and take out their hostilities against themselves or others.

[1] See Part III of the present volume.

Our modern world has conspicuously suffered from the destructive crises nourished by irregularities that we can attribute to lack of control over the machine. Thanks to the rapid introduction of machine methods of production, the carriers of Western European civilization imposed their will upon peoples throughout the world—upsetting established patterns of life, precipitating colossal problems of immediate adaptation.

The abrupt change in the comparative strength of European states intensified the difficulties of harmonious adjustment among the bearers of European civilization itself. Rival arrogances doomed the citizens of every modern power to increasing insecurity of life and limb.

In addition, our world has witnessed the crises generated in the process of modifying the internal structure of every modern society. The rapid emergence of the specialist on market manipulation, on bargaining—the business man—put in positions of influence in society men who were not specialists upon the harmonious adjustment of men in society.

The insecurities that were generated by irregular social development were intensified by the imbalances that were accentuated in the structure of a given society. What does it mean to achieve the rule of balance in society? A balanced social order achieves a commonwealth of mutual deference. To be deferred to is to be taken into consideration—to be consulted, appreciated, and clarified. In a democratic commonwealth there is a relatively general share in power, respect and insight.

To democratize power, then, is to maintain the practice of general participation in the making of influential decisions. Closely associated with the democratization of power is the democratization of respect ; respect is another part of deference. Our own civilization has been conspicuously deficient in the practice of mutual respect. No more flagrant example could be found than the attitude taken up in nominally democratic societies toward those who were thrown out of work in the late collapse. It is true that not many of those who were squeezed out of the processes of production starved to death. Most of them were given enough to keep breath in their bodies. But we were not sensitive to the fact that men who are thrown out of employment are also thrown out of respect. We added insult to injury by stigmatizing these millions as " unemployed ", by treating them as a burden on their fellow-men, a dead weight on the taxpayer, a mass of humanity for whom there was no longer a respected place in society. We kept them from dying, it is true, but we gave them no reason to live. We forgot that men want not only a job ; they want security and opportunity on a respected job. Some of the dictators have been more canny than some of the leaders of states aspiring toward democracy. Instead of a shovel and a job in a make-work programme—open to vaudeville jokes and neighbourhood insult—some of these dictators have given millions of young people a shovel and a job and a gun in the building of a new social order. It is impossible to exaggerate the loathing with which any friend of democracy looks upon many of the measures of totalitarian despotism, but it is unwise to forget that the partial success achieved by these despotisms is that they have appealed to the craving for respect that is a powerful characteristic of human personality.

The psychological sciences put squarely in the forefront of attention the human consequences of all the laws and customs of a given society. By appropriate methods of observation it is possible to discern the degree to which any set of established practices operates destructively upon human nature by stimulating destructive impulses. At the root of destructive impulses lies deficient self-respect. Sufficient self-respect is largely dependent upon a continual inflow of respect from the personal environment—an inflow that enables the child to develop without the warping that arises from an unstable emotional environment and the adult to count upon security and opportunity in a respected place in society.

That we face colossal crises of self-destruction in our historical period is a tragic fact from which no man can escape. And yet there are positive features in the life of our time. There is a blind mass groping for security in a respected place in society, a blind groping for deference that lends itself momentarily to the exploitation of despotic demagogues, but that can gain clarity and vitality if given insight and direction.

It is the province of psychological science to contribute to the development of an applied as well as a general science of politics, an applied science that bears much the same relation to the general science of politics that medical science bears to general physiology. Our task is not to add new general definitions of moral ideas. It is not even to improve upon the sentences that have been used in the past in deriving moral definitions from the key propositions of theology and metaphysics.   In this sense our aim in the cultivation of science is modest.   Yet in another sense our aim is enormously high ; it is nothing less than to give hands and feet to morality, to discern with ever-increasing accuracy the causes and controls of human destructiveness.

LEGAL EDUCATION AND PUBLIC POLICY: PROFESSIONAL TRAINING IN THE PUBLIC INTEREST *

(*With Myres S. McDougal, Yale University*)

A recurrent problem for all who are interested in implementing policy, the reform of legal education must become ever more urgent in a revolutionary world of cumulative crises and increasing violence. Despite the fact that for six or seven decades responsibility for training new members of the " public profession " of the law has in the U.S.A. been an almost exclusive monopoly of a new subsidized intellectual élite, professional teachers of law, and despite much recent ferment and agitation among such teachers, little has actually been achieved in refashioning ancient educational practices to serve insistent contemporary needs. No critics have been more articulate in lamenting this failure than the professional law teachers themselves.[1] What they think they

---

* From *The Yale Law Journal*, March, 1943.

[1] Still the best call to arms is Hohfeld, *A Vital School of Jurisprudence and Law*, *Fundamental Legal Conceptions* (Cook ed., 1923), p. 332. The most useful systematic survey is Faculty of Law, Columbia University, *Summary of Studies in Legal Education* (Oliphant ed., 1928). Among other articles which we have found helpful are Keyserling, " Social Objectives in Legal Education ", *Col. L. Rev.*, vol. 33 (1933), p. 437 (excellent criticism which has not yet received the attention it deserves); Steffen, " Changing Objectives in Legal Education ", *Yale L.J.*, vol. 40 (1931), p. 576 (useful for both criticism and constructive proposals); Riesman, " Law and Social Science : A Report on Michael and Wechsler's Classbook on Criminal Law and Administration ", *Yale L.J.*, vol. 50 (1941), p. 636 (incisive criticism and clear orientation toward policy); Clark, " The Function of Law in a Democratic Society ", *U. of Chi. L. Rev.*, vol. 9 (1942), p. 393; Gelhorn, " The Law School's Responsibility for Training Public Servants ", *U. of Chi. L. Rev.*, vol. 9 (1942), p. 469; Harno, " Disciplines in the Training of a Lawyer ", *B.U.L. Rev.*, vol. 22 (1942), p. 254; Cavers, " New Fields for the Legal Periodical ", *Va. L. Rev.*, vol. 23 (1936), p. 1; Douglas, " Education for the Law " (mimeographed address given before The American Association of Collegiate Schools of Business, April 23, 1936); Bordwell, " Experimentation and Continuity in Legal Education ", *Iowa L. Rev.*, vol. 23 (1938), p. 297; Mechem, " The Proposed Four-Year Law Curriculum—A Dissenting Opinion ", *Mich. L. Rev.*, vol. 38 (1940), p. 945; Frankfurter, " The Conditions for and the Aims and Methods of Legal Research ", *Am. L. School Rev.*, vol. 6 (1930), p. 663; Frey, " Some Thoughts on Law Teaching and the Social Sciences ", *U. of Pa. L. Rev.*, vol. 82 (1934), p. 463; Frank, " Why Not a Clinical Lawyer-School? ", *U. of Pa. L. Rev.*, vol. 81 (1933), p. 907; Gardner, " Why Not a Clinical Lawyer-School?—Some Reflections ", *U. of Pa. L. Rev.*, vol. 82 (1934), p. 785; Gardner, " Specialization in the Law School Curriculum ", *U. of Pa. L. Rev.*, vol. 81 (1933), p. 684; Harsch, " The Four-Year Law Course in American Universities ", *N.C.L. Rev.*, vol. 17 (1939), p. 242.

have done to legal instruction may be recapitalized as a transition from lectures, to the analysis of appellate opinions, to confusion. Not atypical of the common indictment are the words of one eminent self-critic : " blind, inept, factory-ridden, wasteful, defective, and empty." [2]

The major contours of our contemporary confusion have long been plainly visible. Heroic, but random, efforts to integrate " law " and " the other social sciences " fail through lack of clarity about what is being integrated, and how, and for what purposes.[3] Lip-service is paid to the proposition that legal concepts, institutions, and practices are instrumental only ; but the main organizing foci for determining both " fields " and " courses " are still time-worn, overlapping legal concepts of highest level abstraction.[4] Any relation between the factual problems that incidentally creep into particular fields or courses in a curriculum so " organized ", and the important problems of contemporary society is purely coincidental ; and all attempts to relate such fields or courses to each other are frustrated by lack of clear social goals and inadequate criteria of importance. The relevance of " non-legal " materials to effective " law " teaching is recognized, but efficient techniques for the investiga tion, collection and presentation of such materials are not devised. From lack of proper orientation, what appear to be promising ventures into " fact research " produce relatively isolated and trivial results. Professing to include, even as they transcend purely vocational aims, most schools, by ignoring skills in negotiation, personnel management, and public relations— equally essential to-day to caretakers of private clients and public leaders—fail even to do a sound job of vocational training. Grea

---

[2] See Llewellyn, " On What is Wrong with So-Called Legal Education ", Co L. Rev., vol. 35 (1935), pp. 651, 653. Contrast the resurgent optimism of the sam author in " On the Problem of Teaching ' Private ' Law ", Harv. L. Rev., vol. 5 (1941), p. 775, an article in praise of Steffen, Cases on Commercial and Investment Pap (1939).

[3] Katz, " A Four-Year Programme for Legal Education ", U. of Chi. L. Rev vol. 4 (1937), p. 527, writes with an intellectual modesty that borders on diffidenc at p. 531 : " We propose to consider a little more consciously whether anythir worth while can be said as to the ends which law should serve." The shifting courses in " moral and social philosophy " from the college to the law school is n likely to give new direction to legal education. A bolder attitude is taken ar a more promising course on Law and Economic Organization is described in Kat " What Changes are Practical in Legal Education ", A.B.A.J., vol. 27 (1941), p. 75

[4] Its framework is still largely that designed for the training of small-town pra titioners of nearly a century ago. Some changes have, however, been effecte Not long ago a Connecticut judge complained that in the Yale Law School his s had learned how to reorganize a railroad but had not learned how to replevy a do Ironically the son's first job was to assist in the reorganization of a railroad. T records do not reveal that he has yet had opportunity to replevy a dog.

emphasis is put upon historical studies, but too often these studies degenerate into an aimless, literary eclecticism that fails to come to grips with causes or conditions.[5] Despite all the talk of " teleological jurisprudence " and of the necessity of evaluating legal structures, doctrines, and procedures in terms of basic policy, there is little conscious, systematic effort to relate them clearly and consistently to the major problems of a society struggling to achieve democratic values.[6] Some slight integration of legal materials with conventional business practice too frequently passes for evaluation in terms of long-run policy. Indeed, occasional voices still insist that law schools should have no concern whatsoever with policies, goals, or values—that the only proper concern of law schools is method, science disinfected of all preference.[7] Finally, even a majority of those who subscribe to a conception of law as " continuously more efficacious social engineering ", are so obsessed by myopic concern with one institution of social control, the court, that they fail to focus upon newer and, in many instances, more effective forms of organization, or to urge the creative consideration of alternative methods of formulating and implementing public policy.[8]

Proposals for escape from all of this confusion and inadequacy have, of course, been legion. Too often, however, such proposals have tended to get lost in minutiæ, in what one commentator

[5] Compare Boorstin, " Tradition and Method in Legal History ", *Harv. L. Rev.*, vol. 54 (1941), p. 424 ; Holdsworth, " Gibbon, Blackstone and Bentham ", *L.Q. Rev.*, vol. 52 (1936), p. 46.

[6] Thus Hohfeld, *op. cit. supra*, note 1, at p. 351 writes : " I mean to include under critical, or teleological, jurisprudence proper the *systematic* testing or critique of our principles and rules of law according to considerations *extrinsic* or *external* to the principles and rules as such, that is, according to the psychological, ethical, political, social, and economic bases of the various doctrines and the respective purposes or ends sought to be achieved thereby." What we stress is that not only a " testing " of such rules and principles is required but also a conscious pursuit of explicitly defined ends and systematic consideration of alternative doctrines, procedures and structures as means to such ends.

[7] One distinguished authority on Bills and Notes insists that a teacher who expresses a social preference in the classroom should be fired. His preference is for law schools that concern themselves with " law " only as a means to *any* policies, goals or values and not with evaluation or deliberate choice of policies, goals or values. He justifies devoting most of his classroom time to the exposition of the legal literature on the grounds (1) that that literature discloses some of the rules established in the culture for the discourse of lawyers, and (2) that some of the propositions in the literature are part of the pattern of cues or signs to which non-verbal responses have been learned by judges and people generally.

[8] It might be noted that not all experts on legal education in other countries are flattering in their references to American legal education. See Deak, " French Legal Education and Some Reflections on Legal Education in the U.S.", *Wis. L. Rev.* (1939), p. 473 ; Rheinstein, " Law Faculties and Law Schools. A Comparison of Legal Education in the United States and Germany ", *Wis. L. Rev.* (1938), p. 5 ; Riesenfeld, " A Comparison of Continental and American Legal Education ", *Mich. L. Rev.*, vol. 36 (1937), p. 31.

has irreverently called the reverent modification of small particulars.[9] Lecture versus case ; seminars versus courses ; group work versus individual work ; specialization versus " well-rounded " training ; vocational training versus cultural training ; Bills and Notes (substitute any course) in the second year versus Bills and Notes in the third year ; prescribed pre-legal training versus eclecticism ; these and many similar questions have been raised like quills upon the fretful porpentine. No thorough examination of educational problems can ignore such issues. But they are not basic.[10]

A first indispensable step toward the effective reform of legal education is to clarify ultimate aim. We submit this basic proposition : if legal education in the contemporary world is adequately to serve the needs of a free and productive commonwealth, it must be conscious, efficient, and systematic *training for policy-making*. The proper function of our law schools is, in short, to contribute to the training of policy-makers for the ever more complete achievement of the democratic values that constitute the professed ends of American polity.

This end is not proposed as something utterly new or exotic. Indeed most of the recent developments in legal education—from " sociological jurisprudence " to neo-Thomism [11]—have tended, with varying degrees of explicitness, to move in this direction. None who deal with law, however defined, can escape policy when policy is defined as the making of important decisions which affect the distribution of values. Even those who still insist that

[9] See Riesman, *supra*, note 1, at p. 637.

[10] Simpson, " The New Curriculum of the Harvard Law School ", *Harv. L. Rev.*, vol. 51 (1938), pp. 965, 973, thus announces some revision of the rites of the Langdell shrine :
" The revised curriculum of the Harvard Law School attempts to harmonize three different but by no means inconsistent principles. These are :
" ' First : That everyone on the Faculty should be helped and encouraged to develop the best thought that is in him and to put it at the disposal of students to the fullest possible extent ;
" ' Second : That every student should receive a solid foundation of conceptions and methods in each of the great basic legal subjects—such as litigation, crime, tort, property, contract, association, and government—with opportunity as he progresses to pursue the fields of his special interest in greater detail ;
" ' Third : That the courses and their contents should be arranged, so far as practicable, so that the student will proceed to the complex from the simple, and that each course will throw the greatest possible light upon the rest.' "
Note the lack of emphasis in Principle 1 on student self-education, the emphasis in Principle 2 on " legal technicality " as a basis for curricular organization, and the banality of Principle 3. Contrast the broader vision of the same author in " The Function of the University Law School ", *Harv. L. Rev.*, vol. 49 (1936), p. 1068, when he faces no necessity of appeasing colleagues.

[11] See Kennedy, " Portrait of a Realist, New Style ", *Fordham L. Rev.*, vol. 10 (1941), p. 196.

policy is no proper concern of a law school tacitly advocate a policy, unconsciously assuming that the ultimate function of law is to maintain existing social institutions in a sort of timeless *status quo* ; what they ask is that their policy be smuggled in, without insight or responsibility. But neither a vague and amorphous emphasis on social " forces ", " mores ", and " purposes ", nor a functionalism that dissolves legal absolutism for the benefit of random and poorly defined ends, nor a mystical invocation of the transcendental virtues of an unspecified " good life ", can effect the fundamental changes in the traditional law school that are now required to fit lawyers for their contemporary responsibilities. Their direction is toward policy, but their directives are at too high a level of abstraction to give helpful guidance. What is needed now is to implement ancient insights by reorienting every phase of law school curricula and skill training toward the achievement of clearly defined democratic values in all the areas of social life where lawyers have or can assert responsibility.

It should need no re-emphasis here that these democratic values have been on the wane in recent years. The dominant trends of world politics have been away from the symbols and practices of a free society and toward the slogans, doctrines and structures of despotism. Wherever democratic attitudes have declined, institutions connected with democracy have weakened or vanished. In post-Weimar Germany, as in post-parliamentary Italy and certain other countries, elections have become ceremonial plebiscites—rituals of tribal union. Balanced public discussion has given way to discussion directed by a monopoly of government and party. The multiple-party system has yielded to something called a " party ", though in fact an " order ", a privileged monopolist of policy-making. In place of dynamic executive and judicial balance, there has arisen extreme executive concentration. Where institutions named parliaments yet survive, they are mummified into assemblies for the performance of rites of ceremonial ratification of executive decisions. Where there was a balance between centralized and local authority and control, there has arisen extreme centralization. With the sweep of regimentation, the balance is lost between private zones of living and the zones appropriate to official direction. The entire structure of open and competitive markets has been actively threatened by an economic structure of closed and monopolistic markets. Processes of production and distribution that were once carried on by bargaining and pricing depend on negotiation and rationing.

These sweeping transformations in the institutional structure of world politics may be summarized by saying that the balanced skill state has been yielding to the bureaucratic state. This is a reversal of nineteenth-century trends. Despite local deviations, the over-all development of the world was toward the spread of free markets and free governments, and the resulting rise in influence of the specialist on bargaining, the business man. He shared power with other skill groups—the propagandist, whose skill is the manipulation of symbols of mass appeal ; the party boss, whose skill is the negotiation of favours ; the civil official, whose skill is administration ; the military men, whose skill is the management of violence. With the eclipse of the balanced skill state, the bureaucratic state has grown to behemoth dimensions. The line of development can be summarized by saying that the business state, with its balance of skill, gives way to the monopolist state, the propagandist state, or the party state ; and that, if militarization continues, the garrison state will come out on top.[12]

Looking at the plight of freedom in the world to-day, can we fail to ask how the policy-makers of a free society have come to experience such catastrophic rebuffs ? Through what deficiencies of skill or character have they failed to keep the trend of world development in line with their basic objective ? Such chronic failure suggests that the policy-makers of recent times have arrived at their decisions without a firm grasp on reality, and that they have allowed their focus of attention to be absorbed with trivial non-essentials. Long before the present storm, clouds of difficulty were plainly visible. Yet decision-makers in business, government, and in all branches of public life were either oblivious to these portents or remained sterile and ineffective.

The question may be asked whether the lawyer can be held responsible in any significant degree for the plight in which we find ourselves. For a moralist, the question is whether the lawyer can be " blamed ", for a scientist, whether he is an important causal variable ; for a reformer, whether he can be acted upon to produce change. The answer to all of these questions is : most assuredly, yes. It should need no emphasis

[12] On the changing structure of world politics, see Lasswell, *World Politics and Personal Insecurity* (1935) ; Mannheim, *Man and Society in an Age of Reconstruction* (1940) ; Lasswell, " The Garrison State and Specialists on Violence ", in the present volume, Part II.

that the lawyer is to-day, even when not himself a " maker " of policy, the one indispensable adviser of every responsible policy-maker of our society—whether we speak of the head of a government department or agency, of the executive of a corporation or labour union, of the secretary of a trade or other private association, or even of the humble independent enterpriser or professional man.[13] As such an adviser the lawyer, when informing his policy-maker of what he can or cannot legally do, is in an unassailably strategic position to influence, if not create, policy. It is a familiar story, too, of how frequently lawyers who begin as advisers on policy are transformed into makers of policy ; " the law " is one of the few remaining avenues to " success " open to impecunious talent. Successful practitioners of law often receive sufficiently large incomes, from advice and investment, to become powers in their own right and hence gravitate into positions of influence in industry. How frequently lawyers turn up in government—whether as legislators, executives, or administrators, or as judges (where they have a virtual monopoly)—is again a matter of common knowledge. Nor can the policy-making power of lawyers as executors, trust administrators, administrators in insolvency, and so on, be ignored. Certainly it would be difficult to exaggerate either the direct or indirect influence that members of the legal profession exert on the public life of this nation. For better or worse our decision-makers and our lawyers are bound together in a relation of dependence or of identity.

One of the best indicators of the policy-making power of lawyers would, of course, be a complete " job analysis " of the profession. Unfortunately, such an analysis has never been made.[14] In its absence a listing of professional activities which, though it is designed to emphasize the opportunities of lawyers to affect policy, is neither exhaustive nor of consistent level of abstraction, must suffice :

Drafting, promoting, interpreting, and amending constitutions.
Drafting, promoting, and interpreting executive orders, administrative

---

[13] See Rutherford, *Influence of the American Bar Association on Public Opinion and Legislation* (1937), for a chronicling of some of the more organized aspects of the influence of the bar on policy. Cheatham, *Cases and Other Materials on the Legal Profession* (1938), is suggestive of the range of the lawyer's activities.

[14] For the beginnings see American Bar Association, *The Economics of the Legal Profession* (Garrison ed., 1938), pp. 28, 70 ; Bradway, " A National Bar Survey ", *B.U.L. Rev.*, vol. 16 (1936), p. 662 ; Clark and Corstvet, " The Lawyer and the Public : An A.A.L.S. Survey ", *Yale L.J.*, vol. 47 (1938), p. 1272 ; Llewellyn, " The Problem of Undone Legal Service ", *A.B.A.J.*, vol. 26 (1940), p. 38.

rulings, municipal charters, and so on, and attacking or sustaining their constitutionality.

Drafting and interpreting corporate and private association charters, agreements, dispositive instruments, and so on, and attacking or sustaining their validity.

Deciding or otherwise resolving causes or controversies, and making other decisions which affect the distribution of values, as judges, executives, administrators, arbitrators, referees, trial examiners, and so on.

Bringing to, or obscuring from, the attention of decision-makers the facts and policies on which judgment should rest.

Advising clients on how to avoid litigation and controversies and on how to make the best possible use of legal doctrines, institutions, and practices for the promotion of their private purposes and long-term interest. (Clarifying, *inter alia*, intentions as to property disposition, business transactions, and family relations.)

Consulting and negotiating with clients, business men, opposing counsel, and decision-makers of all kinds.

Reading, digesting, and reinterpreting the decisions and reasoning of past decision-makers of all kinds.

Guiding, conducting, and preparing for investigations and hearings (criminal, regulatory, legislative, social-scientific, administrative).

Preparing arguments, legal forms, witnesses (ordinary, expert), trial briefs, and so on.

Selecting courts, juries, arbitrators, negotiators, and other decision-makers.

Selecting clients.

Selecting clerks, associates and successors.

Preparing or supervising press conferences, issuing news releases, preparing radio material, or newsreel material.

Developing influence through participation in civic and other public activities (organizing and directing pressure groups, lobbying propaganda, and other control procedures) and private sociability.

Participating in professional organizations (organizations engaged in selection, exclusion and training of members, and with the maintenance of standards of varying degrees of ambiguity).

Contributing by investigation, writing and lecturing to legal and social science (publishing facts and analyses of the relationship between legal rules and human relations ; reformulation of legal rules).

It should be remembered, furthermore, in computing the sum of the lawyer's influence, that its true measure is not to be found in the more dramatic occasions, such as constitution-making or legislation-drafting, when such influence is exercised, but rather in the cumulative effect of multiple thousands of routine, day-to-day presentations of fact and deliverances of opinion.

Yet, even if it be granted that lawyers are among the most influential of the policy-makers of our society, one question still persists. Is the lawyer not made of the same flesh, blood, eyes, and errors as other men ? Can lawyers be " blamed " for sharing —or be made to share less—the compulsions and obsessions, the false hopes and egregious illusions, which have been, and are largely still, common to his clients and the other policy-makers of our society ? The answer is that the lawyer does bear a peculiar responsibility. The lawyer, it must be recalled, is a member of a learned profession—of a skill group which has the temerity to make a profession of tendering advice to others. It is his responsibility to acquaint himself not only with what the learned have thought, and with the historical trends of his time, but also with the long-term interests of all whom he serves and the appropriate means of securing such interests. For nurturing him in the necessary skills and information society offers him a peculiarly long period of training and incubation ; and, if that period is filled with the proper experiences, he can—our whole educational system is based on the premise—be trained for responsible leadership. To no one else can clients and members of the public reasonably be expected to look for that enlargement and correction of perspective, that critical and inclusive view of reality, that is based on the disciplined exercise of skills which the layman is not given the opportunity to acquire.

Few would contest that during this pivotal era in our history lawyers have flouted both their opportunities and their obligations.[15] It is self-congratulatory falsehood to say that recent catastrophes have come upon us like bolts from the blue, unforeseen by the eye of mortal man ; unheeded prophets have foretold for years what was coming unless appropriate moves were made in time.[16]

The war period is a propitious moment to retool our system of legal education. America's huge plants for the fabrication of lawyers are practically closed for the duration ; yet if the end of the present war in any way resembles the termination of

[15] Compare Stone, " The Public Influence of the Bar ", *Harv. L. Rev.*, vol. 48 (1934), p. 1 ; Douglas, " The Lawyer and the Public Service ", *A.B.A.J.*, vol. 26 (1940), p. 633 ; Jackson, " The Product of the Present Day Law School ", *Calif. L. Rev.*, vol. 27 (1939), p. 635 ; Clark, " Legal Education in Modern Society ", *Tulane L. Rev.*, vol. 10 (1935), p. 1 ; Berle, " Modern Legal Profession ", *Encyc. Soc. Sciences*, vol. 9 (1933), p. 340 ; Shea, " Overcrowded ?—The Price of Certain Remedies ", *Col. L. Rev.*, vol. 39 (1939), p. 191.

[16] Cyclical conceptions of history with many pessimistic applications to the present are summarized in Sorokin, *Social and Cultural Dynamics*, vol. 4 (1941). For a century Marxists have predicted the coming crises of capitalism. Influential modern works are : Lenin, *Imperialism, the Highest Stage of Capitalism* (1933) ; Grossmann, *Das Akkumulations-und Zusammenbruchsgesetz des Kapitalistischen Systems* (1929) ; Luxemburg, *Die Akkumulation des Kapitals* (1921) ; Hilferding, *Das Finanz-kapital* (1910). Non-Marxist pessimism is found in Spengler, *Decline of the West* (1934).

World War I, their doors will swing wide to admit a dammed-up stream of returning soldiers who want legal training.   In the rush of conversion from war to peace the archaic conventions and confusions of the past may win out over the vital needs of our civilization and the doors may open to admit the unwary members of an entire generation into a reguilded vacuum.

What, then, are the essentials of adequate training for policy ? Effective policy-making (planning and implementation) depends on clear conception of goal, accurate calculation of probabilities, and adept application of knowledge of ways and means.   We submit that adequate training must therefore include experiences that aid the developing lawyer to acquire certain skills of thought : goal-thinking, trend-thinking, and scientific-thinking.   The student needs to clarify his moral values (preferred events, social goals) ; he needs to orient himself in past trends and future probabilities ; finally, he needs to acquire the scientific know-ledge and skills necessary to implement objectives within the context of contemporary trends.

Goal-thinking requires the clarification of values.   In a democratic society it should not, of course, be an aim of legal education to impose a single standard of morals upon every student.   But a legitimate aim of education is to seek to promote the major values of a democratic society and to reduce the number of moral mavericks who do not share democratic preferences.   The student may be allowed to reject the morals of democracy and embrace those of despotism ; but his education should be such that, if he does so, he does it by deliberate choice, with awareness of the consequences for himself and others, and not by sluggish self-deception.

How can incipient lawyers be trained in the clarification of values ?   Whatever the difficulties of communication, any state-ment of values must begin with words of high level abstraction, of ambiguous reference.   No brief definition can convey to anyone else much of what the definer means.   Too many persons jump to conclusions about the meaning of terms, regardless of the rules of interpretation intended by the speaker.   At the risk of mis-construction, we offer our brief statement of democratic morals. The supreme value of democracy is the dignity and worth of the individual ; hence a democratic society is a commonwealth where there is full opportunity to mature talent into socially creative skill, free from discrimination on grounds of religion, culture, or class.   It is a society in which such specific values as power, respect, and knowledge are widely shared and are not concentrated in the hands of a single group, class, or institution—the state—among the many institutions of society. This formula-is not new. On the contrary, it states the implicit or explicit assumptions of most of the traditional moralists of democracy. But such a statement of democratic values—and this is the point of our present emphasis—cannot be understood, or implemented, unless it is amplified by rules of interpretation, of varying degrees of generality, that show how observers of specific situations can validly use the terms in describing concrete reality and promoting the occurrence of relatively specific events in harmony with the definition. This task of spelling out values in terms of consistent propositions of varying degrees of generality or of relating general propositions to operational principles, is a long and arduous process. But it is indispensable to clarity and, hence, to the education of policy-makers.

Clarification of values, by relating general propositions to operational principles in representative and specific contexts, must for effective training be distinguished from the traditional, logical, derivation of values by philosophers. Such derivation—that is, exercises by which specialists on ethical philosophy and metaphysics take sentences that define moral standards and deduce them from more inclusive propositions or vice versa—is a notorious blind alley. Divorced from operational rules, it quickly becomes a futile quest for a meaningless " why ", perpetually culminating in " some inevitably circular and infinitely regressive logical justification " for ambiguous preferences.[17] From any relatively specific statements of social goal (necessarily described in a statement of low-level abstraction) can be elaborated an infinite series of normative propositions of ever-increasing generality ; conversely, normative statements of high-level abstraction can be manipulated to support any specific social goal. Prospective lawyers should be exposed, by way of warning and sophistication, to the work of representative specialists in derivation ; relatively little time should be required, however, to teach them how to handle, and how to achieve emotional freedom from, the ancient exercises.

Implementation of values requires, first, trend-thinking. This considers the shape of things to come regardless of preference.[18]

---

[17] See McDougal, " Fuller v. The American Legal Realists ", *Yale L.J.*, vol. 50 (1941), pp. 827, 835.

[18] Thus one of the writers has tried to suggest the kinds of trends which " property " lawyers should study. See McDougal in *Handbook, Association of American Law Schools* (1941), pp. 268, 273.

His goals clarified, a policy-maker must orient himself correctly in contemporary trends and future probabilities.   Concerned with specific features of the future that are ever emerging from the past, he needs to be especially sensitive to time, and to forecast with reasonable accuracy passage from one configuration of events to the next.   For this purpose he must have at his disposal a vast array of facts properly organized and instantly accessible. No one, much less a policy-maker, can do without expectations about the future—expectations about the probability of a short or a long-drawn-out war, of mounting or diminishing taxes, of rising or falling standards of living.   To think developmentally is to be explicit about these anticipations of the shape of things to come.   Every policy proposal and decision, including our recommendations about legal training, turns in part upon a picture of significant changes in the recent past, and expectations about significant changes in the emerging future.   The nature of our picture of recent trends, together with our interpretation of the principal cross-currents of the near-future, have been briefly indicated in our description of the wane of democratic values and of the unrealistic orientation of contemporary policy-makers.   The results of trend-thinking must continually be evaluated by the policy-maker in the light of his goals ; the task is to think creatively about how to alter, deter, or accelerate probable trends in order to shape the future closer to his desire.

Implementation of values requires, next, scientific thinking. While trend information is indispensable, it is not sufficient to enable us to mould the future.   Trends have a way of changing direction ; and often we can contribute to these changes by the skilful management of factors that condition them.   A trend is not a cause of social change ; it is a register of the relative strength of the variables that produce it.   We do not learn about causal factors by passively observing trend ; we must compare many examples of trend before we can build up a body of scientific knowledge.   The laws and propositions of science state invariant interrelations.   We do not have scientific knowledge when we know, for example, that there was a trend toward world war in 1939 ; it is only when we can, by comparing war periods, relate war to conditioning factors that we have science.   When we look toward the future our aim is not a draw of fatalistic series of trend curves in the direction they have been moving in the past.   To extrapolate in this way is necessary, but it is a prelude to the use of creative imagination and of available scientific knowledge in deciding how to influence the future. The very act of taking thought and of acting on the basis of thought are among the factors that determine the future trend of events. In a democratic society a policy-maker must determine which adjustments of human relationships are in fact compatible with the realization of democratic ideals. Which procedures actually aid or hamper the realization of human dignity ? How can the institutions of legislation, adjudication, administration, production, and distribution be adjusted to democratic survival ? What are the slogans and doctrines—in which contexts of experience—that create acceptance of democratic ideals and inspire effort to put them into practice ? In short, the policy-maker needs to guide his judgment by what is scientifically known and knowable about the causal variables that condition the democratic variables.

Effective training in scientific thinking requires that students become familiar with the procedures by which facts are established by planned observation. Most of our sources of information about human experience are not deliberately created records. For the most part we must rely upon whatever inferences can be drawn from " accidental " residues of the past. In recent decades and especially with the rapid expansion of the social and psychological sciences, the observing of human conduct has become progressively more technical and exhaustive. It is not too much to say that the great contribution of modern specialists on the human sciences is less in the realm of general theory than in the perfecting of method by which ancient speculations can be confirmed, modified or rejected. From the laboratory of the psychologist, the field expedition of the ethnologist and the clinic of the physician have come illuminating bodies of data ; and the procedures of observation invented in these special situations have stimulated the development of ways of studying men and women under normal circumstances in our own civilization. The effect of many kinds of human environment—in family, factory, school, army, prison, market—have been subjected to careful scrutiny. The results are continually applied and retested in the selecting of personnel in business, government, army, and other social structures. Systems of incentive are explored for their efficacy in raising production and reducing disciplinary problems. Modes of phrasing are pretested to evaluate their effectiveness as modifiers of buying, giving, voting. Throughout the length and breadth of modern society decisions are modified on the basis of what is revealed by means of intensive or extensive observation of human life, the procedures varying all the way from the prolonged interviews of a psychoanalytic psychiatrist to the brief questions of the maker of an opinion poll.[19]

Acquaintance with various methods of observation not only furnishes a sound basis for policy planning ; it contributes directly to skill in the practical management of human affairs. Another glance at the job analysis of the modern lawyer set forth above indicates something of the range of management problems with which he must grapple. Success calls for skill in direct personal contact with client, partner, clerk, opposing counsel, investigator, witness, juryman, judge ; likewise, there is need of skill in public relations (in the handling of grand jury investigations, conducting trials, conducting legislative hearings).

From all the emphasis which we have placed upon certain ways of thinking, observing and managing, it should not be inferred that we propose to discard or neglect the traditional skills and knowledge of the lawyer. It is the lawyer's mastery over constitutions, statutes, appellate opinions and textbooks of peculiar idiom, and his skill in operating the mechanics (procedure) of both governmental institutions and private associations that set him apart from, and give him a certain advantage over, such other skill groups in our society as diplomats, economists, social psychologists, social historians and biologists. But much of what currently passes for instruction in law schools is a waste of time because it consists of the reiteration of a limited list of ambiguous terms cut asunder from any institutional context that would set a limit to their ambiguities. Thus, a student may learn that if discussion begins with " contact ", it must then proceed by rearrangement of certain meanings to be assigned to a small list of well-known words, such as " offer and acceptance ", " consideration ", " mistake ", " performance ", " condition ", and so on ; but he knows very little unless he has also learned to complete the meaning of these terms by reference to representative institutional contexts and important social values. What we propose is that training in the distinctive core of the lawyer's repertory of skills and information be given a new sense of purpose and new criteria of relevance. It is a fundamental truth of practical and scientific psychology that purpose increases ease of learning ; students can be expected to acquire more

---

[19] Further details are given later in this Chapter, and in Part III of the present volume.

rather than less mastery of legal technicality when the comparatively small repertory of key legal terms is considered in relation to the goals and the vital problems and processes of democracy, rather than in a formalistic framework, unoriented toward policy. The lawyer's traditional storehouse of learning is already too tightly stuffed with legacies from the past to be thoroughly mastered by anyone in a lifetime of devoted scholarship ; a student must, if he is not to choke on triviality, have extrinsic criteria of relevance.   There comes a time, as Mr. Justice Holmes long ago remarked, when energy can be more profitably spent than in the reading of cases.   Given a new sense of purpose and trained in the skills and information which should be common to all policy-makers, the lawyer cannot escape becoming a better lawyer. Schools which prepare themselves to emphasize such purposes and to offer such training may succeed in becoming more truly vocational even as they grow more genuinely professional.

For a quick review of the skills appropriate to lawyers who participate in policy, the following brief table is appended. Later in the Chapter it will be explained in some detail.

SKILL TABLE

1. Skills of thought.
   (a) Goal-thinking.
      The basic values of democracy : how derived, how related operationally to concrete events.
   (b) Trend-thinking.
      Past trends and future probabilities appraised according to the degree of the realization and the distribution of the basic values.
   (c) Scientific-thinking.
      The variables that condition the democratic value-variables.
   (d) Legal technicality (the distinctive skill of the lawyer).
      The command of the vocabulary, citations and procedures that courts and other authoritative agencies expect from counsel.
2. Skills of observation.
   (a) Intensive procedures.
      Observer devotes himself for a long time to a particular person or situation and uses complex methods (detailed personality studies ; detailed studies of historical or current situations).
   (b) Extensive procedures.
      Observer devotes himself briefly to a particular person or situation and uses a simple method (brief opinion poll interview ; cursory report on a situation).
3. Skills of management.
   (a) Primary relations.
      Persons with whom one deals individually.
   (b) Public relations.
      Persons with whom one deals as members of a large group.

So much by way of broad outline. It is now incumbent upon us to spell out in more detail what we understand to be the values of a free society, the variables that condition their appearance, and the ways in which lawyers can be trained in the skills necessary to manage them with a reasonable probability of success.

DEMOCRATIC VALUES AND CONDITIONING VARIABLES

The cardinal value of democracy we have already specified as the realization of human dignity in a commonwealth of mutual deference. Let us now specify in more detail what we mean by a society where the dignity of man is proclaimed and practised. What pattern of value distribution is characteristic of a free society ? By a value we mean an object of human desire.

Three values may be named whose proper relationship determines whether we are justified in calling any group democratic. These values are power, respect, and knowledge. Where the dignity of man is fully taken into account, power is shared, respect is shared, knowledge is shared. A society in which such values are widely shared is a free society. A free society is by no means restricted to these values ; it must, however, make certain that other goal values are not incompatible with them. Within the framework of shared power, respect and knowledge, many other values may be sought, such as a high material standard of living.

We know that the degree of attainment of each cardinal value reacts favourably upon the others. Wherever power is shared it is easier to maintain a sharing of respect and knowledge. Where respect is shared it is easier to share power and knowledge. Where knowledge is shared the sharing of power and respect is simpler. In the same way that they interact with one another, these democratic variables are conditioned by other social factors. One of these variables is balance, in the sense of a balanced distribution of income. One of the earliest discoveries of civilized man was the necessity of avoiding extremes of riches and poverty if human dignity is to be realized and maintained through the years in the life of any community. Still another conditioning variable is regularity in the tempo of social development. A third variable is realism, by which is meant access to a stream of fact and comment that provides one with needed clues to sound policy. No matter how well intentioned the individual may be or how thoroughly equipped with intellectual skill and information, he is dependent upon the reports that reach him through private and public channels of communication in making up his mind on policy questions. A fourth important and very pervasive variable is character. A democratic society is most possible where democratic character prevails ; that is to say, where personalities develop with a minimum of distortion.

The foregoing list of conditioning variables does not exhaust the factors that may aid or retard the attainment of shared power, respect and knowledge, but the list does deal with a cluster of the most important. If we conceive of interpersonal relations as a continuing stream of events through days, weeks, years and generations, we can think of our policy problem as that of maintaining a proper equilibrium among component parts of this perpetual flow. Such a value as power is shared in government, business, church, in varying degree, fluctuating with the passage of time. The magnitude of this variable, indexed by whatever criteria are taken to be most appropriate, increases or diminishes in relation to the other variables we have specified.

The policy task of a free society is to put its own distinctive value-variables into practice and to control the factors that condition their attainment. In addition, other value-variables can be selected to enrich the life of the community.[20] In choosing the following goals of democratic policy we have been influenced by all of these considerations, combining the distinctive values of a free society with conditioning factors and with values that may be sought regardless of the form of society.

DISTINCTIVE GOAL VARIABLES

Shared Power. By " power " we mean participation in or the ability to participate in the making of important decisions. When such participation or ability is general, there is democracy, in so far as the power variable is concerned. The term " power ", as we use it, is equivalent to " the function of government ", which is not to be confused with the " institutions called government ". The power function may be exercised not only by agencies called " government " by the local population, but by private pressure organizations, business enterprises, churches and others. Moreover, we must be on guard against accepting all simple choices as true decisions. It is convenient to reserve the word " decision " for choices potentially or actually sanctioned

[20] Compare the comprehensive statement made in Nat. Resources Planning Board Report, " National Resources Development " (1942).

by coercion. When statutes lapse into desuetude, they have ceased to be decisions in our sense of the word. Coercive sanctions are the " proper sphere " of the state, traditionally conceived as an independent community organized for making and enforcing policy.[21] We do not reject this definition, though the identity of the institutions that exert power can only be determined by proper investigation, and must not be taken for granted through verbal coincidence.[22]

In reviewing the indexes that may be selected to determine the distribution of power in a given community, we may proceed from the institutions locally named " the government " to whatever private pressure associations are in existence. In the United States, we begin with federal, state and local government, and pass on to private pressure organizations that are recruited from, or speak in the name of, the principal groups into which the population is divided. From pressure organizations we pass to businesses, distinguished according to degree of market control (monopoly, competition) and economic function (mining, agriculture, etc.). Private associations may carry on economic functions though not organized as government or business ; an example is the consumers' co-operative. From the economic functions in private hands, we go on to consider all the widely ramifying forms of cultural activity—religious, fraternal, scientific, educational.

When organizations are scrutinized it is first necessary to examine their formal set-up. Beginning with the state, we may declare it to be democratically organized if authority to change the constitution is vested in the people, who may be authorized to act directly by referendum or indirectly through delegates and representatives.[23] The same standard is applicable to the institutions through which the state finds expression ; government is democratic when the majority can change officials or act directly on legislation. We are not satisfied to take the formal rules laid down in constitutions and statutes at their face value ;

[21] The traditional distinctions are in Burgess, *Political Science and Constitutional Law* (1891) ; Willoughby, *The Fundamental Concepts of Public Law* (1924).
[22] Still another distinction may be made in passing : when we refer to " authority " we mean forms ; by " control " we mean facts. The authoritative rules of the code books may be belied by the facts of life. Morgenthau, *La réalité des normes* (1934), distinguishes the " validity " of a rule from its " efficacy ". Some serviceable categories of " power " are in Timasheff, *An Introduction to the Sociology of Law* (1939), especially Ch. 11. See Catlin, *The Science and Method of Politics* (1927) ; Merriam, *Political Power* (1934) ; Russell, *Power* (1938).
[23] For the constitutional structure of the world on the eve of world depression and world war, see Delpech and Laferrière, *Les Constitutions Modernes* (1928–34).

we need to assemble indexes of the degree of popular control in fact as well as in name. Election statistics provide pertinent information.[24] The prevalence of what are called " elections " in despotisms reminds us that high percentages of electoral participation do not necessarily signify majority rule ; we must look beyond the figures to ascertain the degree of coercion, and this calls for properly trained observers. Election returns may reveal a very high degree of non-voting, and while this may signify indifference or hopelessness about influencing important decisions, it may be attributable to other causes. The vital point is to discover whether voters (or non-voters) possess a genuine sense of participation, whether they take it for granted that whenever they feel like it they can make a difference in the decision-making process by utilizing procedures legally available to them.[25]

Another body of participation indexes describes the affiliation of government agencies with the constituent groups of society.[26] To what extent are high, middle and low income groups found in the agencies of government ? [27] What is the relation of office-holders to the distribution of population by sex, age, race, religion, nationality of origin, or occupational skill ? [28] Does the agency receive financial or other aid from special groups, such as foreign governments or business groups ? [29] If there is little participation in office-holding by any specific group, do we find that mobility is fairly high, in the sense that persons who start life in the low income group, for example, often climb to the office-holding level ? [30]

In considering private pressure organizations [31] we must raise

[24] Data and analyses are in Gosnell, *Why Europe Votes* (1930) and Tingsten, *Political Behaviour* (1937).

[25] For attitudes associated with non-participation in elections, the material found in a pioneer study of the subject is still unexcelled : Merriam and Gosnell, *Non-Voting, Causes and Methods of Control* (1924).

[26] A classic of this type is, of course, Beard, *An Economic Interpretation of the Constitution* (1913 ; with a new introduction, 1930).

[27] See Holcombe, *The Political Parties of To-day* (1924), *The New Party Politics* (1933), and *The Middle Classes in American Politics* (1940).

[28] Specimen inquiries : Ewing, *The Judges of the Supreme Court, 1789–1937* (1938) ; Herring, *Federal Commissioners* (1936) ; Laski, *Studies in Law and Politics* (1932) ; Umbreit, *Our Eleven Chief Justices* (1938) ; Cole, " Italy's Fascist Bureaucracy ", *Am. Pol. Sci. Rev.*, vol. 32 (1938), p. 1143 ; Gerth, " The Nazi Party : Its Leadership and Composition ", *Am. J. Soc.*, vol. 45 (1940), p. 517 ; Heinberg, " The Personnel of French Cabinets, 1871–1930 ", *Am. Pol. Sci. Rev.*, vol. 25 (1931), p. 389 ; Hyneman, " Who Makes Our Laws ? ", *Pol. Sci. Q.*, vol. 55 (1940), p. 556 ; Lasswell and Sereno, " The Changing Italian Élite ", in the present volume, Part II.

[29] A succinct introduction is Senturia and Odegard, " Corruption, Political ", in *Encyc. Soc. Sciences*, vol. 4 (1931), p. 448.

[30] See Sorokin, *Social Mobility* (1927).

[31] For recent information see Blaisdell, T.N.E.C. Rep., *Economic Power and Political Pressures*, Monograph 26 (1941) ; Pearce, T.N.E.C. Rep., *Trade Association Survey*, Monograph 18 (1941).

the same questions that we have posed for government, since we are interested in both the forms of authority and the facts of control. Pressure organizations are private associations whose primary object is to influence community decisions. These organizations may be distinguished from one another according to the groups in whose name they speak, from whose ranks they recruit, or from whom they draw financial support. We need to determine which organization is connected with the chief economic divisions of society. As said above, economic divisions can be described according to economic function performed and according to the degree of market control. Another closely related classification separates the skill groups.[32] Chemists and engineers are among the professional groups whose skill consists in the manipulation of symbols of things, and of procedures in dealing with things. Lawyers and social scientists are also professional skill groups ; but their skill is the manipulation of symbols of interpersonal relations, and of procedures for dealing with people. In our inventory of private pressure organizations, we do not stop with economic and skill divisions ; each organization radiates into all the sex, age, race and other identities recognized in society. As with government, we want the facts about internal forms of authority ; and we want to investigate the intensity of participation in control processes on the part of affiliated elements to discover the extent to which the organization puts democracy into practice.[33] The foregoing questions apply to organizations in all the remaining fields of private life, when we pass from pressure organizations to private economic organizations, and from them to all remaining cultural organizations.[34]

In our discussion so far we have referred to the task of assessing the degree of democracy in the internal affairs of any significant governmental or non-governmental organization. But that does not exhaust the problem. We must take external relations into account. With respect to any one area of activity, every degree of organizational control may be found, extending from exclusive control by a single organization to rivalry among many. In world politics the relations among states are deeply conditioned

[32] Consult Lasswell, *Politics ; Who Gets What, When, How* (1936), Ch. 6 ; Carr-Saunders and Wilson, *The Professions* (1933). See Taussig and Joslyn, *American Business Leaders* (1932) ; Schwarz, " Heads of Russian Factories—A Sociological Study ", *Social Research*, vol. 9 (1942), p. 315.

[33] A recent study, representative of the best, is Garceau, *The Political Life of the American Medical Association* (1941).

[34] An enterprising attempt to appraise the state of democracy in an entire community (Akron, Ohio) is Jones, *Life, Liberty and Property* (1941).

by the expectation of violence, the expectation that whether we like it or not, adjustments will probably be made by acts of coercion ranging all the way from light pressure to all-out war. There is no organized world state ; and the typical pattern of world politics has been incessant rivalry among all powers, but particularly among a small number of great powers.[35] Freedom is found when there is one world state which is democratically organized, or when every existing state is democratically organized, or to the degree that democratic states are able to prevent interference by despotic powers.

The pattern of great power politics applies to many areas of economic activity. It is obvious that single economic organizations do not typically dominate one particular product or service throughout the world, although this state of affairs is closely approximated in peace times in nickel and certain other commodities. Inside each region, country and locality an enormous variety of set-ups prevails. Many commodities are dominated by a small number of economic great powers, whose rivalries may vary all the way from total conflict to total sham.[36] In determining the degree of democracy, indexes of the following kinds are in point : degree of monopoly control ; degree of internal democracy. To the extent to which any participant in a market can impose scarcity, he is a monopolist who has broken down a genuinely competitive market structure. He has politicized the market ; scarcity power is among the sovereign powers.

Viewing the world as a whole, it is evident that among the world's most powerful organizations are cartels and trusts that strive for world control of various markets.[37] Some private trusts and cartels add to the manipulation of scarcity by peaceful means the imposition of scarcity by violence, sometimes privately through their police, sometimes indirectly through the armed forces of the governments which they dominate, or which dominate them as instruments of total state policy. In periods of total war, the network of interests that cuts across boundary lines exhibits a

[35] A standard text outlining categories for the study of world politics is Schuman, *International Politics* (1941). A remarkable attempt to formulate interstate relations on a scientific basis is Richardson, " Generalized Foreign Politics ", *Brit. J. of Psych.*, Monograph Supplement 23 (1939).
[36] Consult Lawley, *The Growth of Collective Economy* (1938) ; Plummer, *International Combines in Modern Industry* (1938).
[37] See the vigorous articles by Brady, " Policies of National Manufacturing Spitzenverbände ", *Pol. Sci. Q.*, vol. 56 (1941), pp. 199, 379, 515 ; also Borkin and Welsh, *Germany's Master Plan* (1943).

comparatively simple pattern ; two groups of powers, each seeking to encircle the other, strive to establish totally independent zones of authority and control. So far as shared power is concerned, the general principle is to preserve competition or democratize dominance. In practice difficulties arise from the reluctance of policy-makers to clarify and enforce rules of market control in the areas under their jurisdiction. With respect to markets, notably internal markets, it may be possible to settle on workable rules of balance, to win support for the slogans that incorporate these rules, and to organize the vested and sentimental interests necessary to put them into operation.[38]

Shared Respect. Beyond the voting and arguing relations involved in the making of policy lie many other zones of human contact in which the dignity of the individual is involved.

Respect is shown in ways that may be called negative and positive. The negative side is absence of interference with individual choice, the preservation of large zones of self-determination for the private person. On the positive side respect means equality of access to opportunity for maturing latent capacity into socially valued expression.

We know that communities that share power do not always respect the individual in the sense of reserving for him large areas in which he can go his own way free from compulsion and prohibition. It is notorious that small, tightly-organized and tradition-bound neighbourhoods may hedge the zone of individual expression within narrow limits. This is true of some of the " peasant democracies " and of certain primitive societies that have been reported by ethnologists.[39] The history of sumptuary legislation shows that democracies may even excel despotisms in the austerity of the regime they prescribe for their citizens.[40] Our own principle is that the presumption is against any proposal to pour the individual into a mould ; the justification must be immediate and overwhelming necessity of the community or

[38] On rules of balance see Lasswell, *Democracy Through Public Opinion* (1941), Ch. 10.

[39] Perhaps a word of caution should be given against putting too much credence in the picture of the savage caked with custom who was so movingly described in the earlier ethnological reports. As our investigators have become more familiar with primitive culture they have been less impressed by its uniformities and more struck by personal manifestations. Contrast the point of view of W. G. Sumner and associates in *The Science of Society* (1927) with that of Edward Sapir's students in *Language, Culture and Personality* (Spier, Hallowell, and Newman ed., 1941). None the less, the degree of individualization appears to be lower than in our own highly variegated civilization.

[40] For guidance to the history see the articles on " Blue Laws ", " Prohibition ", " Sumptuary Legislation " in *Encyc. Soc. Sciences.*

clear evidence that men are affected destructively by the prevailing degree of self-direction.

In describing the degree of respect, in the negative sense, that prevails in a given community, certain indexes are pertinent, notably all that has to do with prohibitions, restrictions and compulsions upon the way the individual spends his time. The most extreme degree of disrespect for autonomy is prescribing every move that is permissible by the hour, day and week. In emergency situations, we must acquiesce in such stringent rationing of human resources. But in less critical periods, the zone of personal responsibility can be enormously extended without inflicting damage on others.

Provision for equal opportunity often involves positive measures by the community as a whole. This is notably true with regard to those persons who suffer a temporary or permanent handicap and who cannot realize their full potentialities unless special measures are taken in their behalf. Special exemptions or facilities can be made available to the immature ; to the crippled, injured, and ill ; to the unemployed and the recipients of low incomes ; to those who have received unfortunate early training.[41] Equality of sacrifice is not equality of burden ; the same burden weighs far more heavily on the weak than on the strong. We must make at least a partial application of the maxim, " from each according to his capacity, and to each according to his need ".

As indexes of mutual respect we must examine the extent to which groups participate equally in contact with one another in the non-power spheres of human relations. Scientific field workers know how to make exhaustive inventories of the state of mutual respect among persons divided according to age, sex, race, religion, skill, income, length of residence (and similar characteristics). Rates of intermarriage, access to economic activity, areas of residence, the giving and receiving of social invitations, membership in clubs and cliques, the use of courtesy forms (as in salutation)—these are among the facts of human life open to systematic investigation.[42] Besides the degree of equal

[41] For guidance to the history, see the articles on " Allowances ", " Charity ", " Child ", " Dependency ", " Disaster Relief ", " Family ", " Humanitarianism ", " Institutions ", " Public ", " Labour Legislation and Law ", " Maternity Welfare ", " Old Age ", " Pensions ", " Poor Laws ", " Public Welfare ", " Rehabilitation ", " Social Work " in *Encyc. Soc. Sciences.*

[42] For an exhaustive report on the division of a community into " classes " (respect groups, in our terminology) see the six-volume Yankee City Series in course of publication by the Yale University Press, summarizing the work of W. Lloyd

participation at any given cross-section, it is pertinent to know the facts about social mobility.   To what extent are those who begin life in a low respect position able to rise to more respected positions ?

Shared Knowledge.   One of the basic manifestations of deference to human beings is to give full weight to the fact that they have minds.   People need to be equipped with the knowledge of how democratic doctrines can be justified.   They cannot be expected to remain loyal to democratic ideals through all the disappointments and disillusionments of life without a deep and enduring factual knowledge of the potentialities of human beings for congenial and productive interpersonal relations.   As a means of maintaining a clear and realistic appraisal of human nature, there must be deeply based recognition of the factors governing the formation of human character.   No democracy is even approximately genuine until men realize that men can be free ; and that the laborious work of modern science has provided a non-sentimental foundation for the intuitive confidence with which the poets and prophets of human brotherhood have regarded mankind.   Buttressing the aspirations of these sensitive spirits stands the modern arsenal of facts about the benevolent potentialities of human nature, and a secure knowledge of methods by which distorted personality growth can be prevented or cured. Through the further application of methods that have already achieved partial success, we can provide instruments capable of putting into practice admonitions of the moralists and visions of the dreamers.   Without this knowledge, the intuitions of genius are helpless ; armed with this knowledge, including knowledge of the means of further knowledge, moral intention becomes steadily more capable of fulfilling itself in reality.   There is no rational room for pessimism about the possibility of putting morals into practice on the basis of what we know, and know we can know, about the development of human personality.[43]   Any form of crippling predestinarianism, based on myths about " heredity ", whether of an individual or a race, can be brushed aside.[44]

Warner and associates.   Also : Davis, Gardner and Gardner, *Deep South* (1941) ; Davis and Dollard, *Children of Bondage* (1940) ; Dollard, *Caste and Class in a Southern Town* (1937) ; Powdermaker, *After Freedom* (1939).

[43] In particular see Fromm, *The Fear of Freedom* (1942), and Sullivan, " Conceptions of Modern Psychiatry ", *Psychiatry : J. of Bio. and Path. of Interpersonal Relations*, vol. 3 (1940), p. 1.

[44] See Benedict, *Race and Racism* (1942), for an authoritative summary of the difference between the science of " race " and the ideology of " racism ".

If democratic forms of power are to be full-blooded with reality, the overwhelming mass of mankind must be provided with enough intellectual skill to make a proper evaluation of policy goals and alternatives. These skills include observation and analysis ; and analysis implies intellectual tools for the understanding of human relationships. Our basic knowledge must be ever-expanding ; this makes necessary an organization of scientific work capable of providing more of what we need to know about the factors that mould man and society. At present only crude indexes are available to show the state of knowledge of our people. To some extent we can rely on figures of literacy and of years in school ; [45] more subtle items are not yet described in convenient terms.

THE INSTRUMENTAL OR CONDITIONING VARIABLES

From the goal variables of shared power, shared respect, shared knowledge we now pass to other factors that determine the degree to which deference can be realized. Social processes are explicable as interacting variables ; social life is an ever-moving equilibrium. This applies to the interrelationships of the key variables. They are all in a relationship of ends and means to each other. Distribution of respect affects the distribution of power and knowledge ; in turn the distribution of knowledge affects the distribution of respect and power. More than that, we take it for granted that these key variables are affected by the magnitudes of certain other variables. In such a potential list we propose to select a few. They are chosen because they are believed to be particularly important for the development of policies capable of achieving and maintaining that interrelationship among the key variables that we call democratic. Among the conditioning variables we have chosen the following : balance ; regularity ; realism ; character.

Balance. When we speak of balance we refer to the distribution of income in any given community. By income we mean both monetary and real—the flow of money and claims of all kinds, and of food, housing, medical care, clothing, recreation, and so on. The distribution is relatively balanced when there is a comparatively small number of rich and poor. From the earliest days of systematic political speculation the importance

---

[45] See President's Research Committee on Social Trends, *Social Trends*, vol. 1 (1933), Ch. 7, and Judd, " Education ", *Am. J. Soc.*, vol. 47 (1942), p. 876.

of balanced income for democracy has been explicitly recognized.[46] Throughout the history of Greek and Roman political thought there were continual reiterations of the danger to democracy of an unbalanced distribution of property.[47]   The classics of American political thought take second place to no literature in the amount of emphasis placed upon this theme.[48]   Few political thinkers have been more acutely aware of the intimate dependence of government and economics than the men whose active hands shaped our basic institutions.

Despite the recognition given to the principle of balanced income, there has been an extraordinary failure on the part of policy-makers and their advisers to translate the principle of balance into operating rules applicable to given situations.   In the United States, for example, there is practically no literature that undertakes to stipulate the balances that are compatible with or promote the expansion of production (and hence creation of new income) and the preservation of democratic processes of government.   But it is a commonplace of politics that unless general ideas can be translated into operating slogans. and principles their effect on social life is greatly weakened.   There is little exaggeration in declaring that one of the most flagrant instances of intellectual failure is the existing ambiguity with which the problem is discussed.

It should be noted that discussions of balance often proceed in contrasting " mechanical uniformity " or " dead-level equality " with some other pattern of income distribution.   The idea seems to be that since formal equality is ridiculous, there is nothing more to be said about alternative patterns.   We do not pretend to have formulated in our own minds a final judgment about income distributions in the United States, especially since existing reports evaluate income only in dollar terms that are by no means the same as " real income ".   But certain suggestions with respect to extremes can be formulated.   At one extreme there is the possibility of an income maximum, or of rigorous removal by inheritance taxation of power based on accidental family connection.   At the other, there is the urgent need of a minimum annual income for every family, to be maintained by special

[46] Even before Plato, Euripides stated the point with great clarity in *The Suppliants* (Way's trans.), vol. 1, p. 238.

[47] This recurring theme in political thought can be conveniently followed in Sabine's compact and discriminating *A History of Political Theory* (1941).

[48] No. 10 of *The Federalist* is always in point.   See Pargellis, " The Tradition of Liberty in England and America ", *The Pa. Mag.*, vol. 65 (1941), p. 393.

payments through the Government, if necessary. There is also the possibility of free public education until early adulthood, with payments being made to each student during these probationary years.[49]

Regularity. By "regularity" is meant absence of erratic changes in social development. To-day men are only too aware of the enormous crises of insecurity that have been accentuated by the failure of our processes of production to expand at a fairly regular tempo. Instead, modern states have undergone vast periods of prosperity, promptly followed by devastating collapse.[50] During the swings between prosperity and depression, states have sought to escape from internal difficulties by increasing their impact upon the outside world. This clash of expanding and internally unstable states has bred crises of war and catastrophe, threatening the peaceful development and even the survival of forms of civilization consonant with our ideals.[51]

It must not be lost sight of that the internal structure of modern business states has put a premium on policies that promote irregularity. The economy of the United States, like that of Great Britain, has been an export surplus economy. The investors and merchants of relatively industrialized states have continually extended the scope of their activities beyond the home zone. These groups have, in recent times, curbed the admission of industrial imports in the home area while they continue to operate abroad with surpluses obtained in the internal market.

The possibility of receiving capital returns and repayment from foreign areas depends either upon the preservation of peace and the willingness to receive imports or the winning of a war of conquest that brings the capital equipment—such as mine

[49] In arriving at proximate goals not too far removed from recent facts, it is necessary to consider the data, relations and procedures set forth in such investigations by the National Bureau of Economic Research as : Barger, *Outlay and Income in the United States, 1921–1938* (1942) ; Kuznets, *National Income and its Composition, 1919–1938* (1941). On the crucial significance of every form of balance for freedom, see Mosca, *The Ruling Class* (Livingston ed., 1939).

[50] On the facts about irregularity and the losses resulting from them, see Thorp and Mitchell, *Business Annals* (1926), and National Resources Committee, *The Structure of the American Economy* (1939), Part I. On the relation of acts called " criminal " to economic fluctuations, see Bonger, *Criminality and Economic Conditions* (1916). A particularly elaborate inquiry into crimes against property in Germany is Schwarz, " Kriminalität u. Konjunktur ", *Intern. Rev. of Soc. Hist.*, vol. 3 (1938), p. 335.

[51] On state expansion and conflict see Wright, *A Study of War* (1942). For analyses of fundamental economic sources of maladaptation, consult Clark, *The Conditions of Economic Progress* (1940) ; Meade, *An Introduction to Economic Analysis and Policy* (1938) ; Moulton, *Income and Economic Progress* (1935) ; Robinson, *Essays in the Theory of Employment* (1937) ; Wright, *Economic Adaptation to a Changing World Market* (1939).

machinery, public utilities and manufacturing plants—into an enlarged home zone. To the degree that home peoples share in more values—more income, safety and deference—than they would receive from alternative uses at home, they gain from foreign investment. To the degree that such investment causes the home population to lose income, compromise safety or endanger their power or respect or other deference values, they suffer.[52] Steady inflation of the world price level, together with periodic revaluation of monetary units, are among the factors that contribute to transforming into gifts the exports that were once listed as foreign sales accounts receivable, or as investments abroad. Zones of foreign trade and investment affect more than the structure of world markets—they quietly alter the balance of power, perpetually tilting the scale of fighting effectiveness on the side of Great Britain, or the United States, or Germany, or Russia, or Japan, or of any combination of powers.

Within the structure of world business economies there are focal points of intense pressure on behalf of ever more foreign trade and investment. Banking houses gain underwriting profits from the flotation of foreign loans and great manufacturing industries find it easier to expand the market of established products than to diversify their offerings on the internal market. Whenever an economy passes into the hands of a monopolistic or militaristic ruling class that tries to keep the masses of the population adjusted to a low standard of living as a means of reducing labour costs of production, and of fostering the manufacture of military and commercial export goods, the aggressive-expansionistic tendencies of an economy are at a maximum. The outstanding recent examples, of course, are Japan, Germany, and Italy.

With one exception the industrialized or industrializing economies have not solved the problem of operating a modern system of machine production at a regular tempo. These problems have been postponed to an unspecified future in which it was assumed that the world would be one big market ; and it was implied that some automatic and benevolent process would introduce into the closed world market an internal balance that had never been achieved or thought out for any " closed ", " continental " or " empire " market. The only great state, with

---

[52] Resistance to imports is revealed by protective tariffs and similar restrictive measures. Note especially the resistance of industrial states against receiving indemnities.

an independent as distinct from an export surplus economy, is Russia ; and it may be some cause for foreboding that independence was achieved by means of internal despotism (even though ideological aspirations remained humanistic). Does this mean that one world market will evolve one world boss ? Or are there means of fusing the technical controls appropriate to an independent economy with controls consistent with freedom ? It is probable that within any closed economy regular production can be attained by proper monetary policy. So far, however, the focal points of initiative in our business economies have not put the needed energy behind such monetary measures.

Realism. By " realism " is meant access to a body of fact and comment on the basis of which decisions can be made to implement effectively democratic values. This is not only a matter of skill in thought and observation, for people of great intellectual competence are dependent upon the information that actually comes to their notice when they are trying to make up their minds on policy questions. One guarantee of realism is the provision of proper balance between those who generally emphasize one or another kind of alternative.[53] What appears in the mass media, such as press, radio and film, must provide most of the facts and comments in the light of which sound public judgments can be made. But the problem of realism goes far beyond the content of channels of mass communication. It includes the quality of material made available to decision-makers at every level. Legislators, judges, and juries, administrative commissions, boards of directors, executive committees, must all make their determinations on the basis of what comes to their notice.[54]

The fact that so many unrealistic decisions have been made in the past suggests the importance of providing for a proper balance of fact and interpretation in the future. There is no royal road to truth, but there is reasonable probability of reaching truth when channels are open to the free play of news and opinion, and not closed according to the special prejudices of a few. The vitality of democratic processes, however, cannot be assured by

---

[53] Valuable for the analysis of public opinion remain Arnold, *The Symbols of Government* (1935) ; Dewey, *The Public and its Problems* (1927) ; Dicey, *Lectures on the Relation between Law and Public Opinion in England during the 19th Century* (1905) ; Lippman, *Public Opinion* (1932) ; Wallas, *Human Nature in Politics* (1909), and *The Great Society* (1914).

[54] On the intelligence function see Lasswell, " Policy and the Intelligence Function ", in the present volume, Part I. A penetrating study of the foundations of military decision-making in France is Possony, " Organized Intelligence ; The Problem of the French General Staff ", *Social Research*, vol. 8 (1941), p. 213.

simple acquiescence in the idea that freedom to talk will result in decisions consistent with the preservation of the democratic system.   We have seen too many republics make suicidal decisions to believe that passivity is enough.   Obviously there was not enough affirmative effort in Weimar Germany to clarify the values and conditions adequate to the perpetuation of the Republic. To the ideal of toleration there must be joined energetic determination to find and disseminate truth over falsehood, the better opinion over the worse opinion.   Otherwise democracy can perish by default.

It is technically possible to survey the media of communication to find out whether those who have access to them obtained a balanced " diet " of fact and opinion, or whether the members of some publics are condemned to one-sided reporting and comment.[55]   We can safely say that democracy is endangered wherever the sources are one-sided, and men are allowed to freeze their convictions free from the hot discipline of exposure to contradiction.   Science and common sense are at one in emphasizing the importance of certain factors that influence the quality of debate and final judgment.   Disclosure of source is important,[56] since one who is notified of source is better able to evaluate probable freedom from bias and probable competence. The quality of decision is imperilled when non-relevant matters are allowed to absorb and distract attention from realistic considerations.   It is sound policy to protect the integrity of thought by excluding or nullifying the non-relevant.   Some procedures of thought and discussion aid in clarifying goals and alternatives.[57]

Character.   Character refers to the degree of integration achieved by individual personalities.   The democratic character is distinguished by capacity to respect the self and others.   It has been pointed out by modern psychiatrists that self-love is not to be confused with selfishness ; indeed that selfishness, or domineering arrogance, are evidence of some lack of self-esteem.[58]

[55] Scientific procedures will be described later.   On problems of policy see Catlin, " Propaganda as a Function of Democratic Government ", in *Propaganda and Dictatorship* (Child's ed., 1936).

[56] See Chafee, *Free Speech in the United States* (1941) ; Riesman, " Civil Liberties in a Period of Transition ", *Pub. Policy* (1942), p. 33, and " Democracy and Defamation : Fair Game and Fair Comment—II ", *Col. L. Rev.*, vol. 42 (1942), p. 1282 ; Smith, " Democratic Control of Propaganda through Registration and Disclosure —I ", *Pub. Opinion Q.*, vol. 6 (1942), p. 27.

[57] See Smith, " Propaganda Analysis and the Science of Democracy ", *Pub. Opinion Q.*, vol. 5 (1941), p. 250.

[58] See Fromm, " Selfishness and Self-Love ", *Psychiatry : J. of Bio. and Path. of Interpersonal Relations*, vol. 2 (1939), p. 507.

Within the last two generations the patient, objective study of development during infancy, childhood and adolescence has enormously extended our knowledge of factors affecting the growth and deformation of human personality.[59] Whatever damages the child's respect for himself gives rise to a chain of adjustments that may result in a character dangerous to the individual and to his neighbours.[60] Such secondary attitudes as the acceptance of democratic doctrine may be incorporated in personalities whose basic structure is incompatible with the ideals of mutual respect. Yet very well-integrated characters may live in societies where caste differentiations are taken for granted and these personalities may express secondary attitudes grossly incompatible with democratic ideals. In short, there is no one-to-one correspondence between the total structure of personality and expression in any single sector, such as in the sphere of secondary political attitudes. We know, however, that under stress the underlying character formation exercises profound influence over the conduct of the individual.

A very interesting and important pioneer investigation undertook to probe the relationship between socialist attitudes and character formation in pre-Nazi Germany.[61] The study revealed a very large discrepancy between the characters of many who called themselves socialist and the political attitudes that they professed. This was a basic weakness of the parties that sustained the Republic in Germany. In view of these considerations it is only wise foresight for any society that aspires toward democracy to use every means within its power to make sure that the persons who come to adulthood possess characters whose basic structure is compatible with democratic values.

NON-DISTINCTIVE GOAL VARIABLES

In addition to its distinctive values of shared power, respect and knowledge, any democratic society can rightfully aspire to the achievement of other values. The list that follows suggests with even briefer treatment than was given the distinctive and conditioning variables, a few such non-distinctive values.

Safety and Health. Among the variables non-distinctive of

---

[59] For the early years modern knowledge is authoritatively summarized for general use in Gesell and Ilg, *Infant and Child in the Culture of To-day* (1942). For later epochs, Cole, *The Psychology of Adolescence* (1936).

[60] See, for example, Glueck and Glueck, *One Thousand Juvenile Delinquents* (1934) ; Healy and Bronner, *New Light on Delinquency and its Treatment* (1936).

[61] See Fromm, a manuscript report to be published.

democracy but almost universally sought can be placed safety and health. We might include them as subdivisions of the respect category, in the sense that respect for individuality requires provision of safe, healthy environments. The present plan, however, gives this basic value some of the prominence that it deserves and aids in keeping the category of respect within manageable limits. We know that health and safety are not equally distributed throughout the community but are often directly correlated with income. Sickness is a poor man's burden.[62] Because of the varying incidence of war, various parts of the world differ greatly in safety and the hand of mortality presses with special weight on some elements of the community.[63]

Comfort, Convenience, Taste. Without seeking to expand the discussion we may at least add comfort, convenience and taste as a reminder that they need not be foresworn by democratic societies. As the general material standard of living improves, it presumably affords members of any community wider opportunities for gratifying themselves in new and refined ways.

EXISTING CURRICULUM NOT ORIENTED TOWARD ACHIEVEMENT OF DEMOCRATIC VALUES

It should be obvious that our existing law school curriculum is not adequately oriented toward achieving the distinctive values and conditioning variables of a free society. For the most part the organizing principle still appears to be legal technicality ; problems are defined and classified in terms of overlapping legal concepts of high level abstraction rather than in reference to social objectives. Concerned largely with the traditional, conventional syntax of appellate opinions, the curriculum offers little explicit consideration of alternative social objectives, general or specific, or of justifications for preference or preference priorities. Legal concepts and doctrines, which in theory are instrumental only, are too often presented as if they embodied the prime democratic values of society, and specific decisions are too often appraised or justified, not according to the degree to which they implement these values, but exclusively in terms of their supposed logical derivation from ambiguous definitions and doctrines. Little orientation is given in the historical and contemporary

[62] For guidance to available information, see articles on " Morbidity " and "Mortality " in *Encyc. Soc. Sciences*, vol. 11 (1933), pp. 3, 33.
[63] On war see Sorokin, *loc. cit. supra*, vol. 3, note 16 ; Wright, *A Study of War* (1942).

trends that are most helpful in determining what problems are most important and what objectives are most practicable, and in supplying the background necessary to the formation of realistic judgments about such important problems as do find their way —more often by accident than design—into the present curriculum. Scientific study of the factors that condition the use of old, or the creation of new, social controls (doctrines, slogans and structures) is almost non-existent. Finally, by reason of exaggerated emphasis upon legal technicality, the methods of social control brought to the notice of the student are too much restricted to a single institution—an institution whose rôle in the total process of modern life is of steadily diminishing relative importance —the appellate court and the norms it announces.

Comprehensive and detailed documentation of the above criticisms is no doubt superfluous. It is a matter of common knowledge that the main organizing foci of our existing curriculum are " contract ", " property ", " tort ", " crime ", and the " police power " of government—all much favoured instruments of the *laissez-faire* society that is to-day so desperately navigating the troubled waters of a hostile epoch. From these master concepts, about which are organized our extensive introductory exercises in the conventional legal syntax, stem a plethora of repetitive secondary courses—such as Sales, Insurance, Credit Transactions, Bills and Notes—which, though they may grope after social values and institutional contexts, seldom have the temerity to throw away the blinders of their organizing principle of legal technicality. Cutting across the same factual problems are certain other courses, such as " equity " or " trusts ", which offer exercises in parallel syntaxes inherited from a court system that no longer exists, or such as " wills " or " conveyances ", which take their name and topical organization from certain common legal instruments and their contents. Add a few courses on the rules that are supposed to govern the allocation of power among courts and the rules of fair combat before courts, with, perhaps, a course or two on " administrative procedure " or " legislation ", plus a few faint allusions to " international law ", and the contemporary law student's feast of reason is complete. Small wonder that a distinguished faculty not long ago concluded that it makes little difference in what order the feast is served to the student or the student is served to the feast.[64]

The assumption back of a curricular organization in terms of

[64] See Faculty of Law, Columbia University, *op. cit. supra*, note 1, at p. 58.

legal technicality—an assumption long since explicitly repudiated by most law teachers—is that the body of conventional legal doctrine at once provides comprehensive and well-ordered coverage of the important problems of our society and embodies our preferred values for the handling of such problems. Thus, if a student thoroughly masters such concepts as " offer and acceptance ", " consideration ", " conditions ", " fraud ", " duress ", and " legality ", he will know, it is assumed, what agreements are important in our society, how they affect the distribution of values, and to what extent they will be enforced under what conditions and how. Whether, while mastering these concepts, he focuses his attention on agreements to climb flagpoles or on international cartels is largely immaterial—institutional contexts and modes of adjustment or control other than agreement within such contexts are irrelevant. So also if a student masters the syntactic mysteries of " liability ", " anatomy of fault ", " negligence ", " absolute liability ", " nuisance ", " trespass ", " motive ", and " malice ", the assumption runs that he will be able to handle the redistribution of " unintended losses " in our society in a way that will promote democratic values irrespective of whether the damage is caused by animals, automobiles, blasting, rotten housing, defective consumers' goods, or industrial accident ; institutional contexts are once again largely irrelevant and problems of prevention must be left to the tillers of other syntax. Similarly, the organizing foci of the " property " courses are such concepts as " easement ", " profit ", " servitude " or " land contract ", " deed ", " delivery ", " covenant of title ", or " reversion ", " remainder ", and " executory interest ", and not such goals as the provision of healthful housing, in well-planned communities, for all citizens at prices that they can afford to pay or the promotion of the cheap, secure, and speedy transfer of land, without adventitious restraints having no basis in policy, or the appraisal of doctrines and practices about the transmission of wealth from generation to generation in terms of their effect on a balanced distribution of claims in society. Even the so-called public law courses are still organized with too much deference to " separation of powers ", " jurisdiction ", " due process ", " equal protection ", " interstate commerce ", " police power ", " tax power ", " spending power ", " war power ", " public purpose ", and " public use ". Struggles between governmental units and private groups are isolated from their institutional contexts, and academic investigations into the " public control of business " seldom sweep through all the important businesses and relevant controls or are explicitly oriented toward a full and optimal use of resources.

The traditional language of lawyers and the conventions of judicial etiquette indeed lend spurious plausibility to the assump‐ tion that underlies most of our existing curriculum. The accredited language contains a series of symbols of identification that are available for use in referring to parties who invoke hierarchies of normative statements purporting to specify which relations ought to obtain among such parties when certain factual statements can be assumed to be true and can be subsumed under certain other legal definitions and doctrines. What is commonly called " the law " can, thus, be defined as a syntactic system of propositions composed of terms that are supposedly defined, plus some admittedly indefinable terms, whose modes of combination are governed by certain postulates and rules. In venerable fiction this system, like that of a science or a theology, is internally consistent and complete in its reference ; from its central terms, definitions, and rules, all possible relations can be deduced. If X is a specified entity, X then bears a certain relationship to another entity, Y, or, in more sophisticated form, there is a whole series of interrelationships governed by prescribed rules. If Y performs a specified act, he becomes another entity, Y, and his relations to X are defined by still other rules. Such is the pattern. Courts are confronted by parties who make use of this traditional terminology in describing themselves and the happenings on which they base their claims. Such parties declare that they are " sureties ", or " guarantors of collection ", or " residuary legatees ", or " remainder-men ", and that such and such a defence is " personal " or that such and such an interest is a " con‐ tingent remainder " and hence " destructible ". They ask the courts to apply other identifying terms to the remaining parties to the controversy, and, hence to adopt the rule that is laid down in the authoritative books for governing the interrelations of " entities " so defined. Politely responding to the losers in their own terms, courts allow or disallow the claims advanced by the various parties and justify—and perhaps partly guide—their decisions by invoking the traditional language. Allowing the claims of certain parties, it labels them according to the appro‐ priate identification terminology and declares that its decision is consistent with certain authoritative statements governing such entity relationships. It need occasion no surprise that text-writers, digest-compilers, and curriculum-makers largely work within this framework.

That " the law " consists of a closed, automatic, syntactical system is, as has been suggested above, an assumption too obviously belied by the facts for many to give it conscious credence to-day.[65] Most of the key terms and propositions of the legal syntax are, admittedly, tautological in the sense that they take whatever meaning they have from relations between sign and sign ; [66] they cannot be given meaning in terms of empirical events of behaviour (relations between signs and objects) except by reference to the very judicial responses which they are supposed to predict or justify.[67] But here all resemblance to a true syntactical system ends. The terms and propositions of the legal syntax are neither internally consistent nor comprehensive in their reference. They are, on the contrary, inconsistent, ambiguous, and full of omissions. Mr. Justice Cardozo aptly remarked that legal principles have, unfortunately, the habit of travelling in pairs of opposites.[68] A judge who must choose between such principles can only offer as justification for his choice a proliferation of other such principles in infinite regress or else arbitrarily take a stand and state his preference ; and what he prefers or what he regards as " authoritative " is likely to be a product of his whole biography. Should a judge so beset by antimony, decry " high priori " solution by existing principle and seek the help of more humble induction from previous cases, he does not

[65] For an excellent statement of the traditional view, see the Introduction in Beale, *A Treatise on the Conflict of Laws* (1935).

[66] For an explanation of the distinctions here made see Morris, " Foundations of the Theory of Signs " in *Internat. Encyc. of Unified Science*, vol. I (1938), No. 2.

[67] What empirical observations can be made to determine whether a mortgagee has " title ", or whether a defence claimed by a surety is " personal " or " real ", or whether a right of way is a " licence " or an " easement ", or whether a covenant " touches and concerns ", or whether a group of donees is a " class ", or whether " title " under a power of appointment comes from the donee or the donor? Does the mortgagee get possession because he has title or does he have title because he gets possession? Is the partner an agent because he is a partner or vice versa? Is the promise of a " right-of-way " revocable because it is a licence or is it a licence because it is revocable? Does the covenant run because it touches and concerns or does it touch and concern because it runs? And so on. What, furthermore, is the clear and consistent reference of words like " title ", " personal ", " vested ", and so forth, to either major democratic values or any sub-values? What place have such symbols in a system of policy norms? As Cook has pointed out in " Scientific Method and the Law ", *A.B.A.J.*, vol. 13 (1927), p. 303, at p. 305, we may say that " all gostaks are doshes " and that " all doshes are galloons " and conclude with strictest logic that " all gostaks are galloons " and still not know what we are talking about.

[68] For documentation see Cardozo, *The Paradoxes of Legal Science* (1928), and Oliphant and Hewitt's Introduction to Rueff, *From the Physical to the Social Sciences* (1929).

escape his dilemma. Consciously or unconsciously, if he keeps within the legal syntax, he must beg the very question that he has to decide. The point has been well made by Oliphant and Hewitt : [69]

If the principle . . . " induced " is no broader than the sum of the previous cases which it summarizes, it obviously does not and cannot include the case to be decided, which, by hypothesis, is a new and an undecided case, and, hence, can form no part of the generalization made from previous cases only. If it does not include the case to be decided, it is powerless to produce and determine a decision of it. If it is taken to include the case to be decided, it assumes the very thing that is supposed to be up for decision.

Facts in controversy do not neatly subsume themselves under legal concepts. A judge or other arbiter must create his minor as well as his major premise ; in putting similarities and taking differences, in eliminating the irrelevant and emphasizing the relevant, he must make policy choices. Legal syntax alone— it is no news—does not and cannot dictate decision. [70]

Contemporary legal scholarship has, therefore, largely abandoned the once prestigeful effort to reduce the vast coruscation of traditional legal learning to beautifully terraced unified statements, geometrically laid out with no overlapping, erosion or gaps. In the main modern scholarship works in one of two directions. Certain iconoclasts content themselves with rather fruitless *exposes* of existing imperfection and present " the law " as a chaotic mass of confused and more or less meaningless statements. Other and more ambitious investigators set themselves the task of attempting to determine what courts and other decision-making bodies do, as opposed to what they say they do. Their aim is the legitimate scientific goal of prediction. After making precise summaries of what courts have done in the past they look into the future and forecast what courts will do when confronted with certain affirmations of facts and various patterns of legal language. Such studies enlarge the scope of legal training and bring it in closer relation to the living reality of the judicial process. They escape the stereotype of law as a body of completed rules about entities and the almost equally naïve and sterile iconoclasm of imagining that words have no significance whatsoever in forecasting judicial conduct. In the name of prediction they have

[69] *Idem* at p. xix.
[70] See Dewey, " Logical Method and Law ", *Corn. L.Q.*, vol. 10 (1924), p. 17. Compare Fuller, " Williston on Contracts ", *N.C.L. Rev.*, vol. 18 (1939), p. 1, and Patterson, " Logic in the Law ", *U. of Pa. L. Rev.*, vol. 90 (1942), p. 875.

often gone far enough to provide courts with more concise formulæ for reconciling past inconsistencies than the courts have been able to create themselves and hence, much as business forecasters affect the stock market, predictors have shepherded judges toward the fulfilment of prophecy. Yet this recent emphasis on prediction, however laudable it may be, cannot be said to have brought about important changes in the classification or presentation of legal materials in textbook or casebook. Organizing foci remain all too often in the frame of legal technicality ; prevailing methods of investigation continue at the level of loose impressionism ; and, least heartening of all, the scope of permissible inquiry does not necessarily include the most significant variables affecting judicial response.

Seriously undertaken, the goal of forecasting judicial behaviour poses formidable problems to the legal scholar. The less he is preoccupied with the symmetry of legal syntax and the more with prediction, the less he continues in the rôle of logician to the state and the more he must become a man of science. As scientist, it is his task to account for the occurrence of a selected category of events—to wit : judicial conduct. To account for such conduct he must take into consideration all variables that may significantly determine it. Every resourceful practitioner knows that judicial conduct is affected, not by rival phraseology alone, but by such factors as the nature of the value in controversy, the position of litigant and judge in the structure of society, the personality characteristics of judges, parties, counsel, witnesses and juries, and the method of conducting cases. The legal scholar who would predict the future course of decision must equip himself with skills appropriate to the task of evaluating variables and this means that to his traditional knowledge of legal technicality it is imperative to add naturalistic skills of observation and analysis. As scientist, the legal scholar will conceive that the response of any court is affected by two sets of factors : environmental and predispositional. By environmental factors is meant what goes on when cases are tried ; predisposing factors are how matters stand before the case is opened. Briefs, oral arguments, testimony and exhibits are typical environmental factors (E). The biases of the judge against the very rich or the very poor, the white or the black, the commerce clause or the opinions of Mr. Justice Brandeis, are all part of the predispositions (P) with which the judge approaches the trial, and, in conjunction with E factors, determine his response (R). The final response of the judge is " yes " or " no " to a value claim ; hence he indulges or deprives the parties to a litigation.   If we had scientific laws of judicial decision they would relate given classes of R to E and P. More strictly, such scientific propositions would state the probability of R' (a specified type of decision) to R'' (another type of decision).   Truly scientific propositions of this nature can only rest on data of observation.   Scientific prediction is based on the expectancy that past relations among variables will continue, and that when a given list of variables occurs in the future, their interrelations can be foretold on the basis of proper analysis of observations made on them in the past.   The ordinary forecast is a vaguely qualified assertion, or prophecy, that a given concrete event will in fact take place ; that is, that a certain judge will decide a specific case for the defendant or the plaintiff.   Strictly speaking, such a forecast is not a scientific prediction, even though it may be arrived at partly as the basis of scientific knowledge. Propositions that formulate scientific predictions are statements of the probability that if E and P are so and so, R', not R'', will occur.[71]

Despite the verbal support given to the idea of prediction, existing investigations have not moved very far along the path of science.   Even with the vigorous and outspoken encouragement of a few pioneers (like Walter Wheeler Cook and Underhill Moore), scientific habits of thought are still largely alien to the training of legal scholars.   Little has been done either to make clear the nature of the assumptions involved in any prediction or forecast of judicial response, or to construct the theories and develop the techniques of fact-finding necessary to discover and to interrelate the more significant variables in the environment and predisposition of courts.   Some inkling of the true complexity of the task of framing predictive rules, or of making concrete forecasts, may be gained from the following outline, which is no more than a rough, preliminary categorization of some of the principal variables which may affect the response of a court or other authoritative agency to a controversy.[72]

Claims Presented.   The competing claims presented by the

[71] On the theory of science, see Cohen, *Reason and Nature* (1931) ; Reichenbach, *Experience and Prediction* (1938) ; Nagel, " Principles of the Theory of Probability " in *Intern. Encyc. of Unified Science* (1939), No. 6.

[72] This outline is in part a condensation of one previously used in a criticism of Volume III of the Restatement of Property.   McDougal, " Future Interests Restated : Tradition versus Clarification and Reform ", *Harv. L. Rev.*, vol. 55 (1942), p. 1077.   Many of the sentences should be in quotation.

Whatever the potentialities of the table for predictive, scientific purposes, it has parties to the court (or other agency) : who they are, what they demand, from whom, and why they think they are entitled to their demands.

Objective Facts. The facts which give rise to the controversy as an objective, non-participant observer who utilizes all available sources may determine them. The observational standpoint here must be kept clear. It is not that of the parties ; their view appears as " claims presented ". It is not that of the court ; the judge's view of the " facts " is part of the response to be explained on the basis of the total context of environment and predisposition. The perspective here is that of the disinterested, scientific observer trying to predict human behaviour.

In deciding what to accept as " objective facts " about the original dispute, two sets of sources are available ; namely, allegations made during the trial, and information from other places. It should be noted that the prediction studies may be made on the basis of one or both sets of data. The observer may limit himself to making a critical comparison of everything that was offered in court ; obviously, he may arrive at a picture that differs from the one accepted by the judge, which is included in the R of the court. If the observer has access to other information about the original dispute, he may accept a picture of reality that diverges even more from the view of the facts assumed by the judge.

Two distinct, though related, scientific problems may be studied—one concerned with the response of the parties, and the other with the judge. We have already made it clear that we are interested in how the court responds to " claims presented " and to the " objective facts ". We may also explore what kinds of disagreement are taken before courts, rather than other tribunals, which calls for data about the predispositions of persons

some advantages for expository purposes over the usual dichotomy between " legal concepts " and " operative facts ". The word " operative ", as indicated in the text, conceals three different observational standpoints, that of the parties, that of the court, and that of an objective observer ; in deciding what facts are " operative " a court must smuggle in its own response to the facts as an objective observer would report them. The addition of " policy norms " focuses attention, furthermore, upon the variable which is presumably most significant in contemporary society.

One of the writers has found the table most helpful in exploding the theoretical differences between such concepts as " licence ", " easement ", " profit ", and " estate ", and between " legal " and " equitable " interests and in discussion of such complicated topics as " delivery " of deeds. Its usefulness in clarifying the illusory character of the traditional distinctions between the various categories of future interests was sought to be demonstrated in the article above cited in this note. For further citations on the method of multiple-variable analysis, see that article at p. 1080, n. 7, and Hicks, *Materials and Methods of Legal Research* (3rd ed., 1942), p. 35.

at the time they became involved in disputes. Our knowledge of causal connections is much greater if we can follow the entire sequence that begins with the occurrence of a disagreement. Thus we can hope to predict the probable response of courts and other agencies to probable kinds of objective situations.

Legal Norms. These are the conventional justifications of decisions which judges have become conditioned to give to losing counsel and higher courts,[73] and are the syntactical propositions that appear in legal textbooks and appellate opinions. Most often they are in words found in the peculiar and distinctive vocabulary of lawyers, like " vested ", " contingent ", " executory interest ", " title ", " delivery ", " privity ", " due process ", " equal protection ", and so on. Typically they point to no identifiable social goals ; they are, as indicated above, tautological in the sense that they can be given meaning only by circular reference to the very behaviour which they are usually supposed to justify and predict.

Legal norms enter into scientifically conducted precision studies at several places. The R of the court is partly describable by taking note of the legal norms that are invoked or rejected in support of the decision. Legal norms also enter in the P of the judges ; it can be shown that courts in different jurisdictions are predisposed during a certain period to rely upon different doctrines. Forecasts need continual revision as judicial predispositions change ; every R of the court immediately becomes part of the P of its future response.

There is yet another way in which legal norms are involved in the predictive studies ; they enter into the E of the judges when they are invoked as part of the justification of the " claims presented ". If the spokesmen of the litigants invoke doctrines against which the court is unfavourably disposed in support of a claim, no doubt the court will reject the claim, or at least the probability of such a response is greater than if the claimant's counsel made use of discourse toward which dispositions were favourable. In forecasting the outcome of specific litigation we may ask which claimant is likely to be best represented by counsel who are informed about the P of the court on doctrinal points. This problem, like the question whether a given disagreement will be carried before a court at all, is separable from the narrow task of studying the response of judges, since it calls for an explana-

[73] See Moore and Sussman, " The Lawyer's Law ", *Yale L.J.*, vol. 41 (1932), p. 566.

tion of the response of the claimant. In assembling data about
legal norms for use in prediction studies, therefore, we must
carefully indicate whose norms they are supposed to be, whether
of the judge before or during trial, or of the claimant before or
during trial. Besides those who participate directly in the proceedings, many others—ranging from the general public to specific
elements within it—may take a hand in invoking legal norms ;
and what they say becomes part of the environment, whenever
it is brought openly or privately to the notice of anyone connected
with what goes on in court.

Policy Norms. These are propositions about how values ought
to be distributed, including those to which we have given special
mention. Sometimes the norms are invoked or rejected in propositions of high level abstraction ; often they are condensed into
slogans ; and frequently they are implied by the specific endorsement of concrete measures. As with many legal norms, statements of policy concern prediction studies when they are made by
judges or claimants before or during proceedings. Furthermore,
they may impinge upon the environment of all participants when
they are invoked by the public at large or by specific sectors of it.

Other Norms and Statements. In addition to legal and policy
norms, statements are often made, supported or rejected, that
appeal to such supplementary norms as authority, reason (or
logic), evidence, nature (and science), faith, tradition or administrative convenience.

Personality and Value Position. What judges and juries do is
" human " in the sense that it is affected to some extent by the
impact of personalities upon one another. The interaction of an
aggressive claimant, counsel or witness upon judge and jury may
produce different results than when submissive types are involved.
Besides the factor of personality we must take into account the
constellation of factors that link participants to the value structure
of society. Powerful and respected people interact upon one
another and upon weak and disreputable persons very differently
than the poor react to the poor or the middle-class groups respond
to one another and to those above and below them in value
position.

Judicial or Administrative Structure and Procedure. The result of
litigation is affected in varying degree by the set-up of courts
and related structures and by the procedures actually used.

Skill. We now come to one of the most subtle variables that
determines " law in action " ; namely, skill. This is a matter

of taking advantage of the opportunities afforded in any situation for the achievement of ends by the most economical means. Not only do counsel invoke legal, policy and other norms and statements in influencing the court ; these factors are presented in a certain pattern of interrelationship. Personality and social types may be brought to the notice of the court in ways that strengthen the total impact made on the judge.

Properly adapted, this scheme may be used to include all data required to lay a scientific foundation for prediction. At present, however, the actual content of law school instruction has been relatively little influenced either by the urge to foretell or the skill to predict scientifically. It may be noted that when scientific search for rules of prediction gains the upper hand, legal syntax ceases to occupy the centre of attention. Legal norms furnish only part of the data necessary for the formulation of prediction rules. A law school curriculum, organized around scientific prediction, would be compelled to re-evaluate the significance given to legal technicality. Does this imply, however, that prediction should be accepted as a sound principle of curricular reconstruction ? It is true that in the search for predictive rules, values are given some consideration when policy norms are noted ; but the search does not begin with clarifying value goals. The point of departure is a controversy, and the most prominent initial variable is " claims presented ". When attention is directed to other variables, value objectives are de-emphasized ; hence goal considerations are subordinated in prediction studies. Too much stress on prediction inhibits creative approaches by the student to policy questions ; scientific formalism can be as sterile, in so far as the implementation of democratic value goes, as legal technicality, especially if scientific inquiry is chiefly directed toward the forecasting of judicial behaviour. In predicting decisions as in explaining any response, there is no end to the number of factors that may be taken into account, or the degree of technical refinement to which the gathering and processing of data may be carried. A vast amount of work on the courts may result in comparatively meagre contributions to policy, since it may be doubted whether the opportunity of courts to redistribute values is currently as great as that of legislatures, or of their administrative and corporate creatures. The student who would affect the distribution of values and hence make an influential impact on society must not only bear in mind his policy values, but must try to evaluate and command every control necessary to reach his goal. Imagination should not be too quickly turned toward winning arguments in court or passively forecasting the outcome of litigation, before the previous question has been raised—whether avenues of action other than those provided by the court may not serve the long-term policy needs of a client. Effective policy-thinking must be manipulative, originative, evocative, creative. It cannot substitute the calculation of an endless fan of possibilities for disciplined and imaginative attention to actualizing the most favoured possibility. Unlike logical or scientific thinking, policy-thinking is not primarily contemplative and passive ; it is goal-thinking and provides criteria for the selection of arguments as well as for the control of other pertinent factors. It is developmental, unifying preference and probability.

In the light of the foregoing considerations, we must unequivocally reject both the principles of legal technicality and of scientific prediction as criteria for reconstructing a curriculum for training lawyers to put democratic values into policy.

New Principles of Curricular Organization Directed Toward Policy

At the outset of our positive statement of principles and recommendations, let us make it perfectly clear that we have no hesitation in accepting the traditional assumption that it is imperative for the student to acquaint himself with the established legal syntax. For many generations to come it will be indispensable to persuasive communication. There is, furthermore, no royal road to its mastery. Just how many cases, read for how many hours, discussed for how many hours, described in how many examinations, can turn out a student adequately equipped for the successful manipulation of legal doctrine and procedure ? Certainly no one can successfully demonstrate an exact answer to this question. Nevertheless, we are not entirely in the dark. It is possible to find out how many cases are usually discussed in the various years of a student's work in modern law schools of good standing. The contents of the casebooks provide a clue. Suppose we agree that during his period in law school a student must gain the command over legal technicality that comes from having read and discussed with varying degrees of intensiveness X thousands of cases. The question then becomes by what principles should law teachers select and organize these cases.

Life, like " the law ", is, of course, a " seamless web ". For any event the causal factors are so many and so interdependent that, strictly speaking, it is impossible to tear any one episode from the web of human experience in which it is embedded and treat it in strict isolation from the configuration of which it is a part. Yet classify we must if we are to cope with the " big, booming, buzzing confusion " about us and direct it toward our purposes. Our present major purpose is to promote the adaptation of legal education to the policy needs of a free society. Therefore, our first principle is that all legal structures, definitions, and doctrines must be taught, evaluated, and recreated in terms of the basic democratic values. Not only the legal syntax but also all legal structures and procedures must be related to the larger institutional contexts, the factual settings, that give them operational significance.[74]

We are not so foolhardy as to assume that we can *uno ictu* make the study of the whole social process which is prerequisite to locating every activity in its appropriate context. Nor do we assume that we can get complete consensus upon the values we have stated as the basis of democratic values, or that these or any other values can be neatly segregated for teaching purposes into water-tight curricular departments. What we do affirm is that it is possible to map our seamless web of activities into teachable contexts for the better understanding and eventual promotion of our preferred events (values) and that the events which we teachers prefer should be made as explicit as language can make them. The particular abstract symbols which we have chosen to state our preferences (a " commonwealth of mutual deference ") are not indispensable ; the important point is that we have not been content—nor do we propose to advocate being contented—with

---

[74] For a systematic analysis of the larger context, see Malinowski, " Culture " in *Encyc. Soc. Sciences*, vol. 4 (1931), p. 621, and " The Group and the Individual in Functional Analysis ", *Am. J. Soc.*, vol. 44 (1939), p. 938. Compare Hamilton, " Institution " in *Encyc. Soc. Sciences*, vol. 8 (1932), p. 84 ; Llewellyn, " The Constitution as an Institution ", *Col. L. Rev.*, vol. 34 (1934), p. 1. Malinowski's broadest generalization is, perhaps, that an " institution " is always comprised of a group of people working on a material base, with definite traditions, and organized with reference to a task or purpose which satisfies certain basic or derived needs. His primary concepts are charter (unifying and validating norms), rules (administrative detail), personnel, material equipment, activities, function and needs (basic and derived) ; all these he defines with great precision and in great detail.

Some have suggested that students can be taught legal analysis in one course or year, how to apply this analysis to " vital " problems in still another course or year, and how to synthesize social perspectives in still a third dose. The curriculum of one influential law school is in fact being reorganized along these lines. It would appear doubtful, however, whether the process of evaluation can be so segregated. To give legal syntax operational significance it must, as we have seen, be related to institutional contexts and values. See Marshall and Goetz, *Curriculum-Making in the Social Studies* (1936) ; Green, " Relational Interests ", *Ill. L. Rev.*, vol. 29 (1934), pp. 460, 1041, *idem*, vol. 30 (1935), p. 314, and *idem*, vol. 31 (1936), p. 35.

either the neglect of goal statements or the failure to lay down definitions and exemplifications by means of which terms whose initial meaning is ambiguous can be brought into referential relation to reality. We have already undertaken to specify, at least in a preliminary way, how our key terms are to be understood. They have been given relatively explicit meaning in terms of their relation to people, and so defined they express representative values of our culture. In the light of further experience we may wish to reconsider or redefine these symbols or values. But—and here we take our stand—unless some such values are chosen, carefully defined, explicitly made the organizing foci of the law school curriculum, and kept so constantly at the student's focus of attention that he automatically applies them to every conceivable practical and theoretical situation, all talk of integrating " law " and " social science ", or of making law a more effective instrument of social control, is twaddling futility. Law cannot, like golf or surgery, be taught only as technique ; its ends are not so fixed and certain. What law " is ", and hence what should be taught as " law ", depends primarily, as we have seen, upon the ends preferred. It is not necessary, of course, to have a functional organization of materials for a teacher to disseminate a functional attitude ; many teachers to-day achieve some good results by ridiculing the materials or casebooks with which they work. Truly effective education for policy-making must, however, strive for more than the cultivation of attitude. Its curriculum must offer skill, including informational background and appropriate drill as well.[75]

Several new principles of curricular organization have already been sufficiently tested in American law schools to suggest great promise. The first may be described as organization in terms of the needs of selected, influential policy-makers, such as business managers, government officials, and labour leaders ; existing courses on business units, public control of business, and labour law reflect this principle with varying degrees of consistency. A second principle—still only slightly used—is explicit organization in terms of specified social *values* or clusters of values ; Michael and Wechsler's casebook on criminal law is perhaps the most successful examination of this principle put into practice.[76] Still

[75] Compare the emphasis of an outstanding contemporary professional educator in Kilpatrick, *Remaking the Curriculum* (1936).

[76] See Michael and Wechsler, *Criminal Law and Its Administration: Cases, Statutes and Commentaries* (1940) ; reviewed by Riesman, *loc. cit. supra*, note 1. Other books which might be mentioned, without our purporting to offer a definitive list, as

a third principle, traditional to the American law school curriculum and probably indispensable to any reconstruction, is organization in terms of emphasis on particular skills ; procedure courses, designed to supply the information and drill necessary to operate judicial machinery, are in one sense classic applications of this principle and indicators of its effectiveness. It is not inconceivable that a curriculum thoroughly integrated in terms of these three principles—influence, values, and skills—could lay a basis for effective training in policy-making. Designed to achieve values, through influence and by skills, it offers at least a beginning formula. Let us now explore in more, though necessarily impressionistic, detail what is involved in the full utilization of each principle.

INFLUENCE PRINCIPLE

First, consider organization in terms of the needs of influential policy-makers. Two principles are useful in this connection : selection according to maximum influence and selection according to representative influence. In our society the most influential policy-makers include some government officials, party leaders, business owners and executives. Courses can be arranged according to the problems that confront them, problems connected with maintaining and extending their special values and of integrating their special skills with the general values in which they participate as members of a free society. Policy questions also confront the individual whose position in the value structure of society as a whole is quite modest. Most humble individuals are small property holders, spouses and the like, and legal courses, such as Family Law, can be construed to deal with the range of questions that confront them.

Policy selections need to be made in the light of facts about the structure of society. By the structure of society is meant basic practices in creating and distributing values. In the examination of any society, a list of values for purposes of analysis may be chosen. We have mentioned among others power, respect, knowledge, income, safety. This list is not designed to reflect a general theory of human motivation ; we do not assume that everybody wants the same values with equal intensity all the time or that many people from time to time do not want

tending strongly in this direction are : Green, *Cases on Torts* (2nd ed., 1939) ; Havighurst, *Cases on Contracts* (1934) ; Jacobs, *Cases on Domestic Relations* (2nd ed., 1939) ; Powell, *Cases on Trusts and Estates* (1932).

values different from the ones named in the list.   These values were selected only because they are widely sought by persons brought up in our civilization and there is widespread interest in their amount and in how they are shared.

Power, as we have indicated, means participation in the making of important decisions.   If we examine American society as a whole from the standpoint of shared power, we find that it is convenient to divide the country into six broad social divisions according to their degree of participation.   At the top of the power series stand the policy-makers of monopolistic and basic businesses. Next in the series, and during war time of particular importance, stand public officials.   Farther down the line are the competitive business men.   Lower yet stand the bulk of the professionals and skilled labour groups that find employment in industry and commerce.   The lowest tier is composed of farmers and un-skilled labourers.   Even in a rough over-all sketch of the distribution of power in society it is important to subdivide according to the type of skill by virtue of which the leaders at any level retain their positions of privilege and leadership ; namely the skill in propaganda, skill in violence, and skill in the management of goods and services.   All leaders possess one or more of these skills in high degree.[77]   In the light of this perspective on the distribution of power in our society, we may suggest a series of law courses devoted to the needs of influential and representative persons in each of the major divisions and skills.

It is not difficult for a law student to identify himself in imagination with the problems of a definite policy group.   He easily conceives of himself as a legal adviser to a huge corporation or to one of the most important departments or agencies of government.   He can readily project himself into some of the recurring situations in the lives of persons of modest status.   The business units, public control of business, and labour law courses in our existing curriculum only faintly reflect the possibilities of this principle of organization.

There are, however, certain disadvantages in the organization of courses from the perspectives of particular policy-makers. Students may tend to stereotype their assumptions about the continuity of the social structure with which they become acquainted.   Concerned with promoting the aims of particular

[77] Professor Bruce L. Smith, with the aid of Dr. Rudolph Modley, has set forth the broad social divisions in the United States in a chart published in the *Public Opinion Quarterly*, June, 1941.

groups, they may lose sight of the long-term general interest. Emphasis needs to be put upon training students how to persuade the policy-makers of specific interests to formulate a line of policy consistent with the long-term general interest. The important decisions of our society are, furthermore, often compromises between conflicting influential groups and not the dictates of one group only. It is the direction taken by these compromises that so profoundly affects the general interest. Hence it is advantageous to shift the focus of student attention from the angle of specific groups of influential policy-makers to the consideration of how specific value goals can be achieved by society as a whole. In this way the mind of the student is kept free to assess the adequacy of existing ideas and practices for the attainment of significant policy results.

VALUE PRINCIPLE

Let us, therefore, turn to the principle of curricular organization in terms of specified social values or clusters of values. Here there are several possibilities. Courses could be organized more or less haphazardly about certain important contemporary problems of relatively low level abstraction—such as civil liberties, social security, full employment, democratization of business, democratization of government, farm security, more medical care, food and clothing to more people, protection of consumers, protection of investors, cheaper and better administration of justice, free education to the extent of ability, and so on [78]—without any attempt to run through such problem courses any consistent generalizations of high level abstraction based on some explicit theory of social dynamics, or to harmonize specific values with a general theory of democratic values. Were enough problems taken, it would be possible to achieve a fairly complete, though repetitious, coverage of social processes and legal syntax. Such an organization would have much to commend it over the present principle of legal technicality. In our view, however, the ultimate aim of those who seek better preparation for policy-making should be an attempt to achieve a curriculum organized on the basis of a realistic and comprehensive picture of the structure and functions of society, joined with the best knowledge now attainable of the dynamics of social process, and oriented toward the implementing of a consistent and explicit set of democratic values.

[78] See McDougal, *loc. cit. supra*, note 17.

NON-SYSTEMATIC APPLICATION

To illustrate further the potentialities of even the haphazard aiming of legal doctrines, procedures and structures at specific social goals, let us refer briefly to what is now called the " field of property ".[79]   Take the customary introductory course.   Such organizing foci as " nuisance ", " covenants ", " easements ", and " equitable restrictions " (and their functional equivalents allowed to go by default to other " fields ") could be replaced by the specific goal of implementing the definite, intelligible, and generally accepted norms of community planning experts for building stable and liveable urban communities.   In such an organization the " nuisance " cases would serve only to demonstrate the interdependence of all land uses, the utter anarchy of modern cities, and the ineffectiveness of any judicial handling of the problem.   Covenant, easement, and equitable restriction cases could be used to show both the inadequacies of private agreement to serve the public interest and its continuing indispensability, under existing public controls, to individual security.   But with these legal technicalities the course would just begin.   For achievement of its set goal, it would have to sweep many newer and more effective social controls.   Some indication of the scope it would require may be gathered from a brief outline, which begins at the level of local administration : [80]

A. Techniques for expanding planning area.   Contemporary functional activities have completely burst the arbitrary bounds of existing governmental subdivisions.   Means must be devised to make integrated planning, and governmental control, co-extensive with geographically, socially, and economically integrated areas.

B. Techniques for establishing and maintaining physical design and permissible uses of area.   Past controls have failed not only because of unrealistic planning but also because of a lack of integrated administration of available controls and of a failure to exercise such controls to their constitutional limits.

[79] See McDougal, " Summary and Criticism of Answers to Question 8 of the Property Questionnaire ", in *Handbook, Association of American Law Schools* (1941), p. 268.   In the discussion that follows we draw heavily upon this statement, though a number of new suggestions are added.

[80] Any serious effort to implement the kind of post-war planning now being urged by public and private agencies must require major changes in our existing legal and administrative structures, procedures and doctrines.

1. Zoning. How can this device be made more effective both for controlling new development and for reconstructing areas already built up?

2. "Planning laws". Can affirmative measures be worked out to supplement the negative measures of police power regulation?

3. Subdivision control. What new controls can be devised for both quality and quantity?

4. Private covenants. Can administrative machinery be designed to make these more efficient and secure instruments in both the private and public interest?

5. Future street reservations, parks, etc.

6. Community purchase of land. How can this method of control, used so successfully in Scandinavia, be adapted to this country?

7. Institutional structure. How can all the powers developed above best be integrated for administration? How can long-term planning best be introduced into a short-term political structure? How devise a Special Land Court to determine all land-use controversies?

C. Techniques for promoting public improvements.

1. Capital budget.
2. Special assessments.
3. Revenue bonds.
4. Public authorities.
5. Municipal ownership.

Should we add, in the course now under consideration, to the goal of liveable communities, the further goal of providing healthful and cheap housing—in lieu of the traditional landlord and tenant antiquities of "rent", "caveat lessee", "implied covenants", "independent covenants", "constructive eviction", and so on—the scope of our course becomes even more extensive. A beginning should, of course, be made in the landlord and tenant syntax to demonstrate once again the inadequacies of legal doctrine and judicial control alone to serve the desired social end. With this emancipating exercise completed, attention could be turned again to newer and more effective controls. The following outline, still at the level of local administration, may suggest some of the possibilities.[81]

A. Techniques to provide adequate housing.

B. Controls of condition of premises.

C. Controls of the price of shelter.

The vision of such a course should, however, extend much beyond the level of local administration. To implement an effective national programme—or indeed even an effective local programme—it will be necessary to focus the student's attention upon inquiries at state, regional, and federal levels as well. Thus :

A. At the State Level. What changes must be made in state institutions and laws to enable local communities to exercise all the powers recommended above? How can the planning function best be located in the structure of state government? How allocate powers between state and local planners and administrators?

B. At the Regional Level. How can institutional machinery for making important decisions at the regional level best be set up? By interstate compacts? By public authorities like the T.V.A.? By governors' conferences? By federal administrative agencies? And so on.

C. At the Federal Level. What federal institutions and laws are required to promote an effective and consistent national policy and yet preserve local enterprise? What in detail should be the conditions of the grant of federal funds? How resolve all the attendant legal (constitutional and otherwise) problems?

Indeed, since use of land and other resources for housing purposes is a part of our " whole economy " and effects and is affected by all other economic activities, such as rates of saving and investment and extent of employment, it is possible that certain other general controls for expanding our whole economy—such as, government spending and subsidies of all kinds, lowering of interest rates, rationalization of tax policies removing tariffs and other trade barriers, enforcing anti-trust laws, international organization to reduce expectation of violence, and so on—may

[81] For elaboration see McDougal, Book Review, *Harv. L. Rev.*, vol. 54 (1941), p. 526, and outline of legal questions in *Conference on Urbanism, Harvard University* (Greer ed.), *The Problem of the Cities and Towns* (1942), p. 42.

be even more important for securing cheap and healthful housing than many of the more specific controls outlined above. Though a course which included all of these controls would quite obviously exceed the bounds of management, there is no reason why students should not be kept sharply aware of their relevance.

Take, for a further example from Property, the way Possessory Estates, Future Interests, Wills, and Trusts are commonly taught. The completely complementary possessory estates and future interests are often divorced for separate courses. " Legal " interests and " equitable " interests are treated in contamination-proof compartments as if they had no relation to each other. The formalities for the creation of these interests are taught in one course and the social limitations on their creation in another. Legal technicalities are the organizing foci throughout. Suppose our inquiring student asks what this is all about. He will discover that the courts are here concerned largely with the instruments by which one generation transmits economic power to the next, sometimes through " future interests " reserving a certain amount of dead-hand control, and sometimes escaping a little taxation or avoiding a few creditor's claims. By what norms should he appraise the practices of courts in handling these instruments and toward what ends should his own activities be directed ? The answer is difficult because the requisite scientific studies have not been made. It is probable that the practices for transmitting power from generation to generation which we presently tolerate do contribute to our growing inequalities or over-concentration of wealth. Such over-concentration is, of course, inconsistent with our basic democratic values and it impedes the proper functioning of our economic structure. But an exact determination of what we should do about it would require considerable study of how inheritance claims are distributed in our society and have been distributed in other societies and how such distributions have been correlated with the distribution of such major values as power, respect, and knowledge. It is possible that we would conclude that a certain amount of inheritance should be tolerated for individual security ; how much may depend upon the availability of other functional equivalents such as insurance or governmental " social security ". For the present, in any event, the student must assume that society will tolerate, perhaps even encourage, the private transfer of substantial amounts of wealth from generation to generation. One norm he can set up, however, for appraising the doctrines, procedures and structures by which this transfer is to be effected is that the transfer should be at the least possible social cost and should result in the least possible adventitious disappointment of the reasonable expectations of presumptive beneficiaries.   From such a perspective he will see that most of the traditional syntax of this " field " are not only superfluous but positively harmful.   He can demonstrate that the classic categories, now hopelessly ambiguous, of future interests are disappearing under gradual judicial attrition and should be made to disappear even faster.   He can point out that practically the only difference between " legal " interests and " equitable " interests to-day is in the anachronistic verbiage ;   they are functional equivalents.   The practical problems are the same, the variations in the donor's language are inconsequential, the donor can make the same reference to beneficiary, time, and condition ;   no policy reason can be advanced for invoking a difference in result merely by utterance of a different symbol, and the responses of the courts are in fact largely the same.   The chief function of the surviving language, that of categorizing the various interests and of dichotomizing them into legal or equitable, is to mislead unwary or unsophisticated courts into harsh decisions.

Similar reorientations of other traditional " fields " could undoubtedly be suggested by those who are versed in their mysteries.   It would be presumptuous for us to make the attempt.   We may, however, in an effort at further exemplification suggest some of the initial questions which should be asked about various representative courses.   The following are selected almost at random :

Contracts.   What are the important agreements of our society ? How can we put these agreements in institutional settings that will enable us to assess the effect of the enforcement or nonenforcement or other policing of these agreements on the distribution of major democratic values ?   What is the effect on such values of our present modes of handling such agreements ?   What are the methods of adjustment other than agreement among various component parts of society, and how are they interrelated with agreements ?

Torts.   What are the important injuries, intended or unintended, recurring in our society ?   In what institutional contexts do they occur ?   How does our present handling of these injuries promote or retard major democratic values ?   How could the prevention of injury and the lessening of loss to society as a whole be realized as a goal in addition to the goal of readjusting the redistribution of loss among specific individuals? How can " libel and slander " be handled in a way that will promote respect for civil liberties and realistic reporting and comment in the channels of public communication?

Business Units. What is the effect on the tempo and balance of society of providing the present variety of methods by which persons who wish to engage in speculative activities can limit their possible loss and slough it off on the unsuspecting or the timorous? If it is socially desirable so to encourage entrepreneurs, should not the loss be socialized directly through government provision of capital by means of taxation according to ability to pay, rather than indirectly and haphazardly by present methods? How can business managers be made more responsible to investors, labour, consumers, and the public interest? What are the relative advantages and disadvantages in terms of technological efficiency of aggregates of business capital of varying size in various industries? How can these aggregates be brought to and kept at their most efficient size? Of all the businesses of our society, which are the most important? What are their power structures? How is this power used to affect the distribution of values? What controls are available, and what can be invented, to democratize this power?

Equity. What useful purpose is served by putting this rag-bag of stuff between two covers?

Insurance. What is the effect of the existing system of " distributing " loss upon the value position of various groups in the nation? Are these results " rational " in terms of democratic values? If the most general function of insurance is to make certain by present relinquishments a future flow of stable and adequate income, should not the function be performed by government, since its taxing power can base the required relinquishments on ability to pay? What are the interrelations of " Private " insurance and " social security " in a democratic system?

Taxation. Can the social and economic effects of taxation be appraised and taught in a " general " course on taxation, or must the effect of tax controls be meaningfully considered as an incident of elaborate factual inquiries into the processes of society? Should the tax course be conducted simply as a " skill " course in ways and means of collecting money (or of avoiding its collection) and the policy implications of tax manipulation relegated to richer contexts?

International Law.   How can we build international organizations as effective for promoting democratic values everywhere as we have built for strategy, munitions, and shipping ?   How, in detail, can we build such organizations for the promotion, on an international scale, of full employment, full utilization of resources, technological development, rational fiscal procedures, trade, democratization of business power, and related purposes ?   How can we implement our relinquishment of war as an instrument of national policy and form an international institution authorized to determine aggressors ?

Enough by way of illustrating the kinds of preliminary inquiries required by a more or less haphazard aiming of legal institutions, practices and doctrines at explicit social goals.

Systematic Application of the Value Principle

Let us now turn to a brief examination of curricular organization in terms of a more systematic statement of values and a more explicit theory of social dynamics.   This problem we have anticipated by our formulation above of the values of a free society and of the principal variables upon which the attainment of such values depend.   It is far from fantastic to assume that effective courses may be explicitly organized about these major democratic values and variables.   Consider the following basic courses (no great importance is attached to the order in which they are listed) :

1. Law and control.
2. Law and intelligence.
3. Law and distribution.
4. Law and production.
5. Law and character.
6. Law and community development.

1. *Law and Control.*   The scope of this course is the study of power, the investigation of how power is distributed, and of how legal syntax, procedures, and structures affect, or can be made to affect, this distribution.   Its purpose is to offer a realistic survey of the people or agencies who are actually making the important decisions of our society and of the controls available to keep their power responsible, hence shared.   It is convenient to examine the facts of power in reference to the institutional groups found in society ;   hence the course begins with what is commonly called government ;   from government, the transition is made to private

pressure organizations, and to business and non-business private associations.

Concerned as it is with government, much of the traditional content of courses on constitutional law finds place here. Included are cases that bear on the determination of "the meaning of the Constitution" with respect to the apportionment of authority between federal and state governments, and among all the agencies of government at each level. So far as the sharing of power is concerned, many special problems deserve special attention, such as the legal devices available to the Federal Government in seeking to correct tendencies toward autocracy and despotism in the franchises of individual states.

In addition to problems from the general domain of constitutional law are parts of courses in municipal corporations where the problem is to determine lines of authority between state and local agencies. Here, in particular, it is important to consider the legal doctrines available to adjust governmental areas. With changes in population, with increasing distinctions between work place and residence place, problems of adapting the many kinds of governmental districts to one another are among the most pressing technical problems of government. These issues greatly affect the balance of power among different regions of the country, and among various kinds of economic and other cultural groups.

This course includes some of the topics found in public international law, particularly the concepts relating to the rôle of "sovereign" and "half-sovereign" states, and doctrines of government intervention. Under the rubric of control will come cases that clarify doctrines governing the internal distribution of power in private pressure associations. The problem of access to membership in an association is peculiarly acute whenever the association exercises dominance over the distribution of values, as do certain business cartels, trade unions, and trade associations. The issue is particularly important when groups are able to entrench themselves in private organizations by various methods of coercion. In recent times this problem has been put in the foreground as a result of the efforts of Nazi-controlled and Communist-controlled factions to dominate fraternal, benevolent and other organizations nominally set up for cultural ends.

This course will include the structure of formal authority and of effective control within corporations, partnerships and personal profit-seeking enterprises. Degrees of control over personnel and policy by various classes of shareholders are in point here. This involves part of the material found in courses on corporation law or " business units ".   After examining private pressure and business organizations, attention will be given to the control problems that arise in non-profit economic associations and in other private groupings for non-economic purpose.

2. *Law and Intelligence.* The problem here is how more people can be given access to, and skill in interpreting, the facts necessary to decisions that will promote democratic values.   The realism of the decisions made by the officers or members of any organization depend in no small measure on the quality of the intelligence that reaches them, and the degree of skill with which they are equipped to think.   This raises the whole question of the control and the freedom of channels of communication.

When we examine the question we find that legal devices have already been used in order to improve the factual basis of judgment.   One requirement for an adequate stream of intelligence is disclosure of source, the disclosure of all who have anything to do with directing the flow of communication.   The practices of registration and labelling have been partially adapted to the problem, so that statements of ownership and circulation must be made available from time to time, and advertising matter must be plainly labelled as such.

Besides the disclosure of source, positive means of obtaining access to the media of communication are essential, if public opinion is to be influenced by minority statements of fact and purpose.   Several legal devices have been partly adapted to this problem.   In some instances the government has itself assumed the cost of circulating controversial statements.   This is the effect of the Congressional mailing privilege, and of the dissemination at public expense in certain states of party electoral platforms.   Since freedom of speech involves freedom of access to public attention, topics connected with the use of public property for political meetings and demonstrations are relevant here.

Still a third aspect of the intelligence function is access to facts that interested parties try to conceal (in addition to their identity). Although legislative bodies may have relatively unlimited powers of subpœna, the scope of their investigations are blocked by several legal considerations, notably by a narrow interpretation of the words used to describe the purpose of the inquiry.   It falls within the scope of this course to explore the arsenal of legal attack and defence available to governmental agencies in the exercise of their investigative functions. Also in point are the alternatives available to courts of various jurisdictions to obtain formation, including the barriers involved in confidential communication.

Another requirement of proper intelligence is competent decision-makers. It has long been notorious that some courts and administrative agencies are so poorly equipped and poorly skilled by experience and training that it is ridiculous to expect them to exert effective control over private utility companies. In setting up a judicial and administrative system, one of the positive tasks is to locate jurisdiction at a point where adequate facilities can be brought to bear on problems.

In the conduct of debate and of hearings, certain procedures enhance the probability of a realistic outcome. From this standpoint it is relevant to scrutinize the means by which the attention of the group is protected by the exclusion of the irrelevant (as in the application of many evidence rules), or, if total exclusion is impossible, how protection is found by the nullification of the non-relevant. That all parties to a litigation should have the benefit of counsel is a tacit application of the rule that the effect of mere professional skill on decisions should be nullified by being equalized on all sides. A more positive aspect of procedure is the clarifying of goals and alternatives ; still another is provision for the discovery of new truth. The latter problem carries us over to the study of the set-ups most favourable to enlarging the stock of scientific knowledge available to society. When we consider private pressure organizations, the same questions must be systematically canvassed as for government. Already many legal devices have been invoked for such purposes as forcing disclosure of records to members. Private business organizations are affected by legal means affecting the stream of intelligence at the disposal of prospective investors, and of the shareholders of going concerns. Parallel problems can be taken up for the remaining types of cultural organization.

3. *Law and Distribution.* We have laid down as one of our major policy objectives the achievement and protection of balanced income. The purpose of this course is to examine the effect of legal syntax, procedures, and structures upon property distribution and to consider their potentialities for the attainment of varying states of balanced distribution. The course begins with a study of the present distribution of income, of the correlations between this distribution and the distribution of other values, and generally of the factors affecting distribution. Consideration

will then be given to alternative distributions, their probable consequences, and the compatibility of these consequences with major democratic values. Once preferred distributions are designated or assumed, the course can begin to consider the great variety of controls relevant to redistribution, such as taxation, credit manipulation, tariff policies, control of corporate device, price controls, abolition of restraints on employment, criminal penalties for too obvious shearing of sheep, anti-monopoly activities, and so on.

The authority to tax, for example, is peculiarly relevant here, since it is theoretically possible to mould the pattern of income distribution by the appropriate use of the tax power. At any given time, however, we are confronted by many devices by which exercise of the tax power in the interest of balanced distribution are nullified in practice. In point here is the thorny problem of double taxation, not only among the several jurisdictions within a given nation but by several states of the world. We find a continual struggle between the specialists hired by tax reducers and specialists hired by tax enforcers, and one function of this course will be to get abreast of the current state of this perpetual tug-of-war. In recent times, for instance, we have seen legal syntax connected with the trust made use of extensively in tax evasion.

4. *Law and Production.* The problems centring around production concern regularity and volume. It is apparent that this is one of the continuing and crucial problems of a machine economy. However, regularity is not the only consideration pertinent to the process of production. It is evident that we are also interested in the volume of various types of products. Although the word "production" is made use of to describe man-hours and materials expended, the term covers many diverse operations. There are great differences in the attitude of workers and management when they are engaged in producing instruments of war than when they are at peace. Attitudes differ when heavy machinery or luxury goods are being made. Some processes of production are deeply respected by those who participate in them, while others have no emotional satisfactions whatever. To cover all of these diversified situations by the term "production" is a very preliminary use of the word ; sub-specification is immediately needed.

In this course we pay particular attention to the rôle of money in relation to the technical processes of production. Modern analysis of the monetary (including the credit) system has disclosed the enormous cumulative effect of seemingly isolated transactions upon the ebb and flow of economic activity. When an invested dollar is backed by a saved dollar there can be steady expansion of total production. However, there are many technical devices whose effect is to destroy any constant relationship between dollars saved and dollars invested and to create a pyramiding of money that rests upon no foundation of saving. This process can give rise to enormous booms, but such booms cannot be sustained indefinitely and end in crash. The fabrication of dollars is often obscured by the technical operations involved, the most striking example of which has been a system of financing business through commercial banks. When a bank receives a deposit it assumes a liability to return the money. If it did no more than " warehouse " the depositor's dollars, retaining them as a 100 per cent. reserve until called for, it would make only the money charged the depositor for the performance of this custodial service. When the bank loans out dollars that it has received to businesses, savings are transformed into investment and the income of the bank is increased by the interest charged on the loan. Commercial banks, however, have been permitted to enlarge their profit-making opportunities by the use of procedures enabling them to create dollars. This is what happens when a loan is granted in the form of a deposit, since the bank is now able to loan out some of the deposit that it has just created ; and the pyramiding may go on until an enormous discrepancy prevails between the saved dollars and the number of " invested " dollars circulating. It has been proposed that the warehouse function and the investing function should be clearly segregated in different types of institutions and made subject to rules that keep the flow of dollars invested in stable relationship to the dollars saved in the economic system as a whole. This is but a single example of the complex technical processes of modern institutional life with which we are especially concerned. In this context it will be necessary to appraise not only the consequences of the banking system but of securities markets, exchanges, government budgets, currency regulations, import and export of capital, and the like.[82]

[82] Professor Eugene Rostow has developed courses on (a) The Control of Competition, given three or four times in various forms at Yale, and (b) The Control of Industrial Fluctuations, given in part in Chicago in 1941, and listed for Yale in the spring of 1942. The first course was an effort to study the economic literature on the subject of competition and to use it in analysing a complex mass of data, given in cases, statutes, administrative reports, etc., concerning specific markets for

5. *Law and Character.*   The plan of this series of materials is to consider factors affecting the distribution of respect in society. In studying the relation of legal syntax to respect we will evaluate it from the point of view of increasing or diminishing the zone of individual self-determination.   Included here are many of the limitations on the procedure of public officers designed to protect the individual from arbitrary acts.   In so far as the traditional remedies for many torts are designed to diminish the amount of interference by persons or groups with one another, they will be relevant in this course.

A more positive side of respect is equality of opportunity, and many legal doctrines are designed to facilitate, or can be used to expedite, the realization of equality.   Laws against discrimination on grounds of age, sex, race, religion, provenience in obtaining access to education or jobs, fall in this category.

As a means of aiding character formation, special provisions are often made to affect the rearing of children.   The aim of many of these provisions is to protect the growing child from the character distortions that result when the personality is treated disrespectfully (such as rules to protect offspring from the stigma attached to illegitimacy).

6. *Law and Community Development.*   This is a course which cuts across all our major values and variables.   Its frame of reference is the relation of legal syntax, procedures, and structures to the utilization of resources in communities of varying size.   The areas range from neighbourhoods to village and urban nuclei, to regions, to the broader geographical areas of the world.   In modern times the problem of providing some degree of direction for the use of land and other resources for population groups has become increasingly urgent.   The need is most acute in relation to community and regional planning.   Whenever a problem of community development is in the foreground, the fundamental point is to be clear about the pattern of life that it is proposed to facilitate.   Given our preference for a democratically functioning society, by what legal devices can we give direction to the growth of communities along lines consistent with these ideals ?

coal, oil, milk, steel and other commodities.   The second course was designed on the same pattern to analyse the chief legal institutions of use or potential use in controlling general fluctuations in employment : the banking system, the securities markets, currency laws, international exchanges, as well as more general economic arrangements for controlling wages, prices, etc.   Some experimental materials of this kind were published in Chicago in 1941.   The two courses together were designed both to cover aspects of the problem of economic policy as a whole, and to present an integrated conception of a positive economic programme for democracy.

It is evident that community planning brings into the focus of attention all of the ends and means that we have considered. Certainly the layout of homes and work places exerts a profound effect upon the degree to which democratic character is achieved by the rising generation and the extent to which democratic ideas are put into practice by the older generation. One of the major sectors of this problem concerns the use of legal doctrines and new institutions as means to the achievement of ever-expanding standards of individual health and safety, of individual comfort, convenience and taste. In this context is found most of the traditional content of courses in property, but the syntax of property is given significance in relation to the problems here set forth and much new material is covered. Some indication of the possible scope of such a course has been offered in the discussion of community planning and housing above.

In all the foregoing courses a continuing theme is the relation of the problem at hand to the stage of crisis or inter-crisis prevailing in the nation as a whole. In the crisis of war, every problem must be seen in a somewhat distinctive framework. There are the enormous adaptations involved in conversion from peace-time to war-time production ; and at the end, there are the special problems of " conversion back ". Hence one of the considerations governing the choice of cases throughout will be to exhibit problems that arise in crises of varying degrees of intensity and duration.

SKILL PRINCIPLE

It remains to discuss the third principle of reorganizing the curriculum, the skill principle. The second, or value, principle is the one we have emphasized most, although the first, or influence, principle deserves a larger place than it now has. The immediate problem is to what extent we shall take skill into consideration.

In a sense all courses in the law school exemplify the skill principle, since they provide the student with command of legal technicality. Though we proceed on the assumption that the skill principle in this sense must be applied in whatever curricular changes are introduced, we have asserted that the choice and arrangement of legal technicality should be made from the standpoint of influential groups or key values. There are, however, certain clusters of legal syntax that should be considered separately if we are to avoid tiresome and wasteful repetition.

The traditional courses in procedure have already been instanced as the classical application of the skill principle, in this more limited meaning.   Their function is to train the incipient lawyer how to choose a court for settling his dispute and how to operate a court once chosen to get the result he wants.   Obviously both the " jurisdiction " and the " mechanics " of courts affect the distribution of each of the values in which we are interested, especially power, and are bound to come in for a certain amount of attention in our specific analysis of values.   But the details of court procedure and structure are worthy of special courses. The operating lawyer sees his alternatives of action in this way : Who has authority to settle my dispute ?   Who of this group is most likely to be predisposed in my favour ?   How can I operate on him to get the results I want ?   By what verbal incantations and the like do I get in and out of the scope of his authority ?

It is common knowledge, however, that a lawyer who wishes to operate successfully on his environment does not confine himself to the courts.   Influential decisions are not restricted to judges.   Skill training that stops short with the traditional procedure courses leaves the potential policy-maker hopelessly inadequate for modern conditions.   For he must be prepared to work with—and on—legislators, executives, administrators, arbitrators, negotiators, and other responsible persons.   It is incumbent upon law teachers to make plain to the student not only that there are different ways of settling disputes but many ways of getting results other than by disputation.[83]   As a lawyer moves away from acts that impinge directly on a court, his distinctive skill in handling legal technicality loses application

[83] Compare Assistant Solicitor-General Cox, " Wartime Interpretation of Legislative Orders ", mimeographed address to Society for the Advancement of Management, August, 1942 :
" We lawyers are frequently—and many times justly—accused of having negative minds.   Too often we are disposed to search out and magnify the reasons why something necessary can *not* be done rather than to seek the means whereby it *can* be done.   The counsel's office is the bottleneck of progress in many a government agency faced with the urgent job of putting a new policy into effect or carrying out a directive from Congress.
" The responsibility of the government lawyer in time of war is, above everything else, the affirmative one of finding ways and means by which the decisions of the policy-makers can be most promptly and effectively fulfilled. . . ."
For further indication of what is required here see Frankfurter, *The Public and Its Government* (1930) ; Galloway and Associates, *Planning for America* (1941) ; Landis, *The Administrative Process* (1938) ; Nat. Resources Committee, *The Structure of the American Economy* (1939), Part 1 ; Gray, " The Passing of the Public Utility Concept ", *J. of Land and P.U. Econ.*, vol. 16 (1940), p. 8 ; Lilienthal and Marquis, " The Conduct of Business Enterprises by the Federal Government ", *Harv. L. Rev.*, vol. 54 (1941), p. 545 ; Rostow, Book Review, *U. of Chi. L. Rev.*, vol. 8 (1941), p. 169 ; Tugwell, " The Superpolitical ", *J. Soc. Philosophy*, vol. 5 (1940), p. 97.

and he is compelled to rely more fully upon general policy skills. If the lawyer is to operate on a par with others he cannot afford to foreswear these skills. The years spent in going to law school impose handicaps no less than advantages if they insulate the student from opportunity to acquire or perfect the exercise of the modes of thinking, observing and managing that we call general policy skills.

To a limited extent the existing curriculum looks beyond the doctrines, procedures and structures of the court system and calls the attention of students to other processes by which controls are made operative in modern civilization. Most of these ancillary courses, however, go but a little way toward providing a unified factual picture of the process of dispute-settling and result-getting in our society. Entirely too much concerned with the syntax of "interpretation", and over-cautious in abjuring "policy",[84] courses on legislation rarely come to grips with the fundamental problem of how to get statutes enacted for achieving specified purposes. In control over funds, in power to create new structures and procedures, and in authority to prescribe policy norms of the broadest scope by utilizing words that refer to identifiable social goals, the legislature ranks among our most strategic agencies ; its comparative neglect by the law schools can hardly be justified in a democracy. Surprisingly enough, courses on the executive are conspicuously non-existent. Still over-apologetic about the growth of the administrative function and excessively worried about the " nature " of that function, established courses on " administrative law " seldom succeed in having a sufficiently sustained orientation toward important factual contexts to make the syntax with which they deal meaningful ; moreover, they seldom give explicit and creative attention to how " administration " can be adapted or even further extended for the better promotion of democratic values. Only an occasional catalogue carries an occasional seminar on arbitration, despite the enormous potentiality of this procedure for reducing wasteful litigation. The " public authority " or " public corporation ", fast emerging as one of the most significant agencies of our time, probably with a great international career ahead of it, receives scant notice.

Most of the material describing power processes in our civilization can be furnished to the student in the proposed course

---

[84] See Hurst, " Content of Courses in Legislation ", *U. of Chi. L. Rev.*, vol. 8 (1941), p. 280.

on " law and control ". But every agency engaged in preventing and settling disputes evolves detailed doctrines and procedures ; hence skill courses on the existing operation and possible improvement of each structure should be offered. In all such courses, the minutiæ ought to be mastered first, followed by critical thought about how the detailed modalities of the structure—whether court, legislature, executive, administrative agency, or public corporation—may be moulded into more perfect instruments of democracy. The latter frame of reference follows the value rather than the skill principle ; but there is nothing that forbids compatible principles from being applied in the same course. The influence, value and skill principles are not mutually exclusive ; properly understood they supplement one another.

In the foregoing discussion of principles the main emphasis has been upon mastering the legal technicality needed for the professional practice of law ; at the same time, the objective has been to relate this distinctive skill to the goals and the general skills appropriate to the maker of policy in a society that affirms its devotion to the dignity of man. We assume that " courses " will continue to be the pedagogical framework in which most of the law school instruction will be carried on. We are not opposed to supplementary means of reconditioning the law school environment into a more efficient instrument of pedagogy, but we regard the pattern of classroom instruction as too firmly rooted in our culture to give way in the immediate future. Moreover, it is entirely possible to work within this frame in transmitting policy attitudes and techniques. Individual law professors and adventurous law faculties can revamp the traditional compartments in accord with the principles of value, influence and skill here made articulate ; but the heart of the matter is not the rechristening of courses but the changing of aim and emphasis.

The resetting of legal technicality in a policy-potent framework is an enormous task. During the years of transition toward a policy-training law school, it will be advisable to provide special guides to aid the student in orienting himself. We have already provided a brief synopsis of the skills to be commended for inclusion in the training programme of the future law school. In the skill table we set out, besides legal technicality, other skills of thought, observation and management to which we may now give more extended attention.

SKILLS OF THOUGHT

The mastery of habits of thought and talk can be facilitated by insight into the nature of the tools themselves. Insight is something more than the enrichment that comes from learning and relearning the terms, doctrines and citations of any established field of law. Insight means awareness, not puppet learning ; and one means of enabling the student to objectify his thinking about thought and language is to provide him with knowledge of the rapidly expanding sciences that deal with these two indispensable processes. We understand legal technicality better when we know wherein it resembles or diverges from other forms of expression. These distinctions are all the more pertinent, since in his professional career the lawyer cannot confine himself to the " Yea, Yea ", and the " Nay, Nay ", of the legal idiom. Whether he addresses client or juror, the language of legal technicality gains clarity and impact in the framework of other forms of communication.

In recent years our knowledge of the process of thought and communication has advanced by leaps and bounds, and new insights, properly correlated and kept up to date, should be made accessible to the student.[85] Several frames of reference are often unwittingly invoked by those who purport to state the " law " ; and until these differences are explored, confusion is compounded.

Consider, for a moment, the following statement uttered by a law teacher who is expounding a case, a legal adviser who is arguing with a client, or an advocate who is addressing the court : " This is the law (followed by a statement of a ' doctrine ')." This statement may be treated as a summary of past statements made by sources who are treated as qualified spokesmen (authorities). It may also be taken to refer to future events, predicting what certain authorities will say (even though there is doubt about what they have said in the past) ;[86] or it may be construed as a declaration of preference by the professor, adviser, advocate—a statement of what the speaker thinks the law should be even though the authorities (before or after) dissent.[87] If this last construction is put upon the words, the

---

[85] Consult Ogden and Richards, *The Meaning of Meaning* (1936), with Supplementary Essays by Malinowski and Crookshank ; also Sapir, " Language ", in *Encyc. Soc. Sci.*, vol. 9 (1933), p. 155, " Communication " in *idem*, vol. 4 (1931), p. 78, and " Symbolism " in *idem*, vol. 14 (1934), p. 492.

[86] Obviously the aim of those who accept the " prediction theory of law " is to arrive at future reference statements that will be confirmed by the event.

[87] The " normative conception of law " arrives at such statements, if the speaker takes responsibility for the norms invoked by him.

A.P.B.   D

speaker may affirm that he is misunderstood, since he did not use words that categorically convey preference ; nevertheless, the listener may believe that the speaker lays himself open because so many talkers do in practice say " the law is so and so " when what they mean—in the sense of what they say if challenged— is a preference for the law to be so and so.   Under some circum- stances the statement goes beyond a simple preference and becomes a volition to do whatever is feasible to get the " should " accepted as an " is ".

Hence if we take the statement of the " law " at face value we may find it ambiguous ; and we can call it *normative-ambiguous*, because the word " law " is used, and " law " is a word that refers to norms, even though it is unclear whether the norm in question pertains exclusively to the speaker, whether it is shared by the speaker with others, or whether, though a norm of others, it is not the norm of the speaker at all.   Commonsense experience emphasizes the enormous rôle of such normative-ambiguous statements in the discourse that purports to expound " law " or " ethics " or " Divine Will ".   " That is right (morally) " is a sentence open to all the doubts raised about the " this is the law " sentence ; and " this is God's Will " is no whit less ambiguous. By evoking such word sequences a speaker may conceal his own preference or volition on contentious matters and increase the attention paid to what he says by enunciating norms whose sponsor appears to transcend the speaker.[88]

If we seek to gain objectivity toward our flow of thought— and everybody's flow of language—it is helped to practise using technical categories for classifying the phenomena in question. We have already suggested that some statements may be described as normative-ambiguous ; and there are other useful distinctions to be drawn according to whose norms are understood to be involved.   Thus, " I think the law should be so and so " plainly involves the maker of the statement ; it is a *normative-demand* statement.   " The judges of that period held that the rule was so and so " is a remark about the norms of others ; it is *naturalistic-normative*.   The " fact " statements in litigation are *naturalistic*.

Many normative statements refer to internal relations among a group of propositions.   Assertions that purport to formulate a legal doctrine may be examined in connection with the entire

---

[88] The " illusion of universality " is cultivated by ambiguousness.   For this and similar distinctions see Allport, *Social Psychology* (1924).

family of statements that are taken to be the " law of contract ", or the " law as a whole ", in a given period or jurisdiction. The internal relations among these statements are consistency, economy and degree of generality (universality-particularity) ; statements about these relations are *syntactical*. A well-developed syntactical system is composed of propositions utilizing a limited list of key terms combined according to postulates and rules. The law is but one of the well-developed syntactical systems in our civilization ; every theology is such a system.[89] Where the meaning involves not the internal relations of a body of propositions, but the external references of a statement, we are dealing with the *semantic* dimension of thought and language. The statement that Judge So-and-so made such and such remarks is a semantic proposition ; the statement that certain of his remarks contradicted one another is syntactic.

We are now in a better position to detect the many frames of reference that may be more or less wittingly invoked by those who purport to state a legal doctrine. To the degree that a given statement affirms that something was said in the past, or will be said in the future, it is semantic. To the degree that it characterizes the interrelations of past or future statements according to consistency, generality and economy, the statement is syntactic. It may be that the formulation of the legal rule is accomplished by declarations of approval or disapproval on the part of the statement-maker or of determination to block the recognition of the rule ; these are normative-demand, not naturalistic-normative.

All of the distinctions made thus far have to do with the content of statements rather than their *causes or consequences*. If we assert that the court accepts a certain rule out of deference to a cited authority, our remark purports to explain the judge's conduct. In this instance the explanation offered is to impute to the judge a conscious or unconscious bias.[90] Other types of explanation may, however, be invoked, as when we say that Judge So-and-so favours the corporations because he comes from

---

[89] A valuable contribution to our understanding of the likenesses and differences of modern and ancient logics is Kapp, *Greek Foundations of Traditional Logic* (1942). Note particularly the treatment of the syllogism in Ch. 4. For a succinct statement of syllogistic logic : Treusch, " The Syllogism ", in Hall, *Readings in Jurisprudence* (1938), Ch. 12. For modern " postulationalist " logics : Carnap, *Introduction to Semantics* (1942) ; Korzybski, *Science and Sanity* (1933) ; Tarski, *Introduction to Logic* (1941) ; Ushenko, *The Problems of Logic* (1941) (a criticism). A " psychologistic " logic is Dewey, *Logic, The Theory of Inquiry* (1939).

[90] A general bias toward absolutism was asserted in Frank, *Law and the Modern Mind* (1931).

an upper income family.[91]   In this case we are connecting
conduct with position in the social structure.   The foregoing
statements have been causal ; and statements about consequence
may also refer to personality or social context.   We may forecast
that a ruling will annoy a certain justice on the bench of a higher
court, or predict that the ruling made by the court will hasten
the concentration of wealth.   When we undertake to relate
what is said to its causes or consequences, we are indulging in
pragmatics, as distinguished from *semologics* (which is content).
All pragmatic statements are naturalistic.

Most of the " fact statements " offered in court belong to the
realm of semantic discourse.   The counsel, however, has latitude
in selecting and presenting this material on the basis of his estimate
of the pragmatic probability of acceptance by judge and jury.
Statements put forward as " fact " are continually scrutinized
syntactically in order to expose or cover up lurking inconsistency.

On examination it appears that most of the language used in
presenting claims to the court is syntactic in nature, since it
applies a system of closed categories of identification to all parties
involved in the controversy, and invokes normative standards in
justifying specific demands.   The norms of claimants often run
through a wide gamut of legal, policy and other standards ; but
at every step of the proceedings the counsel governs his choice
of syntactical propositions by his forecast of their pragmatic
effect on the trial and appeal court.   The heavy freight of citation
that appears in every brief is semantic (naturalistic normative)
to the degree that it asserts the fact that authorities have enunciated
norms ; assertions about the interrelations of doctrines are syntactic.   We know that a parade of citations is often designed to
gain the pragmatic end of acceptance by bulk.

For the most part opinions written by appellate judges flow
within the established banks of legal syntactics, though they are
not infrequently characterized, if not distinguished, by forthright
declarations of preference, sustained by norms of policy or theology.
In some jurisdictions it appears that a seat of authority promotes
the flow of normatively ambiguous discourse.

What we have been referring to as " legal syntax " is a short
way of talking about language that purports to state the " law " ;
on closer examination an example of legal syntax may turn out
to be normative-ambiguous, normative-demand, or naturalistic-

---

[91] Such interpretations are stressed in Marxist literature.   See Boudin, *Government
by Judiciary* (1932).

normative. Following some current usage, the entire science of statement analysis may be called *semiotic* ; statements about content are semologic ; statements about cause and effect are pragmatic. Semologic falls into syntactics and semantics.[92]

In our proposals to recast the curriculum we do not recommend specific courses on thought and language, but rather the preparation of materials that can be kept readily available to the law student during all the years of his training. The incentive to master the tools of thought and language should be continually reinforced by a word-consciousness cultivated by teachers in the classroom. As a guide and companion to many of the skills valuable to the law student, it is advisable to prepare and keep up to date through constant revision a collection of materials that may be called " The Skill Book ". Such a volume would contain reprints, original articles by experts, and unpublished research ; it would give " who's who " information on authors.[93]

The categories just developed can be explicitly related to the forms of thinking mentioned above as goal, trend, and scientific. The statement of a goal that is endorsed by the statement-maker is normative-demand ; so, too, are explicit acceptances of more inclusive norms under which it is assumed, or particular applications that are deduced from it. Assertions that a given statement of goal is consistent with a certain norm are not necessarily normative-demand ; the speaker may not himself prefer the norm in question. Normative-demand statements may fall into the preference or volition type (" I accept democratic values " ; " I will work to clarify and execute democratic policy ").

What we have previously called skill in derivation is proficiency in syntactics with special reference to arranging propositions in which affirmations of the democratic values occupy a place. It is the same type of skill involved in legal technicality, save that the lawyer operates with norms imputed to an authority that is assumed to be binding on certain courts, while the authority for moral and other norms may be indeterminate. In connection with derivation, it should be noted, furthermore, that proficiency has little bearing on which values are accepted by

[92] " Semiotic ", " pragmatic ", " syntactic ", and " semantic " are used in approximately the senses here indicated by Morris, *loc. cit. supra*, note 66. Morris does not suggest a convenient term for " content " ; hence we have used " semologic " to round out the system.

[93] In the " who's who " of the science of thought and communication, America's great pioneer, Charles S. Peirce, will be outstanding. Other significant figures will be Carnap in Austria, Tarski in Poland, Couturat in France, Whitehead and Russell in England.

the statement-maker.   After all, the values of a given individual are acquired in the interaction of original nature and the cultural environment in which he grows up.   What may be accomplished by a sophisticated process of derivation is insight ; and by means of insight our actions may be more efficiently integrated toward realizing values.   When we " take our values for granted " we may not only make mistakes, but find ourselves at a disadvantage in the articulate defence of our values when we meet anyone who doubts or rejects them.   Part of the lawyer's training should be familiarity with the thought and speech of those who are currently invoked as authorities in controversies over value.   Hence a place will need to be found in the Skill Book in which are described prevalent modes of legitimizing democratic or anti-democratic values.[94]

Trend thinking, in contradistinction to goal thinking, is conspicuously naturalistic in form, characterizing as it does the structure of past and future events.   Affirmations of approval or of determination to do everything possible in order to increase the probable occurrence of future events are not trend but goal statements.   The thinker or speaker may assign varying degrees of probability to the occurrence of the events referred to ; indeed he must arrive at such estimates if he is to think and act on the basis of the alternatives that the future seems to hold in store. When the speaker's estimate of probability is left vague, the statement is naturalistic-ambiguous.   When probability is assigned by the speaker the degree may be high or low ; or it may be wholly uncertain : " America's balance of government and business will outlive totalitarian forms of state and society " ; " Private enterprise is doomed " ; " I have no opinion as yet about the future of private enterprise."

Scientific thinking, too, is naturalistic in the sense that all propositions are looked upon as confirmed or confirmable by data.   The language of science, however, includes both direct

[94] See, for example, Ducasse, *Philosophy as a Science, Its Matter and Method* (1941) ; Frank, *Between Physics and Philosophy* (1941) ; Perry, *General Theory of Value* (1926) ; Dewey, " Theory of Valuation ", in *Int. Encyc. of Unified Science*, vol. 2 (1939), No. 4. On the democratic values see Anshen (ed.), *Freedom* (1941) ; Dewey, *The Ethics of Democracy* (1888) ; Friedrich, *Constitutional Government and Politics* (1937) ; Jefferson, *Democracy* (Padover ed., 1939) ; Kallen (ed.), *Freedom in the Modern World* (1928) ; Laski, *Democracy in Crisis* (1933) ; Lindsay, *The Essentials of Democracy* (1929) ; Merriam, *The New Democracy and the New Despotism* (1939) ; Mill, *On Liberty* (1854) ; Tawney, *Equality* (1931).   Convenient guides to democratic theory are Coker, *Recent Political Thought* (1934) ; Merriam and Barnes, *A History of Political Theories, Recent Times* (1924).   See also Cargill, *Intellectual America* (1941) ; Gabriel, *The Course of American Democratic Thought* (1940) ; Parrington, *Main Currents in American Thought* (1927-30).

statements about events and statements about these statements. The first are the sentences embodying data and the second are concepts, definitions, rules, laws and hypotheses. Propositions that state interrelations among variables are hypotheses ; they are laws when they receive a sufficiently high degree of confirmation by data. In accounting for the behaviour of courts we have specified a number of variables whose interrelationship is a potential object of scientific investigation. Claims presented, objective facts, legal norms and all the other factors enumerated can be connected with the description of reality by specifying the indices that a given observer is authorized to accept as evidence of the variable's presence, direction and magnitude. It is apparent, therefore, that while the generalizations of science are confirmed or confirmable by data, and therefore rests upon a body of semantic propositions, the semantic statements are composed of units whose definitions and rules of combination are part of a syntactic system.[95]

Certain distinctions cut across goal, trend and scientific thinking ; all statements may be given contemplative or manipulative form. A goal may be phrased in passive, contemplative form when one says, " Let us assume for the moment that we want to increase by 10 per cent. the segment of the population called middle class." Goals may also be phrased manipulatively, actively : " We want a healthy middle class, and that means expanding the middle class sector of the population 10 per cent. in the immediate future." A trend is formulated in a contemplative manner when we say, " We will now consider the possibility that free private enterprise is rapidly moving toward extinction." A more affirmative, manipulative mode of referring to trend is : " The extinction of free private enterprise is probable in the immediate future." Scientific propositions may be couched in contemplative, inactive style, when we say, " X varies as a function of Y and Z ". The same relations may be stated as principles, not as laws, when we say, " To increase the amount of

[95] Scientific relations may be formulated in terms of factor X and factor Y, or systemically. Variables compose a system where changes in any one of them regularly bring about changes in the others that maintain the characteristic pattern of the variables as a whole. Biological processes have been fruitfully considered from this standpoint ; the physico-chemical components of the blood stream, for example, constitute a system. If one of them alters in magnitude, the others change enough to maintain the integrity of the whole. This approach to social processes is advocated in Mayo, *Human Problems of an Industrial Civilization* (1933). For sociological theory, the " one factor-one result " pattern of thought is stated in Durkheim, *The Rules of Sociological Method* (1938 tr.). An example of its application is Ranulf, *Jealousy of the Gods and Criminal Law at Athens* (1933-4).

X, diminish the quantity of *Y* and increase the quantity of Z ". It is plain that most of the sentences that phrase responsible decisions are likely to be phrased manipulatively ; on the contrary initial, tentative and speculative attitudes will be in more contemplative form.   For various pragmatic reasons even the statements embodying fixed determination may sometimes receive contemplative expression.

This carries us to the need of distinguishing the method from the form of thought.   By method of thinking we mean an operation that is carried on with insight for the express purpose of problem-solving.   Manifestly, it is not appropriate to speak of a method of thinking when the process is dominated by unanalysed and unexplored hunch.   The sequence in which different patterns of thought are taken up by the problem-solver may affect the probability that he will arrive at realistic solutions.   Many problem-solving operations go wrong through failure to clarify goal, or to evaluate trend and scientific data.   The deliberate use of each pattern of thinking for the purpose of facilitating the total process is the configurative method of thought.[96]   Practical classroom teaching in the law school will be at its best when it stimulates versatile modes of attack upon any problem ; and supplementary guides to the study of specific techniques of thinking will be valuable if they contribute to insight.

SKILLS OF OBSERVATION

Insight into the process of thought is not sufficient to provide the law student with the orientation needed for policy-thinking. No matter how well equipped the individual is for goal, trend and scientific analysis, his elaborate machinery must work on relevant factual material.   As classroom instruction is progressively revised, the student will be exposed to more facts about the world.   However, it will be necessary for the classroom to maintain a high degree of concentration upon drill in the handling of legal technicality.   When, in connection with specific cases, the facts are in the foreground, the outline of the social system

[96] Lasswell, *World Politics and Personal Insecurity* (1935), Ch. I, and " General Framework : Person, Personality, Group, Culture ", in the present volume, Part II. To think or talk in " equilibrium " terms is to use " variables ", whether in a one-to-one or a systemic pattern.   Thinking or talking may also be " developmental ", in the sense that terms are employed that refer concretely to events.   If, following Cairns, *The Theory of Legal Science* (1941), we choose the term " order " to indicate the frame of reference for legal studies, and consider the variables that affect it, our mode of thought fits the equilibrium mould.   If we consider the post-war prospects of war in Germany, our starting-point is developmental.   In the same way we may begin with, or stress, syntactic or semantic statements.

as a whole may remain too far in the background.   As a corrective of the many distortions of perspective that come from specialization, it will be wise to make available to the law student a guide to social trends, a body of materials to be continuously consulted in the course of his educational and subsequent professional experience.   We have already outlined the justification of factual knowledge of trend, since we have put a great deal of emphasis upon the rational choice of goal, and the disciplined choice of method, on the basis of insight into the structure of the situation in which it is necessary to operate.

As a means of making the point more explicit, we include a provisional outline of a possible " Trend Book ".[97]   To some extent the outline has grown out of trial and error in teaching and policy-advising relationships.   The book is divided into five major divisions, of which the first, having to do with population, provides basic information about the density, distribution and biological characteristics of the people of America and of the world.   The second division is taken up with trends in the utilization of resources.   It brings together information about how people spend their time in production and about the volume and efficiency of output, the level of consumption, the degrees of depletion of potential resources, and the intensity of inventiveness in relation to the exploitation of natural advantages.   The plan is to describe each trend, first in terms of such technical measures as " man hours ", or " *per capita* physical units ", and then in monetary terms, such as " dollar value of output " or " dollars received ".   Summaries are made of the fluctuation of price levels and of general economic activity.

The third part deals with the distribution of values among various groups in society.   The main breakdown is according to deference, income and safety.   Deference is the general term for the distinctive values of power, respect, knowledge.   The fourth division of the " Trend Book " summarizes information about changing methods of getting social results.   Here the lines of division are according to the main instruments by which the human environment can be modified.   To some extent results are obtainable by the manipulation of symbols, as when counsel argues before the court, which reach the public through news releases and interpretative comment.   Besides the manipulation of symbols, results can be achieved by the skilful handling of goods and services.   In this connection we keep track of boycotts,

[97] See Appendix to this Chapter, p. 115.

barter and other arrangements for using economic means for policy ends. Violence, of course, stands out as a method of overwhelming importance to-day. By diplomacy we mean the use of official offer and counter-offer, agreement and non-agreement, as a means of getting results. In this connection we review the practices of mediation, arbitration, conciliation, adjudication, legislation and similar procedures, whose relative significance fluctuates from time to time and place to place. In connection with the treatment of each of these methods it is convenient to give attention to the structural characteristics of the specialized agencies most concerned with them. Here is where details will be found about the structure and operating procedures of courts.

The fifth and last division gathers together trends relating to the value position and methods of groups whose members are rarely if ever gathered in an all-inclusive organization. In the fifth division such topics are considered as the changing place of class, skill, personality and attitude groups. Much of the pertinent information can be cited by cross-references made to the preceding parts of the " Trend Book ". However, there are or can be summaries of the change in the total situation of various components of society, and these will be assembled in the fifth division.

In general, our view is that the material brought together for the use of law students ought to provide them with a concise, inclusive, reliable answer to such fundamental questions as these : How are population characteristics changing? What are the trends in the use of basic resources? What trends are exhibiting themselves in the distribution of each significant value in society? What are the changes in the degree to which different methods of influence are relied upon? What are the trends affecting the value, position and methods of each of the important groups of which society is composed? [98]

Valuable as the trend data are for the education of lawyers and policy-makers, they by no means exhaust the helpful material.

---

[98] In the outline we have referred under each main topic to one or two sample charts or tables. These are intended to give a greater sense of reality about each of the sub-categories and to underline the advantages that come from making our knowledge of social trends available in the compact or graphical forms that have been carried to such a high state of perfection in recent times. This is the " age of visualization ". There is no more effective method of conveying relative magnitudes than by means of charts, graphs and maps.

One result of preparing a " Trend Book " is to disclose gaps in knowledge of significant relations. Our world is still poorly informed about itself, and a continuing inventory of basic trends will reveal the spots where investigation is needed. The questions raised by alert law students will, in many instances, lead to the making of special requests to the census bureau and to other fact-gathering agencies.

The student needs a guide to the best sources of information and analysis about the major fields of national policy. At the present time there is a growing agreement on the convenience of dividing total policy into the fields of strategy, diplomacy, economy and ideology. In the reconstruction of the law school curriculum according to influence, value and skill principles, special emphasis upon value patterns must necessarily lead to familiarizing the student with the considerations involved in total policy.[99]

For this purpose it may be wise to arrange for a series of seminars, available to students in their last year, on each of the four fronts of policy. This idea may be made somewhat more definite by sketching the possible scope of such seminars.

Seminar on Ideology. One function of this seminar will be to give special consideration to the state of democratic ideology in relation to challenging ideologies at home and abroad. Part of the work will be to consider the syntactical structure of major ideological systems, a procedure that has already been discussed in connection with goal thinking. At the same time, however, it will be necessary to describe the actual facts about the ideological state of the world and of the chief trends that have been manifesting themselves in it, together with the possible lines of future development. The well-qualified student will want to have first-hand acquaintance with the most authoritative expositions of major ideologies, prepared by scholars or by persons whose power position in the world entitles what they say to particular consideration.[100] Within recent years there have been important advances in the scientific methods of studying ideological systems.[101] In particular there has been avid study of the effect

[99] Policy thinking, as remarked above, is more manipulative than contemplative ; it is pointed toward possible action in the emerging future. For a masterly exposition see Mannheim, *Man and Society in an Age of Reconstruction* (1940), Part 4 ; see also Lynd, *Knowledge for What ? The Place of Social Science in American Culture* (1939).

A general science of " order " can be developed along the lines proposed by Cairns ; it would call for the " laws " of order and the " principles " of preserving order. Our present concern is with part of the proposed field ; we want to develop the laws, principles, and practices of " democratic order ". Another way to formulate our standpoint is to say that we are concerned with a special field within the general science of values. The general science may be christened " general political science " if desired ; then the name of the special science becomes " the science of democracy " (distinct, for example, from the science of despotism or anarchy).

[100] Besides the pro-democratic statements referred to above, the student will want to familiarize himself with the positions taken by Stalin, Hitler, Mussolini —and equivalents—together with their intellectual progenitors, expositors, and amplifiers.

[101] Notably Pareto, *The Mind and Society* (tr. 1935) ; Mannheim, *Ideology and Utopia* (tr. 1936). On the backgrounds of modern thought consult Carlyle, *Political Liberty, a History of the Conception in the Middle Ages and Modern Times* (1941) ; Curtis, *Civitas Dei* (1934-7) ; McIlwain, *The Growth of Political Thought in the West* (1932).

of organized propaganda, upon the spread and restriction of rival systems.[102]

Seminar on Diplomacy.   The function of diplomacy is to protect and expand values by means of negotiation.   In recent times the term "diplomacy" has been limited for the most part to the conduct of external relations of states ; but there is also internal diplomacy, the process by which the individuals and group spokesmen of society come to terms with one another by various forms of negotiation.

Successful diplomacy is possible only where there is awareness of the changing power position of persons and groups at home and abroad.   Hence the seminar on diplomacy must examine trends in the power of modern states and of the significant groups within them.[103]   By examining historical instances of diplomatic negotiation, it is possible to evaluate the degree to which the technique of negotiation can itself become a significant factor in achieving the policies appropriate to democratic goals.[104]   To some extent books are available to interpret recent and prospective lines of world development.[105]   Indispensable data about the internal structure of American and of other societies have been assembled by many scholars.[106]   Specialists have concentrated upon specific factors or groups of factors that interplay in the total power process.[107]

[102] Examine, for instance, Ashton, *The Fascist, His State and His Mind* (1937) ; Borkenau, *World Communism* (1939) ; Heiden, *History of National Socialism* (1935) ; Lasswell and Blumenstock, *World Revolutionary Propaganda* (1939) ; Rosenberg, *History of Bolshevism* (1934).   General guides to the literature of propaganda are Farago and Gittler, *German Psychological Warfare* (1941) (annotated bibliography) ; Lasswell, Casey and Smith, *Propaganda and Promotional Activities, An Annotated Bibliography* (1935).
[103] For the diplomatic picture see Bemis, *Diplomatic History of the United States* (1936) ; Langer, *European Alliances and Alignments, 1871–1890* (1931) and *Diplomacy of Imperialism, 1890–1902* (1935) ; Steiger, *A History of the Far East* (1936).   On transformations in the social structure of the great powers, consult Ford (ed.), *Dictatorship in the Modern World* (1939) ; Michels, *Umschichtungen in den herrschenden Klassen nach dem Kriege* (1934) ; Neumann, *Permanent Revolution* (1942).
[104] See such detailed studies as Fay, *Origins of the World War* (2nd ed., 1930) ; Schmitt, *The Coming of the War* (1930).
[105] See Burnham, *Managerial Revolution* (1941) ; Lederer, *State of the Masses* (1940) ; Nomad, *Rebels and Renegades* (1932).
[106] On Germany see Neumann, *Behemoth, The Structure and Practice of National Socialism* (1942) ; on France, Ferre, *Les classes sociales dans la France contemporaine* (1934) ; on England, Carr-Saunders and Tones, *Survey of the Social Structure of England and Wales* (1927) ; on China, Wittfogel, *New Light on Chinese Society* (1938) ; on Japan, Lederer and Lederer-Seidler, *Japan in Transition* (1938) ; in general, Weber, *Wirtschaft u. Gesellschaft* (1924), pp. 122, 603.
[107] On geographical factors, for example, see Whittlesey, *The Earth and the State* (1939) ; also an appraisal of Geopolitik by Whittlesey, Colby and Hartshorne, *German Strategy of World Conquest* (1942).
Since we have used the term diplomacy to include all processes of agreement, the inner front of diplomacy includes the structures and procedures by which offers

Seminar on Economy. The task of this seminar is to evaluate the possible contribution to total politics of the skilful handling of goods and prices. Basic data, of course, will concern trends of economic development in America and throughout the world.[108] At the same time it will be necessary to become familiar with the systems of economic thought that are exerting significant influence on the assumptions and actions of influential groups throughout the world.[109]

Seminar on Strategy. Strategy is concerned with the use of armies, navies, air force and police as instruments for the attainment of selected policy goals. The purpose of the seminar is not to turn out future generals or admirals but to prepare policy-moulders for realistic evaluation of the testimony of whatever experts must be relied upon in the calculation of when, and how most effectively to use violence in defending and advancing the basic aims of policy. Such a seminar will concern itself with trends of fighting potential, with changes in the doctrine of war, with innovations in the organization of the armed forces as well as the technology of fighting.[110]

In connection with the work of each seminar it will be expedient to provide for the continuous criticism of current writing and speaking on the subject of America's policy. In this way the student will become more intimately acquainted with " who's who " in the private and public discussions in the course of which policy-makers arrive at the proposals they endorse.[111]

are made and accepted. In point, therefore, are studies of the courts in action, like Clark and Shulman, *A Study of Law Administration in Connecticut* (1937) ; also, investigations of mediation, conciliation, arbitration, collective bargaining, and administrative determination. See, for example, Millis, *How Collective Bargaining Works* (1942).

[108] See Beard, *A History of the Business Man* (1938) ; Bruck, *Social and Economic History of Germany* (1938) ; Day, *Economic Development in Europe* (1942) ; Emeny, *Strategy of Raw Materials* (1934) ; Gilfillen, *Sociology of Invention* (1935) ; Gras, *History of Agriculture in Europe and America* (2nd ed., 1940) ; Haynes, *This Chemical Age* (1942) ; Liefmann, *Cartels, Concerns, and Trusts* (1932) ; Nat. Resources Committee, *Technological Trends and National Policy* (1937) ; Pigou, *The Political Economy of War* (rev. ed., 1940) ; Sweezy, *Structure of Nazi Economy* (1941) ; von Waltershausen, *Die Enstehung der Weltwirtschaft* (1931). See also Hansen, *Fiscal Policy and Business Cycles* (1941) ; Keynes, *The General Theory of Employment, Interest and Money* (1936).

[109] Consult Buck, *The Politics of Mercantilism* (1942) ; Dickinson, *Economics of Socialism* (1939) ; Sweezy, *The Theory of Capitalist Development* (1942).

[110] See Brodie, *Sea Power in the Machine Age* (1941) ; Mitchell, *Outlines of the World's Military History* (1931) ; Rowan, *Terror in our Time* (1941) ; Sloutzki, *The World Armament Race, 1919–1939* (1941) ; Spaulding, Nickerson and Wright, *Warfare* (1925) ; Spykman, *America's Strategy in World Politics* (1942) ; Vagts, *History of Militarism* (1937) ; Werner, *Battle for the World* (1941).

[111] The field of total policy can be considered as a whole, not only in reference to ideology, diplomacy, economy and strategy. The larger structures involved in all of these processes can be examined. This is the place at which the general laws and principles of governmental organization are relevant (the analysis of legislation,

It is evident that the frame of reference of the policy seminars is primarily manipulative, in the sense that the minds of all participants are pointed toward the deliberate pursuit of goals that are persistently being clarified. As indicated before, the chief advantage of shifting the focus of attention from classroom preoccupation with legal technicality is that students can gain by shifting their frame of reference back and forth from details to context and from one mode of thought to another—and supplementary—one. With a knowledge of legal technicality well advanced, it will be possible for the student toward the end of his career in the law school to canvass the larger outlines of the situation in which he must presently find a more active and responsible place.

Whether the student is confronted by data purporting to deal with goal or trend, he is continually faced with the task of evaluating every statement in the light of its probable relationship to reality. Insight into the structure of reality is a never-ending process and every detail of the educational experience of the student can be justified only insofar as it contributes to this all-encompassing need. Yet there are certain forms of special experience that enhance the capacity of anyone to evaluate the truth-value of what is told him. Throughout his professional life the law student will deal with a continuing stream of experts on nearly any conceivable topic. As a policy-maker, he will be particularly concerned with what the specialists have to say about the processes of society and about the formation of human personality. Policy considerations, as we cannot too often reiterate, are " human " considerations the moment we put at the apex of our value hierarchy the celebration and realization of the dignity of the individual.

To some extent it will be possible to furnish law students with guides to the procedures by which qualified specialists obtain their data, together with the conceptual and technical processes by which they rearrange their observations. One part of the Skill Book may, for instance, include handy descriptions of the techniques used in collecting social data. Sometimes a procedure calls for prolonged contact between the observer and the individual or the situation under survey. The scholar who writes the professional or private life of Blackstone, or makes a study of some

the executive, administration, adjudication and control). In recent times the strategy and tactics of administration have received special attention ; see, for example, Metcalf and Urwick (eds.), *Dynamic Administration* (1942) ; Roethlisberger, *Management and Morale* (1941).

living personality with whom he is in prolonged contact, stands at one end of a series of data-gatherers ; at the other end are interviewers who ask a brief list of questions of persons whom they have never met before and never expect to see again.   Obviously the biographers are making use of far more intensive procedures than the poll-taker.   Differentiations in intensiveness, however, do not turn exclusively upon the length of time that the observer devotes his attention to any one individual or situation. Intensiveness is a function of the complexity or simplicity of the method utilized in recording and processing data.   The writer who is equipped to examine personality from the standpoint of modern psychology, psychiatry and sociology is making· use of a much more complex method for deciding what details are data than the man who operates within a framework of " common sense ".[112] The contact of the poll-taker with an individual subject is very brief, yet it may be part of a division of labour in which elaborate mechanical and statistical considerations have been involved in constructing a satisfactory sample of the population ; and the individual interview results may be processed in connection with hundreds or even thousands, of other interviews taken concurrently or during several preceding years.[113]

It is not only convenient to distinguish observational standpoints according to their degree of intensiveness-extensiveness, but we need to take account of the degree to which the scientific observer modifies the situation that he undertakes to describe. What happened to Blackstone during his lifetime cannot be changed by anybody who writes about him in the twentieth century ; but the picture gained of a living figure by a man who sees him every day may be modified by the characteristics of the two personalities.   We may call the observers who have no direct contact with the persons or situations that they describe collectors,[114] distinguishing them from all who are in direct contact with the phenomena they investigate.   Even those who are in direct contact do not necessarily exert the slightest degree of influence over the phenomena ; a spectator [115] who is buried in

---

[112] A book like Alexander and Staub, *The Criminal, the Judge and the Public* (1931), is especially full of insight into deeper personality structure.

[113] See Gallup and Rae, ·*The Pulse of Democracy* (1940) ; Robinson, *Straw Votes* (1932).

[114] Observational standpoints are summarized with reference to political science in Lasswell, " The Developing Science of Democracy ", in the present volume, Part I.

[115] Child behaviour is often studied by observers who are not seen by the children. Some technical procedures developed in these researches are summarized in Arrington, " Time-Sampling Studies of Child Behaviour ", *Psychological Monographs*, vol. 51 (1939), No. 2.

the grandstand does not modify the spectacle if he behaves like everyone else. Interviewers,[116] on the other hand, make people conscious that they are being studied, although false inferences may be made about particular purposes. Participant-observers [117] are those who give no clue that they are studying anybody for any purpose whatsoever, although they are bound to influence to some extent the persons with whom they live.

SKILLS IN MANAGEMENT

We will now consider some of the more active skills of dealing with people, whether individually or as members of groups, that the lawyer needs. There are limits on what the law school can provide in this direction, and most of what can be done must be outside the classroom. To some extent it is useful to acquaint the student with methods of observing people, since it is impossible to improve proficiency in understanding others without picking up pointers about the self. One function of the body of materials we have called the Skill Book can be to impart some of the observational skills that directly affect managerial efficiency.

Consider random movements. Everyone is sensitive to blushing, perspiring, fidgeting, and doodling, usually without insight. We act on the vague inference that the other person is trustworthy, shifty, poised or flustered. Are these " hunches " valid ? And can we learn to see even more in random movements than the ordinary man in the street sees in them ?

When one stops to think about it, the truth comes forcibly home that much of our success and failure in life depends on " reading human nature ", on making correct inferences about the character and even the ability of others on the basis of what we see in ordinary life situations. There is the task of " sizing up " a witness and settling on a line of examination that will improve, or break down, the impression that he is trustworthy. In selecting law clerks, partners and clients, we often have many

---

[116] See Bingham and Moore, *How to Interview* (2nd ed., 1931) ; Roethlisberger, Dickson and Wright, *Management and the Worker* (1939), Ch. 13. See also Moreno, *Who Shall Survive? A New Approach to the Problem of Human Interrelations* (1934) ; Thomas and Znaniecki, *The Polish Peasant in Europe and America* (1927) ; Webb and Webb, *Methods of Social Study* (1932).

[117] See Lindeman, *Social Discovery* (1924) ; Madge and Harrison (eds.), *Britain by Mass Observation* (1939) ; Kluckhohn, " The Participant Observer Technique in Small Communities ", *Am. J. Soc.*, vol. 46 (1940), p. 331 ; Mead, " More Comprehensive Field Methods ", *Am. Anthrop.*, vol. 35 (1933), p. 1. On various methods of self-observation consult Allport, *The Use of Personal Documents in Psychological Science* (1942) ; Horney, *Self-Analysis* (1942) ; Lasswell, *A New Technique of Thinking* (1930), Ch. 3.

sources of information to supplement our unaided guesses. Nevertheless we learn to depend on our judgment, and our success and usefulness is at stake on our "disciplined intuition". If we judge incorrectly, we may select, and unknowingly instigate, a partner who commits suicide at a critical time in our affairs. On the basis of a " hunch ", we may defy the appraisals of others, and entrust a law clerk with great responsibilities ; possibly the outcome will vindicate us.   There is the question of, how far to trust newspaper correspondents with " inside stories " ; a mutually helpful relationship with columnists and commentators may spell the difference between public support of one side and public hostility.   No experienced person banks too much on his " knowledge of human nature ", especially when he has had wide enough experience to find out how complex it often is.   Even those whom we know " like a brother " may turn out to be serious misfits.   The trusted clerk proves to be a falsifier of accounts ; the conscientious partner has a " nervous breakdown ", or becomes suspicious, embittered, unco-operative.

What can be done to improve our " judgment of men " ? There is no royal road, no X-ray eye, no teachable hocus-pocus that gives infallible results.   Two things, however, can be done. The student can be made explicitly aware of what he sees, and the inferences that he draws ; and he can learn to interpret the possible significance of what specialists are able to report.   Law students do not have time to become experimental psychologists, or mental and aptitude test experts, or clinically competent interviewers.[118]   But they can learn how to apply some of the products of scientific research to the daily process of judging men. Actual experience in recording the random movements of others is excellent self-discipline.   If we meet a new person and talk to him for a while, we may decide that he is " untrustworthy ". Very well ; we may practise noting (in an unobtrusive way) some of his specific acts.   Where does he focus his gaze ?   Does he look the other person in the eye, or does his gaze wander up and down and around the room ?   There is popular prejudice against the " shifty-eyed ", and physicians have found shiftiness a useful clue, taken along with others, of neurotic instability. We must keep in mind the " over-compensatory " reaction of keeping the eyes riveted on the other person ; this is often found in slick, bold, impostor types.   What is significant in behaviour

[118] For guidance to the literature consult Allport, *Personality* (1937) ; Murphy and Newcomb, *Experimental Social Psychology* (1937).

is deviation, which may be toward exaggerating a tendency, or toward extreme adjustment in the opposite direction.

Random movements may make " physiological sense ", even though at first glance they lack rhyme or reason. Certain levels of fear are often manifested by an inhibiting effect on some secretions. There is the famous " dry mouth " of stage-fright, connected with reduced salivation, a symptom upon which the Chinese have traditionally depended in detecting false testimony. After all, there is a physiological basis for testing truthfulness according to capacity to chew a mouthful of rice husks.[119] Persons may also indicate anxiety by fingering or picking the nose ; the inner lining often gets dry and irritated under stress. Feelings of helplessness can be betrayed by what appears to be excessive activity of the tear ducts. Some movements can be better understood in the light of the clinical caricature of the tendency that finds only limited expression under ordinary conditions. The uptilting of the chin, with its hint of condescension, is present in many haughty " paranoid " types.[120] ◄ A quick, stereotyped smile may be understood in relation to extreme cases in which excessive fear of being assaulted by others leads to the propitiatory peace-offering of a quick, ingratiating smile.

Lawyers and other members of learned professions often overestimate the creative ability of compulsive and obsessive people.[121] The trained intellectual may have obsessive strains in his own personality ; in any case, seeming sincerity, gravity, orderliness and industry make a favourable impression, where all these qualities are of obvious value. However, when these characteristics are not blended with detachment, revealed in a touch of humour, there is danger that the person in question is too rigid, unadaptable and lacking in improvisation to mature into an individual who can face new and important responsibility. Often we get disappointing results from conscientious people when we promote them into better jobs ; they need definite instructions and a set system, and when they have many alternatives to choose among, the strain is more than they can bear. Suddenly the dependable assistant becomes inefficient, irritable with himself and everyone else, and wholly incapable of smooth adaptation. From

[119] See Larson, *Lying and Its Detection* (1932).
[120] For a view of current psychiatric conceptions see Brown and Menninger, *The Psychodynamics of Abnormal Behavior* (1940) ; Maslow and Mittelmann, *Principles of Abnormal Psychology* (1941) ; Sullivan, *loc. cit. supra*, note 43.
[121] The distinction between obsessive and hysteric types is succinctly given in Mayo, *Human Problems of an Industrial Civilization* (1933), p. 107, based on the work of Pierre Janet.

the " clinical caricature " of types who have " nervous break-downs", we can learn much about the structure of such characters, noting in particular how greatly they depend on routine operations to hold in check their hostile, destructive impulses.   From this group of rigid characters are often recruited stern, self-righteous types who have no insight whatever into the deep, veiled gratifications that they receive from the discomfiture of others. Here are the judges who gain secret joy from cruelty ; in this category, too, we find petty clerks and officials who annoy, where they do not more seriously damage, those who depend upon their application of a rule.[122]

For lack of basic information about human personality, many lawyers have become fruitlessly entangled with ill and even dangerous persons.   To choose a notorious example, there is a type well known to psychiatrists called a " litigious paranoid ", who is continually starting lawsuits, owing to an exaggerated tendency to feel discriminated against, coupled with the ability to tell a plausible story.   Unhappily, such individuals do not impress the untutored as ill, and they may go on for years fomenting trouble.   Some other paranoid types are more destructive.   They are homicidally inclined ; yet often they arouse no suspicion in the layman's mind.   But the lawyer can be given enough familiarity with the picture to keep his guard up.

By closely observing the interplay among those who participate in courts, committees and other recurrent situations, we may discover many valuable facts.   Some judges are intimidated by vigorous, bold, outspoken personalities who challenge opposing counsel constantly and go as far as possible in challenging the court itself.   Usually, of course, judges are amenable to more flattering modes of allusion, if not to opposing counsel, at least to the bench.   In watching witnesses it is often possible to learn to forecast accurately the " breaking point " of the liars and even to distinguish it from the often clumsy fumbling of an honest man with poor poise.   The observer of court proceedings can actually

[122] In addition to random movements, the flow of words may provide helpful clues to the mood of the person with whom one has to deal.   It is convenient to classify statements according to reference.   " Self " references allude to the state-ment-maker ; " other " references to other persons.   Plus references put the referent of the statement in a favourable light (" I am a great man ") ; minus references do the opposite (" I am a flop ").   Furthermore, the standard may be specified ; plus or minus may be in terms of " strength-weakness " or " morality-immorality ", for example.   See Lasswell, " A Provisional Classification of Symbol Data ", *Psychiatry: J. of Bio. and Path. of Interpersonal Relations*, vol. 1 (1938), p. 197.

make a record of the frequency with which given participants refer to themselves and others in various ways, and provide not only self-training in the study of behaviour but contribute to a body of records valuable for deeper understanding of what happens in litigation.[123]

What is seen and heard can be fitted into the perspective of social structure as well as personality type. By accent and manner the upper, middle- and lower-class person—in terms of "respect" position—may be discerned. The "upper-class" manner may be found to include an air of gracious detachment that is difficult for the middle- or lower-class individual to acquire. The clue to a genuinely aristocratic attitude, as has often been pointed out, is that the aristocrat has no compulsion to allow himself to be measured in terms of proficiency in any particular skill.[124] He aristocratically demands respect, not on the basis of sacrificially-gained attainments, but solely for "being"; he expects to be deferred to just because he exists, not because he is "good for something". Part of the code is to maintain an air of imperviousness to the trials and tribulations of the moment; the ego must appear to remain unruffled and uncontaminated by momentary acts of fate. Even enemies may be treated with ceremoniousness. All this, where it is found, contrasts with the sharp "self" and "other" evaluations that are so often on the tongue of the middle-class person, and especially of the more rivalrous "climbers". It may be found that in negotiation, as well as before some of the higher courts, the near-aristocratic benignity may be a more powerful instrument than the "huffing and puffing" of the "over-zealous", or at least over-transparent, middle-class derivative. When tribunals are made up of middle-class personnel, however, certain accents and demeanours may be resented, especially if the person in question is suspected of being "really" middle-class. One of the major points to watch

---

[123] Administrators who came in direct contact with clients were directly observed by Lasswell and Almond, "The Participant Observer, I", in the present volume, Part III. By careful study, it is possible to distinguish between patterns common to a culture and those pertaining to a personality. See Efron, *Gesture and Environment* (1941), a tentative study of some of the spatio-temporal and "linguistic" aspects of the gestural behaviour of Eastern Jews and Southern Italians in New York City, living under different environmental conditions. Correlations between physical type and other characteristics are reported in Sheldon, *The Varieties of Human Physique* (1940) and *The Varieties of Temperament* (1942). See also Murray (ed.), *Explorations in Personality* (1938), and Horst, *The Prediction of Personal Adjustment* (1942). The scientific approach to the entire legal process was advocated and exemplified in the pioneer book of Robinson, *Law and the Lawyers* (1935).

[124] Compare Hobhouse, "Aristocracy", in *Encyc. Soc. Sciences*, vol. 2 (1930), p. 183.

is which participants assume lower-class submissiveness, and which ones react against an inner tendency to submit. " Class points " and " personality points " are continually becoming entangled with one another, sometimes limiting and sometimes reinforcing each other. Middle-class rivalrousness leads to a high frequency level of aspersive remarks ; but from this level may appear conspicuous deviates in the direction of extreme " objectivity ", " sweetness and light ", or " super-cynicism ". The focalizing of stress within our civilization at the middle layers leads to great variety in the forms of solution found by middle-class youth.[125]

In the name of better training for students in these matters it may be possible for law professors to learn more and more of these facts of life and to diminish their own danger to students. All of us have seen promising students fail drastically at some point in their professional training ; often they were gifted intellectually, but suffered from some distortion of personality that might have been rectified had their needs been identified in time and assistance tactfully given by professors who were interested in them. Industrial plants often assume some measure of responsibility in providing modern medical and psychiatric facilities for the executive staff and the working force. Up to the present, however, many professors in our professional schools apparently feel themselves free to damage human personalities at will through unnecessary ignorance and arrogant self-dramatization.[126]

Many of the problems of management involve large groups of people rather than specific individuals and hence are problems of public relations. This is the field which was called ideological policy in the fourfold analysis of policy above. Other synonyms or closely related characterizations are information or propaganda policy. In any case, the problem is to modify response by controlling the symbols that come to the focus of general attention. In operations that concern far-flung governmental, business and other private activities, the time has long since passed when public relations policies are run entirely by hunch. The modern moulding of the human environment proceeds on a factual basis, quite as

[125] See especially Warner and Dollard, loc. cit. supra, note 42. On one of the neglected layers of the middle class, Speier, " The Salaried Employee in Modern Society ", Social Research, vol. 1 (1934), p. 111. For historical perspective, Palm, The Middle Class Then and Now (1936).

[126] A sketch of modern medical and psychiatric services in various institutions is in the Encyc. Soc. Sciences under such titles as " Psychiatry ", " Industrial Hygiene ", " Medicine ".

much as economic, military or diplomatic policy.[127]   Many procedures have been developed for describing the distribution of attitudes on which the future survival of various enterprises depends, and these several procedures may be relied upon to furnish a factual basis for estimating trends and evaluating future probabilities on the basis of scientific knowledge of causal inter-relationships.   In the field of military policy it has long been a commonplace that command depends upon adequate intelligence. The providing of similar facts is what is involved in establishing a solid intelligence basis for public relations policy.

A quick over-all view of significant responses may often be gained by the use of existing methods of polling opinion.   By means of a sample that reflects the structure of a large population in correct proportion, it is possible to obtain a reliable picture of what great numbers of people think by interviewing a small fraction of the persons concerned.   The results of such polling operations are most easy to interpret when the issue before the public is one in which there is very active public interest and with respect to which a few leading alternatives of action are universally known, e.g. an important election.   But we cannot be so sure about the relevance of polling results when public interest is at a low ebb and when a very limited number of alternatives have not been crystallized.   When people are questioned about the structure of a post-war world long before the nature of the leading alternatives is clear, very little can be said about how people will actually respond in future situations.   Under such conditions the brief polling interview tends to become a method of discovering which words are " plus " words and which words are " minus " words.   If the word " planning ", for example, is a " plus " word in the vocabulary of a given sector of the population, the word may be invoked to justify almost any of the alternatives eventually presented in the opinion-forming process.[128]

Deeper knowledge of the way people are disposed to respond can be obtained by the use of other methods of collecting facts. We may for example, conduct prolonged interviews with selected

[127] On propaganda and allied activities of various groups see Culp, *The American Legion* (1942) ; McCamy, *Government Publicity* (1939) ; McKean, *Pressures on the Legislature of New Jersey* (1938) ; Selle, *The Organization and Activities of the National Education Association* (1932) ; Strong, *Organized Anti-Semitism in America* (1941) ; Walker and Sklar, *Business Finds its Voice* (1938).

[128] See Gosnell and de Grazia, " A Critique of Polling Methods ", *Public Opinion Q.*, vol. 6 (1942), p. 378.

persons.[129]   In this way we may discover that people who profess interest in post-war plans will at the same time evince such active distrust of Britain or Russia that the idea of placing the control of certain basic raw materials jointly in the hands of an international agency has little appeal.   On the other hand, it may happen that deep-lying scepticism is encountered about the possibility of providing jobs for all unless there is some form of world economic authority charged with the stimulation and regularization of production in different regions of the world. There may be great loyalty to certain leaders who may at some future time take serious initiatives on behalf of world planning. Skilled workers, unskilled workers, small business men, professional people, government and party employees, owners and top executives of big businesses may reveal at any given time a tangled pattern of inconsistent and contradictory aspirations, expectations and identifications.   By means of prolonged interviewing we may get some of the facts for forecasting the   "priority attitudes"   that prevail among the major social divisions.

The most valuable insight into the structure of collective attitudes may be obtained not by brief or prolonged interviews of the type just described but by the comparative study of the historical background out of which contemporary attitudes have arisen.   In this way it will be possible to rediscover many past experiences that have dropped out of the minds of most of the members of the contemporary generation but which would take on a new birth of vitality under certain future conditions.   By examining the statements and counter-statements made in public and private circles during the struggle of the United States over the ratification of the League of Nations, we may arrive at a more realistic sense of the priority of different factors that may affect adjustment to the post-war environment.   Such fact-gathering operations can be disciplined not only by the knowledge of historians but by the scientific findings of social scientists and psychologists.[130]   In the light of the relationships thus explored and revealed, it would be possible to devise experimental methods

[129] On the use of longer interviews to evaluate attitudes see Cantril, *The Invasion from Mars* (1940) ; Lazarsfeld, *Radio and the Printed Page* (1940).
[130] The convergence of personality and cultural standpoints is creating " social psychology ".   See Brown, *Psychology and the Social Order* (1936) ; Horney, *The Neurotic Personality of Our Time* (1937) ; Kardiner, *The Individual and His Society* (1939) ; Klineberg, *Social Psychology* (1940) ; Sherif, *Psychology of Social Norms* (1936) ; Miller and Dollard, *Social Learning and Imitation* (1941) ; Linton, *The Study of Man* (1936).

both for probing the structure of current attitudes and pre-testing the pragmatic effect of alternative lines of propaganda.

In studying predisposition and response it is important to describe what appears in the media of communication that reaches the focus of attention of different groups and thus operates causally in moulding response. The procedures by which it is possible to describe what is said in speeches, what is sent over the wires of press associations, or what is depicted in newsreels, fall within the general field of " content analysis ".[131] Public relations policy, as we have pointed out, consists in managing the stream of communication, and if this process is to be understood it is necessary to evaluate three groups of factors : content, effect, predisposition. In studying the predispositions, we must give special attention to those who exercise special control over the channels through which news and comment gets to the attention of others. In particular this calls for knowledge of the attitudes of owners, regulators and contributors to press, radio, motion picture and all other mass media. One revealing body of data locates the controllers of communication in the social structure and then shows the value position of those whom they reach through the network at their command. In view of the high concentration of governmental or private ownership control of most of the great modern networks of mass communication, it is apparent that communication flows chiefly from those who occupy high positions in the social pyramids to the rest of the community. Systematic data about the affiliations of those who own, control or contribute to the mass media are peculiarly important in evaluating the function that these media may be expected to perform in future crises.[132] Whether we have to do with a special investigation, or the conduct of significant and protracted litigation, or with the hearings before Congressional committees, or with debates on the floor of legislative bodies, or proceedings before chief executives, departments and agencies, or with presentations to the executive committees and the boards of directors of private pressure groups, business, or private cultural

---

[131] Childs and Witton (eds.), *Propaganda by Short Wave* (1942) ; Waples (ed.), *Print, Radio, and Film in a Democracy* (1942) ; Waples, Berelson and Bradshaw, *What Reading Does to People* (1940) ; Woodward, *Foreign News in American Morning News-papers* (1930) ; Jones, " Quantitative Analysis of Motion Picture Content ", *Pub. Opinion Q.*, vol. 6 (1942), p. 411 ; Lasswell, " The Politically Significant Content of the Press : Coding Procedures ", *Journalistic Q.*, vol. 19 (1942), p. 12.

[132] Representative studies of contributors to media are Rosten, *The Washington Correspondents* (1937) and *Hollywood* (1941). An exemplary study of control is P.E.P., *Report on the British Press* (1938).

organizations—we are engaging in processes that interact with the entire structure of value distribution and condition the fulfilment of democratic goals.[133]

Information about control, content and consequence of communication is necessary to the development of sound strategical and tactical policies. Although democracies and despotisms alike make use of propaganda, the line taken by democratic societies in meeting emergencies is most effective when it adheres to certain differences that distinguish it from despotism. For one thing, the control of communication is not completely subordinated to detailed dictation. Democracies that adhere to their own ideals tolerate self-criticism during crises not as a necessary concession to weakness but as a means of mobilizing their natural strength. However there are conspicuous dangers in permitting unfavourable presentations of democratic leaders, institutions and policies unless these are promptly counterbalanced by favourable material. The basic policy of democracy is neither intolerance nor passive acquiescence in its own destruction ; rather it is vigorous, positive self-defence and counterattack.

The psychic potential of democracy is far higher than that of despotism, since people are at their best when their total energies are released in respected lines of activity. The technique of despotism is to divide and rule ; the masses are divided into echelons that are ordered according to the arrogant self-interest of those in each echelon. At every tier individuals are encouraged to believe that they will gain special privileges by submitting to the echelon just above. The principal advantage consists in permission to impose one's will upon those beneath. Democracies on the other hand, can maintain a conception of power as a shared pursuit of a common goal to which everyone contributes according to capacity. In their propaganda democracies must rule by insight and not by reiteration and imposition, although they must be alert and vigorous in the reaffirmation of their basic principles and in preserving confidence in ultimate success. They can safely allow far more dissent on ways and means than is compatible with the structure of despotism. One tacit admission

---

[133] On general theory see Bartlett, *Political Propaganda* (1940) ; Blau, *Propaganda als Waffe* (1937) ; Chakotin, *The Rape of the Masses* (1940) ; Childs and Witton (eds.), *loc. cit. supra*, note 131 ; Doob, *Propaganda* (1935) ; Merriam, *The Making of Citizens* (1931) ; Pintschovius, *Die seelische Widerstandskraft im modernen Krieg* (1936) ; Taylor, *Strategy of Terror* (1940). See also Bradway, *The Bar and Public Relations* (1934).

of the power of democracy is the spurious simulation of a democratic order by despotic states.   This simulation shows itself in the use of democratic symbols, but it betrays itself by mystical and ambiguous, hence fraudulent, application.   While despotisms offer verbal deference to the masses, they do so on the express understanding that the masses shall not be trusted to have a voice in the selection of leaders or in the determination of policy.

Beyond the Classroom

In the foregoing discussion we have taken it for granted that the classroom will remain the most conspicuous pedagogical device in the environment of the students of the future law school. Hence it will be incumbent upon the professors to make of the classroom a more powerful instrument for transmitting not only the skills in legal technicality that constitute the indispensable core of the lawyer's professional equipment but the additional skills that promise to mould the policy-makers capable of fulfilling the aims and realizing the opportunities of the years ahead.   We have, however, recognized from time to time in these suggestions about curricular reconstruction that other parts of the law school environment can be deliberately remodelled into more effective instruments for supplementing the classroom.

Among these supplementary instruments we give special emphasis to the seminar.   By the seminar we mean a comparatively small group of professors and students engaged in creative analysis and research on problems.   Now there is nothing new about the seminar any more than there is about the classroom— the problem is to refill it with content appropriate to the professed objectives of our curricular reconstruction.   The special advantages of the seminar are well known.   In the intensive work that goes forward skills may be perfected in the organization and presentation of material.   In particular the seminar lends itself to the discovery of new problems and to the patient exploration of new sources and even new skills marginal to the central apparatus of legal technicality with which the student becomes familiarized in connection with the classroom.   In the law school of the future there should be ample opportunity for seminar work, since it seems very plausible to the writers, as to many reformers of law school education, that sufficient grounding in legal syntax and procedure can be gained by a full year of classroom instruction.   Additional work directly looking toward the mastery of legal doctrine and procedure, as well as in the acquisition of general policy skills, can be more productively carried on in seminars.[134]

Without concerning ourselves too greatly with revising the seminar formula itself, we may nevertheless urge the advantages of seminars in which several men of established professional competence take an active hand. Too often the seminar is exploited by a single dominating personality as an instrument for riding his special hobby. This tendency can be held in check by colleagues. The idea here is not to turn seminars into little bullpens, where men of incompatible view and temperament are supposed to conduct interminable jousts with one another. On the contrary, the idea is to create seminars among people who share not only quite general values but specific concern with the achievement of rather restricted objectives.

It is particularly advantageous if seminars can grow into productive centres of continuing research from year to year. In many ways there are advantages if the seminar becomes, even in name, an institute. In addition to the professors in the law school and in other departments of universities, such seminar-institute staffs can be recruited from research fellows who devote most of their time for a period of years to work in a special field. These fellows should be recruited from the regular teaching staff of law schools ; from men who can spend a year or more away from their regular teaching duties whipping into shape some fruitful contribution to the literature of law and policy. To a certain extent, moreover, fellowships may become available to law school graduates who have but a limited interest in teaching but who have great aptitude for fundamental inquiry. Men of this type often have difficulty in making their most distinctive and useful contributions to society, since often they mature into effective classroom teachers late in life when they have the poise that comes from confident mastery of a special field. One of the purposes of the institute-seminar system can be to adapt the whole institutional structure of legal research, teaching and practice to various patterns of individual skill and aptitude. It is difficult to over-emphasize the practical importance of making adequate provision for the encouragement of research along margins of

---

[134] There is merit in Hall's suggestion that legal technicality precede intensive work in the social sciences. However, the courses in legal technicality should not be relegated to the status of drill hours in syntactics devoid of semantic content. Hall, "A 2-2-2 Plan for College-Law Education", *Harv. L. Rev.*, vol. 56 (1942), p. 245.

the traditional field of accepted technicality.   Only too often in the past brave new worlds of integrated law and social science have been proposed ; but a short time afterwards it has been painfully apparent that the high aspirations of the founding fathers had come to little because of the practical difficulties of providing adequate financial and honorific inducements to enable people to " take the long chance " of cultivating marginal problems and skills.[135]

One principle of professional training is to project the student into situations that resemble as closely as possible the circumstances of his future career.   One well-established pattern of this type can, in the reformed law school, be turned into a more productive instrument of legal education.   We refer to the moot court.   It is common in some places to conduct various " autopsies " on the performance of students before these tribunals.   What we propose is that the appraisal should be conducted not only in terms of legal technicality but for the purpose of revealing the total effectiveness of the participant in handling himself in the situation.   By the use of modern recording devices it is feasible to record the speaker's voice and to enable the individual to achieve objectivity toward that all-important instrument.   With the aid of motion picture equipment it becomes feasible to present the total demeanour of the individual to the subject himself.   In connection with the law school, it is practicable to provide technical facilities of many kinds in order to enable the individual to overcome difficulties of trait and skill.   Through proper testing facilities, unsuspected aptitudes may be revealed and the source of many inhibitions on effective expression may be exposed, understood and eliminated.   In some cases it is wise to take advantage of special analytic procedures developed as an adjunct of modern clinical psychology.   For many students intensive coaching in writing is quite as vital as in speaking.

Still another well-established institutional practice is to conduct investigations in the field.   Very often it has been pointed out that the training of modern students deflects their attention from the factual contexts in which legal technicalities are made functional and that this cannot receive entirely satisfactory correction by providing more fact books.   The recommendation

---

[135] A seminar is a convenient pivot around which can revolve the work of preparing and revising such materials as we have referred to as skill book or trend book.   The collaboration of many specialists on different varieties of economic, governmental, psychological and allied forms of data is required for the successful execution of such a project.

is that opportunities be provided for direct contact with courts, administrative agencies and other parts of our social process. It is desirable that at least brief periods of field experience should occur at different times.

So much for the possibilities of the influence, value and skill principles in reconstructing the law curriculum for systematic training for policy-making.   In bringing these proposals to a close, we repeat that they are prepared from the point of view of the needs of a nation that professes deep regard for the dignity of man and that in practice relies to an extraordinary degree upon the advice of professional lawyers in the formation and execution of policy.   In our view the democratic values of our society can only be effectively fulfilled if all who have an opportunity to participate significantly in the forming of policy share certain ways of thinking, observing and managing.   It has been our purpose to deal with some explicitness with those changes in the existing pattern of the law school that will increase the probability that the lawyers of the future will be more effective instruments for the achievement of the public good than they have been in the past.

APPENDIX [136]

(The following citations are intended to illustrate what is meant by each main category of the social trend outline.   Charts are given preference, since they are more concise than tables).

I. Population
    A. Numbers
        x1. Momentum of world population growth, 1650–1930. Snyder, *Capitalism the Creator* (1940), p. 25, chart 2.
        x2. Population of the United States, 1850–1920, and estimates of population 1930–2000.   A. D. Baker, Borsodi, and Wilson, *Agriculture in Modern Life* (1939), p. 20, fig. 3.
    B. Biological Traits (and Families)
        x3. Growth of population of the United States by age groups, 1930–80.   Anderson, T.N.E.C. Rep., *Taxation, Recovery and Defence*, Monograph 20 (1941), p. 284, chart 5.
        x4. Estimated number of private families, U.S., 1920–80. *Idem* p. 287, chart 6.
    C. Spatial distribution
    See atlases.
II. Resource Utilization
    A. Technical
      1. Degree
        x5. Employment and unemployment, 1920–38.´   Gill, *Wasted Manpower* (1939), p. 21, chart 1.

[136] Cf. above, p. 95.

2. Output
    x6. Index numbers of world agricultural and industrial production, 1925–33. Woytinsky, " Social Consequences of the Economic Depression ", in *Studies and Reports*, Series C, No. 21, International Labour Office (1936), p. 21, diagram V.
3. Units (for convenience combined with III, B, 1).
4. Efficiency
    x7. Travel time in days from Boston, 1790–8. Staley, *World Economy in Transition* (1939), p. 8, chart II.
    x8. World travel time in days from Boston, 1938. *Idem.* facing p. 10, chart III.
    x9. Progress of efficiency in the consumption of fuel by large industrial consumers in the United States. Lorwin, T.N.E.C. Rep., *Technology in our Economy*, Monograph 22 (1941), p. 104, chart VI.
5. Consumption and Depletion
    x10. Average *per capita* consumption of principal agricultural products, 1920–37. Meyers, T.N.E.C. Rep., *Agriculture in the National Economy*, Monograph 23 (1940), p. 3, table 1.
    x11. Coal resources of the U.S. (showing original tonnage, amount produced, and estimated waste as of Jan., 1936). Nat. Resources Committee, *Energy Resources and National Policy* (1939), p. 283, table 3.
6. Invention
    x12. Number of British patents granted from 1449 to 1921. 2 Sorokin, *Social and Cultural Dynamics* (London, 1937), p. 168, fig. 8.
B. Monetary
    1. Output
        x13. Value of all construction, 1919–39. Stone, T.N.E.C. Rep., *Toward More Housing*, Monograph 8 (1940), p. 3, chart 1.
    2. Price levels
        x14. Long-term movements of various price series. Macaulay, *Some Theoretical Problems Suggested by Movements of Interest Rates, Bond Yields and Stock Prices in the U.S. since 1856* (1938), p. 230, chart 29.
    3. Income and Outlay (expenditures for consumption, investment)
        x15. Gross national product, capital formation, and consumers' outlay, 1919–40. Altman, T.N.E.C. Rep., *Savings, Investments and National Income*, Monograph 37 (1941), p. 68, table 16.
        x16. Governmental expenditures, federal, state and local, 1923–38. Anderson, *op. cit. supra*, x3, at pp. 52–5, tables 20, 21, charts 3, 4.

4. Cost
x17. Indexes of output per man-hour, average hourly earnings and unit labour cost, United States, 1923–39. Lorwin, *op. cit. supra*, x9, p. 153, chart XII.

5. Activity levels
x18. Percentage distribution of business cycles in various countries and various periods according to their approximate duration in years. Thorp, *Business Annals*, (1926), pp. 56–9, chart IV.

III. Values
A. Total (Relation of an organized group to several values)
x19. Political control of the world's population and land surface by empires. Clark, *A Place in the Sun* (1936), charts p. 81.

B. Deference
1. Power (units, activity, composition)
   (*a*) Government
   (1) Interstate
   x20. Membership of the League of Nations, 1920–40. Middlebush and Hill, *Elements of International Relations* (1940), p. 204, chart II.
   (2) State
   x21. Class, skill and attitude analysis of governmental and party leaders of Fascist Italy. Lasswell and Sereno, " The Changing Italian Élite ", in the present volume, Part II, tables 1–3.
   x22. Age composition of the National Socialist Party in percentages of the total in the years 1931, 1932, and 1935, as compared with age composition of the Social Democratic Party in 1931 and of the total population over eighteen years of age in 1933. Gerth, " The Nazi Party : Its Leadership and Composition " *Am. J. of Soc.*, vol. 45 (1940), p. 530, table 2.
   (3) Intrastate
   x23. Number of local units of government in the United States. Groves, *Financing Government* (1939), p. 636, table 42.
   x24. Distribution according to occupation of all members of thirteen lower chambers and twelve senates during 1925–35. Hyneman, " Who Makes Our Law ? " *Pol. Sci. Q.*, vol. 55 (1940), p. 557, table 1.
   (*b*) Private pressure associations
   x25. Table of meetings of private international organizations, 1840–1914. Potter, *An Introduction to the Study of International Organization* (4th ed., 1935), p. 48, n. 3.

x26. List of national organizations with headquarters at Washington. Blaisdell, T.N.E.C. Rep., *Economic Power and Political Pressures*, Monograph 26 (1941), pp. 197–201.

(c) Business

x27. Indexes of U.S. business population, 1900–38. Anderson, *op. cit. supra*, x3, p. 318, table 24 (appendix).

x28. Intercorporate holdings of voting stock by the John D. Rockefeller and J. P. Morgan and connected interests in companies having substantial holdings in the natural gas and natural gas pipeline industries of the United States as of Jan. 1, 1939. Federal Trade Commission, T.N.E.C. Rep., *Federal Trade Commission on Natural Gas*, Monograph 36 (1940), exhibit 3, facing p. 89.

x29. Growth in the average size of establishments in all manufacturing industries, 1914–37. Thorp, T.N.E.C. Rep., *Structure of Industry*, Monograph 27 (1941), p. 4, table 2.

2. Respect

x30. A measurement of the interconnectedness of the several classes in their associational relations. Warner and Lunt, *The Social Life of a Modern Community* (1941), p. 125, table 1.

3. Insight

x31. Regional variations in high school enrolment. Odum and Moore, *American Regionalism* (1938), p. 534.

C. Income (distribution)

x32. Shares of total individual income received by selected proportions of income recipients, 1918–37. Goldenthal, T.N.E.C. Rep., *Concentration and Composition of Industrial Income, 1918–1937*, Monograph 4 (1940), p. 22, table 2.

D. Safety

x33. Percentage of casualties in four countries from the twelfth to the twentieth century. 3 Sorokin, *op. cit. supra*, x12, p. 337, table 17.

IV. Methods

A. Symbols

x34. Volume of newspaper and periodical advertising revenue, *per capita* expenditures in these media, and ratio of expenditures to national income, selected years, 1865–1937. Borden, *The Economic Effects of Advertising* (1942), p. 48, table I.

B. Goods (and Services)

x35. Federal expenditures for grants-in-aid, 1910, 1918, 1928, 1936 (in thousands of dollars). Bitterman, *State and Federal Grants-in-Aid* (1938), pp. 132 ff.

C. Violence

    x36. Relative indicators of war activities by century periods for nine European countries. 3 Sorokin, *op. cit. supra*, x12, p. 341, table 18.

D. Diplomacy (offer, counter-offer, acceptance, rejection by authorized group spokesmen)

    x37. Work of the Permanent Court of International Justice, 1922 to June 15, 1939, showing chronologically the number of judgments, orders having the force of judgments, and advisory opinions of the Court. Middlebush and Hill, *op. cit. supra*, x20, p. 457, table VII.

V. Groups (The value position and methods of groups that are not as a rule inclusively organized. Governments, private associations, and business organizations are, for convenience, described under II, B, 1).

A. Class

    (Cross reference here the table on " Class Analysis " in x21.)

B. Skill

    (Cross reference here the table on " Skill Analysis " in x21.)

C. Personality

    x38. Distribution of ideational, mixed, and sensate types among popes and kings. 1 Sorokin, *op. cit. supra*, x12, p. 106, table 2.

D. Attitude (data concerning the distribution of symbols at a given time are recorded here, and changes of distribution).

    x39. Shifts in attitude patterns, May to September, 1940. Cantrill, Rugg and Williams, " America Faces the War : Shifts in Opinion " *Pub. Opinion Q.*, vol. 4 (1940), p. 652, chart 1.

CHAPTER IV

POLICY AND THE INTELLIGENCE FUNCTION : IDEOLOGICAL INTELLIGENCE *

The intelligence function adapts itself to changing conceptions of policy and to innovations in the procedures by which facts are gathered, analysed, and presented. New policy ideas are to-day resulting from the vast transformations that are taking place in the structure of society, state, and government. New methods of observing, analysing, and reporting data have arisen as an outcome of the growth of modern social and psychological sciences. So swift is the stream that we may fail in every effort to chart the banks within which it flows ; yet the importance of seeking to understand the complex relationship of policy and intelligence is great enough to justify the risks involved.

A canvass of the existing literature reveals that very little systematic and unified treatment has been given to the intelligence function except in limited spheres, notably in relation to military policy.[1] It has long been an axiom that command depends on adequate intelligence of the resources and plans of the enemy. In the realm of diplomacy there are valuable hints on how information may be obtained.[2] Concern for the internal security of the state [3] and aspirations toward revolutionary action [4] have both inspired contributions to the intelligence problem. The literature of democracy has reiterated the need of an intelligent public opinion ; however, there has been a minimum of advance toward specifying the criteria by which relevant intelligence for the citizen and the official may be recognized.[5]

It is possible to fathom some of the factors that have contributed to the comparative neglect of the intelligence function

* From *Ethics*, October, 1942.
[1] Concerning World War I see Ronge, Maximilian, *Kriegs- und Industrie-Espionage* (Vienna, 1930).
[2] See especially Thompson, James Westfall, and Padover, Saul K., *Secret Diplomacy : A Record of Espionage and Double-dealing, 1500–1815* (London, 1937).
[3] See Book I of *Kautilya's Arthasastra.*
[4] Refer to the secret literature of the Communist International, such as Neuberg, A., *Der bewaffnete Aufstand : Versuch einer theoretischen Darstellung* (Zurich, 1938). (False bibliographical data.)
[5] An effort like that of Merriam, Charles E., in *The New Democracy and the New Despotism* (New York, 1939), is most exceptional. The leads suggested by Wallas, Graham, in *The Great Society* (London, 1914), have never been adequately followed up (Chs. X–XIII).

as a whole. In pre-liberal, pre-democratic states, ideological policy was simple. The aims of policy in this field were to detect sedition at home and conspiracy abroad and to encourage the reverent acceptance of state-friendly religions. In liberal, democratic states, however, there is nothing simple about the ideological goals, if we take these aspirations literally. Democracy means respect for human dignity. Policy is democratic when it is consistent and compatible with human dignity. Obviously this calls for deeper knowledge of reality than the simple recording of momentary approval of contemplated lines of action.

Although the ideal of human dignity is positive, it entered the stage of the large-scale modern state clad in the scanty garments of negativism. Private business men were out to get government out of the market. The expanding business society expressed itself through the competitive market and representative government. The focus of attention of the business man was limited to the market ; the focus of attention of the government man was restricted to auxiliary functions. The postulated pre-established harmony of profit-seeking and national gain was accepted as a moral gloss on the business way of life. " The pursuit of profit is the salvation of the world." [6] No positive conception of the relationship between the parts and the whole of a democratic state was sought. It was not missed.

In recent times the re-expansion of government has redefined the focus of attention of the policy-makers of liberal, democratic states. More and more they are compelled to try to find a unified set of positive objectives, to " reconcile " business and government. At the same moment that the internal structure of the state is changing, the key symbols and symbol elaborations of the state are under attack. Communist revolutionaries deride the democratic aspirations of such states as hypocrisy ; Nazi revolutionaries deride them as decadent and contemptible. The Nazis reject both symbols and practices ; the Marxists reject only the practices.

The sheer intellectual task of clarifying the goals and instruments of democratic idealism has gone largely by default. If we look back to the seventeenth and eighteenth centuries in England, we are impressed by the strength of the intellectual currents that were running toward unity of state aim. When

----

[6] From my notes of a speech delivered by an American business man on his return from negotiating the " Dawes Plan ".

David Hume wrote about social processes, his contributions included not only essays on the balance of trade but on the balance of power.   The doctrines of mercantilism [7] were a rather coherent body of policy ideas : states were conceived as succeeding or failing in terms of power (by which was meant political fighting effectiveness) ; power was believed to depend on stimulating exports in return for precious metals.   Goals were so clearly defined that intelligence operations could count goods and weigh bullion and apply this practical metre stick to the measurement of policy success and failure.

The liberal, democratic state did not succeed in harmonizing professed ideal and effective policy, partly because the democratic elements in the ideal were left undeveloped.   Intellectual life showed the effect of the bifurcation of market and government, and " political economy " became preoccupied with the routines of the market.   In the liberal, democratic state men spoke of " prosperity ", not of " power " ; yet prosperity was not their ostensible goal.   The cardinal value was the dignity of man, but prosperity was not translated in terms of human dignity.   Bentham's calculus of felicity was pointed in this direction, but it was not specified in terms capable of being operationally applied to an extremely complicated division of labour.

Some shortcomings of liberal, democratic states have been failures of policy and intelligence ; the urgent question of the moment is how these deficiencies can be surmounted.   Can the policy-makers who profess ideals of human dignity learn to specify what they mean in operating terms ?   No doubt the intelligence function can aid, to some extent, in the task of clarification ; unquestionably the intelligence facilities of modern society can provide relevant knowledge when goals are put in definite terms.

Modern procedures do make it possible for the first time in the history of large-scale social organization to realize some of the aims of democracy.   Social and psychological sciences have developed procedures that are capable of reporting the facts about the thoughts and feelings of our fellow-men.   By means of quick interviews, we can supplement some of the guesses that are made about what men think ; and by prolonged interviews and participation we can probe more deeply into the texture of experience.   By disciplined methods we can locate the zones

[7] On the full range of mercantilism consult Heckscher, Eli F., *Der Merkantilismus* (Jena, 1932).

of poor democratic performance and determine the factors that contribute to their continuation. We are accustomed to think of production goals for wheat or pig iron and to graph the facts about goal and performance. By using our new instruments of mutual understanding, we can specify our goals and report on their state of realization. The very act of specifying the meaning of human dignity disciplines both our policy-makers and our scientists. The gathering of knowledge can be synchronized with the needs of policy and with the formal standards of science.

We can actually study the thoughts and feelings of each of the major divisions of modern social structure and perfect means of making them fraternally intelligible to one another. Certainly we professional people need to be reminded constantly, and concisely, of the point of view of skilled and organized labour, of farmers, of unskilled labourers, of small and middle business men, of party and government leaders and administrators, of monopolistic and basic businesses. Policy decisions need to be tempered in the light of racial, confessional, and other group attitudes. If democracy includes a decent regard for the thoughts and feelings of others, our procedures can and should be applied to the enormous task of making these facts available to the various components of our society.[8] By examining the contents of the channels of public communication,[9] we may determine the degree to which even the opportunity exists of taking the other fellow into proper account. Up to the present time, it must be conceded, our press, film, and radio channels of mass communication have not adequately performed this task.[10]

Each public policy calls for two types of intelligence : ideological and technical. By ideological intelligence is meant facts about the thoughts, feelings, and conduct of human beings. Other facts are technical. It makes no difference whether the policy goal is phrased in ideological or technical terms ; both kinds of information are involved in any complete consideration

[8] See Smith, Bruce Lannes, " Propaganda Analysis and the Science of Democracy ", *Pub. Op. Q.*, vol. v (1941).

[9] Representative recent contributions to this emerging science include : Waples, Douglas (ed.), *Print, Radio, and Film in a Democracy* (Chicago, 1942) ; Lazarsfeld, Paul F., *Radio and the Printed Page* (New York, 1940) ; Gallup, George, and Rae, Saul F., *The Pulse of Democracy* (New York, 1940) ; Murphy, Gardner, and Likert, Rensis, *Public Opinion and the Individual* (New York, 1938). On content analysis see Lasswell, Harold D., *World Politics and Personal Insecurity* (New York, 1935), Ch. IX ; and " World Attention Survey ", in the present volume, Part III.

[10] See Lasswell, Harold D., " The Achievement Standards of a Democratic Press ", in *Freedom of the Press To-day*, ed. Harold L. Ickes (New York, 1941).

of goals or alternatives.   Ideologically phrased objectives are to strengthen the will to victory of the home population ; to demoralize the fighting will of the enemy ; and to win allies. The attainment of these objectives depends upon many technical considerations, such as geophysical factors affecting radio reception.   If goals are phrased in technical terms (tanks, guns, 'planes), they depend upon data about the thoughts and feelings and conduct of factory workers and of many other elements of the population.   It is evident that we are compelled to pass back and forth between ideological and technical facts in contemplating each and every line of policy.

Whatever scheme is used to classify policy, each policy and each category of policy must be properly integrated with every other.   By policy we understand the making of important decisions.   A decision adds energy and determination to preference ; it is part of an act of striving.   Values, therefore, are not only indorsed ; they are sought by mobilizing a significant part of the values already at hand.   The importance of decisions may be appraised according to the magnitude of this potential mobilization of resources.   In the most vital personal decisions, character, material goods, friendship, and life are at stake.   In the realm of public policy the stakes are comparable : moral integration, material assets, diplomatic position, and continuity.

For any personality, individual or collective, policy is concerned with total value position.   Within the field of total policy, distinctions may be drawn that aid decisions by classifying ends and means.   In the realm of high policy a fourfold classification has often been serviceable, according to which the four fronts of policy are military, diplomatic, economic, ideological.   Each sphere of policy is to some extent an end and to some extent a means ; successful policy proceeds by continuous integration. Thus every proposed military policy must be evaluated with reference to other objectives in the sphere of military policy and to goals in the sphere of diplomacy, economics, and ideology. If the specific military goal is indorsed as consistent and compatible with other objectives, it becomes an end of integrated policy.   Other spheres then become integrated to it as means to end.   In turn, the military sphere must be integrated with policy initiatives that arise in every other sphere.   A diplomatic proposal, designed to aid in the successful negotiation of a trade treaty, may be to offer the inducement of allowing a complement of foreign officers to be trained in American military schools.

Perhaps this is consistent and compatible with military objectives ; hence the military facilities may be made promptly available as means of carrying out the policy. In the economic sphere it may be proposed to conserve our metal resources by increasing imports. The conservation programme may be endorsed on military grounds, and the co-operation of the Navy may be needed to intercept cargoes bound for foreign ports. In the ideological sphere the cultivation of friendship with a foreign power may lead to the suggestion that radio broadcasts be increased to foreign countries from adjacent territory. If the Navy controls bases in adjacent territory, its co-operation is an essential means.

For purposes of brief definition we may sum up the four fronts of policy as ends and means. The end of military policy is predominance over enemies in battle ; the distinctive means are instruments of violence. The end of diplomatic policy is favourable agreement, whatever the substantive character of the agreement ; the distinctive means is negotiation. The end of economic policy is production ; the distinctive means are productive instruments. The end of ideological policy is favourable attitudes ; the most distinctive means are symbols. We may subdivide each policy front into internal and external. If this is done, some clarification is needed about the internal diplomatic front, since usage has limited diplomacy to external relations. In our expanded sense of the word, diplomacy includes offer, counter-offer, consent, dissent, mediation, conciliation, arbitration, adjudication, legislation. Hence it is appropriate to speak of the internal diplomacy of a state. At present, there is no consensus on how these internal processes are classified. Sometimes they are assigned to the internal ideological front. Often what are here called diplomacy and ideology are bracketed together as " political " policy—despite the patent advantages of reserving the term " politics " for the overall term. A threefold division thus results : military, economic, political. Nearly every other thinkable breakdown is sometimes made and is often useful. If a two-term classification is desired, the most satisfactory is the one hinted at above : ideological and technical. In the former the emphasis is upon thoughts and feelings and upon the symbols that circulate through the channels of radio, film, press, and conversation. In the latter the starting-point is material objects. The usual instruments of ideological policy are speeches, news conferences, news releases, magazine articles, photographic stills, newsreels, film shorts, feature films, leaflets, books, cartoons, charts and tables, broadcasts, plays, rumours, maps, exhibits, demonstrations, letters, telephone messages. Propaganda is the positive guidance of such material ; censorship eliminates. Personnel selection for symbolic rather than technical reasons also comes within the field of ideological action. In this theatre of operations personnel choices need to be made in the interest of democratic integration. Army and civilian cadres are made up of varying ratios of persons answering different specifications as to age, sex, size, income, education, residence, religion party (and the like). Some combinations aid democratic attitudes ; others militate against them.

What the intelligence function can contribute to policy may be exemplified in certain simple instances on different policy fronts. The contributions can be summed up in three points : intelligence can (1) clarify goals, (2) clarify alternatives, and (3) provide needed knowledge. First, a military example : Reconnaissance reveals that hill 46 can be enveloped by routes 1 or 2. If orders are not clear, instructions may be requested. It may be pointed out that liaison would be easier to maintain along 1 than 2, but that 5 per cent. more casualties could be anticipated. This statement of alternatives could be supported, if challenged, by facts about the deployment of enemy forces in the immediate sector and by facts about losses under comparable conditions. Second, an example from diplomacy : Policy instructions may be to negotiate a trade agreement, but the time period may be left vague. Intelligence may report that peaceful persuasion would produce the result in about six months ; that an opportunity to receive stock in American business concerns would diminish opposition so much that success could be hoped for in three months. The supporting facts include knowledge of the attitudes of influential leaders. A third example is economic : If available steel is used to reach the tank quota, the shipbuilding quota will suffer by one-fourth. Intelligence may therefore ask for clarification of goal and support the estimates by data about present stocks and production ratios. A fourth example is ideological : Are atrocity stories to be played up more in the future than in the recent past ? Intelligence may report that if more atrocity stories are circulated, among the wives of skilled workers, it may give them a more vivid sense of what war is and stimulate their aggressive interest in helping their husbands keep on the job. This estimate of the probable result may be supported by interview data collected in the field and by the results of an experiment in which more interest in the war is indicated after reports of Japanese atrocities.

These instances have deliberately been selected on a low level of abstraction, but they show the essential interrelations between policy and intelligence. In practice, decision-makers of every level are finding new goals and subgoals, contemplating new alternatives, asking for new information as a means of evaluating future probabilities. Policy thinking is " forward " thinking ; it is manipulative and responsible. It is always guided to some extent by knowledge ; and a recurring problem is to perfect the intelligence function so that it brings to the focus of attention of the decision-maker what he most needs to think about and what he most needs to think with.

We may classify the types of knowledge needed for ideological policy as follows : (1) distribution of attitudes, (2) trend of attitudes, and (3) comparisons of available alternatives with past situations and with scientific findings. In the example above the distribution of attitudes in the homes of war workers is obviously pertinent to war production ; knowledge of whether the trend had been more or less favourable would high-light the seriousness of the problem ; comparison of the results of exposure to atrocity news would be relevant to decision.

Attitudes are hypothetical patterns of reality ; the terms used to name attitudes must be given operational definitions from the standpoint of many different observers. In giving instructions for the identification of carbon, we have no trouble in choosing a definitive index. But this is not true of an attitude, like hatred of the President or of Hitler. We must work with many indices and construct rather arbitrary rules to govern the inclusion or exclusion of the resulting profiles. Attitudes may be inferred from many kinds of data : (1) what people say and do ; (2) what is said to people ; (3) what is done to people.

The organization of the intelligence function calls for the proper articulation of many specialists with policy-makers. Since the science of communication is itself in its infancy, the opportunities now open stimulate both imagination and ambition. Specialists who have become associated with the development of one specific procedure of observation, e.g. polling or psychiatric interviewing, are often prone to exaggerate its place in the total picture.

Policy-makers in business and government are well acquainted with the idea of describing the distribution of attitudes in a given group. They are also familiar with the idea of describing the distribution of politically significant symbols at the focus of attention of a group. The former has come from the counting of votes in elections and in poll interviews. The second has come from the practice of clipping the press of selected groups. Clipping bureaux are long-established institutions inside and outside government. The opinion poll has made rapid progress since the appearance of the American Institute of Public Opinion.

Although the idea of quantitative summaries of significant material is widely accepted, their interpretation is capricious. If you believe in the importance of world-organization after the war, you will probably be less critical of data that purport to show that a great many Americans look forward to such an outcome. If, on the contrary, you reject this goal, you may dismiss entirely the procedure by which the data were obtained or you may engage in vigorous methodological controversies about it. While the words recorded in brief polling interviews are highly valid in predicting elections, they are of indeterminate validity in forecasting how people will respond in situations that are as yet unorganized. The focus of attention of the group is in an advanced state of organization with respect to action when mid-election polls are taken ; but remarks about price regulation may have no more significance than showing that the term itself is a negative word to most of the responders. Hence it may be useful to reselect the validating symbols.

Another difficulty arises from the task of selecting and presenting certain kinds of information in a form deemed useful by policy-makers. Policy-makers are usually poised toward action. They want to choose between clear-cut courses of action. Hence intelligence material must be processed in a way that commends it to decision-makers.[11] Now scientists are accustomed to think in intervariable (" equilibrium ") terms and to appraise their data as pertinent or not if they confirm or disconfirm a general proposition that is part of the systematic structure of their science. Hence they are not accustomed to consider the timing of their results in terms of policy objectives. If they find that experimental animals show more scratching and biting behaviour when they are put on short rations than when

[11] For a classical discussion of " Thought at the Level of Planning ", cf. Mannheim, Karl, *Man and Society in an Age of Reconstruction* (London, 1940), Part IV.

they are cut down in sexual opportunities, they may take it for granted that these results are pertinent to policy. But what policy ? Do they expect policy-makers to cut down on sex opportunities rather than rations ? If so, when and where ? Notice that there may indeed be policy implications ; my only point is that the act of processing intelligence material must find an acceptable relationship to the policy-maker's conception of his policy alternatives.

Scientists who are accustomed to long interviews are faced with the problem of cutting their results down to a form that is valuable for policy and yet preserves something of the depth perspective of their data.

Intensive procedures can be most effectively used when they are guided toward the " sore spots " or the " success spots " revealed by quick, extensive procedures like polling or brief content analysis. Also, intensive procedures can be pointed toward policy problems that can be dealt with at rather long intervals. The effect of withdrawing husbands and fathers from the home needs to be studied, and these investigations are best done by intensive methods. The policy alternatives may grow out of exploratory investigations ; they may, for example, result in vigorous measures to increase the time spent out of the home and in selected community activities.

We are able to adapt to the needs of ideological intelligence many of the presentation forms developed for limited use in our society. In some ways the best and the most characteristic intelligence report is the prospectus offered to potential investors in new undertakings. The prospectus may rest on a foundation of vast research conducted by production engineers, market analysts, and many other technicians. No matter how elaborate the factual groundwork, the final results are put in clear-cut and inviting synoptic form. Photographs and charts illustrate the text, and the text is arranged freely to aid clarity, brevity, and emphasis.

Documentary reports cannot take the place of personal presentation if full advantage is to be taken of research and planning. Ideological material is less definitive than technical reports, and, if it is to be correctly related to policy, the head of intelligence must be a member of the inner policy councils. Only by constant emphasis can policy-makers come to recognize the full degree of their reliance upon certain facts for basic clarification of their task.

The intelligence operation constantly asks for new specifications of objectives. Policy-makers often leave goals phrased in ambiguous language, hence open to misunderstanding. One function of the intelligence branch is to point out any handicapping ambiguousness and to bring about authoritative declarations. Often the goals enunciated by makers of policy are inconsistent or even contradictory ; hence the policy branch must often call for new directives at every level of decision. Often, too, authoritative statements are entirely missing in reference to many zones of action ; one duty of an intelligence branch is to call attention to these omissions.

When the process of goal discovery has been carried to the most inclusive objective, we come to the key ideals of the state. The specialists on integrating the flow of fact cannot bring about goal clarification unless the need of integrated policy is widely felt. Intelligence specialists who try to force rigorous proclamation of purpose may fail to carry the policy group along with them. During our present period of transition from a business-dominant to a government-dominant state, the relationships between those who formulate authoritative declarations of policy and those who perform the intelligence function will be in a constant state of redefinition. To push ahead too far and too fast will often lead to the rejection of disciplined fact-gathering. And yet failure to keep the need of clarity at the focus of attention of policy-makers is to delay needed adjustments to reality.

At present the non-totalitarian states have difficulty in formulating war and peace aims. As a result of World War I legalistic and diplomatic aims were revealed as obviously insufficient to the needs of policy. Of course, we stand for legal order ; but what is the form of social structure that will sustain the sense of justice capable of sustaining a legal order of the type we want ? The influential elements of non-totalitarian states reveal their policy confusion when they are reluctant to put their objectives in basic terms of social structure. We still hear of " victory " as a goal ; but " victory for what ? " is not made manifest.

The crux of the matter is that deep timidities complicate the task of translating democratic aspirations into compelling institutional terms. Slogans like the " Four Freedoms " are not enough unless they are completed by slogans that point to the operating rules of a society that puts freedom into practice.

We are in a war of ideas, but we have not found our ideas. It is essential to face our timidities without fear and to deal with them directly. Some of the reluctance of our leaders of wealth and government springs from basic pessimism about the possibility of maintaining the fundamental characteristics of our pattern of state and society. In one sense, Marxist predestinarianism has conquered the world, for there is deep distrust of the prospects of any order save one distinguished by total governmentalization of organized activity. Our intellectuals have not even clarified in operational terms the meaning of a social order compatible with human dignity and safeguarded by a balanced structure. Despite our quantifying tendencies in production and in the intellectual life, we have not chosen critical ratios of balance and defined in clear terms the fundamental conditions and goals of policy. In these years of stress, however, we may succeed in discovering a unifying conception of democratic policy. When this unity is found, the ideological intelligence function will be smoothly articulated with policy. In the meanwhile there can be a persistent and clarifying interplay between such branches of the intelligence function as can be perfected and those who share in the making of important decisions.

II

HOW TO ANALYSE POLITICS

A. POLITICAL "ÉLITES"

CHAPTER I

SKILL POLITICS AND SKILL REVOLUTION *

I

In recent times we have become accustomed to analyse politics in relation to the rise and fall of national states and social classes. We consider the meaning of events for the unification of Italy or Germany, and for the growth of nationalism in colonial and semi-colonial countries ; or we interpret the consequences of events for the relative position of aristocracy, upper bourgeoisie (plutocracy), lesser bourgeoisie and manual proletariat.

When we consider the meaning of politics from another standpoint, we do not imply that analyses in terms of nation or class are unsound, inexpedient or immoral. The function of an analysis which is executed from a different point of departure is to bring new relationships to the focus of attention. It is true that the contemplation of new differences may lead to the substitution of new loyalties for old. Yet this is not by necessity the case ; old attitudes may gain in rational symmetry, and hence in structural perfection and permanence.

This exercise of skill in analysis involves the statement of conditions rather than the declaration of preferences. It is naturalistic, not preferential. It is preoccupied with the world of the probable rather than with the desirable. This is a methodological limitation made in the interest of clear understanding ; it implies no deprecation of the act of discovering, stating, and justifying preferences.

The scope of skill in analysis is obviously limited when it is applied to the elaboration of accepted standpoints rather than to the exploration of fundamental alternatives. Since the same

* Paper read before the Chinese Social and Political Science Association on November 11, 1937. From *The Chinese Social and Political Science Review*, Peiping, China (October–December, 1937).

persons who are personally or professionally devoted to analysis are entangled in the dominant loyalties of their day and generation, it is not surprising to find that they embellish the old more often than they rough-hew the new. This restriction cannot be accepted as final, for one of the chief functions of the intellectual life is to bring hitherto neglected relationships into the full blaze of critical attention, and in this way to aid the growth processes of history.

Many of the exploratory analyses which are made by intellectuals leave no discernible trace. They lie decently buried in the cabinet of historical curiosities. Only vitalizing sentiment can transform the terms of a contemplative analysis into the slogans of social movements and into the practices of established social institutions. The re-direction of culture requires skill in propaganda, in violence, in organization ; skill in analysis is not enough. The function of the analyst in historical development is to expedite the new by the imaginative charting of new possibilities. The consideration of such possibilities may modify the preferences of enough people with sufficient influence to change the course of history. In a sense the analyst is a focal point of historical growth ; certainly he does not stand outside the flow of historical events, even when he transcends the customary limits of a given time and place.

When the specialist on analysis uses his verbal symbols to refer to relationships, he deliberately seeks to disassociate them from the penumbra of preference with which they have been endowed by previous usage. " Skill politics " in the mouth of the analyst is as devoid of opprobrium or encomium as possible ; the ideal limit toward which he moves is the desentimentalization of his terms. When the specialist on propaganda undertakes to guide the masses, he deliberately steers the opposite course : he attaches as much emotion as possible to certain verbal symbols. He warms the pale signs of thought with the glow of love and rage, and the result is a slogan of mass appeal.

The present analysis is conducted in terms of skill. It considers the significance of events for the relative influence of skill groups. We may speak of *skill* as *a teachable and learnable operation ; a skill group is composed of those who exercise a common skill, or set of skills.* Our definition excludes manual labourers who have no skill, but it includes the workers who have some skill. The professions, of course, are included.

We have now selected our frame of reference : by choosing

to study the distribution of influence among skill groups, we have adopted a standpoint which cuts across the conventional categories of class and nation. Our task is to orient ourselves in the past, present and prospective succession of skill groups in relation to unskilled groups, and in relation to one another. In the course of this effort at orientation, we look for the general factors which condition changes in relative influence.

Class analysis proceeds in the same way : a frame of reference (namely, class variations in influence) is chosen, and the significant features of the total situation are viewed with reference to variations in the chosen category of events. Analyses in national terms pursue a similar path : the relative influence of nations is the selected frame of reference, and the salient aspects of the total situation are noted in so far as they bear upon the shifting position of nations as a whole with reference to other social forms, and of individual nations in relation to one another.

We may now proceed to specify the characteristics of a commonwealth of skill : first, optimum conditions for the acquisition of socially compatible skills ; second, optimum conditions for the exercise of such skills, third, optimum conditions for the control of such skills.

In recent times there have been several large states which, in a very approximate sense, were commonwealths of skill. No doubt the United States of America was rather close to a skill commonwealth during, let us say, the 'seventies and 'eighties of the past century. Free public instruction gave most of the youth an adequate opportunity to develop native aptitudes. The industrial expansion of the East combined with the safety-valve of free public land in the West gave abundant scope for the exercise of disciplined talent. Free competition was enough of a fact to guarantee a high degree of self-control in the exercise of bargaining skill, and suffrage was sufficiently universal to democratize control of governmental decisions. Those who were devoted to fighting (the specialists on violence) were not sufficiently active to be incompatible with specialists on bargaining, which was the dominant road to income and deference.

It is a matter of common knowledge that certain circumstances, manifest even in the 'seventies and 'eighties, were inimical to the realization and preservation of the American commonwealth of skill. Two disturbing tendencies were instability and monopoly. Skill control was curtailed.

It would be correct to say that the growth of social insecurity in the United States was related to obstructions upon the exercise and the control of socially compatible skills. And it would be equally correct to affirm that insecurity crises, attributable to a blockade against skill, occur in communities which are not skill commonwealths. Many South American states are controlled by a few powerful families, and they have shown themselves to be very responsive to economic adversity.

The blockade on skill may not be general, but particular : thus the rising business man, with his skill in bargaining, resented the limitations which were imposed upon the full exercise and control of his skill in aristocratic-monarchical states. Changes in the technical bases of production had introduced a new division of labour which included new opportunities to acquire, exercise and control certain new skills ; the bearers of the new skills asserted themselves against the fabric of society which worked in favour of the older skill bearers.

We have been connecting the departure from optimum skill conditions with certain general factors, such as monopoly. If we set up hypotheses about casual interrelationships, we are using the pattern of analysis which we will call the *equilibrium* pattern. When we attack a problem in equilibrium terms we undertake to state social change as a function of a specified list of interacting variables.

There is another, and a supplementary, way of approaching our analytical task. We may deliberately create *developmental* constructions for the purpose of orienting ourselves in the succession of significant events, past and future. We may, for example, consider the degree to which world political transformations become intelligible as a movement from old forms of social life toward skill commonwealths, as a movement from the plutocratic consequences of the rise of business toward the integration of conditions favourable to optimum skill acquisition, exercise, and control.

Consider, for example, the Russian revolutionary pattern. An essential feature of this pattern was equalization, in the sense that a greater degree of equality in income was sought through the liquidation of the landed aristocracy and the business plutocracy. Since a monopolistic plutocracy is incompatible with the optimum of skill control, the Russian pattern was in the general direction of a skill commonwealth. But free competition was abolished and state monopoly was put in its place, and the state was dictatorially, not democratically, organized. The monopolization of legality in the hands of a single party and the limitation of membership to a small fraction of the population were measures which restricted skill control.   Hence this combination of monopolization with governmentalization is incompatible with a commonwealth of skill.   But it is emphatically denied that this is more than a transition ; accepted slogans look forward to the democratization of party and government at some future time.   This conforms, verbally at least, with some of the specifications of the skill state.

The Russian pattern included the symbol of the proletariat, but the practice thus far has been to consolidate the control of skill groups : specialists on party propaganda, party organization, government departmental organization, engineering.   Differences in material reward for the benefit of skill are held to be justifiable, and the need for production has led to a vigorous emphasis upon the importance of technical knowledge.   Strictly proletarian features are of diminishing importance ; there is no hospitality for the idea that the unskilled or semi-skilled proletarian should monopolize the control of the state and that disabilities should lie permanently against the skilful.

When we turn to consider recent political transformations beyond the borders of the Soviet Union, we are struck by the common features which they present.   Although the symbols of the Fascist movement are vehemently nationalistic and anti-class, they are also directed against the plutocratic consequences of modern business and against the perpetuation of free competition.   Plutocratic and aristocratic elements rallied to the Fascist party as a hopeful alternative to outright expropriation by a party organically connected with Moscow.

The National Socialist movement in Germany was composed of groups which were broadly similar to Italian Fascists : there was the same emphatic use of nationalistic symbols to reject leaders with alien (Russian) connections, the same support from plutocrats and aristocrats, the same rhetorical attacks upon the plutocratic consequences of modern industrialism, the same seizure of office and monopolization of legality by a single political party, the same limitations upon private business by government departments, and the same co-ordination of nearly every phase of organized social life by government departments.

Common to all developments is a symbolic attack upon the limitation of skill control by the growth of private monopoly and the substitution of different degrees of public monopoly.

In the Soviet Union all private business is directed by the state : elsewhere the scope of the government is less inclusive. Common to all is the practice of dictatorial control through organs of party and government. Common to all is the justification of control as a means of advancing the democratic interest of the nation or the class as a whole. In this sense, the slogans are all democratic. But there is a distinction to be drawn between mystical democracy and instrumental democracy. The slogans of the former justify the exercise of authority without emphasizing the procedure by which official personnel is recruited. Instrumental democracy not only justifies the exercise of authority in the name of common ends ; it is careful to demand that the personnel of authoritative agencies be chosen by a procedure which involves the participation of most, if not all, of the community. In Russia the dictatorship justifies itself on mystical grounds : it is the " advance guard of the proletariat " dedicated to the task of constructing the socialist state and eventually the socialist society. But this mysticism with regard to the present is modified with respect to the future. It is both predicted and demanded that the course of development include instrumental democracy ; this is included in the definition of a socialist state and of a socialist society. In Hitler Germany the emphasis upon the " leadership principle ", coupled with the exaltation of " organic " over " mechanical " conceptions of democracy, keeps mysticism in the foreground. Similar symbols are invoked in Fascist Italy, though with more infusion of instrumental conceptions.

Since we are in the midst of a new line of political development in world affairs, it is not to be anticipated that our vision will be any too clear. Yet the thought that all major tendencies of our time move toward the approximation of a basic common pattern need not take us by surprise. When we examine the past of our dominant form of civilization (the Western European), we discover that unity of destination has often been attained by great diversity of means. At the end of the eighteenth century France was the seat of a great political eruption, comparable with the Russian revolution of our times. The élite which seized control in France did it, not simply in the name of Frenchmen, but in the name of all men everywhere (humanity). Élites beyond the frontiers of France who felt themselves threatened sought to defend themselves by denying the justification of the French leaders to speak for all mankind : behind the rhetoric of human rights they said they saw the grim visage of French imperialism. They spoke of the " *French* " revolution, not of the Revolution on behalf of human rights. By the use of such language, they were able to mobilize enough strength to block the expansion of France and hence to restrict the scope of the French élite.

But this did not block the universalization of the basic features of the pattern which made its dramatic appearance in France. As we look over the record of the nineteenth century, we are now able to see how political developments moved toward a common institutional structure. Far beyond the frontiers of France, we see the growth of universal suffrage, parliamentarism, competing political parties, church disestablishment, and the abolition of surviving restrictions on competitive markets. Even some of the symbols as well as the practices were incorporated in the political pattern of many states : " democracy ", and the terms intimately bound up with democracy, were firmly lodged in the ideology of these foreign states.

Such considerations may increase our confidence that the political movements of this historical epoch are moving toward a common institutional form which we are calling the commonwealth of skill. It may increase our confidence in predicting that this unity will be achieved by many nations in many ways, and not by a single simple path. In particular, the unity of this historical epoch is not bound up everywhere with the success of the Third International in universalizing the Soviet Union. In this sense historical processes are more insidious : they occur, not because of the machinations of external propagandists, but because of the shifting correlation of local factors in relation to the general context of factors.

The upshot of this analysis has been to emphasize the extent to which skill politics can make use of national politics, and vice versa. The stronger nations, at least, are likely to move toward a skill commonwealth within the framework of our multiple state system : that is, by the preservation of their independence of organic affiliation with the most recent centre of revolutionary change.

II

Having considered our general problem from developmental and equilibrium standpoints, we are perhaps better prepared to adopt a new point of departure. Let us assume that it is desirable to facilitate the emergence of skill commonwealths ; let us also assume that it is desirable to bring them about as peaceably as possible.   How, in different national contexts, can we accomplish these ends ?   We have now shifted from the contemplative attitude—a manipulative attitude toward events. We have begun by specifying which events we want to expedite, and we are free to consider ways and meaning of bringing them to pass.

I will now briefly discuss this with reference to some of the programmes for the preservation and realization of a skill commonwealth in the United States.   Current programmes include these proposals :

1. Equalize incomes ;
2. Preserve general competition ;
3. Democratize technological monopolies ;
4. Regularize production-consumption ratios.

To some extent the measures which are deemed appropriate to these several ends are interlocking, but we may enumerate them according to major emphasis.   The graduated income tax is a standard device for the equalization of income.   General competition may be preserved in some markets by granting credit facilities to middle-sized enterprises.   Technological monopolies, like some transportation and communication services, may be democratized by governmentalization or by organization into consumers' co-operatives.   Less fluctuating ratios of production and consumption may be obtained by more carefully separating the saving from the investing function.   The most drastic form of this suggestion is in favour of requiring 100 per cent. reserve against deposits, thus eliminating the commercial bank as a source of super-credit expansion in a modern credit economy.

It will be noticed that these proposals for a skill commonwealth leave a place for every form of production control.   Production controls may be classified according to the group which controls the profit (by profit is meant the gains or losses of an enterprise as an operating whole).   We may distinguish three systems of production control on this basis :

1. Public profit system (government ownership and operation) ;
2. Business profit system (private enterprise)
3. Consumer profit system (consumer co-operation)

The consumer profit system may be centralized or decentralized. The traditional Rochdale pattern makes the local manager responsible to the membership of the local branch ; a centralized system would make the local manager responsible to superiors who were ultimately held to account by legislative and executive bodies elected from constituent units.

There is much criticism of the usual plan of administering governmentalized enterprises by government departments. I believe that it is possible to adapt the modern corporation pattern to this difficult administrative task, and to substitute the corporation plan for the department plan. The modern corporation has developed the technique of control by the holder of voting shares who participates directly or by proxy in meetings of the board of directors. In the early phase of corporation history, a share was obtained by those who invested money. In the more recent phases of corporation management, voting shares may be assigned on very favourable terms to those who are believed to be useful to the enterprise in other ways than by investing funds. It is common to include on " preferred lists " some important transportation men, bankers, publishers or politicians. We may adapt this pattern to the problem of democratizing monopoly by assigning shares with voting privileges, not to individuals but to important associations in the community, thus providing a procedure by which the operation in question is regularly brought to the attention of persons responsibly connected with the principal skill groups in the body politic. The administration of enterprises by government departments has suffered, even in instrumental democracies, from " bureaucratism " ; and a large part of the difficulty is to be attributed to the haphazard fashion in which the enterprises in question are brought to the focus of attention of responsible groups. If the corporation pattern were more widely applied to the handling of enterprises of common importance, we would possess a procedure capable of mitigating some of the difficulties often spoken of as " the evils of over-centralization and over-concentration ".

It is not enough to drop the discussion of political programmes with an enumeration of the practices which it is proposed to introduce. Such practices, when effective, are related to the context of relationships in which they are expected to operate. If we propose to lay heavy responsibilities upon administrators, we cannot wisely take the standard of administration for granted. The administration of the large-scale enterprises appropriate to the modern state requires technically competent and impersonally dependable administrators.

The social pattern of impersonal administration appears to have been developed in the West by the Church. Persons forsook their family obligations and devoted themselves to the service of God through the service of the Church. In the language of social psychology, such persons were detached from loyalty to primary symbols and attached to the service of secondary symbols. The practice of poverty, chastity and obedience was perhaps of decisive importance in integrating the pattern of impersonal administration which is so essential for flexible adjustment to a variety of new large-scale enterprises. The modern states of Western Europe were able to take over, not only the culturally established pattern, but in many cases even the personnel of the Church. Our problem of administration in the United States is not that of creating the pattern of impersonal administration, but rather that of preventing certain incompatible circumstances from nullifying it. Elsewhere there is the problem of integrating the pattern itself in relation to a culture which was long able to survive without it.

Political programmes call, therefore, for considering the ways and means of obtaining the skill requisite to the proposed practices. But even this study of the context does not suffice. Political action depends upon the choice of ways and means of eliciting the acts essential to the goals in view. Hence political programmes have their propaganda aspect : they involve the choice of symbols to be invoked in arousing action and the choice of channels through which the symbols can be presented to those who are to be stimulated. Political programmes have their pressure aspect : it may be necessary to consider how to influence the result by the use of violence or by the withdrawal of goods and services. Political programmes also have their inducement aspect : it may be expedient to offer tangible advantages to certain persons in order to get results.

In communities like the United States, where the owners of middle-sized business enterprises are still important, where many farmers preserve their independence, where many professional people of middle incomes are found, and where many skilled workers are organized, the numerical basis exists for concerted action on behalf of programmes which are designed to achieve and protect the conditions appropriate to the acquisition, exercise and control of socially compatible skills.

An important propaganda problem rises, however, from the absence of a unified skill consciousness among these several groups. Fully developed skill consciousness requires a common name, a common outlook, a common programme. Such symbols would constitute the political mythology of the skill groups : we would call it their " ideology " when they are in control.

The skill groups might be brought to accept an invigorating belief in their historical mission by sloganizing some of the relationships which we have been considering from the special standpoint of the political analyst. World history would appear as a struggle toward the attainment and the preservation of skill commonwealths. Crises of social insecurity, often culminating in revolutions, would be treated as a function of skill blockades. From this standpoint the terminology of class consciousness would be understood to be a symptom of grave dislocation in the circulation of skill groups in the community, indicative of a groping after an order of society where socially compatible skill groups would enjoy the optimum opportunity to get, use and control their skills. The problem of creative statesmanship would be that of discovering the conditions of the skill commonwealth and expediting their occurrence by as peaceable means as possible. National sentiment would be harnessed to the task of working out solutions appropriate to the local context, but at the same time capable of stimulating new insight in other national communities, and contributing thus in some special way to the development of world life.

The present stage of partial emergence of the skill community is connected with conditions which have worked in favour of certain special skills. Reverting to our developmental standpoint, we may examine modern states with reference to the relative influence of the following skill groups : Specialists on bargaining, specialists on official organization, specialists on propaganda and party organization, specialists on violence. During the expansion of world markets in the nineteenth and early twentieth centuries, skill in bargaining predominated. The business state spread widely over the world. In the official bureaucratic state, the specialists on the administration of government departments are of outstanding importance. Pre-1911 China was such a state in so far as the affairs of the central government were concerned ; but so great was the strength of family, village and guild organizations that the scope of central authority was restricted.

Even in the expanding period of world economy, specialists on propaganda and party organization were of great importance. Instrumental democracy cannot function on a large scale without parties. But certain parties were devoted to organizing mass discontents against some of the basic features of the predominant forms of state. When Russia was demoralized, control was seized by such specialists (the professional revolutionaries), and the party bureaucratic state emerged. The internal politics of this state revolve about the relative position of the party specialists, the official specialists, and the violence specialists. The party élite, fearful of losing predominance, has not dared to move far in the direction of democratizing control ; it deals with the indirect threats to its supremacy which emanate from other quarters.

The skill composition of Fascist movements is similar to that of the Russian movement. Like Lenin, Mussolini and Hitler were brilliant propagandists and party organizers. It may be questioned whether their successors will be specialists on propaganda ; the internal correlation of factors points, rather, to the rise of the fighters and the officials.

It is evident that the future of the struggle among skills and for a skill commonwealth depends, in large measure, on the intensity of insecurity crises. Under the stress of prolonged war and near-war, the specialists on violence may predominate, with the resulting liquidation of the residue of private business, and the consolidation of garrison states.[1] In the interest of preserving the morale of the masses the skill commonwealth would, in some respects, be approximated. But the democratization of government control under the garrison state would obviously depend, as it does in the party bureaucratic state, upon the context of factors which affect the level of insecurity.

It is plainly the well-established business states, with their traditional respect for competitive bargaining and competitive propaganda, which have the best chance of protecting and attaining the skill commonwealth with a minimum of violence. The philosophies and programmes of positive, rather than negative, liberalism are endowed with the greatest symbolic vitality, in such states and are most favoured by material conditions.

These last comments upon the general factors affecting the survival of the skill commonwealth are made from the equilibrium standpoint. They remind us of the high importance of

[1] See the next chapter.

diligent search for the degree of interrelationship among the factors which affect the optimum acquisition, exercise, and control of socially compatible skills.

Our present exploration is at an end. We have chosen as our frame of reference the consideration of variations in the relative influence of skill groups in the past, present and future. We have dealt with our problem by the configurative method of analysis : hence we have deliberately passed back and forth between the standpoints of contemplative and of manipulative analysis, and the two forms of contemplative analysis, the developmental and the equilibrium. The consideration of these differences illustrates the function of the specialist in analysis. Whether this analysis will modify our loyalties, our outlook or our programmes, we do not venture to predict.

CHAPTER II

THE GARRISON STATE AND SPECIALISTS ON VIOLENCE *

The purpose of this chapter is to consider the possibility that we are moving toward a world of " garrison states "—a world in which the specialists on violence are the most powerful group in society. From this point of view the trend of our time is away from the dominance of the business man, and toward the supremacy of the soldier. We may distinguish transitional forms, such as the party propaganda state, where the dominant figure is the propagandist, and the party bureaucratic state, in which the organization men of the party make the vital decisions. There are mixed forms in which predominance is shared by the monopolists of party and market power.[1]

All men are deeply affected by their expectations as well as by their desires. We time our specific wants and efforts with some regard to what we reasonably hope to get. Hence, when we act rationally, we consider alternative versions of the future, making explicit those expectations about the future that are so often buried in the realm of hunch.

In the practice of social science, as of any skill in society, we are bound to be affected in some degree by our conceptions of future development. There are problems of timing in the prosecution of scientific work, timing in regard to availability of data and considerations of policy. In a world in which the scientist may also be a democratic citizen, sharing democratic respect for human personality, it is rational for the scientist to give priority to problems connected with the survival of democratic society.

The picture of the garrison state that is offered here is no dogmatic forecast. Rather it is a picture of the probable. It is not inevitable. It may not even have the same probability as some other descriptions of the future course of development. What, then, is the function of this picture for scientists? It is to stimulate the individual specialist to clarify for himself his

---

* From *The American Journal of Sociology* (January, 1941).
[1] For a preliminary discussion of the garrison state see my " Sino-Japanese Crisis : The Garrison State versus the Civilian State ", *China Quarterly*, vol. XI (1937).

expectations about the future, as a guide to the timing of scientific work. Side by side with this " construct " of a garrison state there may be other constructs ; the rational person will assign exponents of probability to every alternative picture.[2]

Expectations about the future may rest upon the extrapolation of past trends into the future. We may choose a number of specific items—e.g. population and production curves—and draw them into the future according to some stated rule. This is an " itemistic " procedure. In contrast, we may set up a construct that is frankly imaginative though disciplined by careful considera-tion of the past. Since trend curves summarize many features of the past, they must be carefully considered in the preparation of every construct. Correlation analysis of trend curves, coupled with the results of experiment, may provide us with partial confirmation of many propositions about social change ; these results, too, must be reviewed. In addition to these disciplined battalions of data there is the total exposure of the individual to the immediate and the recorded past, and this total exposure may stimulate productive insight into the structure of the whole manifold of events which includes the future as well as the past. In the interest of correct orientation in the world of events, one does not wisely discard all save codified experience. (The pictures of the future that are set up on more than " item " basis may be termed " total ".)

To speak of a garrison state is not to predict something wholly new under the sun. Certainly there is nothing novel to the student of political institutions about the idea that specialists on violence may run the state. On the contrary, some of the most influential discussions of political institutions have named the military state as one of the chief forms of organized society. Comte saw history as a succession (and a progression) that moved, as far as it con-cerned the state, through military, feudal, and industrial phases. Spencer divided all human societies into the military type, based on force, and the industrial type, based on contract and free consent.

What is important for our purposes is to envisage the possible emergence of the military state under present technical conditions.

[2] We use the term " subjective probability " for the exponent assigned to a future event ; " objective probability " refers to propositions about past events. The intellectual act of setting up a tentative picture of significant past-future relations is developmental thinking. See Lasswell, Harold D., *World Politics and Personal Insecurity* (New York and London, 1935), Ch. I : " Configurative Analysis " ; Mann-heim, Karl, *Man and Society in an Age of Reconstruction : Studies of Modern Social Structure* (London, 1940), Part IV : " Thought at the Level of Planning ".

There are no examples of the military state combined with modern technology. During emergencies the great powers have given enormous scope to military authority, but temporary acquisitions of authority lack the elements of comparative permanence and acceptance that complete the garrison state. Military dictators in states marginal to the creative centres of Western civilization are not integrated with modern technology ; they merely use some of its specific elements.

The military men who dominate a modern technical society will be very different from the officers of history and tradition. It is probable that the specialists on violence will include in their training a large degree of expertness in many of the skills that we have traditionally accepted as part of modern civilian management.

The distinctive frame of reference in a fighting society is fighting effectiveness. All social change is translated into battle potential. Now there can be no realistic calculation of fighting effectiveness without knowledge of the technical and psychological characteristics of modern production processes. The function of management in such a society is already known to us ; it includes the exercise of skill in supervising technical operations, in administrative organization, in personnel management, in public relations. These skills are needed to translate the complicated operations of modern life into every relevant frame of reference—the frame of fighting effectiveness as well as of pecuniary profit.

This leads to the seeming paradox that, as modern states are militarized, specialists on violence are more preoccupied with the skills and attitudes judged characteristic of non-violence. We anticipate the merging of skills, starting from the traditional accoutrements of the professional soldier, moving toward the manager and promoter of large-scale civilian enterprise.

In the garrison state, at least in its introductory phases, problems of morale are destined to weigh heavily on the mind of management. It is easy to throw sand in the gears of the modern assembly line ; hence, there must be a deep and general sense of participation in the total enterprise of the state if collective effort is to be sustained. When we call attention to the importance of the " human factor " in modern production, we sometimes fail to notice that it springs from the multiplicity of special environments that have been created by modern technology. Thousands of technical operations have sprung into existence where a few hundred were found before. To complicate the material environment in this way is to multiply the foci of attention of those who live in our society. Diversified foci of attention breed differences in outlook, preference, and loyalty. The labyrinth of specialized " material " environments generates profound ideological divergencies that cannot be abolished, though they can be mitigated, by the methods now available to leaders in our society. As long as modern technology prevails, society is honeycombed with cells of separate experience, of individuality, of partial freedom. Concerted action under such conditions depends upon skilfully guiding the minds of men ; hence the enormous importance of symbolic manipulation in modern society.

The importance of the morale factor is emphasized by the universal fear which it is possible to maintain in large populations through modern instruments of warfare. The growth of aerial warfare in particular has tended to abolish the distinction between civilian and military functions. It is no longer possible to affirm that those who enter the military service take the physical risk while those who remain at home stay safe and contribute to the equipment and the comfort of the courageous heroes at the front. Indeed, in some periods of modern warfare, casualties among civilians may outnumber the casualties of the armed forces. With the socialization of danger as a permanent characteristic of modern violence the nation becomes one unified technical enterprise. Those who direct the violence operations are compelled to consider the entire gamut of problems that arise in living together under modern conditions.

There will be an energetic struggle to incorporate young and old into the destiny and mission of the state. It is probable that one form of this symbolic adjustment will be the abolition of " the unemployed ". This stigmatizing symbol will be obsolete in the garrison state. It insults the dignity of millions, for it implies uselessness. This is so, whether the " unemployed " are given a " dole " or put on " relief " projects. Always there is the damaging stigma of superfluity. No doubt the garrison state will be distinguished by the psychological abolition of unemployment—" psychological " because this is chiefly a matter of redefining symbols.

In the garrison state there must be work—and the duty to work—for all. Since all work becomes public work, all who do not accept employment flout military discipline. For those who do not fit within the structure of the state there is but one alternative—to obey or die. Compulsion, therefore, is to be expected as a potent instrument for internal control of the garrison state.

The use of coercion can have an important effect upon many more people than it reaches directly ; this is the propaganda component of any " propaganda of the deed ". The spectacle of compulsory labour gangs in prisons or concentration camps is a negative means of conserving morale—negative since it arouses fear and guilt. Compulsory labour groups are suitable popular scapegoats in a military state. The duty to obey, to serve the state, to work—these are cardinal virtues in the garrison state. Unceasing emphasis upon duty is certain to arouse opposing tendencies within the personality structure of all who live under a garrison regime. Everyone must struggle to hold in check any tendencies, conscious or unconscious, to defy authority, to violate the code of work, to flout the incessant demand for sacrifice in the collective interest. From the earliest years youth will be trained to subdue—to disavow, to struggle against—any specific opposition to the ruling code of collective exactions.

The conscience imposes feelings of guilt and anxiety upon the individual whenever his impulses are aroused, ever so slightly, to break the code. When the coercive threat that sanctions the code of the military state is internalized in the consciences of youth, the spectacle of labour gangs is profoundly disturbing. A characteristic response is self-righteousness—quick justification of coercive punishment, tacit acceptance of the inference that all who are subject to coercion are guilty of antisocial conduct. To maintain suspended judgment, to absolve others in particular instances, is to give at least partial toleration to counter-mores tendencies within the self. Hence, the quick substitute responses —the self-righteous attitude, the deflection of attention. Indeed, a characteristic psychic pattern of the military state is the " startle pattern ", which is carried over to the internal as well as to the external threat of danger. This startle pattern is overcome and stylized as alert, prompt, commanding adjustment to reality. This is expressed in the authoritative manner that dominates military style—in gesture, intonation, and idiom.

The chief targets of compulsory labour service will be unskilled manual workers, together with counter-élite elements who have come under suspicion. The position of the unskilled in our society has been deteriorating, since the machine society has less and less use for unskilled manual labour. The coming of the machine was a skill revolution, a broadening of the rôle of the skilled and semi-skilled components of society.[3] As the value of labour declines in production, it also declines in warfare ; hence, it will be treated with less consideration. (When unskilled workers are relied upon as fighters, they must, of course, share the ideological exultation of the community as a whole and receive a steady flow of respect from the social environment.) Still another factor darkens the forecast for the bottom layers of the population in the future garrison state. If recent advances in pharmacology continue, as we may anticipate, physical means of controlling response can replace symbolic methods. This refers to the use of drugs not only for temporary orgies of energy on the part of front-line fighters but in order to deaden the critical function of all who are not held in esteem by the ruling élite.

For the immediate future, however, ruling élite must continue to put their chief reliance upon propaganda as an instrument of morale. But the manipulation of symbols, even in conjunction with coercive instruments of violence, is not sufficient to accomplish all the purposes of a ruling group. We have already spoken of the socialization of danger, and this will bring about some equalitarian adjustments in the distribution of income for the purpose of conserving the will to fight and to produce.

In addition to the adjustment of symbols, goods, and violence, the political élite of the garrison state will find it necessary to make certain adaptations in the fundamental practices of the state. Decisions will be more dictatorial than democratic, and institutional practices long connected with modern democracy will disappear. Instead of elections to office or referendums on issues there will be government by plebiscite. Elections foster the formation and expression of public opinion, while plebiscites encourage only unanimous demonstrations of collective sentiment. Rival political parties will be suppressed, either by the monopolization of legality in one political party (more properly called a political " order ") or by the abolition of all political parties. The ruling group will exercise a monopoly of opinion in public, thus abolishing the free communication of fact and interpretation. Legislatures will be done away with, and if a numerous consultative body is permitted at all it will operate as an assembly ; that is, it will meet for a very short time each year and will be expected to ratify the decisions of the central leadership after

[3] See Sogge, T. M., " Industrial Classes in the United States ", *Journal of the American Statistical Association*, June, 1933 ; and Clark, Colin, " National Income and Outlay ", in Pigou, A. C., *Socialism versus Capitalism* (London, 1937), pp. 12–22. Sogge's paper is a continuation of an earlier investigation by Alvin H. Hansen.

speeches that are chiefly ceremonial in nature. Plebiscites and assemblies thus become part of the ceremonializing process in the military state.

As legislatures and elections go out of use, the practice of petition will play a more prominent rôle. Law-making will be in the hands of the supreme authority and his council ; and, as long as the state survives, this agency will exert effective control.

What part of the social structure would be drawn upon in recruiting the political rulers of the garrison state ? As we have seen, the process will not be by general election but by self-perpetuation through co-option. The foremost positions will be open to the officers' corps, and the problem is to predict from what part of the social structure the officers will be recruited. Morale considerations justify a broad base of recruitment for ability rather than social standing. Although fighting effectiveness is a relatively impersonal test that favours ability over inherited status, the turnover in ruling families from generation to generation will probably be low. Any recurring crisis, however, will strengthen the tendency to favour ability. It seems clear that recruitment will be much more for bias and obedience than for objectivity and originality. Yet, as we shall presently see, modern machine society has introduced new factors in the military state—factors tending to strengthen objectivity and originality.

In the garrison state all organized social activity will be governmentalized ; hence, the rôle of independent associations will disappear, with the exception of secret societies (specifically, there will be no organized economic, religious, or cultural life outside of the duly constituted agencies of government). Government will be highly centralized, though devolution may be practised in order to mitigate " bureaucratism ". Not only will the administrative structure be centralized, but at every level it will tend to integrate authority in a few hands.

We have sketched some of the methods at the disposal of the ruling élites of the garrison state—the management of propaganda, violence, goods, practices. Let us consider the picture from a slightly different standpoint. How will various kinds of influence be distributed in the state ? Power will be highly concentrated, as in any dictatorial regime. We have already suggested that there will be a strong tendency toward equalizing the distribution of safety throughout the community (that is, negative safety, the socialization of threat in modern war). In the interest of morale there will be some moderation of huge differences in individual income, flattening the pyramid at the top, bulging it out in the upper-middle and middle zones. In the garrison state the respect pyramid will probably resemble the income pyramid. So great is the multiplicity of functions in modern processes of production that a simple scheme of military rank is flagrantly out of harmony with the facts. Summarizing, the distribution of safety will be most uniform throughout the community; distribution of power will show the largest inequalities. The patterns of income and respect will fall between these two. The lower strata of the community will be composed of those subject to compulsory labour, tending to constitute a permanent pariah caste.

What about the capacity of the garrison state to produce a large volume of material values? The élites of the garrison state, like the élites of recent business states, will confront the problem of holding in check the stupendous productive potentialities of modern science and engineering. We know that the ruling élites of the modern business state have not known how to control productive capacity; they have been unwilling to adopt necessary measures for the purpose of steadying the tempo of economic development. The rulers of the garrison state will be able to regularize the rate of production, since they will be free from many of the conventions that have stood in the way of adopting measures suitable to this purpose in the business state. The business élite has been unwilling to revise institutional practices to the extent necessary to maintain a continually rising flow of investment. The institutional structure of the business state has called for flexible adjustment between governmental and private channels of activity and for strict measures to maintain price flexibility. Wherever the business élite has not supported such necessary arrangements, the business state itself has begun to disintegrate.

Although the rulers of the garrison state will be free to regularize the rate of production, they will most assuredly prevent full utilization of modern productive capacity for non-military consumption purposes. The élite of the garrison state will have a professional interest in multiplying gadgets specialized to acts of violence. The rulers of the garrison state will depend upon war scares as a means of maintaining popular willingness to forgo immediate consumption. War scares that fail to culminate in violence eventually lose their value; this is the point at which ruling classes will feel that blood-letting is needed in order to preserve those virtues of sturdy acquiescence in the regime which they so much admire and from which they so greatly benefit. We may be sure that if ever there is a rise in the production of non-military consumption goods, despite the amount of energy directed toward the production of military equipment, the ruling class will feel itself endangered by the growing " frivolousness " of the community.[4]

We need to consider the degree to which the volume of values produced in a garrison state will be affected by the tendency toward rigidity. Many factors in the garrison state justify the expectation that tendencies toward repetitiousness and ceremonialization will be prominent. To some extent this is a function of bureaucracy and dictatorship. But to some extent it springs also from the preoccupation of the military state with danger. Even where military operations are greatly respected, the fighter must steel himself against deep-lying tendencies to retreat from death and mutilation. One of the most rudimentary and potent means of relieving fear is some repetitive operation—some reiteration of the old and well established. Hence the reliance on drill as a means of disciplining men to endure personal danger without giving in to fear of death. The tendency to repeat, as a means of diminishing timidity, is powerfully reinforced by successful repetition, since the individual is greatly attached to whatever has proved effective in maintaining self-control in previous trials. Even those who deny the fear of death to themselves may reveal the depth of their unconscious fear by their interest in ritual and ceremony. This is one of the subtlest ways by which the individual can keep his mind distracted from the discovery of his own timidity. It does not occur to the ceremonialist that in the spider web of ceremony he has found a moral equivalent of war—an unacknowledged substitute for personal danger.

The tendency to ceremonialize rather than to fight will be particularly prominent among the most influential elements in a garrison state. Those standing at the top of the military

[4] The perpetuation of the garrison state will be favoured by some of the psychological consequences of self-indulgence. When people who have been disciplined against self-indulgence increase their enjoyments, they often suffer from twinges of conscience. Such self-imposed anxieties signify that the conscience is ever vigilant to enforce the orthodox code of human conduct. Hence, drifts away from the established order of disciplined acquiescence in the proclaimed values of the garrison state will be self-correcting. The guilt generated by self-indulgence can be relieved through the orgiastic reinstatement of the established mores of disciplined sacrifice.

pyramid will doubtless occupy high positions in the income pyramid. During times of actual warfare it may be necessary to make concessions in the direction of moderating gross-income differences in the interest of preserving general morale. The prospect of such concessions may be expected to operate as a deterrent factor against war. A countervailing tendency, of course, is the threat to sluggish and well-established members of the upper crust from ambitious members of the lower officers' corps. This threat arises, too, when there are murmurs of disaffection with the established order of things on the part of broader components of the society.

It seems probable that the garrison state of the future will be far less rigid than the military states of antiquity. As long as modern technical society endures, there will be an enormous body of specialists whose focus of attention is entirely given over to the discovery of novel ways of utilizing nature. Above all, these are physical scientists and engineers. They are able to demonstrate by rather impersonal procedures the efficiency of many of their suggestions for the improvement of fighting effectiveness. We therefore anticipate further exploration of the technical potentialities of modern civilization within the general framework of the garrison state.

*   *   *   *   *

What are some of the implications of this picture for the research programme of scientists who, in their capacity as citizens, desire to defend the dignity of human personality?

It is clear that the friend of democracy views the emergence of the garrison state with repugnance and apprehension. He will do whatever is within his power to defer it. Should the garrison state become unavoidable, however, the friend of democracy will seek to conserve as many values as possible within the general framework of the new society. What democratic values can be preserved, and how?

Our analysis has indicated that several elements in the pattern of the garrison state are compatible with democratic respect for human dignity. Thus, there will be some socialization of respect for all who participate in the garrison society (with the ever-present exception of the lowest strata).

Will the human costs of a garrison state be reduced if we civilianize the ruling élite? Just how is it possible to promote the fusion of military and civilian skills? What are some of the devices capable of overcoming bureaucratism? To what extent is it possible to aid or to retard the ceremonializing tendencies of the garrison state?

It is plain that we need more adequate data from the past on each of these problems and that it is possible to plan to collect relevant data in the future. We need, for instance, to be better informed about the trends in the skill pattern of dominant élite groups in different parts of the world. In addition to trend data we need experimental and case data about successful and unsuccessful civilizing of specialists on violence.[5]

Many interesting questions arise in connection with the present sketch about transition to the garrison state. What is the probable order of appearance—Japan, Germany, Russia, United States of America? What are the probable combinations of bargaining, propaganda, organization, and violence skills in élites? Is it probable that the garrison state will appear with or without violent revolution? Will the garrison state appear first in a small number of huge Continental states (Russia, Germany, Japan [in China], United States) or in a single world-state dominated by one of these powers? With what symbol patterns will the transition of the garrison state be associated? At the present time there are four important ideological patterns.

FOUR WORLD-SYMBOL PATTERNS

In the Name of	Certain Demands and Expectations Are Affirmed
1. National democracy (Britain, United States)	Universalize a federation of democratic free nations
2. National antiplutocracy (also antiproletarians) (Germany, Russia, Japan, Italy)	Universalize the "axis" of National Socialistic powers
3. World-proletariat (Russia)	Universalize Soviet Union, Communist International
4. True world-proletariat (no state at present)	New élite seizes revolutionary crisis to liquidate "Russian betrayers", all "National Socialisms" and "plutocratic democracies"

The function of any developmental construct, such as the present one about the garrison state, is to clarify to the specialist the possible relevance of his research to impending events that concern the values of which he approves as a citizen. Although they are neither scientific laws nor dogmatic forecasts, developmental constructs aid in the timing of scientific work, stimulating

[5] For analysis of trends toward militarization in modern society consult Hans Speier, whose articles usually appear in *Social Research*.

both planned observation of the future and renewed interest in whatever past events are of greatest probable pertinence to the emerging future. Within the general structure of the science of society there is place for many special sciences devoted to the study of all factors that condition the survival of selected values. This is the sense in which there can be a science of democracy, or a science of political psychiatry, within the framework of social science. If the garrison state is probable, the timing of special research is urgent.[6]

[6] Robert S. Lynd is concerned with the timing of knowledge in *Knowledge for What? The Place of the Social Science in American Culture* (Princeton, 1939). The book is full of valuable suggestions ; it does not, however, specify the forms of thought most helpful to the end he has in view.

CHAPTER III

THE CHANGING ITALIAN ÉLITE *

(With Renzo Sereno, the University of Chicago)

Study of the governmental and party leaders of pre-war Fascist Italy may contribute to our understanding of the Fascist state, whether we are concerned with public law, comparative government, or comparative politics. The application of the rules of law by any public law agency is affected by the characteristics of those who constitute the agency. Whatever affects the social position or the relative strength of the groups with which an agency is affiliated affects the relative strength of the agency. Hence it is important to ascertain the class, skill, personality, and attitude characteristics of officials in relation to the composition of the community as a whole.

The present analysis therefore begins by classifying the agencies of the Fascist Italian state into those which, when examined from the viewpoint of public law, are " rising ", and those which are " falling " (or at all events not rising). We shall eliminate from consideration those agencies consisting of a single individual, like the king and the chief of the government. Among the pre-Fascist organs of government, two have risen : the cabinet and the prefects. The cabinet has attained more freedom from the control of Parliament, and widened its legislative scope. The prefects have more authority, including direct control over local government. The following organs of pre-Fascist Italy have fallen (or not risen) : Senate, Chamber, ministers of state, and *podestà*. All of the new agencies introduced by the Fascists are obviously " rising " (when compared with pre-Fascist institutions).[1]

I

Much of the material assembled in this study of governmental and party élites [2] is on public record. The communiqués of the

* From *American Political Science Review* (October, 1937).
[1] For basic distinctions, reference may be made to Romano, Santi, *Corso di Diritto amministrativo* (1931), and Ranelletti, Oreste, *Elementi di Diritto Pubblico Italiano* (1933).
[2] The term élite is used in no invidious or romantic sense. It designates those who exercise the most influence in a given situation in which influence is appraised, for purposes of analysis, in a determinate way.

Ufficio Stampa (later the Under-Ministry and finally Ministry for the Press and Propaganda) are usually short and matter of fact. The editorial comment which follows a biography often yields more information than the biography, because the official news stresses the relationship between the individual and his new job, and the editorial eulogy often provides more intimate details. The Italian " Who's Who " (*Chi è? Dizionario degli Italiani d'oggi*) is more devoted to literary than to political figures. A special dictionary concerned wholly with politicians (*La Nazione Operante*, Edoardo Savinio, Milan, 1934) contains three thousand biographies and is indispensable for the minor hierarchies. Supplementary details have been gleaned from local publications and interviews.

Critical comparison of sources has been relied upon to reduce the distortions which arise from tendencies to reconstruct biography to fit the values of the new order of things. How far this revision may go is shown by some sporadic cases of politicians who moved their birthplace closer to the cradle of Fascism and copied the encomiums appropriate to Romagna. No biography of Mussolini forgets to play on the Romagna and the Romagnolo, for popular tradition has it that Romagna is the country of sunshine, wheat, and wine, and the Romagnoli are bloody, fierce, and picturesque.[3]

Table 1 shows the number of cases tabulated in this investigation, and the data relating to class and skill. The number of cases reported does not necessarily correspond to the number of offices, since no person has been counted twice. He has been assigned to his most important office. *Il Duce* has not been included. In order to emphasize the more active elements in Parliament, the whole membership has not been studied. The 190 senators who have taken the most active part in the senatorial sessions since 1929 are included, and the 187 deputies ratified in the plebiscites of 1929 and 1934 are reported. In general, the data depict the situation prior to the Ethiopian War.

For purposes of this investigation, four terms have been used to designate class origins and present status. Aristocracy includes persons from families with titles of nobility and persons who have acquired titles in their own right (Fascist and pre-Fascist). Plutocracy covers persons enjoying high incomes. When the individual is among the wealthy few in his region, he is included

[3] A representative biography in this vein is *L'Uomo Nuovo* by Antonio Beltramelli (Milan, 1923).

TABLE I

CLASS ANALYSIS

	Number of Cases.	Proletariat.		Lesser Bourgeoisie.	Plutocracy.	Aristocracy.
Rising Agencies :						
Cabinet	24	O	3	12	7	2
		P	0	0	20	4
Grand Council . . .	9	O	0	7	1	1
		P	0	0	7	2
Party Executive Com. .	7	O	0	6	0	1
		P	0	2	4	1
Provincial Party Sec. .	66	O	3	50	9	4
		P	0	20	42	4
Chief Exec. Nat'l Unions and Associations . .	12	O	0	10	1	1
		P	0	0	11	1
Prov. Secs. Union Agric. Workers	53	O	0	53	0	0
		P	0	53	0	0
Prov. Secs. Union Industrial Workers . .	51	O	0	51	0	0
		P	0	46	5	0
Prov. Secs. Union Commercial Workers . .	43	O	4	39	0	0
		P	0	43	0	0
Prov. Secs. Employers Associations . . .	43	O	0	26	12	5
		P	0	4	34	5
Declining Agencies :						
Senate	190	O	3	87	54	46
		P	0	60	78	52
Chamber	187	O	16	93	50	28
		P	0	95	64	28
Ministers of State . .	16	O	0	6	3	7
		P	0	1	7	8
Podestà	38	O	3	5	18	12
		P	0	3	23	12

O = origin.   P = present status.

among the plutocracy, although he may not qualify from the standpoint of the nation as a whole.   About 15 per cent. of those called plutocratic in this list would be excluded if we were to classify them according to the national income pyramid.   The lesser bourgeoisie takes in everyone who falls short of inclusion in the plutocracy, but who stands outside the proletariat.   Skilled workers, professional persons of middle or low income, independent business men, and executives of middle or low income are thus considered lesser bourgeoisie.   The proletariat includes unskilled workers in industry and agriculture.   At least 95 per cent. of the aristocracy are sufficiently wealthy to be classified with the plutocracy, although double classification is not used in this report.

Table 2 exhibits the data about skills, which are defined as teachable and learnable operations.   Skills are classified into those acquired and exercised before entry into politics, skills bringing the individual into politics, and present skills.   In each of these sub-categories, the principal skill is recorded and other skills are omitted.   Skill in ceremony is perhaps the most novel.   It includes persons who are masters of etiquette, e.g. aristocrats or retired army officers and high officials.   It also includes individuals who have high symbolic value because they stand for some traditional distinction with which the new regime desires to associate itself (like descendants of illustrious personages).   A third and smaller sub-category refers to individuals who, having attained eminence (like a famous scientist or engineer), are attached to some official agency as a symbolic gesture.   Bargaining is a distinctive skill of those engaged in business ; organizing refers to the co-ordination of non-profit-making activities, public or private.   Propaganda specialists include newspaper men, personnel of information offices, and teachers of controversial subjects.   The term " attorneys " includes bar and bench.

II

The outstanding contrast between rising and declining agencies is the lesser bourgeois origin of the personnel of the rising agencies. Three-fourths of the provincial party secretaries, and an overwhelming proportion of all other Fascist party agencies, come from the lesser bourgeoisie.   Half the cabinet is from this social formation.   Less than a seventh of the *podestà*, a declining agency, spring from the lesser bourgeoisie, and only a little over a third of

TABLE 2
SKILL ANALYSIS

		1	2	3	4	5	6	7	8	9	10	11
Rising Agencies:												
Cabinet	O	2	1	—	—	4	2	1	5	4	5	—
	E	—	1	—	—	7	2	—	5	4	5	—
	P	—	—	—	—	3	2	2	8	4	5	—
Grand Council . . .	O	1	1	—	—	—	—	—	—	2	3	2
	E	—	—	—	—	2	1	—	3	2	2	—
	P	—	—	—	—	—	1	1	3	2	2	—
Party Executive . . .	O	1	1	—	1	—	—	—	1	1	2	—
	E	—	—	—	—	—	—	1	3	1	2	—
	P	—	—	—	—	—	—	1	3	1	2	—
Prov. Party Secretaries .	O	1	3	4	4	—	4	1	12	10	13	13
	E	—	3	2	2	29	4	—	12	8	6	—
	P	(all exercise 5, 8, 9)										
Chief Ex. Nat'l U. and Assoc.	O	1	—	1	—	—	—	3	2	3	2	—
	E	—	—	—	—	—	—	3	4	3	2	—
	P	(all exercise 7, 8)										
Prov. Sec. Agric. Wkrs. .	O	—	—	4	—	2	—	24	—	—	5	18
	E	—	—	—	—	7	—	—	37	8	5	—
	P	(all exercise 7, 8, 9)										
Prov. Sec. Ind. Wkrs. .	O	—	2	1	—	1	—	—	26	7	14	—
	E	—	—	1	—	8	—	—	37	—	5	—
	P	(all exercise 7, 8, 9)										
Prov. Sec. Commer. Wkrs.	O	6	—	—	—	3	—	13	2	2	5	12
	E	—	—	—	—	7	—	—	31	—	5	—
	P	(all exercise 7, 8, 9)										
Prov. Sec. Empl. Assn. .	O	—	4	3	—	2	—	19	—	5	10	—
	E	—	—	—	—	2	2	19	7	3	10	—
	P	(all exercise 7, 8, 10)										
Declining Agencies:												
Senate	O	—	8	4	10	20	32	10	15	18	73	—
	E	(Same)										
	P	(Same)										
Chamber	O	(Missing)										
	E	12	17	2	8	27	20	19	18	23	41	—
	P	(Same)										
Ministers of State . . .	O	—	1	—	—	3	7	—	1	9	3	—
	E	—	—	—	—	3	7	—	1	2	3	—
	P	(Same)										
Podestà	O	—	3	1	2	5	14	3	3	1	6	—
	E	(Same)										
	P	(Same)										

O = original skill.
E = skill by which entry made into politics.
P = present skill.
1 = manual and semi-skill.
2 = engineering.
3 = physical science.
4 = medicine.

5 = violence.
6 = ceremony.
7 = bargaining.
8 = organizing.
9 = propaganda.
10 = attorneys.
11 = no skill.

the ministers of state.   Half of the Senate and Chamber cases derive from this class.

There is evidence of a slight recovery of aristocracy under Fascism.   Table 3 gives the percentage of deputies in the Chamber who were aristocrats :

TABLE 3

ARISTOCRATS IN THE CHAMBER OF DEPUTIES*

Year.	Per cent.	Year.	Per cent.
1861	37·6	1919	5·7
1904	19·5	1921	5·4
1909	18·1	1924	7·5†
1913	15·3	1929	9·0‡

* Ubaldo Baldi-Papini, " Le condizioni presenti della Nobiltà italiana ", *La Nobiltà della Stirpe*, II, vol. 1 (1932), p. 141.
† First election after the March on Rome.
‡ First plebiscite.

Fifteen per cent. of our sample of the Chamber elected in the plebiscite of 1934 are aristocrats.   The new regime has conferred titles of nobility sparingly, although somewhat more freely than under the Liberal order.   Biographers carefully point out (particularly when the aristocracy is old or the title ranks high) that the subject is a nobleman who, " instead of . . ." pursuing a life of leisure and sport, has devoted himself to public service.

Leaders of proletarian origin are sporadically found, which continues the situation under the pre-Fascist regimes.[4]   The extent to which the lesser bourgeoisie contributes to the present plutocracy exhibits the opportunities for climbing which have been afforded by the rising agencies.

To choose, almost at random, typical careers of those who have risen from the lesser bourgeoisie to the new plutocracy :

Renato Ricci, born in 1896 in Carrara ; war volunteer ; member of Fascist party since 1919 ; organized a local of the party and rose to be vice-secretary of the national party ; initiator and organizer of the Fascist youth movement ; leader of governmentalized sport activities ; became under-secretary of education, thus controlling physical education all over Italy ; member of the cabinet.

Rino Parenti, born in 1895, in Milan ; non-commissioned officer

[4] Michels, Roberto, *Storia critica del movimento socialista italiano* (Florence, 1921), Ch. 6.

during the war; became Fascist in 1919, participating in local squadrist action; constantly held local party jobs; federal secretary for Milan.

Cases typical of other careers :

Ugo Cavallero comes from a very modest family and was made a count in 1928; born in 1880 in Casale, province of Asti; entered military academy and fought during the War; in 1918, became general; after War, became director of the Ansaldo of Genoa, an iron and steel concern manufacturing armament; appointed senator in 1926, and then called to the Ministry of War. When in 1928 he left the ministry, he was named count.

Pompeo Cattaneo, born in 1885 into a wealthy family of Pavia; decorated with a war cross; joined party in 1921, and remained in local politics; cheese manufacturer and secretary of the provincial employers' association for commerce.

Marquis Mario Laureati, born in Ascoli-Piceno in 1867, of the most outstanding noble family of the province; entered military school and fought in the first Ethiopian, Turkish, and World Wars, retiring as general; joined party in 1921; became secretary of employers' association for agriculture.

Edmondo Rossoni, born in 1882 in Ferrara into proletarian family; emigrated to United States, where he worked as a track labourer for railroads in Pittsburgh, Chicago, and New York; prominent in the radical labour movement among Italians in America, he later became an exponent of socialism with nationalistic colouring; organized the labour unions on a national scale under the Fascist regime; an exponent of the syndicalist versus the corporative tendencies; was the leader of the labour unions and publisher of *Lavoro Fascista*; later under-secretary of the interior and then secretary of agriculture; draws salaries from the *Banca del Lavoro*, from several social insurance institutions, and from the sea salt corporation of Italian Somaliland.

III

Possibly the outstanding revelation of the skill analysis is the relatively narrow recruiting base of the rising agencies. The personnel either has no original skill or wields a skill very closely connected with the functions performed in the party or governmental hierarchy. The older agencies, in addition to skill in organization, are recruited from a wider variety of specialties. In a sense, the new personnel made their own jobs through the organization of the party and the seizure of governmental authority. The new agencies are thus staffed by a highly specialized governing group.

Conspicuous, of course, is the importance of informal violence as a means of entering politics. Observe, for a striking instance, the provincial party secretaries, twenty-nine of whom particularly distinguished themselves in the squadrist phase of Fascism. Most of these had served in the War, 1915–18, and many of them had become officers, rising to a social status higher than they had enjoyed before. After the War, they were unable to live up to the new standard of life which they had come to demand ; hence the bitter resentment, from which direct action sprang.

As the internal organization of the centralized regime has consolidated, careers have become more regularized (which is to say, bureaucratized). There is a growing tendency for persons to be appointed federal secretary in provinces where they have never been active in politics, thus gradually transforming the party itself into a true bureaucracy. Under such conditions, there is less possibility that the central party leadership can be challenged effectively by local party machines. The future of this privileged group is determined chiefly by the central party figures.

There are now few examples to be found of new men who enter party or governmental positions without an original skill of some kind. A university degree has become increasingly necessary for the corporative appointments. Some of the agencies conduct rigid competitive examinations. These offices are not civil service positions, though the distinction has little practical significance. Somewhat less certainty of tenure is compensated by higher emoluments and prospects of more rapid advancement.

It should not be ignored that the older bureaucratic agencies have been infiltrated by persons who owe their careers to Fascist party service. In 1928, the diplomatic and consular services were flooded with party men (the *ventottisti*), such as Cantalupo, Bastianini, Mazzolini, and several consuls-general. Among the first-class prefects, we find twenty-two (of forty-nine) appointed from outside the administration. Nine of these have records of vigorous squadristic action (Foschi, Tamburini, Uccelli, for example). Most of the high bureaucracy in the Ministry of Corporations originated outside the government service.

Skill in ceremony is very prominent in the case of the *podestà*. The decline of local government in Italy has meant an enlarging sphere for the prefects and the provincial party secretaries. As a compensation for the loss of effective local control, the *podestà* have been chosen from individuals of local eminence. Both the Senate and the ministers of state show a substantial proportion of ceremonial personages. It will be noticed that the Chamber has seventeen engineers. No doubt it would be consistent with our analysis of ceremony to include all of these in the ceremonial category. They owe their preferment to their symbolic significance in the ideology of Fascism, which has glorified the technical man at the expense of the " windbags " of the democratic parliament. Despite all the emphasis, however, it is interesting to notice that the engineers are few and far between in the most effective agencies. They are still footmen of the chariot of state, not chauffeurs.

Despite the diatribes which have frequently been directed against attorneys, their number has not declined and their rôle in the state appears to be about what it was before. The number of lawyers is now restricted, but the number of students taking the bar examinations is very large. The law schools actually train most of their men, not for the private practice of law, but for posts in the government. In this connection, it may be observed also that the professors of law, philosophy, and social science have been reduced to their pedagogical function. Before the Fascist revolution, the professors contributed a very high proportion of political leaders to Italy ; indeed, 85 per cent. of all of the prime ministers were professors. Thus far, professors (of law and education, for example) have been named only to specialized ministries.

Although journalists have been frequently and fervently praised, they have been practically bureaucratized by the establishment of the Ministry of Propaganda and the Syndicate of Journalists. Editorships of important newspapers have occasionally been treated as party spoils.

The importance of skill in bargaining has declined with the general decline in the amount of business left in private hands. The manual and the semi-skills contribute infinitesimally to the leadership of government and party. The twelve members of the Chamber who fall in this category are chiefly of ceremonial significance.

Representative careers include the following :

Renzo Chierici, born in 1895 in Reggio, Emilia ; lesser bourgeois family ; lieutenant during the War ; joined party in 1919 ; went to Fiume with D'Annunzio, later identifying himself with the Balbo group ; perhaps the best known squadrist in Italy ; established himself in Ferrara, becoming provincial party secretary.

Giuseppe Avenanti, born in 1898 at Arcevia, province of Ancona, of modest bourgeois parents ; volunteered in the War and became lieutenant ; joined party in 1919, engaging in local squadrist and journalistic activity ; became provincial party secretary for Ancona ; transferred as party secretary to Zara (apparently on account of shady activities) ; later transferred as federal secretary to Gorizia.

Renzo Morigi, born in Ravenna in 1895 ; corporal during the War ; comes from fairly wealthy landowning family ; joined party in 1919, and led squadrist action throughout region of Emilia ; very proud of his Romagnolo descent ; world's pistol-shooting champion, Los Angeles Olympic Games, 1932 ; provincial secretary of Ravenna and actual boss (ras) ; several times connected with central committee of the national party.

Paolo Boldrin, born in Padua in 1906 of lesser bourgeois family ; joined party in 1922 ; shared squadrist activity and organized students ; took Ph.D. later and became provincial party secretary for Padua ; docent in public law, University of Padua, and author of scholarly publications.

Epaminonda Pasella, born in 1875 in Pombino ; modest family origins ; engineer in royal navy, serving in this capacity during the War ; joined party in 1919, organizing seamen's union, co-operating with Costanzo Ciano ; provincial party secretary for the island of Elba.

Nino Vicari, born in Pesaro in 1894, of lesser bourgeois family ; captain in the army during the War ; later employed in postal service ; active in propaganda and newspaper work, and made honorary member of the party in 1923 ; provincial party secretary for Parma.

Rodolfo Vagliasindi, baron of Randazzo, born in 1887 at family seat at Randazzo, province of Catania ; served as captain in the War ; as Nationalist, took part in local politics ; joined Fascist party in 1921 ; comes from family of wealthy landowners and is himself actively engaged in agriculture ; took a doctorate in chemistry and has published scientific contributions ; provincial party secretary for Catania.

Count Pier-Ludovico Occhini, born in 1874 in Arezzo ; wealthy landowning and noble family ; served in War as officer attached to propaganda services ; Nationalist until 1919, when joined Fascist party ; holds doctorate in literature ; contributor to and editor of several art reviews ; æsthete and poet of the D'Annunzio school ; interested in local history and art ; podestà of Arezzo.

Gugielmo Marconi, born in Bologna in 1874 ; father, Giuseppe Marconi, mother née Annie Jameson ; family wealthy ; passed early life in Italy and England ; early experiments worked out on his family estate, Pontecchio, and in England where first successful results were obtained ; aided by both Italian and English governments ; recipient of several honorary degrees and Nobel Prize, 1909 ; senator, 1914 ; delegate to Versailles Peace Conference, 1919 ; 1928, named president of National Research Council ; 1929, named Marquis ; September, 1930, president of the Royal Academy and member of Fascist Grand Council.

Alessandro Mazzucotelli, born of poor parents in Lodi in 1865 ; began as a blacksmith's helper ; became independent iron worker ; established himself in a country house near Milan ; interested in popular education and inaugurated the biennial exposition of decorative arts in Monza ; has been appointed commissar of the arts for Milan and elected a member of the Chamber of Deputies ; has attained international renown in his craft.

Among the less readily defined skills which have been the basis of successful careers in the Fascist state is skill in " fixing ". The fixer is a negotiator who enhances his private income by exercising, or seeming to exercise, governmental and party influence. He may be put on the board of directors of a corporation in the expectation that he will prevent the government or the party from making trouble for the corporation ; he may be put on the board at the direct initiative of the political leaders themselves.

The fixer is prominent in Italy because monopoly has almost, but not quite, supplanted competition, and all organized hierarchies are not quite co-ordinated in a totalitarian unity. The fixer is not a simple broker who brings persons of equal bargaining power together to make a deal according to publicly understood rules. He is the go-between when the parties to an arrangement must consider many other matters than simple profit. He plays a part when a resort to violence or to coercive pressure may occur at different stages of the transaction.

Fixers tend to stabilize the existing state of tension between private and public hierarchies by building up vested interests in existing ambiguities. Owing to the confidential nature of the transactions mediated by the fixers, it is impossible to arrive at a satisfactory objective estimate of the relative importance of this skill. It is plain, however, that politicians of the second and third rank very commonly trade on their supposed power. This applies particularly to the members of the rather innocuous Chamber of Deputies and of some of the unions and associations. Owing to the great centralization of the party and government, the fixer functions as a go-between who seeks to adjust local to central interests. The growth of the newly rich members of the Fascist party is often to be attributed to income derived from fixing.

Here are two examples :

A. was a modest lawyer in an important industrial centre ; a brother occupies a high position in the party and the government ; hence he has been generally assumed to exercise a considerable degree of influence ; by using the name of his brother, he has been able to settle controversies, often very delicate and important, between unions and associations, industrial firms and banks.

B. was a fairly prominent industrialist who felt apprehensive for the security of his business ; at the beginning was not sympathetic with Fascism, but joined the party after 1925 in order to protect himself ; became very active in politics, financing his own campaigns ; having attained some prestige in politics, he used his position not only to protect his business but to extend his connections ; corporations appointed him to their boards of directors, and he extended the range of his operations on a national scale.

IV

Another important aspect of governmental and party leadership is the degree of ideological incorporation in Fascism. To some extent, this can be shown by studying the length of time that the members of different agencies have been identified with the Fascist party, and the nature of their previous party affiliations. By Fascists *della prima ora* (from the first hour), we mean those who joined the party before the March on Rome in October, 1922, and had no previous party connections. The Nationalists supplied many members of the Fascist party before March, 1923, when the older party officially amalgamated with the Fascists. Some Liberals enlisted under the emblem of Fascism before October, 1922. (The date, August, 1922, is taken for the northern provinces ; this marks the successful breaking up of the general strike in these provinces.) The Liberals were the right wing of the old Parliament (Monarchists, Constitutionalists, Liberals, Conservatives, Democrats). Some of them passed over to Fascism between the March on Rome and the establishment of the dictatorship, January 3, 1925, which followed the Matteoti crisis. Some joined afterwards, when adherence to the Fascist party had become practically compulsory.

The members of the Popular (Socialist-Catholic) party who went over to Fascism can be grouped into the three periods used for the Liberals. The same subdivisions likewise apply to the Socialistic groups (Syndicalists, Official Socialists, Reformists, Maximalists, Communists).

Table 4 is constructed to show these differences.

The declining agencies show the most laggards in affiliating themselves with the new and ultimately successful party. In rising as well as declining agencies, there are some examples of former Socialists who went through the same transition as Mussolini himself. In all cases, the change was made before the March on Rome. Ex-Socialist members of the cabinet include

TABLE 4

PARTY ATTITUDES

1. Fascisti della prima ora, no previous affiliations.
2. Nationalists
    (a) Fascist before March, 1923.
    (b) Fascist after March, 1923.
3. Liberals
    (a) Fascist before October, 1922.
    (b) Fascist between October, 1922, and January 3, 1925.
    (c) Fascist after January 3, 1925.
4. Popular
    (Same subdivisions as above)
5. Socialistic groups
    (Same subdivisions as above)

	1	2a	2b	3a	3b	3c	4a	4b	4c	5a	5b	5c
Rising Agencies :												
Cabinet	6	1	3	3	—	—	—	—	—	6	—	—
Grand Council . . .	6	—	1	1	—	—	—	—	—	—	—	—
Party Executive . . .	6	—	—	—	—	—	—	—	—	1	—	—
Pr. Pty. Secretaries . .	46	2	4	—	1	—	—	—	—	—	—	—
Chief Ex. Nat'l Unions and Associations . .	3	1	2	1	—	1	—	—	—	4	—	—
Declining Agencies :												
Chamber	113	3	9	5	13	33	—	2	3	6	—	—
Ministers	1	1	1	—	3	6	—	—	—	—	—	—
Podestà	7	4	2	—	12	3	—	5	—	—	—	—

Note : Unaccounted for : Cabinet 5 ; Provincial Party Secretaries, 13 ; Ministers of State, 4 ; *Podestà*, 5, with possible Popular affiliations.

Razza, Rossoni, Benni, Tassinari, Cobolli, and Lantini. An ex-Socialist member of the executive committee of the party is Marinelli, who was a bookkeeper on the *Popolo d'Italia* from its founding in 1914. Chief executives of national unions and associations include Barni, Ciardi, Pala (socialistic leanings), Racheli. These four were trade union organizers. Members of the Chamber of Deputies include Bolzon, Ciarlantini, Lanfranconi, Malusardi, Orano, and Paoloni.

The Italian Senate had practically no members of socialistic groups even before Fascism. More than half of the Senate was changed in 1922, and the new senators, if not party members, are at least in agreement with the regime. At least twenty-three of the 190 senators in our sample were formerly connected with the *Partito Popolare*, or were prominently identified with pro-clerical organizations. Five senators are ex-Socialists (Rossini was a trade union organizer ; Professor Achille Loria introduced historical materialism into academic circles). No more than ten senators can be identified as *Fascisti della prima ora*. Fascism glorifies youth, and the widespread recognition that the Senate is a declining, decorative post for old men means that appointment to it has been more resented than sought after by active leaders.

In considering the ideological characteristics of Fascism, it is of interest to discover the extent to which the party is recruited from the nation as a whole, or from particular regions. The higher party councils give extraordinary prominence to persons from Bologna and nearby provinces : Grandi, Manaresi, Biagi, Oviglio (Bologna) ; Balbo, Rossoni (Ferrara) ; and the *Duce* (Forlì). During the formative years of Fascism, this region was the most active scene. The social structure of the area reveals some significant features. Some cities provided employment for urban proletarians ; these cities were situated close to agricultural regions which depended upon city factories to process their products (sugar beets, hemp). In the production of these commodities, use was made of a large body of unskilled casual labourers (*braccianti*). Workers, both urban and rural, were organized, and the post-war years saw the high-water mark of union activity. The lesser bourgeoisie, except the section directly connected with the unions, were alienated by the dislocation of public services through frequent strikes, and by the improving status of the manual toilers. Small tradesmen were exposed to the ever-sharpening competition of the co-operatives, which were supported by the unions. Some degree of social disorganization was endemic in this region ; illegitimacy rates, for example, were higher than anywhere else in Italy. The refineries in Ferrara were operated by corporations which were not locally owned ; the city was constantly losing members of the rising bourgeoisie to other centres.

The further down one goes in the party and governmental hierarchy, the more completely does the personnel become representative of the nation as a whole. Indeed, many persons are advanced chiefly because they are identified with localities rather than for conspicuous party service. The most striking cases are from Sardinia or southern Italy in general.

V

The data assembled here about the governmental and party leaders of Italy refine in some degree our picture of Italian, and indeed of world, developments. By comparing the rising and the declining agencies of Italian public law, we have ascertained the degree to which certain social formations are becoming more or less influential. Outstanding is the extensive contribution made by the lesser bourgeoisie to leadership in the state. Equally plain, however, is the extent to which a section of the lesser bourgeoisie rises to a plutocratic level of income, thus establishing vested interests which are in many respects contradictory to the logical development of a lesser bourgeois polity.

In terms of skill, the rising agencies exhibit the relative predominance of those who are devoted to the arts of government and politics in the narrowest possible sense. There are found many who owe their entire career to skill in violence and who had no antecedent skill before their entry into politics. Party organization and party propaganda, with no previous skill acquisition, was the foundation of other careers. With the consolidation of the new regime, preliminary technical training assumes greater importance as the bureaucratizing tendencies of party and government manifest themselves. Among the less formalized skills, skill in fixing plays a prominent rôle. Totalitarian patterns of organization are not yet crystallized ; hence private and public hierarchies continue in unstable relationship to one another. The fixers capitalize existing insecurities and develop strong vested interests in preserving present ambiguities.

The ideological integration of the state around the symbols of a single party has gone forward with the broadening local basis of party and government. The association of the older aristocratic and plutocratic formations with the activistic section of the lesser bourgeoisie has tended to conserve older values, and to militate against the emergence of distinctive practices.

The data here summarized are but a fraction of all that one might desire for developmental interpretation of political events. The facts given have not been related to many facts about the circumstances in which transformations occurred in Italy. Nor have they been presented in relation to an explicit description of the social structure of Italy. They do, however, constitute a step on the way toward relating public law agencies organized in particular ways to the social contexts in which they operate.

CHAPTER IV

THE RISE OF THE PROPAGANDIST *

America's debt to propaganda is very great. The propagandist of religion walked beside or a little in advance of, the explorer, trader and occupier of the broad acres of the New World. The natural reluctance of men to pull up stakes and settle overseas was overcome, in part, by the incessant use of propaganda. " The land of opportunity " is a tribute to the tireless propaganda of the colonizing and shipping interests on both sides of the Atlantic Ocean. There is no doubt of the efficacy of propaganda in overcoming the hesitation of men to move themselves and to risk their capital in America. This, perhaps, is America's greatest debt to propaganda.

The internal consolidation of America went along with the specialized use of propaganda. Religious propaganda (in the form of home and foreign missions) has been a powerful outlet for American energy.

Benjamin Franklin did a superlative propaganda job in Paris during the triumphant struggle to secede from the British Empire.

With the democratization of suffrage and the westward bulge of the nation, America developed remarkable devices of electoral propaganda, like torchlight processions, that stirred the rank and file to a virile sense of participation in the great decisions of the hour. The secret societies proselyted across the nation for new members and occasionally inaugurated crusades on controversial matters. The great agitations—against slavery, against the liquor traffic, against monopoly, for women's rights —were psychic waves that swept across successive generations. In war—whether war between the States, with Britain, with Mexico, with Spain or with the Central Powers—propaganda played a growing part. The great humanitarian causes—educational, recreational, curative—called for skill in inducing gifts.

The main stream of propaganda, however, was neither religious, partisan, reformist, official, nor philanthropic. It was commercial. It was advertising. Its purpose was to control buying habits. In a world of spectacular technical advances in the creation of new goods, and in a world where ancient habits

* From *American Scholar* (1939).

were upset by migration, advertising bounded to undreamed-of heights. With some rhetorical licence one might say that if Columbus found the continent the advertiser formed the nation.

Although the broad lines of the story of the place of propaganda in American history are evident, exact information is scarce. How much money has America spent on propaganda per year since the sixteenth century? What proportion of our gainfully employed have been manipulators and handlers of propaganda? The moment we pose questions of this kind we are at a loss. Research has not caught up with curiosity. Some facts are known. We know about what is spent every year for advertising. For instance, the gross income of the National Broadcasting Company in 1937 was $39,000,000. The Columbia Broadcasting System took in $29,000,000 and the Mutual $2,000,000. For radio advertising as a whole (including the chains) the total was no less than $125,000,000. For national newspaper and magazine advertising the total was close to $800,000,000.

The rapid expansion of publicity activities by the Federal government during the Great Depression led to the inquiry instituted by a Senatorial Committee (Senator Harry F. Byrd of Virginia, chairman). A report prepared for this committee by the Brookings Institution gives some information about the scope of Federal activities in 1936. $600,000 was the salary bill of publicity men. On October 1, 1936, there were 146 persons fully occupied with publicity and 124 partially so. Salaries of $5,000 or over were paid to 26 persons in the first class and to 21 persons in the second. There is no reliable figure for the amount spent on the various forms of publicity work. We know, of course, that the new or the rapidly-expanded agencies of government are the most active in public relations. Contrast, for example, the staid Treasury with the bouncing record of the P.W.A. The Department of Agriculture belongs to the " rapidly-expanded agencies " and possesses one of the most elaborate and inventive publicity machines in the nation.

America's propaganda bill would include much of the money spent by the hundreds of trade and professional associations. This " Third House of Congress " has not been recently and authoritatively examined ; but no one who follows public affairs has the least doubt of the vigour of the Chamber of Commerce, the American Federation of Labour, the Congress of Industrial Organizations, the American Farm Bureau Federation, the

American Medical Association, the National Educational Association, the National Manufacturers' Association and the like. The mere enumeration of some of the chief trade associations connected with different media gives a solid sense of reality : Association of National Advertisers (who control the big commercial budgets) ; Association of Advertising Agencies (who collect 15 per cent. of the amount charged by the media) ; American Newspaper Publishers' Association ; National Association of Broadcasters ; National Association of Accredited Publicity Directors, etc.

The most distinctive group engaged in propaganda, however, falls almost entirely outside the categories mentioned above. The most specialized propagandist is the " public relations counsel " who serves several clients. Often he is an " idea man " and works with a small staff (the late Ivy Lee was a famous example). Or he may run a shop large enough to turn out a metropolitan newspaper (one operator in New York has at least 325 employees).

In addition to independent public relations men there are specialized public relations officers inside every large modern enterprise. Only research based on intimate knowledge of " who does what " can ever give us any dependable report on the prevailing situation. We know of corporations in which the head of the publicity looks after the public relations ; elsewhere the job is done by a Vice-President. Sometimes the key man is in the law department—or he may be in the sales department. He may be on the Board of Directors. In large law firms, with many partners and clerks, some partners specialize in different kinds of " contacts ". Investment banking houses doubtless search for a Thomas Lamont.

Part of the difficulty in understanding what is going on derives from the lack of standard terms. The problem, as usual, is not to quarrel about words but to find out what they mean to the person using them. Suppose you define *propaganda* as I do, as *the use of symbols to influence controversial attitudes* ; you must at once lay down many special rules before you can deal with reality. For many Americans Presbyterianism or Catholicism are controversial matters : shall we include the entire budget of all the denominations in the propaganda bill of the country ? Or shall we say that the term propaganda applies only to efforts to convert the unbeliever, thus restricting ourselves to the amounts expended on foreign and domestic missions ? I speak of these problems with no intention of implying that they are insoluble but for the sake of showing why caution is needed if we are to understand the language in this field. Let us take another example. In writing of the " publicity activities " of the Federal government or of a trade association or of a corporation we may be referring to quite different kinds of material. A government film on " How to Grow Hogs " may be useful to the agricultural colleges that are trying to teach skill in hog raising, but the film may be a total loss as general entertainment. " The Plough That Broke the Plains ", on the other hand, is full of dramatic interest to the casual audience. It is capable of arousing people to accept the proposition that soil conservation is a national need and that the agencies now engaged in it should be supported. Films—or words of any kind—inculcate attitudes and transmit skill in varying degrees. For exact comparisons it is useful to segregate the material of low skill-content from material of high attitude-content (and it should not be overlooked that the two go together in varying proportions). A consideration of these technical difficulties is vital to sound judgment on the treacherous subject of propaganda. Here, as elsewhere, the making of distinctions is the beginning of wisdom.

Whatever our degree of dissatisfaction with our present ignorance of propaganda we are on firm ground in asserting that Americans spend more and more on propaganda and that the propagandist plays an ever more decisive part in the policy of official and unofficial agencies. In short, we have to do with the expansion of an old function and the concurrent rise of a special skill-group concerned with the function. The propagandist is exerting more control over the fruits, and even the honours, of society.

Is the rise of the propagandist a feature unique to American civilization or is this a general trend in world affairs ? When we undertake to answer this question we come upon data of exceptional interest.

It is probable that in Germany there has been a sharp drop in the total volume of propaganda since 1933. Party propaganda is monopolized in the hands of a single political party and private business is subjected to minute regulation in the name of the needs of the Third Reich. Judged by the volume of commercial advertising the effect has been to diminish the stream of paid persuasion. The number of newspapers and magazines has declined sharply and total circulation has contracted. There has also been a decline in total propaganda in Fascist Italy as in Germany.

But decline is not invariably associated with totalitarian governments : there has been a rise in the volume of propaganda in Russia. Pre-Soviet Russia was illiterate and Soviet Russia has enormously widened the circle of the literate. Pre-Soviet Russia was chiefly rural and little given to advertising ; Soviet Russia is far more industrial and has revolutionized the basis of agriculture. The stupendous transformations in the style of Russian life have been accompanied and fostered by unceasing propaganda. The vigour of the new regime is such that more people have been induced to do more things in more different ways than ever before. And the volume of propaganda is responsive to precisely these variables : the number of people, the number of acts, the number of novel acts (per period of time).

If we examine the German case with more patience we find that the crucial point is not the volume of propaganda but the change in the relative position of propaganda and propagandists. Although there is less propaganda in German society there is more government ; the sphere of business has shrunk. And those who occupy the glittering posts in the government are recruited to a marked degree from men who specialize in propaganda and the organization of mass parties. The conclusion is this : the business man has lost out to the party man ; bargaining skill has become less influential than propaganda skill.

We have now isolated a feature characteristic of all totalitarian states, whether the total volume of propaganda has gone up or down in recent years. The disappearance of the business man is most complete in Soviet Russia, of course ; the men who run Russia are recruited from specialists in propaganda and mass party organization. This was more marked in the early days of the Revolution than it is to-day : the great names of 1917 were the names of powerful orators and effective organizers. The orator has given way to the organizer (Stalin, Kaganovitch) ; and to-morrow the party man may give way to the military man. But the fact remains that as the business man went out, the propagandist—and the mass organizer—came in.

The German case is instructive if we look at it another way. Just before the taking of power by the Nazi party, Germany was a seething cauldron of clashing propaganda. Communists, Social Democrats, Nationalists, and many other sizable and fractional parties were at one another's throats. Business, though not booming, was engaged in vigorous promotion. In those critical times practically every component element in the structure of the German nation became conscious of its special interests and used propaganda to advance them. Germany was at the peak of a rising curve of propaganda that extends back over many years. The position of German business was undergoing a subtle transformation. Business was accustomed to buy advertising skill. As the situation became more acute, business began to buy more skill in political propaganda. Its subsidies were scattered among several parties : the significant point is that they increased in amount. As social insecurity was intensified the amount of social energy that went into propaganda was augmented. Then a profound change occurred in the relative position of the propagandist. That sector of the propaganda group that stayed in the pay of business (and continued to be in business for itself) lost out. It lost to that fraction of the propaganda group that played active politics. And it ultimately lost to that minority of propagandists who combined propaganda with mass organization and with mass violence. German business began by paying for more profits ; then it paid for protection ; and it ended by paying for its own destruction.

After this glance at the general trend of world affairs we bring our eyes back to America with renewed interest. We see that America pays more for propaganda as the nation grows less secure. Business has always divided its contributions to advertising and to political parties. To-day, in the form of public relations, there is a broadening of the scope of advertising. Is this the preliminary to even greater dependence upon the propagandist—and, eventually, upon the political propagandist ? Under the forced draft of the Great Depression, developments have been particularly rapid. The Great Collapse impaired the prestige of business, and men turned with hope to government. As the sense of emergency abated, business began a counter-offensive in a series of tremendous advertising campaigns (notably the " March with Business to Better Times " campaign of the United States Chamber of Commerce in 1936). The overwhelming defeat of the Republican candidate in 1936 was a jolt to many leaders of business and they took stock of their position. They redoubled their efforts at advertising and they undertook to improve their total public relations. Big business corporations felt particularly isolated from smaller business and from other elements in the nation. Already, however, a successful campaign had shown the way to better results. In 1935 the chain stores defeated the proposed chain-store tax in the state of California by identifying themselves with the locality, with the workers and with the consumers. Business at large saw the wisdom of seeking to turn every conceivable contact into account.

For better or worse the future of business is bound up with propaganda. If propaganda can remove the basic causes of the recurring crises of insecurity in our society, propaganda will continue to be a business, and a servant of business. If propaganda cannot lead to action that removes the sources of difficulty, political propaganda may well become the master here as elsewhere.

B. POLITICAL ATTITUDES

CHAPTER I

THE TRIPLE-APPEAL PRINCIPLE: A DYNAMIC KEY *

I

Psychoanalysis divides the personality into three main divisions, which include biological needs, socially acquired inhibitions, and the testing of reality. The new-born infant is a biological organism characterized by nutritive, excretory, and allied necessities, and by capacity to be impelled by sexual impulses when certain glands shall have matured. Very few of the primitive biological needs of the individual can be directly gratified, owing mainly to the restrictions which are imposed by representatives of the particular social order into which the individual is born. When these restrictions are no longer dealt with as obstacles in the outer world, but are observed on the basis of acquired modifications of behaviour, the individual has achieved a new and important personality structure, which is technically known as the "super-ego". The perceiving of external relationships, and the modification of impulses in the light of current reality, are the special functions of the third division of the personality, the "ego". In the technical language of psychoanalysis, the *original biological needs are the "id"*, the *inhibitions are the super-ego*, and the *reality adaptations occur in the ego*. About the proper connotation is conveyed by speaking of personality as divisible into the realms of impulse, conscience, and reason, although some distortion is involved in this usage, inasmuch as the conscience and the reason are not categorically different from the impelling drives of the individual, but rather complications which arise in the process of elaborating drives in relation to one another and to surroundings.

Since social and political processes take place among people, there can be no major contribution to the understanding of personality which fails to carry with it certain immediate implications for the analysis of collective processes. Within the last thirty or forty years psychology has received a new and powerful

* From *The American Journal of Sociology* (January, 1932).

impetus from the study of those major deformations of personality growth which we speak of as mental diseases. Where this study has been conducted with full attention to the interconnection between processes capable of description in physiological terms, and processes capable of description in psychological or sociological terms, significant progress has been made. Investigations that began in the clinic with some single distortion of personality refine and generalize their methods and their theories until a comprehensive account of personality development in both its healthy and its pathological aspects is the result. In all this Freud is the epochal figure, and it is to psychoanalysis with its insight into the tripartite structure of personality that we may recur in search of a promising starting-point for the reconsideration of politics and society.

If the personality system is divisible into the reaction patterns assignable to impulse, conscience, and reason, it follows that the meaning of any social object to any particular person is to be interpreted in terms of its appeal to one or more of these main divisions. Persons, institutions, occasions, policies and practices, doctrines, and myths and legends may be examined for the purpose of discerning their appeals to impulse, conscience, and reason. And we may go further : In so far as politics is the science and the art of management, politics must direct its means to the three levels of personality structure. The principle of tripartite division implies the principle of triple appeal as a method of political management.

We may begin our exploration of the applicability of the tripartite principle by studying the relations which subsist between one person and the cluster of persons who have some fairly constant connection with him. In view of its significance for the theory and practice of administration, I shall first recite some extracts from an intensive study of the personality of a successful executive, who had associated various subordinates with him in the conduct of his daily work. It was possible to carry through a very intensive inquiry into the conscious and the unconscious motives which led him to choose and to abide by his choice of personnel. In certain cases there appeared to be a clear-cut predominance of an appeal to but one of the principal portions of his personality. We shall take as representative the case of the controller, the private secretary, and the field representative.

The case of the controller was very simple indeed. Here was a middle-aged, taciturn, conscientious technician, whose expertness and dependability had been recognized before the executive himself had assumed his present responsibilities. No one doubted his skill and integrity, and although he was colourless and tiresome in purely social situations, his position was secure beyond criticism. He was distinctly an ego selection, since his utility for the specific purpose in question was undisputed.

The significance of the private secretary was not so simple. When you first met this hatchet-faced New England spinster, and heard her sharp, querulous voice, you wondered how she could possibly keep her job. And when you knew the details of her daily round, you wondered yet more. Miss X. was one of those individuals who worked so over-scrupulously that her work was chronically in arrears. She was exasperated almost beyond endurance at the slightest error, or at the slightest deviation from office routine. Punctually at eight-thirty she sat in front of her desk, brushing mostly imaginary flecks of dust off the chair, the desk top, and the shade of the droplight. Her stationery, her pencils, and her erasers were invariably in order. Office assistants came and went, usually leaving a trail of complaints about the impossibility of working with Miss X. The executive was himself not infrequently rallied good-humouredly about his " office nurse ", but he passed off every comment with a shrug. The truth was that in spite of her admitted inefficiencies, he found it unthinkable to do without her. During the course of the study of his personality he candidly admitted that he was as much at a loss as anybody to understand why he should cling so tenaciously to Miss X. He just did, that was all.

Whenever there is a striking lack of proportion between an act and the reasons alleged for it, there is a presumption that some unconscious impulses are involved in the act. So it proved in this instance. In the course of his long self-scrutiny by free-association methods, it eventually appeared that Miss X. owed her hold on this man to the very fact that she caricatured those rules of promptness and exactness which he found so onerous. Mr. Z. was one of those impetuous, imaginative, somewhat erratic individuals who are in some measure hampered by their juvenile consciences, with all the demands of conscience for consistent conformity to prudent rules. He was continually violating this inner and quite unconscious legacy from his youth, and this led to much inner discomfort. He put up with Miss X. because she made a powerful appeal to his conscience, and his curious timidities in her presence were penances for his self-indulgences. Like all such primitive reactions of conscience, this one was rather extreme and was clumsily adjusted to efficient living. There were certainly many more agreeable secretaries available to provide the standing model of diligence and precision, without overdoing the matter. It was the appeal to the non-rational, in this case to the conscience, which secured Miss X. her place in Z.'s entourage.

Another member of his staff seemed to offer more serious difficulties to his retention than did Miss X. After all, the secretary was principally a nuisance. But the young man who served as field representative was often a serious problem. Everyone agreed that he possessed exceptionally captivating ways, and that he bound prospective clients to him by his open-handed generosity, his never-failing good humour, and his great personal charm. But these very assets were frequently expended upon dangerous quests which seriously damaged his own reputation and that of his superiors. He was continually becoming involved in clandestine love affairs with the wives of his associates—affairs which were not always handled with that discretion which, in the absence of true abstinence, is the better part of safety. The tenacity with which Z. stood behind the young man was a matter of continual amazement as well as embarrassment to the influential members of his organization. His attitude appeared all the more remarkable because the private life of Z. was well known to be exemplary, and in spite of a certain gusty looseness of language, he had been known to deal severely with men who allowed sex to interfere with professional obligations. As for Z. himself, he was never quite at ease in discussing the matter, usually asserting tartly that he believed the young man had very good stuff in him, and that it would be a mistake to act too harshly without giving him a chance to settle down. Every responsible person agreed that the young man was promising enough, but opinion was practically unanimous that he had so repeatedly and so shamelessly imposed upon the tolerance of his superiors that he had forfeited all claims to special consideration in the future.

In the confidence of the analytical situation, Z. said that he was himself at a loss to understand his own position, since he had much respect for the judgment of those who criticized the excesses of the field representative. It was only gradually that the private background of Z. became sufficiently illuminated in reminiscence to disclose the unconscious motivation which accounted for his quite exceptional loyalty to this young man. Z. had gone through many years in youth during which he had been harried by keen feelings of his own incapacity, especially in the specific field of sex. An accident in early childhood had damaged him physically, and his morbid reveries about himself were not wholly without foundation. A boyhood companion of Z. had played the rôle with girls which Z. had secretly envied. This companion had been carried off early by an infection, and Z. had always felt a sorrowful and protective attachment to his memory. Quite without being conscious of it, Z. had read into his young field representative his own admiration and attachment for his boyhood friend, the emotional power of which is indicated by his long-suffering forbearance. In part, Z. secured an indirect gratification of his own deeply buried impulse life by virtue of this identification.

It would be a mistake to imagine that the history just referred to is, in principle, exceptional. The details of the picture vary as individual backgrounds vary, but the main point is clear enough. We select our personal circles according to the appeal made to the principal components, both conscious and unconscious, of our personalities. It may be that within our official rôle as superintendent, director, department head, bureau chief, manager, foreman, editor, or publisher we are principally governed by rational calculations of efficiency in our choices of personnel, and that our intimates are chosen from among those who appeal to the life of impulse and conscience. But the study of actual administrators has shown that this subordination of discretion to considerations of mere utility is never fully achieved. Private motives of the kind mentioned not only continue to operate, but not infrequently predominate, in the choice of personnel.

Since this highly schematic presentation has referred to marginal instances, it may be well to stop for a moment to emphasize the fact that every relationship between persons involves appeals to every phase of the personality, and that thorough analysis of any particular case is extremely intricate. Every enduring personal relation implies a fusion of meanings derived from each of the principal personality levels, although any one level frequently does predominate.

Since the selection of personnel is subject to influences which modify simple considerations of efficiency, the history of institutions may be examined from the point of view of assessing the relative importance of these modifying factors. Do we find that though a given enterprise required great ruthlessness to succeed, the moral scruples (consciences) of the original founders led to the choice of men incapable of the acts of illegality and brutality necessary to success? Do we find, reversely, that the brutal aggressiveness of the original clique, traceable to defective conscience formation and to great sadism, brought together a band of men who ruined the enterprise by needlessly provoking the resentment of society? Or do we find that the organization was handicapped by internal strife, owing to the selection of men representing extremes of over-scrupulousness and over-ruthlessness by the founder, as the asocial or the conscientious parts of his personality won temporary ascendancy? Do we find that the organization is left in the hands of men who are incapable of taking the initiative in modifying their policies to changing circumstances—men who appealed to the original leader precisely because of their inability to challenge his narcissistic satisfaction in originating all policies himself and in looking after the details of their execution?

If it is necessary to remind one of the relevance of these considerations, I may refer to the personality factors which are alleged to have influenced Woodrow Wilson's cabinet selections, or to have enabled Lincoln so to subordinate himself in the selection of prominent collaborators as to attach them to the service of the government. Or, in the field of business, one may remember that one factor in the decline of a great packing-house was the policy of picking socially agreeable and " fast young men " who were boon companions to those in high positions.

The study of the personality factors which affect the course of institutional growth is a matter of general interest to the scientific student of culture, and it is not devoid of relevance to the task of social engineering. An adviser on personnel policy who can assist in creating a certain self-awareness in these matters can do something to protect organizations against the destructive tendencies which are released within it, owing to the complication of judgment by irrelevant unconscious impulses. A new and important chapter in the management of personnel in government, industry, and ecclesiastical institutions can be written when the factors affecting productive adaptations among personnel have been carefully studied.

So far, in this discussion of person-to-person appeals, reference has been exclusively made to those who are choosing associates and subordinates. The point of view is equally applicable to the study of the behaviour of those who are responding to " superiors ", " leaders ", or " models ". Since the rank and file of mankind is in no position to know many relevant facts about the men whom it trusts, who may, to all intents and purposes, be as remote as God, it is compelled to project its loyalty by a simple act of faith, if it would escape the barely tolerable state of suspended judgment or of bitter scepticism. Few characteristics of men are so obvious as their capacity for strong emotional attachments and aversions in respect to a handful of public characters. Since this can scarcely be said to rest upon extensive first-hand observation and sifted knowledge, it must rest chiefly upon the appeal value of the few to the non-rational components of the many.

Man is prepared for dependence upon others by the circumstances of his early relationship to his social environment. Every infant passes through a period in which the one who performs the maternal rôle looks after its primary needs without specific recompense, thus furnishing the experiential base for the infant's primitive mother-sentiment.[1] This primitive mother-sentiment becomes detached from particular individuals in the environment as restraints are imposed by those in custody of the infant and child, but the early sentiment leaves its residue in the form of a deep yearning for the re-establishment of complete dependence. This underlying sentiment is reinforced in many ways by subsequent sentiments, but it is always present, capable of becoming attached to some substitute object like God, or some human symbol of universal, protective omnipotence. So man is prepared to trust those whom he cannot rationally assess, and his seemingly inexhaustible yearning for dependence, for submission, for worship, for admiration, for loyalty, is so generally noticed that many theorists have imputed a biological basis to it.

Little less conspicuous than man's willingness to defer is his revulsion of feeling against many of those whom he has once loved. Here, again, we are compelled to invoke the aid of those who have studied the early growth of the personality, and who have come to stress the importance of the reactive structures which are built up quite early in individual development. They notice that the foregoing of direct gratifications of primitive

[1] I follow the terminology here of Harry Stack Sullivan.

drives. is accomplished with considerable discomfort to the organism. One of the native reactions to an outside obstruction is destructive operations upon that obstacle ; when the social environment outlasts or outwits the developing individual, and the personality takes over the socially imposed inhibition, many destructive impulses are repressed in the process. Repressed destructive drives do not die, but rather they show themselves in the form of indirect attacks upon substitute objects. Hatreds organized within the family circle are partially repressed, and partially discharged against public targets.

These hatreds come out in sensational reversals of public sentiment. Wilson in 1918 was a saviour ; in 1920 Wilson was a fiasco. These protests against the sanctioned social order are made manifest, also, in the sentimentalization of spectacular rebels and criminals. The exploits of distinguished pirates, bootleggers, highwaymen, rebels, and imperial mistresses are a cherished heritage : " . . . Jesse James was a three-gun man. . . ."

The other component of the unconscious structure of the personality may be relied upon to create saints and martyrs. There are heroes of conscience, who stand for the virtues of renunciation, self-sacrifice, generosity, and peace. There is Jesus the Christ, Gandhi, Jane Addams, and the long list of saints and martyrs.

In some measure there are heroes of expediency, men whose utility to socially sanctioned purposes has been demonstrated more objectively than usual. I refer here to those the worth of whose contributions can be shown by some complex technical procedure to a trained public. Many philosophers, scientists, and engineers come in this category ; but it should be said that as far as the wider public is concerned their fame rests upon appeals to those portions of the personality which impute wonder-working power and omniscience so readily. We certainly need not assume that the vogue of Einstein in the public mind of our day rests upon informed estimates on the part of the rank and file, whatever may be the expertness of the few to whom he primarily appeals.

II

The tripartite analysis, which has been applied to person-to-person relationships, can be applied with no less cogency to the study of the meaning of those patterns of social life which are

so firmly rooted that they deserve to be named " institutions ".
Institutions, conceived as social objects, likewise appeal to human
personalities as the price of their perpetuation, and their appeal
may be highly specialized to impulse, conscience, or reason.
Spranger has classified the institutionalized achievements of man
into economic, political, religious, social, æsthetic, and scientific.
Each one is stylized in innumerable ways from culture to culture,
and from epoch to epoch.   To Spranger's sixfold classification
we may add a seventh, which we shall call the " technological ",
the justification for which has been extensively dealt with by
Fritz Giese.

It is the economic, political, scientific, and technological which
appeals to the reason of man, demanding continuous modification
of ends in terms of the limits imposed by reality.   Politics is
peculiarly the sphere of expedient calculation.   Demands which
at first sight appear irreconcilable short of violence may be
harmonized in relation to goal symbols and special practices.
When the arbitrament of violence is involved, the same swift
calculation of disposable means to sharply defined ends is implied.
The province of economics is that of the articulation of men
and materials for the production of rather tangible objects and
services ; science disciplines the imaginative flights of man by
requisitioning attention to the nature of unfolding reality.
Technology is concerned with the elaboration of means, with
scant reference to general principles of economy in relation to
the market.

The inhibitory structure of the personality is appealed to
mainly by religious institutions, which sanction the relinquishment of direct impulsive gratifications by the young at the behest
of their elders.   These denials are powerfully buttressed by
appeals of a symbolic order to the primitive cravings for universal
protection and for cosmic participation.   In so far as law involves
the enforcement of standards concerning which there is practically no dissent within the community, law is to be classed
with the religious institutions.   Those " laws " which enunciate
an imperative which depends upon bare majorities or pluralities
are not in the same category but fall within the world of the
debatable and the shifting balance of power (politics).

The world of æsthetics makes a strong appeal to the primary
springs of the personality, permitting direct pleasure in the
smudging of liquids and the moulding of solids, in undisciplined
reverie, and in the discovery of forms which indirectly gratify

the asocial or the antisocial cravings of the personality. The artistic imagination admits no duty of external relevance to govern the choice of proportion, design, and colour. Limits which are imposed by imperfect materials or undiscovered manipulative techniques are merely obstructions, and not, as in the case of science, ruling conditions. The fact that art may be used to adorn symbols of the super-ego is a tribute to the necessity of reinforcing the imperative orders of conscience by more seductive devices.

Art, viewed from the standpoint of the established order, always shows much waywardness, that is, many concessions to the primitive nature of man. Much the same tendency to get out of hand, to go beyond the conventions, and to neglect solemn obligations is shown in the world of social intercourse. Institutions are for ever being dissolved in the wayward heat of affections which transcend them. Intimacies bridge chasms between lawful and lawless, high-born and low-born, rich and poor, white and black. The conventionalizations which are imbedded in the super-ego, and which are externally buttressed by proper conduct in formal social situations, together with institutional ceremonialism and symbolism, give way under the impulsive pressure of private, intimate ties. Friendship has often been called the enemy of law, for friendship motivates exceptions to the rule on behalf of the one who is understood, admired, and loved.

Our institutional paradigm so far reads : The appeal to expediency is predominant in economic, political, scientific, and technological institutions ; the appeal to conscience is that of religion and fundamental law ; the appeal to natural impulse is that of art and sociability. Needless to insist, politics involves appeals to hatreds, omnipotence, lusts, and submissive urges ; economics includes appeals to powerful acquisitive, retentive, and potentially expulsive drives ; and science offers much opportunity for isolated imaginings, aloofness from many ordinary demands of society, and underlying sadistic designs against the reality which it pretends to serve. Thus no institutional pattern falls into any pigeon-hole with any more than an approximate fit.

Great variability in meaning is particularly characteristic of those complex patterns called government. I have already taken occasion to observe that laws which rest upon unanimity are essentially religious institutions, and that other laws are political. Both, of course, are " governmental ". Political science as a living discipline is actually composed of specialists who are interested mainly in the governmental and secondarily in the political.   G. E. G. Catlin has already thrown down the gauntlet on behalf of those who want to be political scientists and who want to deal with the governmental only in so far as it is political. Those who desire some substantial homogeneity of subject matter, capable of abstract treatment, will be in sympathy with Catlin's viewpoint ; but the external homogeneity of the governmental will no doubt continue to exercise its predominance upon the minds of " political scientists ".

The ambiguity of the governmental is very far-reaching indeed.   Many of the movements which are studied by students of the governmental are not primarily political, or even techno-logical and social, in the meaning of Spranger ; many of them are religious.   Imperialism, whether conceived as the extension of an empire or the fomenting of world-revolution, is a form of religion.   Its pretensions are universal and categorically absolute. A nationalism that becomes conciliatory and tractable ceases to be a religion and becomes a rather weak, sentimental union, essentially social and political in character.   Indeed, any sect which becomes tolerant and compromising has ceased to be a religion and becomes a denomination.   After the Protestant Reformation, which ultimately brought about an accommoda-tion among ecclesiastical institutions in the Western world on the basis of 'tolerance, the Catholic Church became less of a religious and more of a socio-political institution, for the adjust-ment of ecclesiastical differences became a discussible, debatable proposition.

III

So far the tripartite principle has been applied to person-to-person and person-to-institution relations.   The next step is to consider person-to-occasion relationships.   Every culture includes many special occasions which are stylized in relation to particular institutions, and which might quite properly have been discussed in the previous section.   But they may usefully be considered separately, since the same institution may provide episodes which appeal to quite different components of the personality than the one to which the major appeal of the institution is addressed. We were previously concerned with the most general aspect of the relation between an institution, considered as a whole, and the personality ; we are now in a position to refine the analysis somewhat.

In spite of all the attendant complications introduced by irrelevant motivations, elections—particularly referendum elections —are episodes in government in which rational considerations are emphasized. The situation is defined in terms of definite alternatives for which preferences are to be expressed in a peaceful procedure. This is a definite contrast to the major appeal of patriotic holidays, when the graves of fallen soldiers are decorated, or where patriotic dogmas are ceremonially reiterated. Such occasions are appeals to conscience, stressing unity with the collectivity and devotion to shared values. And there are celebrations and carnivals of all descriptions where the customary restraints of propriety are swept aside for the nonce, and where the primary impulses are allowed to express themselves unveiled by the customary cloaks. The war crisis is essentially religious in character, demanding, amid greatest excitement, the fulfilment of the imperative obligations of the good citizen. There is no time to deliberate ; there is but time for consternation and prompt action.

Acts of popular justice are under the domination of the conscience, but they display the peculiar character of primitive punitive measures in that they likewise involve the direct gratification of very deep destructive tendencies. Mobs which form when the moral order is supposed to have been outraged by a brutal sexual assault, or by the hoarding of food in time of want, or by acts of aid and comfort to the enemy, are forms of popular justice. They very often display semiformal modes of action which lend a certain air of responsibility to what they do. A " court " is set up for the hearing of the charges, and " sentence " may be passed with the greatest solemnity.

The close association between the indulgence of the primitive nature of man and the exactions of the authoritarian order is shown in the close association which has historically existed between rites of worship and sexual orgies. It is notorious that religious fervour among sectarians is often closely connected with orgiastic indulgences. When waves of patriotic enthusiasm capture the masses, the soldiers are offered and permitted exemptions from more commandments than " Thou shalt not kill ".

The tripartite analysis of institutionalized occasions may be extended to the policies and practices of institutions. Many of the intricate practices of governmental agencies are conspicuously concerned with safeguarding the operations of the ego function. Court processes show the most involved web of formalities of this character, but the purest case of ego dominance is in the laboratory work of the physical scientist. Legislative practices, administrative curbs to irresponsible discretion, and personal modes of politeness in discussion are all germane to the preservation of ego operations with a minimum of distortion from appeals to prejudice or lust.

Reminders of duty are conveyed in the solemn trappings of state. The national emblem figures prominently in every decorative scheme. The practice of opening legislative sessions with prayer is reminiscent of the days when theocracies held sway in various sections of our own country. The solemn declaration or oath which is taken by incoming officials and court witnesses, the references to duty and conscience which commonly figure in the charge to the jury, and the moralistic denunciations and admonitions so frequently heard from the judicial bench are all supposed to reinforce the claims of the super-ego portion of the personalities involved.

The whole drama of litigation and punishment is profoundly linked to the exactions of conscience. A considerable number of those who fall foul of the law have been driven to make clumsy errors which led to their detection owing to the unconscious self-punishment reaction of their own consciences. They demand punishment to relieve the inner discomforts of living. Many of them, as soon as they have paid off the debt they owe to conscience, are once again free to indulge their antisocial impulses in destructive acts against society.

The spectacle of any violation of the accredited order arouses the repressed impulses of the spectator to indulge his own antisocial whims. This produces a crisis of conscience within the personalities of those who see and hear of the violation, and the individual is driven to relieve himself of his own discomfort by externalizing his aggression against those in the environment who threaten the inner equilibrium of his own life. To punish and to have punished the performer of a criminal act is to perform a vicarious act of propitiation of one's own conscience.

It is to a comparatively limited sphere that the conscience analysis applies in interpreting the significance of legal penalties. When the law rests on no moral consensus, an unsuccessful violation is little more significant than an unsuccessful business venture. The individual has often calculated in advance that his chances of being fined or imprisoned were " so and so ", and he wipes off a " bum rap " to profit and loss.

Society is so organized that it gives many opportunities for the direct gratification of exceedingly primitive impulses of the personality. The oral (mouth) pleasures are among the most elemental of all, and the examination of our culture shows that oral pleasures may be indulged in biting, smoking, swallowing, chewing gum and tobacco, talking, singing, cheering, and spitting ; the anal pleasures are permitted to a very limited extent. Handling and touching are permitted in the handshake, the permissible embrace of good fellowship, and kissing. All these primary satisfactions are involved in different varieties of the sexual act.

Many opportunities for brutality are offered in society, especially in the field of conflict, or politics. Killing and maiming may be enjoyed by soldiers and by policemen, and judicial murder by judges, prosecuting attorneys, and a prurient, bloodthirsty public. Codes of decency in intimate intercourse may be violated in the heat of electoral and parliamentary oratory. Hostile tendencies may be indulged in anti-authoritarian crusades of various kinds, and in the corruption of officials. The ubiquity of bribery in society is due to the fact that it is learned as a by-product of the experience of being a weak child in a world of strong adults. Indulgences can be secured from nurses and parents if one is willing to make " amends ", especially if one is able to make available something that they desire. Bribery is one of the most common of all the techniques by which the weak or the preoccupied can deal with the strong or the obstructive. It has the special lure of damaging the authoritative object even as he is being granted tangible advantages, and as such is particularly designed to throw authority into contempt, and to gratify the antisocial impulses of the personality. Keen pleasure is taken by many bribers in the very act of corrupting those who profess to represent the pomp and circumstance of the conventional order.

It would be possible to make an extensive analysis from the tripartite point of view of the meaning of social doctrines, myths and legends. Some popular sayings appeal to the ego : " Doubt is the beginning of wisdom." Some appeal to the conscience : " Honour thy father and thy mother." Some appeal to the id : " You're only young once." Stories of heroic and villainous acts, prophecies of heroic and villainous events, theories of social permanence or social flux—all combine to arouse different components of the personality, stimulating the ego, reinforcing the super-ego, and unleashing the id.

IV

Thus far our analysis has been essentially classificatory and static as we discussed the predominant appeal of persons, institutions, occasions, policies and practices, doctrines, myths and legends.[2] The tripartite principle is particularly promising when applied to the problem of social dynamics, since it implies not only the concept of equilibrium, but indicates the specific dynamisms of the process by which the moving equilibrium is continually redefined.

It is not within the scope of the present paper to develop this further. The essential principle may be succinctly formulated as follows : Prolonged ego and super-ego indulgence produces redefinitions in directions gratifying to the id ; prolonged ego and id indulgence produces redefinitions in directions gratifying to the super-ego.

---

[2] Cultural patterns which predominantly appeal to the super-ego of most of the personalities in a group are the " mores " of current sociological theory. The patterns which predominantly appeal to the id may be called the " counter-mores ". The patterns which predominantly appeal to the ego may be called the " expediencies ".

CHAPTER II

GENERAL FRAMEWORK : PERSON, PERSONALITY, GROUP, CULTURE *

The four terms Person, Personality, Group, and Culture are among the cardinal terms in the science of inter-personal relations. The purpose of this discussion is to clarify the method by which their meaning may be made explicit. The terminology owes something to the Cambridge Logical School, and especially to A. N. Whitehead.[1] The debt is evident in the use of such expressions as " event " and " event manifold ".

Perhaps it is not beside the point to remind ourselves of the interest in the study of meaning which has been so acute among social scientists and psychologists in recent years. A great impetus was given to " word consciousness " by the publication of *The Meaning of Meaning* by Ogden and Richards, with a valuable appendix by Malinowski.[2] It is significant that this book was a collaboration of specialists on different aspects of psychology and culture. Ogden was a psychologist, Richards was a literary critic and humanist, and Malinowski was a social anthropologist. This is typical of the many quarters from which interesting contributions have been made to the understanding of words and their meaning. Specialists on general linguistics like Sapir, clinical psychologists like Freud, child psychologists and educators like Piaget and Thorndike, have had something to offer.

It was no accident that the *Meaning of Meaning* came from England and that it was profoundly influenced by the " Cambridge Logical School ". Since the migration of Whitehead to Harvard there has been a growing body of scientific speech in the United States which makes use of the " event " categories which were so profoundly shaped by Whitehead. Developments similar to those in England and the United States were taking

* From *Psychiatry*, vol. 2 (1939). This is part of a larger memorandum which dealt with personality, culture, and education, and which was prepared for the use of a seminar on educational measurement organized under the auspices of the General Education Board. Used by permission.

[1] See especially Whitehead, Alfred North, *An Enquiry Concerning the Principles of Natural Knowledge* (Cambridge, 1919) ; *The Concept of Nature* (Cambridge, 1920) ; *Process and Reality, an Essay in Cosmology* (New York, 1929).

[2] Ogden, Charles K., and Richards, I. A., *The Meaning of Meaning : A Study of the Influence of Language Upon Thought and of the Science of Symbolism* (London, 1944).

place at the same time in the other intellectual centres of Western European civilization. Perhaps the group of most interest to Americans was the logical positivists of Vienna. (Probably the names best known in this country are Carnap and Reichenbach.) A Polish philosopher, Korzybski, long resident in the United States, has attracted a great deal of popular and some scientific attention by his systematic treatise, *Science and Sanity*.[3] Arthur Bentley, an American social psychologist, has also published in the newer idiom.

One result of this discussion among logicians has been to clarify three dimensions of word analysis. The relationship of words to words may be called logic—syntactics ; the relationship of words to their events of reference may be called semantics ; and the relationship of words to practical causes and practical results may be called pragmatics. Distinctions of this kind have been clearly made by Charles W. Morris in the *International Encyclopædia of Unified Science*.[4]

Among historians and students of comparative history, word-consciousness has been of growing importance for at least one hundred years. The study of words and their place in society has been closely connected with the revolutionary movements of the nineteenth and twentieth centuries. The group which centred modern attention upon the symbol was largely made up of critics of the dogmas with which Western European civilization entered the nineteenth century. The students of comparative religion developed secular interpretations of religious ritual and belief. Students of comparative economics and politics challenged the " ideology " of modern capitalism. One of the great names in connection with the analysis of the religious tradition of Western Europe is Ludwig Feuerbach. Marx made use of some of the categories of Feuerbach in analysing other forms of accepted language in our society. It was Marx and Engels who were chiefly responsible for the controversies which have centred around the term " ideology ".

The word " ideology " was used by them to refer to all of the words, and supporting subjective states, which contributed to the survival of capitalism.

As the number of specialists on social science increased, more

[3] Korzybski, Alfred, *Science and Sanity* (Lancaster, Pa., 1933).
[4] The *Encyclopædia* is in process of publication at the University of Chicago Press under the general editorship of Otto Neurath, with the assistance of Rudolf Carnap and Charles W. Morris. Professor Morris has developed the " Foundations of the Theory of Signs " in vol. 1, No. 2.

attention was given to the examination of ideology. One result was to generalize the concept of myth· (Sorel). In recent usage the term " myth " is impartially employed to refer to any words in the name of which social groups undertake to advance or defend their position in society. The mythology of the established order is ideology and, following the terminology of Karl Mannheim, the mythology of those who attack an established order is called Utopia.

The analysis of the myth has gone forward simultaneously in every centre of European life. In recent times France has contributed Durkheim ; Italy has been represented by Mosca and Pareto. The most important name in the history of English thought in this connection is Jeremy Bentham, with his *Theory of Fictions*.[5]

The growth of word consciousness has another interesting aspect. The study of words has encouraged the study of the word user. Indeed, one distinguishing mark of the intellectuals of our time is the growth of that special form of tool consciousness which is word consciousness. As the intellectuals have become more aware of their distinctive tools, they have become more aware of themselves. Hence, intellectuals have been taking themselves as objects of scientific investigation. They are a segment of the skill specialists of modern society. Their distinctive skill is the manipulation of symbols.

The problem of the intellectual was sharply posed in the writings of Marx and Engels, who gave attention to the alleged parasitism of the intellectual. They thought of the intellectuals as dependent upon the dominant economic classes.

As systematic reflection on the problem of the intellectual in society has increased, new hypotheses have been advanced. One of the most interesting was that of the Polish-Russian revolutionist who wrote under the name of Wolski, and whose ideas have been made available in the West by Max Nomad in *Rebels and Renegades*. Instead of dismissing the intellectuals as a subordinate social formation, Wolski spoke of the intellectuals and the semi-intellectuals as constituting a new social class which was in process of rising to power. The " capital " of the intellectual is his knowledge, and the intellectual is rising at the expense of aristocracy and plutocracy. As a means of rising, the intellectuals have allied the manual workers with them by means of an

[5] Bentham, Jeremy, *The Theory of Fictions* [with an Introduction by Charles K. Ogden] (London, 1932).

inclusive symbol—by speaking in the name of the proletariat. Thus the rising intellectuals got the jobs in a state like Russia, benefiting from the revolutionary energy of the workers.   In the nineteenth century the rising intellectual class created the orators and bureaucrats and journalists of the socialist political parties, the trade unions, and the consumer co-operatives ; and in the twentieth century they take the jobs in the Russian bureaucratic state and in Fascist movements or Fascist states.

Another contribution to the theory of the intellectual was made by a vivacious literary critic, Benda—author of *The Treason of the Intellectual*.[6] His point was that intellectuals in modern society are grasping for power by talking to the masses rather than by talking to themselves and adhering to the austere pursuit of truth as judged by scholarly standards.   This, says Benda, has brought about a steady disintegration of the integrity of the intellectual and has contributed to the barbarization of our time.

The problem of the intellectual and his place in history is commonly spoken of as an aspect of the " sociology of knowledge ", to which Max Weber was an influential contributor.[7]

Culture Trait and Personality Trait

As a result of modern concern with the analysis of words and word users, the key terms of our present discussion—personality, culture, person, group—have received new connotations.   More important, we have become aware of methods by which meanings could be fixed for an observer who occupies a specified position, in relation to a field of events of potential reference.   The observer and his words are events among events.   The term " field " refers to the event at the observer's focus of attention. In the manifold of events, observers may take different positions, standpoints.   Observations may be calibrated from standpoint to standpoint by comparing observations with regard to what is taken to be the same field.

Suppose we begun by referring to the position of an observer in a strange community who has just noticed that the one who addressed him made a certain gesture.

Suppose the observer writes in his notebook : "At eleven a.m.

---

[6] Benda, Julien, *The Great Betrayal (la trahison des clercs)* [transl. Richard Aldington] (London, 1928).

[7] For a convenient summary see Parsons, Talcott, *The Structure of Social Action : A Study in Social Theory with Special Reference to a Group of Recent European Writers* (New York, 1937).

X., a child, came to see me and rubbed his right ear with his right hand when we greeted one another. I don't know whether this was a gesture of politeness, or whether it shows that X. is embarrassed." The observer has two possible relations in mind with reference to the act of ear rubbing. He wants to place it in terms of culture and personality.

In order to determine whether the act is a culture trait, the observer collects *testimony* and notes *occurrences*.

Suppose that he asks a group of those who participate in the culture whether they expect to have this particular gesture made when two persons meet. The answer may be unanimous: " We expect this gesture to be made when a younger person meets an older person who is in authority over him." Suppose also that the observer follows a series of situations in which younger persons meet older persons in authority over them and the gesture always appears.

We will not complicate the discussion at this point by raising questions of the reliability, adequacy and validity of the samples.

Some of the acts noted by the observer may not be easy to describe. Suppose the observer is told that the knee should be bent at' the same time that the ear is rubbed whenever a younger person meets an older relative of his mother. Assume that all testimony is unanimous on this point. Yet the observer finds that the act of bending the knee fails to occur in five out of ten situations which correspond to these specifications. Or suppose that the observer faces still another complication : A disagreement among those whom he asks to testify. Assume that seven out of ten say that they expect a given gesture under specified conditions. Is the gesture a culture trait? The observer must set rather arbitrary limits for what he is going to call a trait. The frequencies which he selects are of no direct interest to us here. Assume that the observer decides to use the expression " trait of this culture " when six, or more, of ten testifiers agree that it is expected, and when the expected act occurs in no less than six of ten possible situations.

We ought to stop at this point to say that the working social scientist very seldom finds it possible to keep his records as carefully as our hypothetical observer. The working observer of a primitive community only approximates these strict requirements. Even the published monographs which describe our own culture do not in practice meet these standards. When the Lynds describe Middletown, they make no effort to specify the frame of reference of their words as carefully as our hypothetical observer.[8]   Our remarks do not imply that it is always advisable to operate within the framework of super-strict requirements. The aim is only to make entirely clear what is necessary for very refined observation and communication.

We have carried our observer to this point : He has standardized his terminology so that he (and perhaps others) can understand what he is talking about.   He uses the expression *" trait of a specified culture " to refer to an act which is expected to appear and which does occur with at least a specified minimum frequency in a given field of observation.*   Our observer may use the word " conduct " to refer to an act which conforms to a culture trait and the word " behaviour " to refer to an act which does not conform.   We may note that an act which is behaviour in one community may be conduct in another community, but it is also possible that an act may conform to no pattern anywhere.   The latter act would be behaviour in all observed communities.

Our observer has succeeded in placing the act of ear rubbing in one dimension of the context in which it is found.   He is also interested in placing the act in proper relationship to another dimension of this manifold of events.   The act is one of the acts which compose the career line of the actor.   Some of the acts are representative of the person under specified conditions.   If our observer watches the future acts of the same person, or records the past acts of the person, under the same conditions, the results may be as follows :   " The politeness gesture was made in ten of the ten occasions when there was an opportunity to make it." Or, " The politeness gesture was made in seven of the ten occasions when there was an opportunity."   *The frequency of occurrence of an act on comparable occasions in the career-line of a person is a trait of the personality.*

Personality traits are thus described in relation to acts which are related to culture.   But all events which enter into the act are not necessarily defined in the culture.   Our observer may borrow Chester W. Darrow's portable psychogalvanometer and induce the subject to wear it.   As a result he may learn that ear rubbing is preceded by a sharp increase in skin conductance. Our observer can be quite sure that the participants in the culture do not entertain any expectations whatever about the electrical reactions of the skin.

[8] Lynd, Robert S., and Helen M., *Middletown : A Study in American Culture* (London, 1929) ; and *Middletown in Transition : A Study in Cultural Conflicts* (London, 1937).

The reason the observer bothers to describe skin conductance at all is that he expects to make use of these data in examining the personality-culture manifold. For purposes of concreteness we may consider the following possibility : the observer may find the same individual differs markedly in skin conductance reactions when addressing people whom he loves or hates, and when addressing persons to whom he is indifferent. He may find that measuring skin conductance reactions of subjects who are exposed to pictures of different individuals is an economical way of discovering the emotionally active, or the emotionally indifferent, relationships of élite or non-élite groups in the culture. Tests of the presence or absence of the " startle pattern "—as defined by Carney Landis and associates—may be devised for different personality-culture manifolds.[9] This indicates how " physiological " events may be used in the examination of personality and culture.

As a matter of convenience our observer may use the following terms : " *response* " for the acts, including parts of acts, which are the objects of expectation in a culture ; " *reaction* " for the acts, including parts of acts, which are not objects of expectation in the culture : Ear rubbing is thus a response in the context in which our hypothetical observer has been at work. Skin conductance is a reaction.

Now all of the acts which are expected in a culture are not necessarily approved by the participants in the culture. Politeness expressed in ear rubbing may be expected. But the occurrence of violations may also be expected. That is, while it is agreed that morality and propriety dictate this gesture, it is recognized that some immoral and improper breaches are likely to take place among those who belong to the culture. Contrast this with the expectations which prevail regarding incest with a small daughter. The very idea that such a thing could occur may be alien to those who share a given culture. They may be shocked to have the possibility mentioned and they may know of no examples of it. Intimate observers of the culture may agree that this simply doesn't happen. We know from general study of culture that when events of this kind do take place the participants in the culture refuse to recognize that anyone capable of sharing their culture would perform such an act. They do not regard it as compatible with human nature. The shocking and outrageous event is treated as subhuman.

[9] Landis, Carney, and Hunt, William A., and Strauss, Hans, *The Startle Pattern* (New York, 1939).

The distinctions which we have just made can be fixed in our terminology by setting up the following conventions : *mores traits* of a culture are recognized to be obligatory by the bearers of the culture, and this is signified by the indignation with which violations are met. *Counter-mores traits* of a culture are acts which violate the *mores* and are recognized to occur, regrettable as they are. Acts which fall completely outside culture traits are not conduct at all. They are, as mentioned above, behaviour. The term *mores* came into the language of modern social science by way of Sumner.[10] The expression *counter-mores* has been proposed to emphasize a neglected though tacitly recognized aspect of cultural analysis. To round out the terminology : for cultural traits which are not *mores* or *counter-mores*, we may use the expression " folkways " or " expediencies ".

Personality and Culture as Wholes

Although we have defined culture trait and personality trait, we have not defined culture or personality. These terms refer to wholes, and as wholes they include not only the traits of which they are composed, but the interrelationships of these traits. When we describe ear rubbing as a trait, we have not located it with reference to the culture or personality until we show how it is interconnected with the other traits of which personality or culture is composed.

An observer knows that the number of traits which can be isolated for purposes of description is legion. The length of trait lists is largely a function of the imaginative subtlety of the one who makes them. Hence our observer seeks to avoid sinking in the never-ending task of enumerating traits. There is no event so inconspicuous in the field of observation that it cannot be subdivided, since every whole of reference may be referred to as composed of parts, and each part can be taken as a whole, which in turn is composed of parts, and so on without end. The description of a trait as ear-rubbing-with-the-right-hand may be useful for some purposes, but there are questions which call for splitting this trait into two traits. There is ear-rubbing-of-the-lobe-of-the-ear-with-the-right-hand, and there is ear-rubbing-of-the-entire-ear-with-the-right-hand ; and there may be very meticulous workers, who, for purposes best known to themselves, count the fingers of the right hand involved in ear rubbing, describe slight

[10] Sumner, William Graham, *Folkways ; A Study of the Sociological Importance of Usages, Manners, Customs, Mores, and Morals* (Boston, 1906).

inclinations of the head, indicate whether palm is in or out, and so forth.

Since the trait list is unlimited, our observer undertakes to orient himself with reference to the whole context of personality and culture by using a limited list of words to refer to the principal features of each context.

What are some of the words which may prove serviceable in referring to the whole of personality or culture?

As students of human relations we are—by definition—concerned with interpersonal relations.[11] The significant feature in the environment of any personality is another personality, and the significant feature in the environment of any culture is another culture.

Interpersonal relationships are *indulgent* or *deprivational*—or indifferent. Hence the interpersonal environment of any personality or culture is indulgent or deprivational—or indifferent. Through any period, the interpersonal environment is indulgent when the value position of a personality or a culture is improved, and deprivational when it is impaired. For many research purposes, an indulgent environment may be indexed by *increase*—or *promised increase*, or *avoided loss*—in deference, income, and safety. A deprivational environment may be indexed by *decrease*—or *threat of decrease*, or *lost gain*—in these values.

It is evident that the acts of a personality or a culture in relation to its interpersonal environment are also indulgent or deprivational—indulgent when they increase the deference, income, and safety of the other personality or culture, and deprivational when they diminish deference, income, and safety.

We have now selected a frame of reference for our inquiries—" interpersonal relationships of indulgence and deprivation ". *" Personality " is the term used to refer to the way a person acts toward other persons. " Culture " is the term used to refer to the way that the members of a group act in relation to one another and to other groups. A " group " is composed of persons. A " person " is an individual who identifies himself with others.* Our observer may find it difficult at first to determine whether individuals identify themselves with one another sufficiently to constitute a group—or, to say the same

[11] The phrase " interpersonal relations ", first launched and emphasized by Harry Stack Sullivan, has established itself rapidly. J. L. Moreno and the " sociometry school " have been among those to incorporate it into their terminological system. Cf. Sullivan, Harry Stack, " Psychiatry ", *Encyclopedia of Social Sciences*, vol. 12 (New York, 1931-5) ; and Moreno, J. L., *Who Shall Survive? A New Approach to the Problem of Human Interrelations*, Nervous and Mental Disease Monographs (Washington, D.C., 1934).

thing another way, it may not be easy to decide whether individuals who are persons in some relationships are sufficiently identified with others in certain situations to be called persons in the latter.

Observers have reported that some primitive people for whom we have names share no symbol of identification. Margaret Mead found that the mountain Arapesh have no name for themselves, nor have their neighbours any name for them.[12] They use names to distinguish small locality groups varying from 150 to 250 people. Although there is no shared symbol, investigation would probably reveal that those who live in certain villages believe that they are more like those who live in mountain villages than they are like the villagers of the plains or beach. Under such conditions, the observer must do more than make a simple inquiry for the name of the tribe.

A group may be distinguished from an aggregate of individuals by the degree to which they share symbols of mutual identification. The individuals who live near the fortieth parallel, north latitude, are not a *group*, but they constitute an *aggregate*. They have no name for themselves—like " forty parallelers "—and they have no sense of being more like one another than they are like thirtieth parallelers. If our observer studies these people at a time when " parallel-consciousness " is a rising social trend, he may find that one in a million have attained " parallel-consciousness " by 1945. He will need to select the critical frequencies which will enable him to separate a group from an aggregate. He may decide that three out of every four persons living near the fortieth parallel must identify with an inclusive symbol before the term group is applied to them.

So far the term " culture " has been used here as if it were a synonym for the collective practices of any group. However, there is no advantage in using the word culture as a synonym for all group customs, no matter how trivial. There has been a tendency in recent social science to use the term indiscriminately. We often speak of culture patterns when we are talking about the customs which prevail in Muncie, Indiana, or in the Middle West as a whole, or in the United States, or in all countries sharing Western European civilization. There is no advantage in having such a term as culture unless it is reserved for the most representative and distinctive group practices found in the world

[12] Mead, Margaret (ed.), *Co-operation and Competition among Primitive Peoples* (New York, 1937).

of to-day and of yesterday. It would be desirable to classify the group practices which prevail over the face of the world to-day, and which have prevailed in the known past of mankind, and to lay down criteria of importance and distinctiveness. This task has not been performed by the students of comparative culture in a way which gives general satisfaction. In the interim, therefore, we are perhaps justified in retaining the terms culture and culture pattern when we refer to the practices of a group.

When our observer uses the expression " a personality " or " a culture ", the terms are very poor in meaning until they are exhaustively elaborated. The process of elaboration is the study of traits and their interrelationships. We need to know how the traits vary in relation to one another when the environment changes. Our observer must relate the gesture of politeness to the other traits of the culture or the personality under various environmental conditions.

The crucial relationships of a person or a culture are to other persons or to other cultures.

The immediate environment of the person making the gesture of politeness which we have been discussing is an older person in authority. By proper means of investigation our observer can find out what mutual expectations prevail in this situation. The person in authority expects to be indulged by this gesture. It is probable that the subordinate expects the superordinate to act in a certain indulgent way toward him. On the basis of these expectations, we can classify the degree of indulgence and deprivation. When a subordinate uses an abrupt or sketchy gesture, his act is less indulgent than when he makes a full gesture. When the superordinate is less attentive than expected, a deprivation has been inflicted upon the subordinate. The following combinations are possible in the situation :

ENVIRONMENT	INDULGENT	—POLITE GESTURE
ACTIVITY	INDULGENT	—POLITE GESTURE
ENVIRONMENT	INDULGENT	—POLITE GESTURE
ACTIVITY	DEPRIVATIONAL	—IMPOLITE GESTURE
ENVIRONMENT	DEPRIVATIONAL	—IMPOLITE GESTURE
ACTIVITY	INDULGENT	—POLITE GESTURE
ENVIRONMENT	DEPRIVATIONAL	—IMPOLITE GESTURE
ACTIVITY	DEPRIVATIONAL	—IMPOLITE GESTURE

The situation may be read as indulgent or deprivational in

several ways. The subordinate's gesture of politeness may be met by politeness, and hence the subordinate's gesture may be termed "successful" in eliciting a gain (indulgence) from the environment. If the subordinate's gesture is met by impoliteness, it is a "failure". If the authority enters the situation with an impolite gesture, the subordinate then makes a polite gesture, and the authority comes through with a polite gesture, the subordinate's gesture may be called "successful", in the obviation of threatened loss. If the superordinate is very polite at the start, the subordinate is polite, and then the superordinate is less polite, the gesture by the subordinate may be judged a "failure", a loss of promised gain. In general, indulgence is gain, promise of gain, and obviation of threatened loss ; deprivation is loss, threat of loss, and obstructed gain.

The environmental events E and the activity events A are treated as concurrent.

It is not enough to connect A with E, and to explain the variation of A as a function of E. A is also a function of certain previous events which we call predispositions, P. The frame of reference of the term P may be arbitrarily defined to suit the convenience of the observer who operates with reference to a given field. The P may be defined to mean the "ten preceding comparable situations in which the person was observed".

Our observer has now arranged his data in time order. If he is fortunate, these dated data may disclose—after proper analysis—the functional interrelationships of varying magnitudes of A as a function of EP.

But the probability is that his data will soon prove to be inadequate. The data about the politeness gesture may describe very completely how the authoritative person conducted himself in the presence of the subordinate. And it may summarize a great many situations in which the subordinate and the superordinate interacted upon one another. Yet the data may not suffice for the purpose of displaying the significant interrelationships of the trait in question with other traits of the personality. Expectations founded upon the data may be of little use in predicting how the person will act in the next series of situations which involve authority. Our observer may be prepared to see the subject respond politely to an authoritative person who initiates the situation with a very polite gesture.

But, no ! The next few occasions may show a wholly unpredicted series of acts by our subject. He may snub authority, as he has never done in the past which we have recorded. Always in the past we have seen him meet politeness with politeness.

Our data obviously left something to be desired. How could we improve our observer's efforts to locate the politeness gesture correctly in reference to the personality in question?

THE PERSONALITY AS A SYSTEM

Our observer may allow himself to be guided by the thought that the personality is a going concern which is constantly relating itself as a whole to the environment in which it is living.

To say that a personality is a going concern means that we expect it to act in such a way as to maintain a certain degree of internal consistency among its parts. We expect it to display the characteristics of a system—if one part of the whole is changed, substitutive changes occur among the other parts of the whole. This means that a person may be accustomed to receive a great deal of indulgence from authority, and to maintain this indulgence —if it diminishes—by withholding indulgence from authority until authority again becomes indulgent. It is quite thinkable to our observer that something like the following may account for the unexpected response of the subject to authority :

Our subject may have expected to receive a gift from his father on every occasion when his father is away from home. For the first time since he can remember his father was away from home and no gift came. He had an impulse to withdraw indulgence from his father, by pouting, for example. But father was out of reach. At this point the child goes to school and receives the polite greeting from another authority, the teacher. Our observer sees that the child responds by making a sketchy gesture that constitutes a deprivation of the teacher.

As we said, our observer did not see the hypothetical events to which these words refer. He is quite prepared to regard such a sequence as plausible because he is thinking of the personality as a system. If certain expectations are not fulfilled by the environment during a given period of time, he expects that the personality will exhibit substitutive activities. The substitutive activities, the observer predicts, will be in the direction of restoring the level of expectation which is usual for the person. We understand the personality if we are able to demonstrate, during any period of time, which changes occur in the personality if there is a change in any part of it. Our observer would have understood the child if he had known what change in its expectations of indulgence would be followed by what substitutive changes.

It is plain that our observer was not using the method of observing the child which provided him with the data which he most needed for understanding the personality of the child. Our observer saw the child in a single situation—one which involved certain subordinate and superordinate relations. He made a great many observations in situations in which the child participated. But he was not prepared for the sudden appearance of impoliteness in relation to the politeness of the teacher.

Our observer may alter his procedure. He may try to understand the personality as a system, not by stationing himself at one vantage point through a long period of time, but rather, by focusing his attention upon all the activity of his subject over shorter time periods.

For this scrutiny of the career line as a whole through a given cross-section, he may choose some recurring cycle, like days, or weeks, or menstrual periods. The events of each full cycle period he may describe by means of a fixed list of terms (variables). Each term (variable) refers to some part of the whole pattern of events. The observer has achieved formal completeness when he can correctly state the changes in all the variables which occur upon a given change in the magnitude of any one of them. When he has found the pattern of intervariable relationship which is maintained, promptly re-approximated after interference, he has found the " dynamic equilibrium " of the system.

The technical problem of our observer is to discover the terms and the indices (measures), which will enable him to execute this programme. Students of personality and of social science are still groping after satisfactory terms and procedures. The mathematical and statistical problems involved are already exemplified in several fields of science ; but the sticking point among psychologists and social scientists has been the task of finding categories and procedures which are appropriate for the specific event manifolds with which they are concerned.

THE RESISTANCE TO " SYSTEMIC " ANALYSIS

To some extent, there has been resistence against this mode of conceiving the task of students of personality and culture. It may be worth while to say something about the methodological situation in this respect.

A sterling example of the successful use of the equilibrium

pattern of thought in the sciences is furnished by the work of L. J. Henderson and associates upon the blood as a physico-chemical system.[13] Henderson has been an enthusiastic exponent of this methodological standpoint for the psychological and sociological sciences. He was deeply impressed by the sociological system of Vilfredo Pareto, then went out of his way to bring it to the attention of scientists and laymen in this country.[14] Henderson's influence on the study of personality is explicitly acknowledged by Henry A. Murray and associates at Harvard.[15]

The formal pattern of thought which is needed in equilibrium analysis is congenial to anyone trained in the calculus of variations. But it should be remembered that the dominant methodological tradition in social science has favoured a different mode of thought. At the risk of seeming to stigmatize this mode of thought in advance, we may speak of it as the " one factor—one result " pattern of analysis. This pattern of thinking does not disregard the multiplicity of factors which operate in psychological and sociological relationships. But it specifies that the goal of analysis is the discovery of the necessary factor which determines a given outcome. John Stuart Mill's logic helped to standardize this mode of thought, especially when it was generalized for the field of sociology by Émile Durkheim.[16]

An interesting re-application of Durkheim is found in the work of the influential French sociologist, François Simiand.[17] Simiand was committed to the " one factor—one result " goal of sociological research. But he insists upon the importance of conducting research upon évent series which are found in a given cultural setting. Simiand took the fluctuation of wages in France as his problem. He made a long list of factors which might conceivably affect this variable. He abstained from hypotheses—except in so far as the choice of a factor implied the expectation that it might be important. In abstaining from hypotheses he paralleled the logic of many other multiple-factor studies. Simiand then analysed the wage data with reference to each variable in turn.

[13] Henderson, Lawrence J., *Blood: A Study in General Physiology* (New Haven, 1928) ; and *Pareto's General Sociology: A Physiologist's Interpretation* (Cambridge, Mass., 1935).
[14] Pareto, Vilfredo, *The Mind and Society* (London, 1935).
[15] Murray, Henry A. (ed.), *Explorations in Personality: A Clinical and Experimental Study of Fifty Men of College Age* (New York, 1938).
[16] Durkheim, Émile, *The Rules of Sociological Method* [8th ed., translated by Sarah A. Solovay and John H. Mueller, and edited by George E. G. Catlin] (Chicago, 1938).
[17] Simiand, François, *Le salaire: l'évolution sociale et la monnaie; essai de théorie expérimentale du salaire, introduction et étude globale* (Paris, 1932).

Ultimately he arrived at what he considered to be the critical factor which accounted for wage fluctuations.

It is not wholly correct to say that resistance to the " systemic " approach among some social scientists is to be attributed to their lack of knowledge of the calculus. Many psychologists who are well equipped mathematically have gone ahead for years with a " non-systemic " approach. They have operated with variables, but they have not undertaken to select a list in terms of which they could describe the fluctuations of the whole personality in relation to the environment. The essential point about the " systemic " pattern of analysis is not that it uses variables, but that it chooses a list whose interrelations are studied with regard to fluctuations in the environment.

Biologists are the scientists who have found it most useful to think " systematically ". L. J. Henderson derives from Claude Bernard, and a physiologist like Walter B. Cannon easily puts his researches into the " systemic " framework.[18]

In this respect biologists differ from physicists, who are able to carry on successful work with no selective conception of an " organic pattern " which maintains itself in an environment. Whatever may be the forms of thought which aid in the exploration of cosmic evolution, or which explore the " individuality " of certain sub-atomic forms, the prevalent physics is " non-organismic ". These non-systemic traits of physics are particularly prominent in elementary physics, and elementary physics is often the only physics which enters at any time into the training of future social and psychological scientists. Physics seems to operate with a list of variables which can be treated as dependent or independent at the convenience of the experimenter. The picture of scientific method which is obtained by those who learn physics—chiefly elementary physics—is " non-organismic ". When they undertake to apply quantitative procedures to psychological and social events, they expect to operate with much the same freedom in the handling of variables as the physicist.

In appraising the resistance which " systemic " patterns have often encountered, we should not overlook the sterility with which they have often been associated. Pareto was both pretentious and sententious. And if his sociological system made a clear programmatic statement of the advantages of an " equilibrium " approach, it should not be forgotten that it furnished a clear example of failure to achieve definitive results by its application.

[18] Cannon, Walter B., *The Wisdom of the Body* (New York and London, 1932).

There has been no dearth of " systemic " proposals for a science of personality and of culture. The difficulty has been the inadequacy of the specific categories and modes of observation with which these proposals have been associated. Meanwhile, science seemed to be growing by the discovery and exploration of new standpoints, and by the discovery of interpart relations independent of explicit modes of describing " wholeness ".

The " organismic " vocabularies have encountered stout resistance in some quarters on political grounds. " Organic " metaphors were part of the language of the conservative movements that came in the wake of the French revolutionary epoch. Respect for the " organic " was supposed to defeat the claims of reason, and to disparage the " rationalism " of eighteenth century reformers and revolutionists. Organismic analogies have been abundant in the thinking of modern anti-individualists like Othmar Spann. It is characteristic of many Protestant thinkers that they are suspicious of " organic " phrases on account of the frequency with which these phrases have been used by Catholic theologians. It is not one of the least distinctive achievements of Whitehead that he has lifted the conception of the organic from the battle-scarred phraseology of preceding centuries.

If our period in history is one in which the individual is in at least temporary eclipse in the presence of collective demands, we may predict the further diffusion of " systemic " methods of thought. This diffusion may have nothing to do with technical superiority. The popularity of categories of wholeness may be a means by which the harassed and insecure individual minimizes some of his insecurities by identifying with the whole. Preoccupation with the whole, familiarity with ideas of the whole— these are possible means of seeking to abate the anxieties bred of the instabilities of our epoch.

To call attention to these possibilities is not to stigmatize, nor to endorse, the use of systemic ideas. It is to suggest how our own intellectual processes can be related to the context in which they operate. If we obtain insight into the factors which dispose us to accept, or to reject, a certain pattern of thought on non-rational grounds, we may be better prepared to accept or reject the pattern on rational (technical) grounds.

Observing the Whole Personality

We left our observer confronting his task of personality analysis, intent upon finding the most economical ways of discovering the interrelationship of traits under various environmental conditions. We left him dissatisfied with the results of observing a trait in one recurring situation, because he saw that he had no means of exposing the systemic activities of the personality as a whole.

The chief difficulty in this programme of total observation is how to station the observer in relation to the whole gamut of events. Direct observation of the activity cycle is only possible with adults or adolescents when they are confined to very circumscribed situations—penitentiaries, hospitals, boarding schools—or when the participant observer is in a very intimate relationship to the subject—an inseparable companion.. Indirect observation is possible if subjects are willing to make diary notes of how they spend their time.[19]

Each of these observational standpoints has distinctive possibilities and limitations. And one common limitation is that the subject who is being observed may not be exposed to a sufficiently wide range of environmental changes during the cycle of study to reveal many of the important facts of trait interrelationship. It is always possible, of course, that we happen to be observing somebody who loses his dearest friend and makes a suicidal attempt ; or we may be on hand to see how a man takes a great political or business victory. But there is some " waste " in observing many persons who do not happen to be subjected to the shifts in the environment whose effects we want to study.

A solution of this difficulty readily springs to mind in this experimental age. Subject the personality to a gamut of environmental changes of the kind which we want to study ! But there are practical limitations in the path of such a procedure. It is not feasible to arrange an accident in order to crush the leg of a subject, and to see how he responds to this form of deprivation. It is also difficult to arrange for the sudden advancement of a subject in order to study the response to such indulgence.

The experimental approach is not entirely hopeless, of course, but it quickly tends to move over into a test situation. The test situation requires validation, while the experiment does not. The test is an economical change in the environment of a subject which is supposed to be the equivalent of changes in the natural environment to which that subject is exposed. This equivalence

[19] One of the most recent uses of this method of indirect observation is by Sorokin, Pitirim, and Berger, Clarence Q., *Time-Budgets of Human Behaviour* (Cambridge, Mass., 1939).

must be demonstrated by comparing test with non-test data. An important example of what may be done experimentally is the Western Electric experiment under the auspices of Elton Mayo, T. N. Whitehead, and associates.[20] The work situation was systematically varied. One of the ideal, though scarcely attainable, methods of validating a personality test would be to examine the responses of the same person as he passes through cycles of deprivation and indulgence.

THE CULTURE AS A SYSTEM

Our observer has been engaged in the task of placing the politeness trait with reference to personality. When he undertakes to locate the trait with reference to culture, his problem is similar, but the relevant context of events is larger. It is necessary to show the position of the culture as a whole with respect to other cultures in its environment.

Suppose that our observer finds that the culture which he is studying is going through a period of humiliation at the hands of all surrounding cultures.

Observations on politeness gestures between subordinate and superordinate now take on new relevance. Suppose that our observer found that politeness was declining during the period of his studies. Subordinates were becoming less respectful of authority, and authority, in turn, was growing suspicious of disloyalty and supersensitive to criticism. The provisional picture seen by our observer is something like this, then : culture A has been subjected to deprivation at the hands of other cultures, but the authorities of A, feeling weak, have done nothing about it ; this has weakened the deference given to authority, and in turn diminished the indulgence shown by authority to subordinates. Broadly speaking, the culture has responded to deprivation, not by acting upon the outside environment, but by acting upon itself. In the situation referred to, the authority-subordinate relationships have been sharply reduced in number and in mutual indulgence. Study may show that more people spend more time out of contact with others (indulging in private fantasies stimulated by the increased use of opium, for example).

By studying the fluctuations of a given culture we may discover the interrelationship among its component traits. In our symbolic statement, we treat the A of the culture as a function

[20] Whitehead, T. N., *The Industrial Worker : A Statistical Study of Human Relations in a Group of Manual Workers* (Cambridge, Mass., 1938).

of *EP*. We may choose cycles for investigation—from victory to victory, or from defeat to defeat in war, for instance. None of our cycles will be conditioned by the succession of biological phases, as are the cycles along the career line of the individual. Many efforts have been made to speak of biological phases of cultures, of young and old cultures, but no one has demonstrated a recurring series of patterns comparable with the recurring series along the career line of the individual from birth to death.[21] A culture appears and disappears ; but the succession of patterns does not display the regularity and irreversibility of the phases through which the individual passes.

Without pursuing the subject much further, an additional remark may not be out of place in this connection. The idea that the career line of the individual is composed of an irreversible succession of patterns has been very helpful because of its " obviousness ", an " obviousness " which has been conspicuously lacking in regard to culture histories. But " obviousness " is becoming less and less as the control of the environment is perfected. In experimental embryology we see that more and more processes are reversible. By reversibility is meant the capacity to resume a state congruent with a former state. Tissues may be permitted to differentiate in the direction of one pattern, then shifted toward another pattern, and ultimately brought back to the initial direction. There are limitations upon this procedure, to be sure ; but these limitations are fewer and fewer. It is no longer a paradox to say that we have less " heredity " than we used to have.

From the comparative study of culture we expect to learn how different cultures interact with their cultural environments. And from the comparative study of personality we expect to find how different personalities meet their personal environments.

If we want to think " systemically " of culture or personality, how may we proceed ? Suppose we explore the following line of thought : During any given period, any personality or culture tends to maintain a certain pattern of subjective events. This is the " dynamic equilibrium " of the whole, and it is evidenced by the tendency toward prompt restoration of the pattern when it is subjected to interference.

Consider the act which puzzled our observer, the sudden

[21] The most elaborate treatment of the subject of cycles in history is found in some of the publications of Pitirim Sorokin. Sorokin, Pitirim, *Social and Cultural Dynamics* (New York, 1937–41). See vol. 2.

appearance of impoliteness. He tried to make it more intelligible by allowing for such possibilities as these : The impoliteness toward the teacher was a displacement of hostility which was originally directed toward the father, but which could not express itself against an absent father, who had neglected to send an anticipated gift.

Careful study of the child during daily—or other—cycles might reveal the following characteristic pattern : The child entertains high expectations from authority, and if these are not fulfilled, the child feels somewhat resentful and withholds some indulgence from authority. If, on the contrary, expectations are fulfilled, the child promptly evolves a new set of high expectations until authority fails to come through. Then the resentful-aloofness-pattern makes its appearance. Investigation may show that the person spends about the same time every day being a little injured and a little aloof from authority. It is the tenacity with which this pattern maintains itself, despite many changes in the environment, that shows that it is part of the pattern of dynamic equilibrium characteristic of this personality.

The pattern which we have been describing may involve everybody, whether authority objects, or colleagues or subordinates. In extreme instances the cycle may occur repeatedly with everyone : large expectations are evolved until they are unfulfilled, followed by resentfulness and aloofness.

The study of personality may be expected to disclose the presence of many different patterns. From general experience we are more or less acutely aware of some of the more extreme forms. There is the enthusiast, the person who maintains a state of incessant enthusiasm about the self and others, despite adverse environmental factors. There is the detachment pattern, whose distinguishing mark is the restoration as promptly as possible of subjective states free of vivid love, enthusiasm or anger.

Ruth Benedict has classified cultures on the basis of the characteristic subjective event which they tend to maintain in the lives of those who are exposed to the culture. In her classification, the Pueblo Indians are Apollonian : they avoid intense subjective states. The Plains Indians are Dionysian : they facilitate intense subjective states.

The formal ideal of research on the dynamic equilibrium of personality and culture remains the same : To explore the interrelations of equilibrium patterns. Freud's bold speculation about the " life and death instincts " is an equilibrium pattern for the

career line as a whole.   The existing data are far too fragmentary
to confirm or to disconfirm such inclusive ideas.

GENERAL CATEGORIES

What general categories are useful in personality study ?

We may profitably distinguish between internalized and
externalized acts.   *An act is externalized when it involves the environment* as it runs to completion.   *When the environment is not involved,
the act is internalized.*   Through a given period, the acts of a person
or a culture involve measurable degrees of internalization and
externalization.

The person who sits alone and thinks is internalized during
that period.   The person who is greeting other persons is externalizing.   Those who bear a given culture may withdraw from
contact with neighbouring cultures by physical migration or
non-intercourse.   Acts are collectively externalized within a
culture when individuals act in concert upon other individuals—
in a business enterprise, a political party, for example.   When
individuals act in concert upon themselves, acts are collectively
internalized within the culture—in a sect which devotes itself to
secret rites.

We have already had occasion to speak of acts as destructive
when they endanger the wholeness of a personality or a culture.
Suicide is the extreme form of internalized destructiveness.   But
there are self-destructive acts short of suicide, such as drug
addiction.   Many bodily diseases are " functional " in origin and
belong to the self-destructive reactions.[22]   Other destructive
internalizations are moods and fantasies irrelevant to reality,
autistic reactions.   Collective autism occurs when there is collective participation in the encouragement of fantasy, as in some
forms of the peyote cult.   The ceremonies of the cult consist in
chewing a plant, thus stimulating visions which are later communicated.[23]   A more extreme example of collective autism is
the observance of a lifetime vow of silence by Trappist monks.

The categories of indulgence and deprivation have already
been introduced.

Studies of culture from the standpoint outlined here have

[22] A convenient handbook of the experimental work on mind-body relations is
that of Dunbar, H. Flanders, *Emotions and Bodily Changes.   A Survey of Literature on
Psychosomatic Interrelationships, 1910–1933* (Second Edition with Supplementary Introduction and Additional Bibliography) (New York, 1938).

[23] La Barre, Weston, *The Peyote Cult* (New Haven, 1938) ;   and Lasswell,
Harold D., " Religious Cult as an Internalized Response to Deprivation ", *Zeitschrift
üfr Sozialforschung*, vol. 4 (1935).

begun, and many existing studies are partially relevant. The most explicit published research is that of Philleo Nash on revivalism among the Klamath Indians.[24] Revivalistic movements were studied in three groups, and the distinguishing characteristics of the different movements were accounted for by referring to the degrees of deprivations and indulgences to which the groups had been exposed, and the antecedent state of cultural predisposition. The sequence of events was established from historical records and from living informants.

A comparative study of three modern nationalistic movements has been made from this point of view, but the findings are not yet available in English. Dinko Tomasic studied nationalistic movements during the same period in Serbia, Croatia and Slovenia.

A general theory of response to economic indulgence—prosperity—and deprivation—depression—was stated by the present writer in Chapter VII of his *World Politics and Personal Insecurity*.[25] (Douglas Waples has considered the bearing upon these hypotheses of data about reading habits in *People and Print*.[26]) This book also presented some preliminary formulations relevant to the rise and fall of élite.

These allusions are intended only to indicate that a body of specialists are finding it convenient to work with similar categories for the statement of their problems and the communication of results. Terminological parallelism is, as we have repeatedly had occasion to say, far less important than inclusiveness of formulation from any specified standpoint. We have deliberately used terms to refer to the whole observational field of the observer, and equivalent terms are usually in the vocabulary of an observer who is accustomed to think of his field " as a whole ". The " part reference words " are more readily understood when they are arranged with explicit relationship to " whole reference words ".

There has been an increasing tendency to use a language of wholeness in many fields. Quite often the change comes by the redefinition of a vocabulary that was once restricted to part-ness as distinguished from wholeness. To choose but a single example,

[24] Nash, Philleo, " The Place of Religious Revivalism in the Formation of the Intercultural Community on Klamath Reservation ". Eggan, Fred (ed.), *Social Anthropology of North American Tribes* (Chicago, 1937).
[25] Lasswell, Harold D., *World Politics and Personal Insecurity* (New York and London, 1935).
[26] Waples, Douglas, *People and Print* (Chicago, 1938).

the language of stimulus-response has been thoroughly overhauled by Clark Hull and his collaborators at the Yale Institute of Human Relations.[27]

Another example is the spread among psychologists and social psychologists of categories connected with topological and " Gestalt " psychology. It came as a distinct revelation to many psychological and sociological workers that there could be " non-quantitative " categories employed in the name of the most rigorous of all the traditional sciences—mathematics. This is one of the factors in the extraordinary release of creative insight which has frequently accompanied the discovery of topology. Some experimenters who were unaccustomed to allow themselves to think freely about total contexts were genuinely emancipated. Formerly they studied only what they could be very precise about. They used words whose frames of reference they defined very carefully : there were exact measures specified for the limited aspects of the environment of the animal that were called " stimuli ", and of the limited aspects of the animal that were called " responses ". Topology supplied these experimenters with language—properly sanctioned as mathematical—for thinking about the relevant wholes—the context—in which they were making observations. It was now possible to use words like " field " and " barrier "—and to draw diagrammatical representations. New experimental insights have arisen as a result of this new freedom in using words of reference to a whole—the whole that was formerly treated as the vague sum of all the parts, if you ever got around to adding them all up. Quite apart from any other advantages or disadvantages, Kurt Lewin has performed this valuable function by his topological emphasis.[28] For many special students of perception, the equivalent release came through the earlier Gestalt psychology.

How to Observe Changing Developments

We are in an earthbound universe of interpersonal events. Like the students of wind and ocean, we need a network of observation stations over the face of the earth. Like the student of vulcanism, and of the emergence and subsidence of continental blocs, we need large-scale organizations equipped to gather inclusive data. Like the student of the morphology of landscape,

[27] Dollard, John, and others, *Frustration and Aggression* (London, 1944).
[28] Lewin, Kurt, *Principles of Topological Psychology* (New York, 1936).

the physiographer, we need observers and mappers of on-going processes. Like the student of plant and animal ecology, we need to spot the distribution and succession of many forms of life in time and space.

The planned observation of the emerging future is one of the tasks of science. Important data are irrevocably lost unless they are collected by contemporary observers of events. Wise planning is needed if well-equipped observers are to be stationed around the world to make proper use of the latest and best tools of scientific observation. When the observation of the emerging future is provided for, we may expect to follow world developments with greater insight and to obtain data which confirm or disconfirm our basic theories. Although most of the data will be non-experimental, we can arrange in advance for the experimental control of at least a few situations.

As students of personality and culture, we are professionally concerned with the changing interrelationships of personality and culture through time. This calls for systematic world-wide observation. Already mankind is partially organized for systematic self-observation. Every modern state has extensive census agencies for the gathering of social facts, and one of our special functions as social scientists is to contribute to the steady improvement of official and unofficial observation and analysis.

At the present time the gap between what we need for scientific purposes and what we have is enormous. Whenever the social scientist looks into any standard yearbook, like the *Statesman's Yearbook*, he is reminded of the great discrepancy between what he needs to know and what is readily available. Most of the yearbooks have not yet begun to make use of many of the modern devices for the meaningful presentation of data. Even atlas-makers have stayed close to conservative ways—with the ever-stimulating exception of Otto Neurath.[29]

In exploring culture and personality, we can divide culture into *situations*, and we can study the way *persons* are related to these situations. *Personality* is revealed when we study all of the situations in which specific persons are placed during given cross-sections of their career-lines. We can describe *culture* only when the data are in about the component situations of the culture,

[29] Neurath, Otto, *Gesellschaft und Wirtschaft, bildstatistisches Elementarwerk ; das Gesellschafts-und Wirtschaftsmuseum in Wien zeigt in 100 farbigen Bildtafeln Produktions-formen, Gesellschaftsordnungen, Kulturstufen, Lebenshaltungen* (Leipsic, 1930).

and about the surrounding cultural environment.[30]   Some of our observations on persons may relate the persons to a number of situations, and yet provide us with inadequate information about personality.   It is necessary to follow the same person through his whole gamut of exposure to situations before we have described personality.

It is evident that there are several different though interrelated starting points for exploring the manifold of events which comprise personality and culture.   We may enumerate the patterns found in specific situations.   We may start with persons who share a common characteristic, like age or sex, and enumerate all of the situations in which such persons are found.   We may begin with specific persons, and examine all of the situations in which they function.   Each set of observations is potentially related to those which are made from any other starting point. Observers who study the third form situation are providing us with some of the data for studying, for example, the situations in which all of the twelve-year-olds of a given culture are found. And some of the data can be related to the context of personal relationships which involve particular persons, and thus reveal their personalities.   By relating the third form situations to the other situations of the culture, and of the environemnt of the culture, we contribute to the understanding of the culture as a whole.   No matter what our point of departure, we may illuminate the entire manifold of events, if we bring all of our data into the proper interrelationship.

Any cross-section which it is convenient to use in observing culture and personality is somewhat protracted.   The Lynds were in direct contact with Middletown for several months and most of the studies which have been made of primitive societies have required months or years.   When the time interval is rather long, it is possible to discover *developmental profiles* within the period.

Assume that our observer chooses a two-year period for observational purposes.   During this period many profiles will have altered.   The *situation profile* of the third form, for example, may change in at least a few respects.   Third form pupils may pay more attention during the second year to contemporary events,

---

[30] The term " *society* " may be used to include the members of the " aggregate " composing a " group ", plus their " culture " ; the term " *individuality* " may be employed to refer to an " *individual* " who has become a " person ", plus the patterns constituting his " personality ".

and they may be less submissive to their teachers. By comparing the two third form profiles, we arrive at the *developmental profile of the situation.*

During the same two-year interval, the *person-to-situation* profiles may have changed. There may be a smaller proportion of the community's twelve-year-old youngsters in the third form during the second year than the first. By examining the contrast in the total range of situations in which the twelve-year-old group operates, we have the *developmental profile of the person-to-situation* relationship. If data are collected for the same individuals, and their personality profiles described, we have the *developmental profile of personality.* By viewing the totality of relationships which constitute culture, and the environing cultures, we have the *developmental profile of the culture.*

The data not only establish developmental relationships ; they also have an important bearing on all our theories about the relationship of activity A, to environment E, and to predisposition P. It may be possible to relate the change in self-confidence and aggressiveness which is noted in the second year of the study to the presence of a more indulgent environment, and to the growth of self-confidence and aggressiveness during the first year of the study. The growth during the first year is called a " predisposition " with respect to the environment during the second year. The data gathered by our observers have a double relevance therefore : they bear upon developmental patterns and upon equilibrium patterns of relationship.

We may undertake to expose one of the most complicated profiles of development, namely, that which concerns *personal position.* We saw how third-form pupils—or twelve-year-olds— in the first half of the two-year period differed from the third form pupils—or twelve-year-olds—of the second half of the period. Can we determine at the beginning of the third form period which person will probably occupy which position in the distribution of personal traits at the end of the sixth form? For example, can we examine the least aggressive tenth at the start of the third form and determine what their relative position will be at the end of the sixth form, assuming a specified environment during the third form ? The same question can be asked for *personality position* among the personal positions.

For several purposes it is convenient to arrange data in sequences in which the groups which follow one another in time are composed of different persons :

First Year	Second Year
FOURTH FORM	FOURTH FORM
THIRD FORM	THIRD FORM
SECOND FORM	SECOND FORM

For other purposes it is convenient to arrange the data in sequences in which the groups which succeed one another are composed of the same persons :

First Year	Second Year
THIRD FORM	FOURTH FORM
SECOND FORM	THIRD FORM
FIRST FORM	SECOND FORM

The second plan of arrangement may be called the " *inter-lapping* " *method* to distinguish it from certain overlapping methods of arranging data which do not follow precisely this selective principle.[31]   If we plan our observations so that they fall readily into the interlapping method, we can summarize longer profiles of development than when we use the first plan.

THE INTERLAPPING METHOD OF OBSERVATION

The interlapping method of observation is by no means restricted to the study of school situations or of age groupings. Suppose the civil service of the community is divided into fifteen classifications. We can apply the method of interlapping observation to the study of the interrelationships which are found within, and among, these several classifications. As students of inter-personal relations, we should like to be able to say which persons, e.g., who enter class 1, or who act in certain ways during their period of service in class 1, will act in a predictable way in class 2. The entire profile of development can be summarized by the interlapping method during a two-year cycle of observation. Observers can follow persons during the first year who are in rank 1, and who pass to rank 2, at the same time that another group is being observed which passes through ranks 2 and 3. Since the change from one civil service classification to another does not always follow a regular chronological sequence, many of the data gathered in a two-year cycle of observation would not bear directly on the developmental problem to which we have referred. Many persons may stay in the first rank for five years, in the second rank for six years, and so on. The same problem is well known in the study of school forms, since some children

[31] Lasswell, Harold D., " The Method of Interlapping Observations in the Study of Personality in Culture ", *J. Abnormal and Social Psychol.* (1937).

remain in the same form for more than one year. In order to get most satisfactory results in the study of the civil service, we may need to work with a basic cycle that is longer than two years. But if the two-year cycle is chosen, the data will illuminate at least some developmental sequences. Thus we are interested in following the changes of experience from year to year in each classification of the service. There is a widespread impression that originality and zeal diminish with experience, and these relationships can be explored to advantage by means of the method of interlapping observation.

In general, we may say that the events which are suitable for the use of the method of interlapping observation are those which pass through easily identifiable and regular phases—and all phases are always exemplified by many examples.

There are many organized activities in society which answer to these general requirements. The civil services of government are in some ways less amenable to study by the method of interlapping observation than the armed forces.

Family situations are suitable for study by the method of interlapping observation. Children are passing from the status of the only child to the eldest child of two, to the eldest child of three . . . and so on. Parents are passing from the status of providing a home and support for children to the status of providing a home and support for more children, or fewer children . . . and so on through an infinity of possibilities which are potentially relevant to the study of culture and personality.

Persons are constantly changing their income classification in society. Many persons are rising or falling in deference—passing from one social class to another. Persons are rising or falling in safety—passing from peaceful civilian life to civilian life in a beleaguered city, or vice versa.

States are constantly rising or falling in influence in the world balance of influence. Other institutions—churches, businesses, colleges, hospitals—are passing up and down in the scale of influence. These changes are less amenable to fruitful study by the method of interlapping observation because the change in influence does not follow prearranged phases.

For the same reason communities lend themselves less readily to interlapping studies. Yet villages are always passing from a few hundred to a few thousand people, while towns are dropping from a few thousand to a few hundred. Brunner and Lorge have made observations on a large number of rural communities in

America over intervals of about ten years.[32]   Some of the data are no doubt amenable to treatment by an interlapping procedure over twenty-year cycles.   The categories could be set up, not simply in terms of population, but of more or less prosperity, more or less cultural homogeneity in the population, and the like.   The Lynds have made two observations on a middle-sized western manufacturing community.   If similar investigations were conducted simultaneously in other urban areas, we would greatly enhance the value of each inquiry.   For the future we might select a number of towns and cities in all the continents, and follow them at five- or ten-year cross-sections.   Serial data are already at hand for some communities.   Peking, China, for instance was surveyed by the Sociology Department of Yenching University.[33]

It is abundantly evident from the foregoing that the time-interval of culture and personality studies is subject to much expansion or contraction to fit the emerging expediencies of the problems in hand.   The method of interlapping observation, while not universally applicable, can be adapted to the study of many more problems than those to which it has been applied in the past.

If we try to extend our observations backward in time there are kinds of data which for ever elude us.   We cannot hope to psychoanalyse Napoleon, nor to watch the psychogalvanic reactions of Brutus to Julius Cæsar.   Some data require contemporary observation of events ; and we must carefully plan in advance if we are to have competent observers on the spot.

What are the cross-sections which lend themselves to the study of different problems of culture and personality ?   We spoke of extending our cross-sections forward and backward in time.   But the sheer magnitude of the potential field of personality and cultural events is overwhelming.   Some data can be obtained by total enumeration through time, like bank clearings.   But other data are less amenable to total enumeration and serialization.

THE WORLD SURVEY OF INFLUENCE

There is still a great deal of uncertainty about the sampling procedure which is best adapted to the study of world changes

---

[32] Brunner, Edmund de S., and Lorge, Irving, *Rural Trends in Depression Years : A Survey of Village Centred Agricultural Communities, 1930-36* (New York, 1937).

[33] Published in Series C of the publications in Sociology and Social Work of Yenching University.

in influence. Some important indices of influence are abundant for modern states. Income stratifications are fairly well known, but stratification by deference, or stratification by personality form, are inadequately known, and such data as exist are of varying degrees of adequacy and reliability.

Under these circumstances it seems wise to set up some provisional goals of comparative research. The present writer has suggested that we undertake to build up the best possible picture of the distribution of influence throughout the world at five-year intervals. Several scholars have voluntarily agreed to adopt this procedure wherever convenient.

Our knowledge of the main sequences of influence throughout the world is rapidly being improved by modern research. Karl A. Wittfogel has recently completed an elaborate investigation of the social origins of the Chinese bureaucracy during several centuries. Preliminary contributions are published in the *Zeitschrift für Sozialforschung* from time to time. There were many valuable studies of social and economic stratification in pre-National Socialist Germany by Emil Lederer, Theodor Geiger, and many other economists, sociologists and political scientists. Among all nations, however, the most exhaustive work appears to have been done by Scandinavian scholars on Scandinavian sources. A mine of information about the distribution of influence in the past is found in Gaetano Mosca's classical work on *The Ruling Class*.[34] Abundant material is in the encyclopædic contributions of Vilfredo Pareto, Pitirim Sorokin, and William G. Sumner.

We may consider world politics with reference to the rise and fall of skill groups, but the "sociology of the professions" and of other skill groups is of relatively recent origin. The existing state of knowledge may be conveniently appraised by examining the work of A.M. Carr-Saunders.[35] There is a growing body of data upon the social origins, the economic position, the prestige and the activities of the teaching profession. Some other exploratory studies have been made of the social attitudes of boards of education, and of the social origins and affiliations of these boards in different communities.[36] Outside pressures of organized groups upon the schools have been treated in several mono-

---

[34] Mosca, Gaetano, *The Ruling Class (Elementi di Scienza Politica)* (New York, 1939).
[35] Carr-Saunders, A. M., and Wilson, P. A., *The Professions* (Oxford, 1933).
[36] A representative monograph on the activities of the teachers themselves is Selle, Erwin, *The Organization and Activities of the National Education Association:. A Case Study in Educational Sociology* (New York, 1932).

graphs.[37] As a general criticism, it may be said that most of these researches, valuable as they are, fall short of placing the school firmly in the framework of the chief stratifications of the community. There are many questions connected with the effects of upper- and lower-class teachers upon upper- and lower-class pupils which have yet to be subjected to methodical study.

The study of the changing influence of skill is newer than the study of class changes. The powerful effect of Marxist sociology is everywhere discernible in this sphere, since it was Marx who first set up, and made influential, political analysis in terms of class successions. Because of the prominence given to class, and to the world revolutionary sequence, it may not be amiss to give a little more attention to these potentialities.

"The analysis of world politics . . . implies the consideration of the shape and composition of the value patterns of mankind as a whole. This necessitates the comparison of world élites in terms of social origins, special skills, personality traits, subjective attitudes, and sustaining assets, such as symbols, goods, and violence. Attention is particularly aroused by any fundamental change in the characteristics and methods of élites. A *revolution* is rapid and extensive change in the composition and the vocabulary of the ruling few; *world revolutions* are those which inaugurate new principles of élite recruitment and new reigning ideologies in the political life of humanity.

No doubt the French and Russian revolutions were major innovations in the world history of rulers and ruling symbols, although we may entertain some reservations on our judgment when we remember the extent to which we are saturated in the details of European history, and the meagreness of our information about oriental, "primitive", and ancient peoples.

If the significant political changes of the past were signalized by revolutionary patterns which rose and spread until they were blocked or superseded by new revolutionary innovations, the future may follow the same course of development. Hence our " present " would be transition between the latest and the impending world revolutionary emergent.

Correct self-orientation would therefore consist in discerning the principle of élite recruitment and the predominant symbols to appear in the next phases of world political change. Sound political analysis is nothing less than correct orientation in the continuum which embraces the past, present, and future. Unless the salient features of the all-inclusive whole are discerned, details will be incorrectly located. Without the symbol of the total context the symbols of detail cannot be data."[38]

[37] Notably, Beale, Howard, *Are American Teachers Free? An Analysis of Restraints upon the Freedom of Teaching in American Schools* (New York, 1936).
[38] Lasswell, H. D., *World Politics and Personal Insecurity* (New York and London, 1935), pp. 3-4.

"A great question mark in world politics then is this : . . . Regardless of local failures or concessions, will the trend of history be toward world union in the name of Communism ?

We are not wholly at a loss for objective ways of approaching this question. From one point of view it is a problem of diffusion and restriction, and such processes have been studied by several specialists in the social sciences. The most vigorous discussion of the technical issues involved is in the literature of students of comparative history and of primitive society. Some of their methods may profitably be applied to the understanding of the political events with which we are concerned.[39] Russia may be taken as the world centre from which a revolutionary pattern is spreading. Beyond the boundaries of the Soviet Union the Third International rises and falls in influence. Its geographical dispersion at any given time is the net result of the factors which affect the total process of diffusion and restriction. Our problem is to discover the relative strength of these factors, and in the light of the total world picture to evaluate the possibility of development toward inclusiveness.

World revolutionary waves are not unique in the history of modern civilization. Those who seized control in France at the end of the eighteenth century spoke in the name of all mankind, prophesied the age of reason, and demanded active support for the realization of the rights of man.

The world revolutionary waves of the past have come short of universality. The élite which seized power at the world revolutionary centre was restricted by the play of the balance of power.

Our judgment of the world-unifying potentialities of the Communist revolution depends upon the analysis of the relative strength of factors making for diffusion and restriction of world revolutionary initiatives.

Among the possibilities we may distinguish the following :

Total diffusion. The world beyond the boundaries of the Soviet Union may eventually adhere to the new order, and the new order may retain its revolutionary characteristics.

World unity with restrictions from within. The world adheres to the Soviet Union, but in the meantime the revolutionary characteristics of the centre are modified by the reactivation of older social patterns.

Restriction of the scope of the world revolutionary centre from without by the reactivation of older social patterns. One well-established pattern is loyalty to local regions (national territory) ; and nationalistic sentiment may be utilized to block the spread of control from Russia. This may be called restriction by geographical differentiation.

Restriction by partial incorporation. The restriction of the élite in control at the centre may proceed by incorporating some of the distinctive characteristics of the revolutionary pattern. Some incorporation may

---

[39] An important theoretical statement by Edward Sapir is "Time Perspective in Aboriginal American Culture, A Study in Method", *Geol. Survey of Canada, Memoir 70, Anthropological Series 13,* 1916. Useful discussions are found in the publications of Roland Dixon, Leslie Spier, Alfred Kroeber, Paul Radin, Bronislav Malinowski, Ralph Linton, Wilson Wallis.

be limited to symbols : " Socialist revolution ", " soldiers' and working-men's councils ".   Some may include practices : the monopolization of legality by a single political party, the governmentalization of organized social life.

Restriction by functional differentiation.   The restriction of the élite at the centre may involve the rejection of the claim of the élite to bear the true revolutionary burden, and a call for a new revolutionary initiative.

The understanding of the diffusion-restriction process calls for case studies of communities of different characteristics at varying distances from the centre of the world revolutionary wave." [40]

"It may be that world revolutionary waves themselves are one of the permanent as well as basic features of the western European pattern of civilization.   Before the Russian upheaval was the French upheaval ; both of them were marked by the cataclysmic emergence at a circumscribed centre of an élite which invoked new symbols to justify its control and new practices for the benefit of hitherto " under-privileged " class formations. . . .

If we decide to extrapolate the past into the future, we may add to our description of the world revolutionary waves as permanent features of western European civilization the following statement : the élite which seizes power at the eruptive centre of a new revolutionary movement does not succeed in unifying the world.   Another conspicu-ous feature of the western European pattern of civilization is the multiple state system, which is sustained by such symbolic formations as the demand for " sovereignty " and the expectation of violence. Most potent of all, the multiple state system is supported by national-istic sentiment. . . .   Thus it seems highly improbable that world unity will occur by the incorporation of all states within the U.S.S.R.

To predict that the scope of the élite which seizes power at a world centre will fall short of the world does not imply that all elements of what was called before " the world revolutionary pattern " will fall short of universal diffusion.   We must distinguish the *original* world revolutionary *pattern of the* revolutionary *centre* from the world revolu-tionary *pattern of the epoch*.   The first—the original centre pattern—is no doubt destined to be restricted ; the second—the epoch pattern —is moving toward universality among the major powers.

If we look back at the French case, we plainly see in the perspective of subsequent happenings that many of the innovations in symbol and practice which took place within the borders of France also appeared beyond France, without formal affiliation of the other states with the eruptive centre.   That is, practices concerning the relation-ship of governments to economic processes which favoured the rise of the bourgeoisie at the expense of the aristocracy became more and more universal during the nineteenth century, although the world remained separated into independent states.   The same may be said for a series of other practices—universal suffrage, supremacy of legisla-tures over executives—as well as for certain symbols " rights of man ".

[40] Lasswell, Harold D., and Blumenstock, Dorothy, *World Revolutionary Propaganda ; A Chicago Study* (New York, 1939), pp. 13-15.

In all of these cases the connection between them and the élite of the eruptive centre of revolution in France was severed. It is evident, too, that the most extreme features of the original revolutionary pattern did not persist, even in France.

What are the features of the Russian centre of world revolution which are also components of the world revolutionary pattern of our entire epoch? Perhaps one may attribute a predominant place to the *moderation of income differences* by the abolition of private ownership in the instrumentalities of production, unaccompanied by reinstatement of differences of the same magnitude within governmentally controlled enterprises. Possibly another pattern is the increasing *governmentalization of organized social life.* Another is the *predominance of a party with a privileged status.*" [41]

"No doubt the tendency to abolish unemployment—at least symbolically—will prove to be as universal as the tendency to moderate income differences." [42]

We can bring into the purview of our world studies the data from areas of primitive culture. Already some of the students of social anthropology have organized research in a way which fits neatly into the programme of world observation which is here outlined. Robert Redfield is studying a series of communities which it is planned to re-survey from time to time in the future. [43] Rough studies were made of the distribution of primitive traits in Lower Mexico and Guatemala.

Although most of the primitive cultures which lie dispersed over the face of the earth are of minor political importance in contemporary world politics, since they are under the domination of the superior technology of Western civilization, they should not be completely underestimated. The native Indians of Central and South America, and the native African tribes of that huge continent, are not entirely " passive " factors even at the present time. And studies of the diffusion of the dominant symbols and practices of the Great Powers cannot by any means ignore the primitive cultures. I encountered an Indian in a New Mexico pueblo who dreamed of going to Mexico where " the Indians really amounted to something ", so that some day he could join in introducing soviets all over the American continent.

The students of primitive culture have gone far enough in the study of the " remnant Cultures " for us to include them in the general programme of world observation which is here proposed. By bringing the world picture to the focus of attention of anthro-

[41] *Ibid.*, pp. 354-6.   [42] *Ibid.*, p. viii.
[43] Redfield, Robert, *Chan Kom, a Maya Village* (Washington, D.C., 1934); *Tepoztlan, a Mexican Village; A Study of Folk Life* (Chicago, 1930).

pologists, new questions will occur to them ; and new data—and even new hypotheses—may come to the social scientists who specialize upon the study of the Great Powers. Some of the primitive groups are still almost wholly isolated from the rest of mankind. But there is evidence that no primitive group is wholly without outside connections. This is the sense—no matter how tenuous—in which it is no romantic exaggeration to say that the present history of man is a common enterprise.

In connection with the contact of Western civilization and other cultures, there are many opportunities for study within the boundaries of the United States. There are still remnants of the Indian cultures which were vanquished in the struggle for the control of this continent, and in some cases it is not too late to gather data of unusual importance for the understanding of personality and culture. The schools which are operated by the Department of the Interior are excellent vantage points for the pursuit of these investigations. How can the world-view of our Western civilization—and its accompanying techniques—be communicated to the carriers of the surviving cultures in a way that simplifies, rather than complicates, the problem of transition ? Some of these cultures provide children with a view of the world that is strongly reminiscent of the dominant outlook which pre- vailed in Europe until the Enlightenment. The boundary between " being alive " and " being dead " is not nearly as sharp as modern scientific knowledge has tended to make it. The supernatural influences are less remote than in our modern world- view. There is a more active sense of kinship with many forms of life. We know from the gory history of Europe the difficulties which arise as the new scientific method of thought, coupled with technology, comes in contact with pre-scientific views of the world. It seems probable that more work is being done on the problem of managing these transitions in the Soviet Union than anywhere else in the world. But many opportunities survive for funda- mental research on culture and personality.

Social Areas

We may think of the different kinds of data we need in terms of different geographical distributions. There are different kinds of *psychological* (*symbolic*) *areas*. The *attention area* is occupied by the persons who share a common focus of attention. The atten- tion area of New York is composed of all people who have New

York brought to their attention with at least a specified frequency —one reference a month, for example.[44]

The study of the attention groups with which young people are connected is a matter of very special significance. What is the relationship between the attention areas which include the children of a given form in school, and their parents, teachers, or colleagues of like age who are out of school? The milieu of a person is defined by what he thinks and muses about, and the attention area is defined by those who share a common object of reference, with or without knowledge of the similar pre-occupation of the other person. The study of the daily cycle of activity of representative young people may provide more and more of the relevant information. To what extent is the daily cycle of attention distributed among newspapers, magazines, radio programmes, motion picture films, books, lectures, conversations; and how are the specific objects of attention—direct and in imagination—to be classified? Because of our special interest in the subjective-expressive cycle which constitute personality, we are especially interested in references to the self in relation to others; and, among others, to members of the immediate and the remote environment classified according to the social structure of the community. Thus the very low class person in the deference pyramid may pay a great deal of attention, direct and in fantasy, to persons of the same class; persons of the middle classes may focus upon the upper classes; and persons of the upper classes may focus upon one another. The pre-occupation with the self may be greatest among the middle classes. If more class distinctions appear on the basis of the criteria which are selected, distinctive attention patterns may be demonstrated. Subjective events may also be classified as pro or anti, hence pro- or anti-self, and pro- or anti-other. Moods with no symbol of reference may be classified " euphoric " or " dysphoric ", agreeable, disagreeable. Anxiety is a subjective event which shows acute dysphoria, and stress toward action. On the basis of these fundamental distinctions, the subjective cycle of the person may be explored, and the degree to which he shares a common focus of attention with other persons may be discovered.

The relation of the focusing events to the dynamic equilibrium

. [44] The reading areas of metropolitan newspapers in 1920 and 1929 are summarized in *Recent Social Trends* (New York, 1934), Ch. IX. Some of the book-reading areas of the United States are outlined in Wilson, Louis R., *The Geography of Reading : A Study of the Distribution and Status of Libraries in the United States* (Chicago, 1938). Radio listening areas are described in publications put out by the radio industry.

of personality is very important in this connection.   If we are dealing with personalities which, at a given period, reinstate light fear states, these fear states may be procured on exposure to radio or motion picture ; and if not forthcoming from these media, the individual may provide his own nightmare, or act provocatively toward someone in the environment.

The *public* is a psychological area which is made up of those who make debatable demands for action.   The public is smaller than the attention area, since it is composed of those who occupy a sufficiently direct relationship to certain activities to expect to influence them.   The New York attention area is vast ; but the New York public is comparatively circumscribed.

Another psychological area is the *sentiment* area, and is constituted by those who share common sentiments.   Racial, nationalistic, regional, and many other groups share common sentiments, and determine the area.

Besides psychological areas we may speak of *activity* and *organization* areas.   An organization area has an explicit hierarchy, an activity area does not.   The organization areas include legislative districts, administrative districts, official school districts, judicial districts ; activity areas include zones of trade, travel, and fighting.

Modern social science has accumulated a huge amount of information about all kinds of social areas.   Under the name of " ecology " many distributions have been charted.   The analysis of spatial distributions, particularly in urban sociology, received a vigorous impetus from Robert E. Park.[45]   Many rural sociologists and economists have worked out the relationship between small population nuclei, like villages, and areas defined by those who came in to trade, to attend church, to go to a lodge or school and the like.   In the field of world politics, the study of boundaries and of the zones of conflict, has developed a huge literature.   The " human geography " of France has stimulated much scientific interest in regional phenomena.   In the United States this interest is conspicuously served by sociologists like Howard E. Odum, and by many other social scientists besides professional geographers.[46]

The charting of data in space and time is an excellent exercise in social reality, but it leads nowhere in particular unless it is

[45] Park, Robert E., " Human Ecology ", *Amer. J. Sociol.* (1936), Vol. 42.   For a selected and annotated bibliography see Caldwell, Morris Gilmore, " The Sociological Tract : The Spatial Distribution of Social Data ", *Psychiatry* (1938).
[46] Odum, Howard W., *Southern Regions of the United States* (Chapel Hill, 1936).

given significance by means of developmental constructions, or equilibrium analyses. We have had, as yet, comparatively few studies of the interrelationship among areas. Hence we have had few investigations which pivot around problems like these : If the psychological areas are modified in a given way, how will the activity and organization areas be modified ? If the activity and organization areas are modified, how will the psychological areas be changed ? Alfred Weber's theory of industrial localization remains one of the few elaborate systematic works in this field.[47] Students of administration, notably educational administration, have undertaken to find the criteria for the optimum size of school district. The data which are called for in such investigations are of very general importance for social science, as well as practical administration.[48]

In bringing this discussion to a close, it is perhaps pertinent to repeat that useful work in the field of interpersonal relations does not depend upon the achievement of a uniform vocabulary. After all, the field of the social and psychological studies has expanded with phenomenal rapidity in the last hundred years. Observers are always taking up new standpoints as social scientists become more numerous and their activities more diversified.

The rapid exploration of any continent imposes certain limitations upon the explorers. They grow a little apart from one another. Each new band of pioneers is rather completely taken up with the occupation of a new river valley, a new plateau, or a new peninsula. Local loyalties grow up and strange differences in dialect appear.

If each body of specialists upon the life of man displays some of the less congenial characteristics of isolated men, we must not forget that a degree of isolation is necessary to complete the general map of human knowledge. If these hardy adventurers speak a dialect very much their own and not always simple to understand, we may take solace in the reflection that these scientific vernaculars have not only grown up in isolation, but that they bear some relationship to the task of conquering the jungles and swamps of the local region where they are found.

For many reasons we find dialectical differences among

[47] Weber, Alfred, *Alfred Weber's Theory of the Location of Industries* (Chicago, 1929). For an admirable discussion of the problems connected with culture area studies, consult Kluckhohn, Clyde, " On Certain Recent Applications of Association Coefficients to Ethnological Data ", *Amer. Anthropol.* (1939).

[48] The area problem is given attention at many points in White, Leonard D., *Introduction to the Study of Public Administration* (New York, 1939).

specialists less irritating than we did a few short years ago. We are learning the technique of understanding and translating speech. A new optimism has begun to pervade the world of scientific work—an optimism born of confidence in the degree to which barriers of language can be overcome. Partly this is a matter of new technique. New ways of understanding words have come to us from modern logic. From logic we learn how to translate from one set of scientific symbols into another and we learn to emphasize the standpoint of the particular observer in relation to the whole. From modern psychological and sociological research we have gained new insight into the attitudes which tend to colour our conduct in the presence of alien speech. Why is it so common to hate the strange, and especially the strange word? Among the many relevant factors in this problem some are both suggestive and liberating. Words were once the property of the adults who surrounded us when we were children. With words, adults could live in a private world beyond our grasp. Commanding the tools of speech they screened themselves from us, and dictated our destiny. In many of us the childish feeling of weakness in the presence of words has not been entirely left behind. When we meet a strange word we draw back in alarm and frown in resentment.

To-day, we do not disregard the advantages of common speech, but we are learning to deal with differences of speech without annoyance. This new detachment has led us to inspect our own language. We find that the same word in the mouths of two persons may betray us. The word seems to refer to the same event, but often it does not. Thus the word-awareness with which we greet the scientific stranger is turned toward the scientific colleague—and then toward the self.

When we try to state what we ourselves see, we find it wise to recognize the limitations imposed upon us by professional terms, by the traits of our own personality, and by the cultural surroundings to which we have been exposed. We take it for granted that we always speak more or less for ourselves—but at the same time we seldom speak exclusively for ourselves. And as the work of verification proceeds among social scientists and psychologists, we hope to widen the area of stable communication.

THE PSYCHOLOGY OF HITLERISM AS A RESPONSE OF THE LOWER MIDDLE CLASSES TO CONTINUING INSECURITY *

Since a political order which fails to coincide with an era of international prestige and domestic prosperity is endangered by the accumulating animosities of the community, it need occasion little surprise that a mass movement of protest swept aside some of the conventionalities of orderly government in Germany. Smarting under the humiliation of defeat, burdened by the discriminatory aftermath of Versailles, racked by the slow tortures of economic adversity, ruled in the name of political patterns devoid of sanctifying tradition, the German mentality has been ripening for an upsurge of the masses.

It is less the broad fact of mass action than the specific direction of discharge that demands explanation. The lower middle classes have become active factors in the struggle against the " proletarian " and the " Marxist " on behalf of an order of society in which the " profit system ", though excoriated, is none the less protected. Powerful trades unions have been demoralized as potent instruments in maintaining wage scales ; " Marxist " bureaucrats in public offices and private unions have given way to loyal National Socialists from the bourgeoisie ; restless young men, usually sons of the impoverished middle classes, have been inducted into the violence department of the state ; Jews have suffered personal outrage and economic boycott. The torrents of inflammatory rhetoric against the foreign enemies of Germany have culminated in no impulsive martyrdom in the Rhineland, or in Silesia, or along the Polish Corridor ; it is obvious that the rearmament of Germany has not gone far enough to repel the French. The separately manufactured parts of heavy artillery and tanks require from six weeks to two months to assemble, and French arms could devastate the West at once. Most of those who were in material want before Hitler are in material want to-day, though many of the materially cramped have been emotionally rejuvenated by the crusade to regenerate the German nation. New meaning has come to life, symbols are welcome

* From *Political Quarterly* (London, 1933).

substitutes for bread, and a lowered standard of living is but a sacrifice to the cause of national resurrection. The vast discrepancy between promise and performance in high politics and emergency economics is worthy of attention, for it reveals the peculiar dependence of Hitlerism on abracadabra.

In so far as Hitlerism is a desperation reaction of the lower middle classes it continues a movement which began during the closing years of the nineteenth century. Materially speaking, it is not necessary to assume that the small shopkeepers, teachers, preachers, lawyers, doctors, farmers and craftsmen were worse off at the end than they had been in the middle of the century. Psychologically speaking, however, the lower middle class was increasingly overshadowed by the workers and the upper bourgeoisie, whose unions, cartels and parties took the centre of the stage. The psychological impoverishment of the lower middle class precipitated emotional insecurities within the personalities of its members, thus fertilizing the ground for the various movements of mass protest through which the middle classes might revenge themselves.

The insecurities of the class were reflected in the small bourgeois youth who furnished the basis of the German youth movement during its formative years. One of the first significant political expressions of the lower bourgeoisie was the Pan-German movement among German-speaking subjects of the Hapsburg monarchy. Pan-Germanism and Christian Socialism profoundly influenced Adolf Hitler during his years in Vienna ; later he was able to adapt the nationalistic, socialistic and anti-semitic features of these agitations to his own uses.

Nationalism and anti-semitism were peculiarly fitted to the emotional necessities of the lower bourgeoisie. Rebuffed by a world which accorded them diminished deference, limited in the opportunities afforded by economic reality, the members of this class needed new objects of devotion and new targets of aggression. The rising cult of nationalism furnished a substitute for the fading appeal of institutionalized religion in a secularizing world. Anti-semitism provided a target for the discharge of the resentments arising from damaged self-esteem ; and since the scapegoat was connected with the older Christian tradition, guilt feelings arising from lack of personal piety could be expiated by attacking the Jew.

Anti-semitism gave a plausible alternative to the uncompromising indictment of capitalism circulated by proletarian socialists. The proletarian doctrines offended the middle classes less by denouncing the extremes of wealth fostered by capitalism than by praising the "workers" and insulting the "bourgeoisie". The chief aspiration of the thrifty little manual worker, his self-esteem was openly wounded by the taunts, jibes and sneers of the proletarian agitators. He was often alienated from the political parties which were conspicuously identified with the older aristocracy and the new plutocracy, yet he could not endure the humiliation of associating with the "proletariat". He drifted uncertainly toward the democratic parties of the middle, but democratic republicanism coincided with want and humiliation in the post-war years. The lure of anti-semitism lay partly in the opportunity which it provided for discharging animosity against the rich and successful without espousing proletarian socialism. It was not capitalism but Jewish profiteering which was the root of modern evils. The international character of finance, with which the Jews were so conspicuously connected, was apparently irreconcilable with fervent nationalism, and the crusade against the Jew became a legitimate act of devotion to the idols of Germanism.

The prominence of the Jew in proletarian socialism enabled the lower bourgeoisie to rationalize its hostility to the wage earners as resentment against the Jew. This paved the way for a political alliance with those wage earners who were sufficiently "Germanic" to renounce Jewish doctrine, which could be distinguished from "socialism" by naming it "Marxism". Thus by hating "Marxists" middle-class elements were able to discharge enough hatred of the wage-earning class as a whole to permit limited co-operation with wage earners who would espouse a truly "national" form of "socialism". By adopting the word "socialism" in a vague, emasculated sense, the lower bourgeoisie directed some of its hatred against the bloodsuckers who ran chain stores and exacted high profits, without being constrained to join with the most insolent spokesmen of the wage earners. And it was evident that some flirting with the Left could improve bargaining relations with the Right.

The growth of anti-semitism also favoured political collaboration of the lower middle classes with the landed aristocracy, despite conflicting economic interests. The aristocracy cherished the old-fashioned hatred of money-making by the use of mobile capital. The hatred of modern capitalism by the aristocracy would be rationalized as hatred of the Jew, the money-lender of tradition ; by hating Jewish capitalism the aristocracy is enabled to work off its hostility to capitalism as a whole, and to collaborate with some capitalistic elements. When the petty bourgeoisie utilized the Jew as a scapegoat, a common hatred favoured political association with the aristocracy. By flocking into a separate party, the lower bourgeoisie emancipated itself to some extent from the tutelage of the old order, but remained able to co-operate with it on the basis of common loyalty to " Germanism " and common hatred of " Semites ".

In some measure the use of the Jewish scapegoat is an incident in the struggle for survival within the intellectual class, which includes many members of the bourgeoisie. The growth of the vast material environment in modern society has been paralleled by the unprecedented expansion of specialized symbolic activity. Medicine, engineering and physical science have proliferated into a thousand specialities for the control of specific aspects of the material world. Those who master the necessary symbol equipment are part of the intellectual class whose " capital " is knowledge, not muscle. There is a sub-division of the intellectual workers, the " intellectuals " in the narrow sense, who specialize in the symbols connected with political life. The growing complexity of modern civilization has created a vast net of reporters, interpreters, pedagogues, advertisers, agitators, propagandists, legal dialecticians, historians and social scientists who compete among themselves and with all other classes and sub-classes for deference, safety and material income. These specialists in the invention and transmission of political symbols can reminisce about history, argue about morals, law, philosophy and expediency, inculcate myths and legends, or exemplify rituals and ceremonies. Lenin dismissed the " intellectuals " as classless prostitutes hired out to the highest bidder. It is evident that a " brains trust "—to use a current American expression employed to describe President Roosevelt's expert advisers—is a useful form of political armament on all sides, but the tremendous growth of symbol specialists in The Great Society suggests that we have to do with the emergence of a potent social formation with objective interests of its own, some of which can be fostered, paradoxically enough, by encouraging symbolic warfare among its members.

During times of economic adversity the symbol specialists suffer deflation like the rest of the community, and if colleges, universities and other agencies for transmitting skill are not proportionately curtailed, the difficulties of the " intellectuals " are accentuated. Weimar Germany abolished many limitations upon university training, and German universities pumped an increasing volume of trained talent into an overstocked market. The prominence of the Jew in law, medicine, acting, literature, journalism (indeed, in all branches of the intellectual arts) contributed to his vulnerability as an object of mass attack led by rival intellectuals, with or without the aid of other social classes.

The position of the Jew in German society has been further weakened by the frequency with which he has appeared as an enemy of the *mores*. His activity as an intellectual of necessity brought him into conflict with the conventional patterns of German bourgeois life. A Jewish physician in Vienna invented psychoanalysis, which scandalized, even as it fascinated, the middle classes. A Jewish physician in Berlin attained celebrity by identifying himself with the cause of the homosexuals. Jewish writers and actors have produced plays which horrified the provincial conscience. Indeed, one of the avenues to money, prestige and heightened self-importance which is open to the intellectual is sensationalism, which usually involves some defiance of accepted taboos. The Jew was relatively free from the parochial loyalties of gentile Germans, who were often bound to the sentiments of the separate cultural islands throughout the German-speaking territories. Less entangled by local tradition, the Jews were able to seize the opportunity to cater to the whole German market, and to supply many of the symbols which were capable of appealing to all Germans everywhere.

Modern urban culture is fatal to the simple prescriptions of the rural and provincial conscience ; to the moralists of the hinterland the cities defy the laws of god and man. The middle-class code of sexual abstinence, thrift, work and piety crumbles before the blandishments and the concealments of the city. The vulnerability of the conventional code under urban conditions has resulted in crises of provincial conscience ; these anxieties have been adroitly turned against " cultural Bolshevism ", which means the urban, intellectual, Marxist Jew.

Hitlerism is a concession to cultural fundamentalism in a far deeper sense than that it defends property from communist expropriation. Hitler has come to stand for the re-affirmation of the cardinal moral virtues whose neglect has weakened the whole fibre of the German nation. Putrid literature, putrid drama, putrid practices are imputed to the foul Jew who desecrated the homeland whose hospitality he so long enjoyed. The stress of battle, under-nourishment, inflation, and unemployment during these eventful years has exposed many men and women to temptations which they could not resist, and the accumulated weight of guilt arising from these irregularities drives many of them into acts of expiation. In some measure the " awakening of Germany " is a cleansing gesture of aspiration for a feeling of moral worth, and the Jew is the sacrificial ram.

Such is the meaning of the emphasis in Hitler's public personality upon abstinence from wine, women and excess ; this is the clue to the appeal of the humourless gravity which is one of his most obvious traits. The irreverent urbanites of Berlin find Hitler dull, and his appearances have been relatively infrequent and as ceremonial as possible. The biting Goebbels is the darling of the city ; the sober Hitler is the lion of the provinces. This pious deacon with the silver tongue is the articulate conscience of the petty bourgeoisie.

Hitler's appeal to the conservative mothers of Germany derives from their resentment against all the slogans which have been associated with a world in which their sons have been killed or demoralized since 1914. Through Hitler comes revenge against the immoral monsters who have defied the immutable principles of human decency and divine order. Through Hitler comes the hope of rescue for sons, who may learn discipline and self-respect in the uniform, the exercises, and even the dangers of the National Socialist movement. The sons of German mothers who were sacrificed in vain, betrayed by the alien Jewish cankers in our midst, are to be avenged. The traitors shall not go unpunished. The dawning day of resurrection is nigh. The organized might of German manhood shall rise to purify the state and to recover the honour of Germany on the field of battle. Our blood shall not have been shed in vain. The flesh of our flesh shall not decay ; it shall live in the glories of immortal Germany.

There is a profound sense in which Hitler himself plays a maternal rôle for certain classes in German society. His incessant moralizing is that of the anxious mother who is totally preoccupied with the physical, intellectual and ethical development of her children. He discourses in public, as he has written in his autobiography, on all manner of pedagogical problems, from the best form of history teaching to the ways of reducing the ravages of social disease. His constant preoccupation with

" purity " is consistent with these interests ; he alludes constantly to the " purity of the racial stock " and often to the code of personal abstinence or moderation. This master of modern Galahadism uses the language of Protestant puritanism and of Catholic reverence for the institution of family life. The conscience for which he stands is full of obsessional doubts, repetitive affirmations, resounding negations and stern compulsions. It is essentially the bundle of " don'ts " of the nursemaid conscience.[1]

In yet another way Hitler has performed a maternal function in German life. The disaster of the 1918 defeat left the middle classes of German society shocked, dazed and humiliated. The " we " symbol which meant so much was damaged, and they were left shorn of means of revenging themselves upon their enemies. When an individual is suddenly deprived of his customary mode of externalizing loves and aggressions the resulting emotional crisis is severe. In extreme cases, the aggressive impulses which were formerly directed against the outside world are turned back against the personality itself, and suicide, melancholia, and other mental disorders ensue. Most thwarted people are protected from such extreme reactions by finding new objects of devotion and self-assertion. Emotional insecurities are reduced by hating scapegoats and adoring heroes, and in so far as politics provides the formulæ and the activities which satisfy these requirements, politics is a form of social therapy for potential suicides.

Hitler was able to say, in effect : " You are not to blame for the disaster to your personality involved in the loss of the war. You were betrayed by alien enemies in our midst who were susceptible to the duplicity of our enemies. Germany must awaken to the necessity of destroying the alien at home in order to prepare to dispose of the enemy abroad." The self-accusations which signify that aggressive impulses are turned against the self are thus no longer necessary ; not the " sacred ego ", but the Jews are to blame. By projecting blame from the self upon the outside world, inner emotional insecurities are reduced. By directing symbolic and overt attacks against the enemy in our midst, Hitler has alleviated the anxieties of millions of his fellow Germans (at the expense of others). He has also provided fantasies of ultimate victory over the French and Poles, and

[1] This analysis of Hitler's public rôle among middle-class conservatives carries no implications concerning his private life.

arranged marches and special demonstrations as symbolic acts of attack upon the outer as well as the inner enemies of Germany. Hitler has offered himself as the hero and Germanism as the legitimizing symbol of adoration. These partially overt but principally magical acts have provided many distraught Germans with renewed self-confidence either to ignore or to face the rough deprivations of daily life. From one point of view, Hitler's rôle resembles that of the nurse who tells her crying charge that the neighbour boy was very naughty to hit him ; but Hitler's reassurances stir up trouble within the household by diverting animosity against the Jewish fellow-national.

When realities do not facilitate the discharge of aggressive tendencies against the outer group, these impulses are often turned back against sub-groups within one's own community. This is one aspect of the larger proposition stated before that impulses which are denied expression in the outside world rebound against symbols more closely associated with the personality.

As aggressive impulses are turned against the self, those aspects of the personality are chosen which are deplored as particularly weak or immoral. Germans have long lamented the absence of a unified German nation, attributing this weakness in part to the dogmatic pride of opinion which is so deeply rooted in German pride of mind. Unity has been partially attained by the superficial co-ordination of external motions ; " the German national dance step is the goose step ". Beneath the façade of external harmony survive the legacies of disunion. Since the Germans hate most in themselves, as a collective unit, cultural diversity and intellectual virtuosity (qualities which they simultaneously admire), it is scarcely surprising to discover that they have turned upon the Jew as the most typical exponent of their own limitations. German devotion to the symbols of uncompromising nationalism is constantly threatened by contrasting loyalties and intellectual scruples. In the Jew, the eternal scapegoat, they can expiate their own sins against the collective god.

In the hope of contributing to the consolidation of the German nation many elements of German society have condoned the " excesses " of the National Socialists, and welcomed the vigorous centralization and inspired fervour of the movement. Accustomed to submissiveness within the hierarchy of home, army, bureaucracy and party, Germans have assumed the yoke of Hitlerism in the name of freedom, socialism and nationalism.

The appeal from the politics of discussion to the arbitrament of violence and dictatorship came readily in Germany. The symbols and practices associated with the Weimar Republic have meant comparatively little to anybody. The failure to liquidate the symbols of the old régime is shown in the battle over the national colours, and in the persistence of the older personnel in the universities, in the schools, and in the principal organs of administration. Civic training on behalf of the Republic has been formal and uninspired; for some time after the inauguration of the Republic, the schools continued to use the old Imperial textbooks. Perhaps no amount of skill and ingenuity could have built up a body of myths capable of sustaining the Republic under the unfavourable conditions of the post-war era, but in some measure the battle of Weimar was lost by default.

Just as the influential Jews failed to see the handwriting on the wall and lulled themselves into a false sense of safety, the nominal heads of the Republic neglected to intervene boldly and aggressively in the unfolding situation. The fear of the Communists by the bureaucrats of the Social Democratic party and the trades unions drove them into collaboration with their class enemies. Socialist and union officialdom denounced Communist workers to the employers; the Communists were frequently weeded out and superseded by National Socialists. The bureaucratizing tendency of the labour movement in Germany has long been notorious; a job in the union or in the party transformed the fervent agitator into a model bourgeois, anxious to keep his job by preserving discipline among the masses.

That the bourgeoisie of Northern Germany has never fought and bled for republican institutions is connected with the belated industrialization of the country. The English middle classes and the French struggled for responsible government, but the rising Prussian bourgeoisie first connected democratic internationalism with the French invasion; later they began to fear the proletariat as the menace on the Left, which drove them steadily to the Right. Thus national parliamentarism is not deeply enshrined in the loyalties of the classes most closely associated with it in the West.

The future of the middle classes in Germany depends on the success of the new ruling régime in improving their material prospects and psychological rewards. Unless this problem is solved, enthusiasm for the new symbols will gradually die away, and the resulting disillusionment will gradually transform the middle classes into mere passive supporters of the reigning order of society. They will then conform more closely to the rôle which the older revolutionists expected the middle classes to play in the class struggle. Events in Italy and in Germany have given rise to the reflection that the political activism of the middle classes has been grossly underestimated, for they contributed sons to supply the sinews, money to defray the cost, and ballots to sustain the candidates, of potent alternatives to proletarianism.

The abandonment of so many of the forms of democratic government has corroborated the communist teaching that such trifles will be cast away whenever the class struggle seems to render it imperative for the protection of the profit principle. This convincing demonstration may be expected to dissolve much of the democratic romanticism which enabled the tiny bureaucrats of the older labour movement to drift and not to fight.

Communism may supply the symbol in whose name mass hostilities will ultimately discharge themselves against bourgeoisie and aristocracy. No doubt this is improbable, short of military defeat in war, or long-protracted war, when foreign war may be transformed into civil war. In the meanwhile, it is sound tactics to preserve the integrity of the term " Communist " by refusing to associate it with its near rivals. Small disciplined bands of revolutionaries may one day use the uncontaminated symbol and the technique of the *coup d'état* to ride the waves of mass discontent to the seats of power.

It is worthy of comment that the lower middle classes, stung from political passivity into political action, have been able to furnish their own crusading leadership. Hitler, the self-made semi-intellectual, son of a small customs official in the service of the Hapsburgs, stirs his own class to an unwonted spurt of political aggressiveness. Other social groups, like the wage earners, have so often been led by men who were social renegades from the older social strata that this self-sufficiency of the bourgeoisie inspires respectful interest.

Influential elements of the upper bourgeoisie of Germany have partially financed the Hitler movement in order to break up the collective bargaining system which was sustained by the powerful German trades unions. This was impossible in the name of the older parties of the Right, who were too intimately connected with the plutocracy and the aristocracy. Only a movement thoroughly nationalistic and demagogic could stir the lower bourgeoisie to enthusiastic action, and make substantial inroads in the more passive elements of the wage-earning class. In general, the symbols of Hitlerism have assuaged the emotional conflicts of the lower bourgeoisie, while the acts of Hitlerism have lowered the labour costs of the upper bourgeoisie.

CHAPTER IV

RADIO AS AN INSTRUMENT OF REDUCING PERSONAL INSECURITY *

As long as radio reflects the interests of an individualistic society, there will be " psychological " programmes, programmes devoted to the explanation and handling of human nature. The child who is born into an individualistic society develops acute consciousness of his own ego, since he is trained to compare himself incessantly with all potential rivals. He is taught to discipline his own impulses in the interest of success, and by success is meant the improvement of his control over such values as power, respect and income. In return for work well done, success is said to be sure.

The taste for psychology may be found among all men everywhere, but only among individualistic societies does the taste become a craving that approaches the magnitude of an addiction. Within the general framework of such a culture, there are zones of special emphasis upon individualistic achievement. The child who is reared in a middle-class family usually grows to share the middle-class aspiration to rise in the world. The middle-class child is the quintessential climber in a society of climbers.

Whatever conflicts are found in the culture as a whole are brought to burning focus in the lives of middle-class children. The ideological structure of our own society is no homogenous unity, since it contains ideals that are difficult to hold in balanced relation to one another. There is great stress upon individual achievement ; but this is mitigated by the virtues of service and loyalty. Within the occupational network of our culture are found too sharply contrasting types, one devoted to the pursuit of money, the other to the service of non-pecuniary aims.

The double standard of success and service creates enormous difficulties in the lives of middle-class boys and girls. If the middle class is the germinating bed of ambitious climbers, it is also the custodian of morality, of ideals of sacrifice on behalf of values that transcend the limits of the individual ego. The typical conflict within the personality of the middle-class youth is between " ambition " and " ideals " ; the individual suffers

* From *Studies in Philosophy and Social Science* (New York, 1941).

from contradictory emphases that are found throughout the total structure of an individualistic society.

Given the individualistic traditions of American life, we know that the taste for psychology will be particularly active during periods of social difficulty. When they meet rebuff severe crises are generated within the personalities of all who share individualistic traditions. From the earliest days they have been trained to appraise the value of the ego in terms of success and failure. If they proudly accept responsibility for what they achieve, they seem bound to accept the onus of blame for what they do not attain. When they are thrown back upon themselves, they seek escape from the keen anxieties that arise from the feelings of futility and guilt. At such times the need of insight, the need of clarification of the position of the person in relation to the whole of experience, is most acute ; and " psychology " is one of the symbols of reference to those who claim expert knowledge of human nature. Hence the prominence of " psychology " in the interest scale of insecure people ; hence the truth in the prediction that as long as the media of mass communication in an individualistic society reflect popular sentiment, they will concern themselves with psychology—to some extent at all times ; to a greater extent in times of general insecurity.

Explanations of human nature, popular or scientific, fall in three convenient categories. Stress may be put upon the impulses and ideas of the person, upon the environment to which he is exposed, or upon a balance of internal and external factors. Strictly speaking, there is a continuous gradation from one extreme to the other, hence there are varying degrees of balance and imbalance in between. For the sake of clarity we may speak of Type A, concerned with the internal environment, Type B, descriptive of the external environment, and Type C, presenting a balance of the two sets of factors. The scientific point of view is Type C. It is, of course, taken for granted that there are large degrees of difference in the amount of stress put upon internal or external factors among various groups of specialists.

Type A may be illustrated by the following excerpt from a broadcast by the present writer [1] :

[1] No. 12, "Human Nature in Action", Sustaining Programme of the National Broadcasting Company, April 5, 1940. The script collaborator was Albert N. Williams of N.B.C.

In accordance with the plan of the series, the " Dictator " type of personality was shown from four successive standpoints : conventional, intimate, unconscious, formative.

(1) An example of characterization from the conventional standpoint :

MAN : Well—let me tell you one thing. You may be Mayor of this town—but you don't any more run this town than you run my business—my business is this town. . . .

ANALYST : We will call this man the hyperaggressive type, which means simply that here is a man who imposes his personality upon other people to an intense degree. This man could have been a dictator. In fact, he is definitely of the stuff from which Napoleons are made. . . .

(2) From an intimate point of view :

MAN : Huh ! Look down their noses at me because I never went to college. . . . I don't know modern art. . . . I don't know literature. . . . I think I better have my secretary get me some books on modern art and the next time I have a dinner-party I'll teach those people a thing or two about their own subjects. . . .

ANALYST : You see what the psychology of this man is ? Every time he feels inferior because of a blind spot in his intellectual make-up he immediately takes drastic measures to correct that fact. He is a very imaginative, well-trained man ; he is a highly disciplined person who knows his weaknesses, and takes immediate steps to correct them. . . .

(3) From an unconscious point of view, as reflected in his dreams :

(DREAM TECHNIQUE)

MAN : This art gallery of mine . . . this great art gallery . . . those pictures cost a million dollars . . . each one cost a million dollars . . . they are the greatest pictures in the world and nobody can see them except me . . . ohhh . . . it's pulling off my arms . . . it's pulling off my right arm . . . and ohhh that picture . . . is pulling off my right leg . . . I'm being killed . . . those pictures are pulling off my arms and legs . . . ohhhhhhhh . . .

ANALYST : Yes . . . the pattern of his dreams is quite similar . . . great possessions and then final destruction. . . .

The foregoing extracts concentrate attention upon the inner life of the subject, and relate behaviour and conduct in the immediate present chiefly to other parts of the internal environment. The dream life is brought prominently into the focus of attention as an index of the incompatible tendencies that are found within the " Dictator's " personality. Taken out of its context, we have here a rather good example of Type A.

The following excerpts deal with the formative years of the same man :

BOY : Have to work at a paper stand all day long . . . I can play baseball . . . I can have a good time like the other kids . . . but mother says that I've got to work at a paper stand all day long . . . never have any fun, never have any time to play baseball . . . never any money to go to the movies. . . .

ANALYST : Yes . . . he was a victim of poverty . . . he couldn't enjoy a free life of boyhood, but had to work. . . .

These sentences relate the boy to his external environment, emphasizing both his poverty and the exactions of his mother. Taken by themselves, we would not hesitate to classify them in Type B of the explanations mentioned above. Taken in conjunction, as part of the same script as Type A, they justify the inclusion of the broadcast in Type C, the balanced type.

For the proper study of psychological broadcasts, as of any broadcast, content analysis is essential. If we are to discover the effect of psychological programmes upon the listening audience, we must make use of the methods adequate to the task of describing them. In the foregoing example, we have illustrated a very crude variety of content analysis. Excerpts have been selected that answer two opposite specifications : Presentation of the subject as dependent upon his internal environment ; presentation of the subject as dependent upon his external environment. More refined methods would make it possible to describe relative degrees of such presentations within the limits of these selected excerpts. The soliloquy about the rebuff at the dinner-party (2) obviously refers to an interpersonal situation in the recent past of the subject. The connection of the dream sequence (3) with an external situation involving people is not evident on the face of the record. Hence the dream sequence falls entirely within the category of the subjective event without explicit reference to an immediate feature of the personal environment.[2]

Why is it important to distinguish carefully among the forms of psychological explanation that are current in our society ? Chiefly because there are very searching hypotheses about the alleged effect of these various forms upon political and social movements. We have no adequate data at present that enable us to confirm or to disaffirm any seriously-held hypothesis about the effects of psychological programmes upon those who listen. However, the possibility that research may yield data on signi-

[2] For the problem of content analysis, see Lasswell, H. D., " A Provisional Classification of Symbol Data ", *Psychiatry*, 1938.

ficant questions is presumably increased when we guide our investigations by important hypotheses ; and with this in mind, we have put in the very forefront of this discussion the classification of programmes according to the stress given to internal or external factors in the causation of conduct and behaviour.

And what are the socially significant hypotheses that lay so much emphasis upon the type of psychological explanation ? With the greatest succinctness, the hypothesis (a compound hypothesis) is that in an individualistic society in our historical period Type A has reactionary, Type B has revolutionary, and Type C has adjustive effects. Let us consider what is meant by the suggestion that Type A has reactionary results upon the auditing group. It is said that such explanations of human activity lead the individual to concentrate his attention upon the subtleties of private experience, and to divert his gaze from the broad situations in the culture that need to be changed, if more healthy private lives are to be made possible. Explanations of Type B, on the other hand, fix attention upon the broader outlines of the institutions of society, and attaches to them major responsibility for the distortion of human personality. It is predicted that those who accept explanations of the B type are more disposed to participate actively in social and political movements for the fundamental reconstruction of the social order.

In passing, it may be suggested that the first hypothesis is plausible, as stated, only if immediate effects are taken into consideration. It is doubtful if passivity is the enduring response to incessant stress upon subjective factors. On the contrary ; if the level of general insecurity continues high, more and more members of the community may be expected to be " fed up " on " little Willie stories ", upon childhood memories to account for difficulties that seem plausibly accounted for by the threat of unemployment and of invasion from abroad. If the revulsion against " Hamletism " rises to significant dimensions, the choice of activistic symbols depends upon the alternatives available at the moment (revolutionary, counter-revolutionary).

In any case Types A and B are probably connected with rigid and dogmatic ways of responding to the difficulties of adapting a richly complicated social structure to internal and external stress. Type C is the pattern of psychological explanation that may be expected to nourish and sustain the progressive adjustment of an individualistic society to the needs of the time. In

Type C the emphasis is balanced, correcting over-emphasis upon an individualistic ideology without flying to the opposite extreme of dogmatic anti-individualism.

It is not easy to give currency to balanced explanations of the C type. We know only too well that specialists as well as laymen have their difficulties when they try to clarify the complex interrelationships of internal and external environments. Among scientists the inept days of opposing such ambiguities as " heredity " versus " environment " are practically at an end. Yet among laymen echoes of the past continue to resound in the overtones of popular speech. We have not made proper use of our modern instruments of communication to clarify the community as a whole about the nature of human nature, about the complex interrelations between one person and another. We can demonstrate in many instances the connection between timidity and the kind of maternal care received by the individual ; yet these distinctions, often corroborated by common experience, are obscure when the layman begins to think about " human nature ". He is unprovided with a vocabulary appropriate to the context. Subtle interconnections are dramatized in his mind around crude expressions like " heredity " or " environment " ; there is little perception of the variable degrees of effectiveness to be assigned to the internal or the external environment at a given moment. No doubt the use of such expressions as " interpersonal relations " will polarize many realistic associations in the minds of laymen. Eventually it may be possible to talk quietly about different kinds of interpersonal situations, and to estimate the relative influence of internal and external factors upon the adjustment of each participant.

It is necessary to experiment with different ways of bringing language about the internal and the external environment into the same universe of discourse. The present writer has experimented in this direction by inviting attention to focus upon " impulses " and " practices ", with special reference to " destructive impulses " and " destructive practices ". Human destructiveness is thus expressed in two forms, directly through destructive impulses that are unchecked, and less directly through institutional practices that provoke crises by creating situations in which destructive impulses are sharply stimulated. The task of reducing human destructiveness is to discover and to spread proper methods of controlling destructive impulses, once aroused, and of reducing the occasions that prod them into concentrated life.

In addition to a common language that balances internal and external factors in the explanation of human nature in action, there is need of common language about important specific factors. The writer has experimented in this direction by calling attention to " hurt ego " as a major cause of human destructiveness. This method of analysis was presented on the radio in two forms, one a series of lectures, and the other a series of dramatizations with analysis.[3]

Quite apart from the question of whether these specific formulations are fortunate or not, the urgency of directing radio research toward the study of the effects of different kinds of psychological broadcasts is great. If any of the basic hypotheses about Types A, B and C are true, they are of the gravest importance for understanding the human consequences of radio as an instrument of communication in American society. It should not be forgotten that psychological explanations are not only given currency over the radio in broadcasts that happen to be called " psychological ". In fact, the most important effect of radio upon the popular understanding of psychological causation may take place in " commercial " broadcasts that have never been conceived as disseminating psychological information or misinformation. If, in this discussion, we refer to explicitly labelled " psychological " (or near psychological) programmes, we do not lose sight of the total problem of assessing, through any period of time, the total psychological content of the broadcasts to which the listening audience is subjected.

For the guidance of research and policy in reference to psychological broadcasts, let us specify in more detail the objectives to be sought. We assume, at the outset, that the socially significant purpose of these broadcasts is insecurity reduction. The reduction of the national level of insecurity can be sought by means of broadcasts that contribute to insight, recognition, and selection.

(1) *Insight.* To some extent the anxiety level of individuals

[3] The first series of " Human Nature in Action " began May 17, 1939, and concluded August 9, 1939. The second (dramatized) series began January 12, 1940 and ended December 17, 1940 (with No. 46). The writer proposed the idea of combining dramatization with analytic comment some time before the series. He was fortunate in having assigned to him a talented writer and director, Albert N. Williams, who had been experimenting along many new programme lines, including the combination of drama with comment. The experiments were undertaken at the instance of James Rowland Angell and Walter Preston, Jr., of N.B.C. The contrast between the lecture-question method and the drama-analysis pattern may be seen with special clarity by contrasting the last episode of the first series with " The Dictator ".

can be reduced by insight, rendering them less tense, less worried and irritable, less compulsive in their attitude toward themselves and the world.

(2) *Recognition.* Persons can be trained to recognize personality conditions that require expert assistance.

(3) *Selection.* Assuming that dangerous conditions can be recognized, there is the added step of selecting competent experts.

Patient research is needed to translate these standards into the specifics of practical application. It would be unwise to underestimate the complexity of the problems involved at each step in the inquiry.

Taking it for granted that conscientious and skilful investigation will reduce the ambiguity of these standards, we may take the further step of formulating the characteristics of programmes compatible with them.

1. *Cautious Optimism.* Optimism is needed if listeners are to feel reassured about the possibility of freeing themselves (and others) of anxiety. Yet there is need of restraint in reference to the removal of noxious subjective states, since optimism can be carried so far that it arouses incredulity and leads to frustration. False optimism can prepare the way for crushing disillusionment. Hence the need of cautious optimism—for calm, matter-of-factness, for balanced and unexaggerated statement.

2. *Restrained Endorsement of Specific Means.* In a sense this is a sub-category of " cautious optimism ", but it is singled out for co-ordinate emphasis because of the frequency with which it is disregarded in current practice. Our dependable knowledge of human nature is regrettably meagre, and restraint is needed in the endorsement of any diagnosis or of any therapeutic expedient.

3. *Balance of Internal and External Factors.* We have dealt extensively above with the need of maintaining a balance between internal and external factors in the explanation of human activity.

4. *Balance of Prestigeful and Non-prestigeful Instances.* There is danger in crippling the usefulness of psychology if it is popularly understood as a system of innuendo. This impression can be gained when psychological explanations are invoked only to account for the Hitlers and never for the Churchills. It is true that we seek psychological insight chiefly to get rid of disturbing personal relations ; yet there is a theory of " successes " as well as " distortions ".

5. *Guidance to Competent Specialists.* If the listening audience is to act wisely with reference to dangerous human situations,

there is need of definite instruction about how to identify such situations, and how to get in touch with competent specialists. But who, it may be asked, are the competent specialists? Our knowledge of human nature has been growing with startling rapidity in recent years, and the onrush of new data has not been critically evaluated and finally assimilated into our social inheritance. No one body of specialized observers can justifiably claim to monopolize useful knowledge of man and his works. Yet there are certain extreme conditions in which it is imperative to establish contact with a qualified physician, and preferably a psychiatrist. Over the years, no doubt, guidance will present less delicate problems than it does to-day; it is unlikely that we will suffer from another inundation of interpretations and methods quite as extensive as occurred during the past generation. (Contrast Sigmund Freud, for example, with Ivan P. Pavlov.)

Let no one assume that the present writer is under the impression that the series of programmes to which reference has been made in this article constitutes a model of conformity to these standards. Without passing judgment upon the degree to which the " Human Nature in Action " broadcasts as a whole measure up to these requirements, certain deficiencies may be specified at once. It is probable that the " optimism score " of some of the broadcasts would be low. " The Dictator ", for example, contained little if any explicit suggestion that tendencies toward the formation of dictatorial personalities could be brought under control. To some extent, of course, any balanced explanation of human personality contributes to optimism, since it suggests that what can be understood can be partially directed. Some of the broadcasts were explicit in suggesting that certain noxious situations had been cleared up by means of proper methods of thought and of adjusting the external environment. But in the main the series was diagnostic, and offered a bare minimum of specific therapeutic suggestions. For this reason the series would obtain a high score on a " restrained endorsement " scale. In fact one irate listener expressed the sentiment of an unknown number of his colleagues when he wrote :

I would like to be delivered from the recital of case after case of neurotic aberration, from Psychiatry, " our latest experiment in ignorance ", into some hope of sanity through mental hygiene,—the only constructive hope for relief and upbuilding. From long and close study of the methods of so-called psychiatrists, I am convinced

that they tend to deepen every morbid tendency—instead of leading
out and up and on into sanity and balance. From dealing with sub-
normal and diseased, you seem to accept them as typical. Surely
there is no hope or uplift on that line.

Probably, too, the broadcasts would rank high on " balance
of internal and external factors ". There would be a lower
score, and possibly a much lower score, on the " balance of
prestigeful and non-prestigeful instances ", although the second
third of the second series had to do with historical personages
of some eminence.

We need much careful investigation to determine the effect
of psychological programmes in general, and of specific patterns
in particular, upon various listening audiences. The effect will
depend, in part, upon the varied predispositions latent and
active in the personalities of those who listen. Indeed, one of
the most interesting questions to be raised in connection with
psychological broadcasts is who listens to them at all. This is
what Paul F. Lazarsfeld calls the pre-selective effect, the self-
selecting not only of radio as a channel of communication, but
of specific types of programme.

Very few facts are known about those who listen to psychological broadcasts. From the general theory of response, however, we may propose certain hypotheses as a guide to future
study. Any response is a function of two sets of factors, environmental and predispositional (R is a function of E and P. P is
equivalent to the expression " internal environment " used above).
The probability of a positive rather than a negative response to
any given environment is increased if past response to the dominant features of the environment have been followed by gains
rather than losses. Now who are the people who may be said
to be predisposed toward listening to a psychological programme ?

Certainly we may expect that one listening group will be
composed of (1) those who talk or want to talk about psychology.
By watching the technique of the broadcast, they hope to improve
their own skill in talking about the subject. In the past they
have often gained vocabulary by exposing themselves to the language of others about psychology ; hence we may expect them
to continue until their gains drop down.

The following references to those who listened to the " Human
Nature in Action " programmes are intended to add concreteness to general hypotheses here outlined about the pre-selective
effects of psychological broadcasts. It was not possible to study

the listening audience with enough care to create an inclusive picture.

One listening group was composed of colleagues in various universities who were interested in the problem of talking about psychology to laymen, and who wanted to form a first-hand impression of the drama-analysis technique of presentation. The writer received a steady trickle of criticisms from these colleagues, many of whom were not personally known to him. One distinguished psychiatrist and social psychologist wrote as follows :

Unfortunately I heard only three so far but I think that is enough to get some impression of the whole. . . . It seems to me that the idea of blending theoretical explanation with slight dramatization is an excellent one. It makes the whole thing very much alive and at the same time in no way cheapens it. . . . I think it might be a good idea to emphasize somewhat more that given such and such childhood background, this background is not the simple " cause " for a specific outcome but that certain other factors which complicate the picture and which cannot be dealt with in the broadcast make for the one or other outcome. In other words, I feel that although one should show the listener the general lines of development, one should also make him feel how complex the causal relationship between early experiences and later personality development is.

Another social psychologist with psychoanalytical training, too, wanted more explicit references to the part of the social structure in which the child was reared. He was inclined to the view that the use of " psychological " language obscured the correlation of the conduct discussed with facts of social structure. Thus some of the situations depicted in the broadcasts were typical of lower middle-class families in which an ambitious mother believes that she has married " beneath her position ", and strives to realize through the children the career that she " threw away ". And in the text of the analytical comments there were no explicit references made to these important facts about the position of the family in the structure of society. These remarks, it will be noted, bear on the all-important question of the proper balance between internal and external factors.

Incidentally such appraisals show how broadcasts on psychology can be critically used for educational purposes. It would be a mistake to imagine that radio broadcasts can be a substitute for textbook or lecture. The chief rôle of the psychological broadcast in relation to classroom work is supplementary in two directions. To some extent the broadcast can enliven the interest of some classes in the subject, and confer a sense of vivid reality upon some of the words in the text, or in the lecture delivered by a familiar teacher. Of more importance is the critical study of the material included (and excluded) in the broadcast. To what extent is a balance held between internal and external factors? To what extent is the terminology chosen consistent with particular schools of systematic thought? To what degree is the vocabulary clarifying to the layman, and consistent with a scientifically defensible framework?

Among the many specialists who communicated with the writer were sociologists, social psychologists, psychologists, political scientists, anthropologists, economists, philosophers, psychiatrists, physicians, social workers, adult educators, army morale officers, educational directors in C.C.C. camps; college, junior college, and high-school administrators; high-school teachers of the social studies; clergymen; librarians; graphologists; nurses; students.

From the foregoing listeners who use or want to use language about psychology, we pass over to a group (2) that is aware of the problem of manipulating other people (without necessarily wanting to talk about the theory of it). The manipulators include public relations counsels, advertising men, display consultants, salesmen, playwrights, lawyers, receptionists, dentists, teachers of music and art.

The last group (3) in the present list includes the enormous total of those who suffer from anxiety or uncertainty about the self or others. In this group are some of the patients in mental and other hospitals, mothers left behind by their children, jilted suitors and partners in marital splits, elderly persons concerned about senescence, young parents, disturbed adolescents, anxious bachelor women (more often than men), and the like.

Systematic study would enable us to locate the zones in the social structure that, at a given time, give rise to the most disturbed personalities. We have already called attention to the conflictful middle classes; but an inclusive survey would explore all classes of society.[4]

What are the forms of response available to the groups that pre-select psychological programmes? Since we have selected

[4] A suggestive inventory by a contemporary psychiatrist is by Plant, James S., *Personality and the Cultural Pattern* (New York, 1937). For a more comprehensive and systematic picture, consult Mannheim, Karl, *Man and Society in an Age of Reconstruction; Studies in Modern Social Structure* (London, 1940).

insecurity reduction as the social purpose of psychological broad-casting, it is convenient to consider responses as follows :

(1) Immediate or eventual reduction of anxiety in the self, (a) with the reduction of anxiety in others, (b) with the increase of anxiety in others ;
(2) Immediate or eventual increase of anxiety in the self, (a) with increased anxiety in others, (b) with decreased anxiety in others.

From case studies we know that the reduction of anxiety in one person is not invariably followed by reductions in the anxiety of those whom he affects. If a timid husband becomes more assertive as he overcomes certain internal limitations, he may precipitate severe difficulties in the personality of his wife, if she is unstably integrated. We know, too, that increasing anxiety may reduce anxiety in others, if the effect of augmented anxiety is to reduce the provocative intimidation of another person.

Reliable data about the effects of psychological broadcasts must come from observers who obtain a total, intensive view of persons who pre-select such radio programmes. It is futile to attempt to infer effects from the classification of the mail received from the listening audience. We do not know who writes, as distinguished from who listens and does not write ; and we do not know what connection there is between what is written, and the effect of the broadcast upon the level of anxiety.

However, the mail received from the radio audience need not be ignored entirely, since we may classify it into groups and undertake to do the field work needed to discover the correla-tion between the manner of man who writes in a given vein, and the total effect of the broadcast.

It is convenient to separate the mail received from the listen-ing audience into those containing no special requests and special requests. Another interesting classification is according to plus or minus references to the speaker and the programme.

Among those who make no special requests, several responses may be distinguished. Some go no further than to note examples of the types described by the speaker. Often the writer says no more than that he, himself, or someone known to him, is a " perfect example ".

Sometimes the correspondent raises a general question that bears no avowed or obvious relationship to a worry. The prob-lem is posed in the general spirit of intellectual inquiry ; and there may be original disquisitions upon problems touched upon, or suggested by, the speaker.

Often the dominant trend of the letter seems to be self-justification. One example is a pencilled note from a New England farmer's wife :

You be careful what you say of the woman who can't make up her mind, the silly talking woman. She isn't as silly as you think. Just her way of doing business is with her heart and intuition which sounds pretty foolish to a hard-headed business man. I graduated at 21 and tried every way to be a business woman. After six years I decided I was getting nowhere fast. At the time I had three or four men friends, and so I selected the one I thought would make a good husband and father. We were married. He is a smart young man and I have done everything to push him ahead. We own our own home and have three beautiful children. Perhaps you will call me a drudge. If so, I still like it. I don't like the little social clubs. They push me around too much and I haven't the time or it isn't worth the energy to push them around. Then I stay at home a lot. I have plenty of work. . . .

The special request communications ask for discussions or replies over the air, by special correspondence, or by personal consultation.

One group poses a problem for discussion that is apparently not a problem that disturbs the writer, but is intellectually stimulating. One woman from a high-income group, active in civic affairs, writes to suggest the analysis of two fellow townsmen, whom she describes in friendly, and somewhat puzzled, fashion. A receptionist describes a fellow worker in detail, exhibiting no animus, and betraying no concern about the other worker as a serious problem.

Some write of problems in the handling of others (sometimes disguising the fact that the type described constitutes a specific problem to the writer). Representative is this terse, straightforward letter of a cultured woman from a farm community in the West :

Because of a problem which is confronting me—the problem of a young woman who, though she seems normal in other respects, has a tendency to literally fall in love with other women (and at present with my young daughter, a perfectly normal girl) I am writing for any available books, pamphlets, or printed information on the subject of perversion of this kind. I want, if possible, to help this strange young woman to understand herself, and in order to do so, I need information myself. Perhaps you can help me in any way by sending such information if you have it, or by directing me to any source where it can be obtained ?

Much of the special request correspondence asks help in relation to the self as the dominant problem. Sometimes there is a slight disguise—as in the case of an alcoholic who called up over the long-distance telephone during a broadcast to ask for a discussion of the psychology of alcoholism, which he assured us would be of great benefit to the whole world.

Using these various categories of correspondence, it will be possible to select subjects from among those who respond to future psychological broadcasts, and to learn more about the impact of these programmes upon determinate portions of the population. Such full knowledge of representative persons will enable us to test the revolutionary, reactionary, or adjustive effect of psychological programmes of Types A, B, and C. Only when further investigation has been done can we translate general programme standards into the specifics of effective policy, and embark with certainty upon the fundamental task of reducing the level of personal insecurity by the proper articulation of radio with every agency of mass communication.

III

HOW TO OBSERVE AND RECORD POLITICS

CHAPTER I

THE PARTICIPANT-OBSERVER : A STUDY OF ADMINISTRATIVE RULES IN ACTION

(*With Gabriel Almond, Brooklyn College*)

(*a*) THE OFFICIAL *

I

Some officials apply rules with scrupulous rigidity, and not plasticity. Some are stimulated by bold and demanding behaviour to misapply rules and discriminate against, or in favour of, the other person. Others are susceptible to flattery or over-react against efforts to curry favour with them. Some over-ride the submissive ; others go out of their way to indulge the meek.

Rules are one of the principal devices of control in business, government, and general administration. It is common experience that the relationship between the phraseology of a rule and its application is subject to many influences. If the wording is ambiguous, differences in application will arise from varying constructions put upon the words. If bribery or intimidation occurs, an administrative staff may bend the rules to personal profit. If certain philosophies of administration prevail, rules may be twisted for the benefit of or against the " under dog ". It is universally conceded that many discrepancies between rule and act originate in the unconscious interplay of personalities.

Is it possible to discover the relative importance of " unconscious " or " broader personality factors " in the relation of salesman and customer, foreman and worker, official and client, and in some degree to remove them from the realm of hunch to the realm of fact ? Then there would be an adequate basis for practical psychotherapy in the daily practice of administration.

This paper reports a study of the relationship between rules and rule application in an administrative situation which was sufficiently simple to expose the unconscious personality factors.

* From *The Personnel Journal*, April, 1935.

Clients on public relief in many districts in the city of Chicago in 1932–3 were expected to make complaints in person at the complaint desk which was maintained at district headquarters. Complaint aides decided whether the request entitled the client to wait to see his case-worker personally. The judgment of the complaint aides at the Halsted office, where this investigation was conducted, was supposed to be guided by a very explicit code of rules which defined the nature of requests which would entitle the client to see his case-worker. A certain number of days of delay in food or coal orders merited waiting, as did health emergencies and final eviction notices. Many clients came to the office on appointment, or for routine " waiting ", such as for street-car tokens, tickets for the purchase of ice, or for correction in orders. With these exceptions, all requests were to be delivered to the case-worker in the form of a written message and the client sent home.

It will be seen that the definiteness of these rules practically eliminated the possibility of deviations arising from uncertainties about the meaning of words.

Certain possible sources of deviation between official act and rule can be dismissed as of small importance in this relief client-complaint aide relationship. Intimidation, bribery or philosophy of administration were not significantly operative. This statement rests upon the testimony of those who were in constant and intimate contact with the particular aides during the observational period.

With these possible sources of deviation minimized, resulting discrepancies between rule and act can be mainly attributed to that broad category of influences called unconscious personality factors. It was decided to note the ways in which clients approached the complaint aides in making their requests, and by connecting this with departures from rules to detect the magnitude of the effect of different approaches upon various administrators.

Classifying Behaviour

The complaint aides agreed upon a list of adjectives to characterize the various degrees of behaviour exhibited by the clients in making their requests. " Non-aggressive " behaviour was " requesting ", " pleading and complaining ", " formal and reserved ", " submissive ", " confused ", " compulsive ", or " insistent ". Aggressive behaviour was described as active

" demanding ", " threatening ", " arrogant ", and " clear cut and concise " ; or as passive, " wise cracking ", or " curries favour ". It was considered to act as a strong stimulus upon the personality of the other to comply with or to reject a request. Non-aggressive approaches lack intense impact upon the personality of the other ; they arouse indifference. The aggressives impinge decisively upon personalities they touch, impelling them to do something—favourable or unfavourable—for the persons concerned. The distinction between aggressive and non-aggressive approaches is made in terms of the conscious appraisal of the administrators affected. This act of appraising the impact of the personality of the other is not to be confused with the act of indulging or denying the request. It is precisely the spread between this initial estimate and the final official act that constitutes a significant difference.

The complaint aide noted the behaviour of the client on the slip which was used to record the request and its disposition. The aides who kept these records over a six months' period were experienced workers. Reliability was checked by having one of the aides observe the behaviour of the clients toward the other aides, and by comparing his notations with those of the aides in question. The results showed almost complete agreement on the broad categories of " aggressive " or " non-aggressive ".

It was not certain at the beginning that the method would be sufficiently refined to disclose significant differences in the behaviour of the complaint aides. But striking divergences did in fact emerge. These will be discussed in three cases on which data are unusually complete. Aide 1 departed from the rules to favour those who made non-aggressive approaches, but Aides 2 and 3 gave less than the rules called for, to those who made such approaches.

This comes out very clearly in the analysis of the contacts between 200 relief clients and these complaint aides. These 200 clients made requests of the three complaint aides 1, 2 and 3 exactly 1,012 times. 432 of these contacts were with Aide 1, 273 with Aide 2, 307 with Aide 3.

Aide 1 was approached submissively 86 per cent. of the time. On 21 per cent. of these occasions, he departed from the rules. Detailed analysis of the total number of instances in which he deviated from the rules when non-aggressively approached, shows that in the overwhelming number of cases the clients got the benefit of the deviation. Thus in 87 per cent. of the instances of departure from rules, Aide 1 permitted individuals to wait to see the case-worker in contravention of the regulations.

On the other hand, when confronted by aggressive behaviour by clients, Aide 1 showed a pronounced inclination to discriminate against them. The result was unfavourable to the client 78 per cent. of the time.

A tendency of almost equal strength in the opposite direction appears when the records of Aides 2 and 3 are closely examined. If they deviated from the letter of the rule when non-aggressively approached, the applicant lost rather than gained. Aide 2 discriminated against them 80 per cent. of these occasions, and Aide 3 discriminated against them 72 per cent.

RESPONSE TO AGGRESSIVENESS

Their responses to active aggressive behaviour is a little different. With Aide 3, 62 per cent. of deviations worked to the disadvantage of the client. Aide 2, on the other hand, was evidently somewhat submissive, since 67 per cent. of her deviations from rules were favourable to the aggressive client. This, it will be recalled, is the reverse of her reaction to submissiveness.

When confronted by passively aggressive behaviour Aide 1 is paired with Aide 2 and both contrast with Aide 3. In 75 per cent. of the instances in which Aide 1 deviated from rule, the passively aggressive client benefited. This holds in 60 per cent. of similar instances for Aide 2. Aide 3 shows no significant tendency to favour the one or the other, the percentages being 48 favourable, 52 unfavourable.

The foregoing results distinguished rather clearly between forms of behaviour in administrative situations. Aide 1 discriminated in favour of those who approached him submissively and discriminated against those who were actively aggressive. Aide 2 favoured those who were aggressive, and deprived those who were non-aggressive. Aide 3 discriminated against submissive approaches, and showed no particular sensitiveness to passive aggression.

II

Such variations in rule application are no doubt typical of many administrative situations, and it seems probable that self-awareness among administrators can be fostered by records of this type.

Yet another aspect of the matter is of general interest. Who are these administrators who behave like Aides 1, 2 and 3? Can we specify some of the antecedent characteristics which predispose to behaviour of each kind?

Behaviour in any setting is partly predictable if the past experience of the participants with prominent features of the present situation are known. In the administrative situation just described, the rules stand for constituted authority, and the official is expected to identify himself with this authority, and to conform to its prescriptions. The administrator who departs from the rules for the benefit of the client is himself assertive against authority. If he departs from the rules to discriminate against the client, he aggrandizes authority.

The clearest case of anti-authoritarian liberality in the application of rules is that of Aide 1, who indulged those who displayed submissive approaches. The roots of his attitude were found to be deeply embedded in his relationship to authority in his family circle. He was a young man of 23. It was learned that his early family relationship was marred by frequent and violent quarrels between his parents, who were otherwise congenial and indulgent. Under these circumstances, he was unable to rely upon the emotional stability and indulgence of the environment. Very much attached to his parents, he did not express his resentments directly, neither did he completely repress his hatred of authority. He became conciliatory and diplomatic, endured inner discomfort and suffering, and became notably gentle and kind in dealing with all whom he fancied to be in trouble. Here was the basis of the relatively extreme sensitiveness which was exhibited in ignoring the rules for the benefit of non-aggressive clients.

His masochistic tendency and craving for affectionate indulgence made him susceptible to good-humoured wheedling and to similar passive approaches.

His discrimination against those who approached him aggressively is not at first sight consistent with the conciliatory pattern which has been described as typical of his approach to people. In the home and in all professional and social connections he was genial and detached, and was often known to be imposed upon by more aggressive natures. However, this was not the whole story. It appears that the enduring of discomfort was but the initial phase, and that this was followed by over-reactive efforts to escape from disagreeable situations. During his early days in the service, he was no doubt intimidated by the bolder approaches. As he became aware of his own tendency to take passive rôles in dealing with assertive people, he sought to escape from this passivity. His discrimination against aggressive clients is his second phase of adjustment to the situation confronting him.

Aide 2 had a stable and dependable relationship to her parents, but as a child she had been somewhat overshadowed by the physical attractiveness of a sister. The resulting resentment was not directly expressed, since she was attached to the sister and to the code of conduct sponsored by her parents. The evidence suggests that most of her hostility against the disappointing features of her family life was successfully repressed, although some mild difficulties of adjustment persisted. We noticed how she discriminated somewhat in favour of those who flattered or " kidded " her ; this suggests a strong craving for the affectionate attention which was to some extent denied in her family, owing to the attractiveness of the sister. Intimate knowledge of her reactions showed that she had moods of depression attended by reveries of self-pity. This tendency to devalue the self led to some suspicion of those who made advances toward her ; it was noticed that she frequently complained of those who tried to curry favour. Special tabulations of her administrative behaviour showed, in contrast to Aides 1 and 3, that she was very unstable in dealing with passive approaches, often becoming suspicious and discriminating against those whom she at first indulged.

Perhaps the comparative ease with which Aide 2 accepted authority in the home had something to do with her failure to project upon others such discomforts as she experienced. (We find no special indulgence of the non-aggressive, as with Aide 1, and no evidence of striking sensitiveness to the needs of others. Her connection with the relief service was considered by her to be temporary, and she looked forward to a business rather than a professional career.) There were, to be sure, slight traces of over-scrupulousness about what was expected of her. Thus in one administrative shake-up, another aide thought he had some authority over her. She resisted this firmly, but when it was clear that the new rules made this provision, she wholeheartedly accepted the situation. But when the demands of the regulations and the demands of the applicant were conflicting, she yielded to the more immediate and insistent ; hence her deviations in favour of active aggressive conduct.

Aide 3 was a young woman of 24, brought up in a stable

emotional environment and was a general favourite because of her physical beauty. Since her emotional development was unwarped, she took for granted the flattery and appreciation which was given to her by the environment, treated it casually, and was not much influenced by it, as confirmed by her reactions in the administrative situation.

Her counter-assertiveness in dealing with aggression had a very different basis from that of Aide 1. She was directly expressing her annoyance at being deprived of her customary indulgence.

III

This study of rules and their application corroborates the impressions of common sense, that personalities differ widely in their response to the same manner of approach. The data bring out quite vividly what is meant by the play of unconscious motives and past experiences in determining conduct. Observational methods of the type used here can be employed to promote self-knowledge among administrators of all kinds disclosing the effect of hitherto unnoted biases upon action. The source of these components of behaviour can be sought in the earlier history of the person.

Hence it is possible to lay the foundation for more impartial administration of rules, or at least for administration which, if not impartial, has frankly and not inadvertently rejected the ideal of impartiality.[1]

(b) THE CLIENT *

From the equilibrium standpoint, changes in any variable in a total situation involve substitutive changes among the other variables (including the political variables). When deprivations are inflicted suddenly upon many members of a community, as in economic depression, efforts to re-establish income involve concerted action toward the authoritative patterns and practices of the community (including government). If restitutions in the form of " relief ", and presently of " recovery ", occur, the former equilibrium is reinstated ; but prolonged failure to re-establish income leads to the re-definition of the local equilibrium on a new level (by revolution).

Special interest attaches to the study of those who respond

---

[1] See also the next chapter.
* From *American Political Science Review*, 1934.

to deprivation by acting with maximum directness upon the environment, since their rôle is very important in political re-adjustment. We may say that they are probably recruited from among those who have had most experience in asserting themselves in situations of the type now confronting them ; and also that they include those who have made relatively large demands on the world, and hence have suffered relatively large recent losses.

Recasting in more definite form for purposes of this investigation, we may say that those who display aggressive behaviour toward public relief authorities are probably those who have had most experience with relief agencies, and with government ; that they have previously been assertive against authority in general ; that they have been experienced in manipulating a personal rather than a material environment ; that they have made relatively large demands on the real world for gratification, and suffered most substantial recent deprivations. The situation in which the relief clients find themselves is thus conceived to elicit behaviour which has been organized in earlier situations involving relief, government, authority, and persons ; and it is seen as an incident in the sequence of claims and deprivations in the careers of the persons affected.

The study of aggressive behaviour in Chicago in 1932–3 [2] is of interest to theorists of political development since it discloses the situation in a major centre of industrial capitalism in the interior of a continent far removed from the radiating nucleus of Communism, and remote from the anti-Communist dictatorial movements in Europe. The year during which these observations were conducted was marked by the emergence of one of the most spectacular of these defensive dictatorships in Europe, bringing the pattern somewhat closer to Chicago, especially in the psychological sense, because of the large numbers of persons there of German or Jewish origin.

While several industrial centres in Western Europe were in acute crisis, the extent to which crisis exhibited itself in Chicago was mild indeed. Rarely did the clients on public relief resort to other than individual symbols and individual efforts to get what they demanded. This comes out very clearly in the sample reported upon in this study ; and it is confirmed by supplementary investigations of the organizations in the name of the unemployed, and of organizations which frankly adopted some

---

[2] See the preceding chapter.

" revolutionary " name. From the data collected in 1933 we have established some bases of comparison which may be utilized in following the subsequent transformations of aggressive behaviour, especially the possible growth or further decline of resort to organized methods of rendering individual demands more effective. If the centre of revolutionary and counter-revolutionary dictatorship moves closer to Chicago, the accompanying re-definitions of behaviour may be very clearly exhibited by studies conducted by the present method ; if additional layers of the population become " radicalized ", we shall see whether their characteristics square with the indications found in the present inquiry.

This particular investigation was conducted by procedures which are in some respects novel. It was decided to devise a standard method of recording the behaviour exhibited by relief clients and to see whether the " aggressive " group (contrasted with a " submissive " group) was recruited from among those anticipated on the basis of our hypotheses. The missing personal data could be secured from the case-records prepared independently. A sample of 100 aggressives and 100 submissives was selected from the total number observed, and their case-histories tabulated, with results which are reported here. The 200 were selected from clients with whom there were five or more rated contacts. Examination of the census data for 1930 was made in order to determine the representativeness of the sampling. Checking against the community by means of such indices as population composition, occupation, home-ownership, and rental revealed that the sampling fell within the community norms.

The first hypothesis as to a possible differential between the aggressives and the non-aggressives related to the degree of familiarity achieved through length of contact with the Halsted district of the Unemployment Relief Service and agencies similar to it in purpose and procedure. Tabulation of the data revealed that the bulk of the aggressives made first application during the eighteen months from July, 1931, to December, 1932. The bulk of the non-aggressives made application during 1933. Taking broad averages, the typical aggressive would have had the advantage of two years' experience with the Halsted district office, the non-aggressive but one year.

Tabulation of the data relating to previous experience with welfare and relief agencies indicated that 60 per cent. of the aggressives had contact with social agencies between 1911 and 1930 and 68 per cent. of the non-aggressives between 1930 and the present. The typical aggressive had contact with welfare and relief agencies dating back to 1926, the typical non-aggressive since 1930. The first hypothesis, therefore, relating to previous experience with similar public and private agencies was documented rather impressively by the above summarized differentials.

The relationship at the relief office was judged, secondly, as one of applicant and government. Previous contact with government, it was conjectured, would play a predisposing rôle. Government as defined here includes party authorities, such as precinct captains or ward committeemen. Both frequency and type of previous contact with government are relevant. Governmental or party authorities could have played an indulgent rôle by giving jobs, interceding at the relief office, or conferring bonus or disability allowance for war service. Governmental authority could have played a penalizing rôle by imposing sanctions in all degrees of severity ; and it could have played an impartial rôle, granting citizenship, calling to jury service, or judging between parties in civil suit.

TABLE I—POLITICAL JOBS

Kind of Employment.	Percentage.	
	Aggressives.	Non-Aggressives.
Election canvassing and employment	9	0
Permanent job	11	1
None	80	99

Table I indicates that 20 per cent. of the aggressives had some kind of government employment as opposed to 1 per cent. on the part of the non-aggressives. Eleven per cent. of the aggressives once had relatively permanent work with some governmental agency. This clear differential can be interpreted as yielding two insights into the problem. First, the aggressive had seen government from the " inside " ; second, he had so manipulated politicians in the neighbourhood that he was rewarded with this employment.

A similar interpretation would hold for Table II, where, it appears, 17 per cent. of the aggressives as opposed to 5 per cent. of the non-aggressives had resorted to political intercession at

TABLE II—POLITICAL INTERCESSION

Number of Letters.	Percentage.	
	Aggressives.	Non-Aggressives.
1	7	4
2	6	1
3	3	0
4	1	0

the relief station. The differential is even more impressive if one considers the frequency of intercession, for the figure would then be 27 per cent. to 6 per cent. Contact with authority in the form of precinct captains, aldermen, ward-committeemen, state senators and representatives, and federal congressmen indicates, first, evidence of familiarity with authority, and, second, evidence of the facility of the aggressives in exploiting manipulative techniques.

The question arises as to the effect of a penal contact with government. Here we are dealing with an offender against that part of the *mores* which has been crystallized in law. Such an offence is penalized in all degrees of severity. Presumably the gravity of the offence would be commensurate with the severity of the punishment. We may therefore consider the following tables in terms of the degree of the penal sanction, assuming that the gravity of the offence would be indicative of the degree of aggressive behaviour involved in the offence.

TABLE III—PENAL CONTACTS WITH PUBLIC AGENCIES

Number of Contacts.	Percentage.	
	Aggressives.	Non-Aggressives.
0	78	89
1	15	8
2	5	3
3	1	0
4	1	0

Table III records penalties applied by agencies such as the Court of Domestic Relations, the Juvenile Court, or the Juvenile

Protective Association. The sanction may be in the form of an admonition, close supervision of the family, and in some cases imprisonment for desertion or for non-payment of alimony. The supervision of the children by the Juvenile Court or the Juvenile Protective Association usually involves some punishment of the parent or parents, such as taking the children out of the home or subjecting the home to close supervision. We find 22 per cent. of the aggressives with one or more contacts with these or with similar agencies, contrasted with 11 per cent. of the non-aggressives. Differential damage at the hands of these agencies can be interpreted as contributing to aggressive behaviour in so far as contact with governmental authority would render it a more familiar symbol; damage at its hands would provoke resentment against government; and offence would indicate earlier aggressive behaviour.

TABLE IV—OFFENCE AGAINST " MORES "

	Percentage.	
	Aggressives.	Non-Aggressives.
Offence . . .	37	7
Arrest . . .	20	3
Imprisonment . .	11	2

The offences recorded in Table IV are those for which there are penal sanctions, some of which have not been applied, possibly because of clemency, non-discovery, or non-apprehension. The ratio of 37 per cent. to 7 per cent. for the incidence of offence among the aggressives as contrasted with the non-aggressives yields a clear differential in respect of this important factor. The differential of 20 per cent. to 3 per cent. in arrests and 11 per cent. to 2 per cent. in imprisonments is again significant as indicating the gravity of the offence.

Contact with the courts in civil suits and evictions was also judged as a predisposing factor in the orientation of the client in the relief agency. Tabulation of this data indicated a contrast of 29 per cent. to 19 per cent. with respect to such contact. Being a party to eviction proceedings or a defendant in a civil suit would involve, because of the poverty of the individuals under consideration, some loss or damage through the agency of government. It is probable that such damage would be attributed to government, and serve as a source of resentment against governmental authority.

The hypothesis was verified that conflict with non-governmental authority and with non-legal *mores* predispose toward aggressive behaviour. Non-governmental authority refers to family, church, occupational, and similar relationships—parents, priests, employers. It refers also to uncodified usage and social bias, the sanctions for which are less palpable. The early family history of these individuals not being readily available, only a few of the many possible indices were isolated.

The following offences against the *mores* or authoritative standards were considered to be revealing : 10 per cent. of the aggressives as contrasted with 1 per cent. of the non-aggressives had offended by drunkenness and disorderly conduct ; 4 per cent. of the aggressives as contrasted with 1 per cent. of the non-aggressives were guilty of petty thefts ; and 16 per cent. of the aggressives as contrasted with 2 per cent. of the non-aggressives had deserted their families one or more times.

Intermarriage and church attendance were also considered as relevant indices to previous anti-authoritarian behaviour. The two cases of intermarriage which most gravely flouted authority were found among the aggressives, a white-coloured intermarriage and the marriage of a Jew and a Gentile. Seven per cent. of the intermarriages by aggressives were between Protestants and Catholics ; there were none on the part of non-aggressives. Thirteen per cent. of the aggressives married outside their nationality as compared with 5 per cent. of the non-aggressives. In summary, 26 per cent. of the aggressives, as compared with 8 per cent. of the non-aggressives, married outside their affiliations. We have here an index, first, to anti-authoritarian, anti-*mores* behaviour, and second, to the relatively wider range of social affiliations within which the aggressives operated.

The neighbourhood from which the sampling was taken was one in which church attendance is more or less taken for granted. Consistent non-attendance would thus represent a relatively serious break with the community norms. Six per cent. of the aggressives, as contrasted with 1 per cent. of the non-aggressives, had made such a break.

The relationship between complaint aide and client has been predicated as firstly, a relief, secondly, a governmental, thirdly, an authoritarian, and fourthly, a personal relationship. What background factors would lend facility to the client in manipulating a personal, in contrast with a material, environment? Three factors were judged to be peculiarly relevant, and many of the above and following indices may be used as cross-references. The first relationship was occupational. A distinction can be drawn between occupations in terms of the objects upon which the individual operates, whether persons or machines and materials. Is the individual a salesman, a foreman, a street car conductor? Or is he a mechanic, a machine tender, a common labourer? Seventeen per cent. of the aggressives, contrasted with 9 per cent. of the non-aggressives, dealt with persons in their occupations.

The second factor was formalized collegial affiliation, such as union and lodge membership, where an individual might acquire facility in stating his demands and working with others. Twenty-four per cent. of the aggressives, as contrasted with 9 per cent. of the non-aggressives, were members of the trade unions.

Education is an index to the acquisition of such a significant skill in dealing with persons as verbal facility. Forty-five per cent. of the aggressives, and only 10 per cent. of the non-aggressives, had completed grammar school.

The client-aide situation was also defined in the preliminary hypotheses as one of demand and deprivation ; hence the demand and deprivation history of the client would play a significant rôle in the evocation of aggressive behaviour. Under this heading of claims, or demands and deprivations, are considered the income, debt, and wealth history, the relative familiarity with the environment, the age range, danger in or shifts in occupation, and physical and psychic damage. The claims or demands referred to are those made upon the real environment, upon the socially defined goods and services.

Tabulation revealed that the majority of the aggressives earned incomes between $21 and $40 a week, the majority of the non-aggressives between $10 and $30. The relative wage of the aggressives and the non-aggressives would serve as an index, first, to their differential demands upon the values in society, second, to their skill in asserting these demands, and last, to their damage through unemployment and application for relief.

Six per cent. of the aggressives and 1 per cent. of the non-aggressives had formerly occupied some managerial position. This contrast would seem to reflect relatively higher claims upon income and prestige, relatively higher skill in assertion, and relatively more grave damage by the present reversal of rôles.

A supporting index to differential claims, skills, and deprivations is revealed in tabulation of rents before and after application for relief. The majority of the aggressives paid rents between $16 and $25 before application for relief, between $11 and $20 after. Among the non-aggressives, we find the majority paying rents before application from $5 to $20 and after application from $5 to $15.

Tabulation revealed that the average age of the aggressive was 35 years, that of the non-aggressive 42 years. The majority of the aggressives were between 31 and 35 years of age, of the non-aggressives between 41 and 45. The older the individual the more have his aims and wants been circumscribed and defined. May we assert that younger persons over-assert their claims, since their expectations are higher?

Relative familiarity with the environment exercises some effect upon claims and skills in assertion. How can this particular environment be characterized? First, it is an American community; second, it is an urban community; and third, it is an industrial community. Presumably individuals who have spent the larger part of their lives in an American, urban, industrial community will have higher claims upon the values, and relatively more skill in asserting them than others. Our hypothesis was that as the background of an individual was in degree dissimilar to the current environment, his claims and his skills in assertion would diminish.

Seventy-one per cent. of the aggressives, as contrasted with 42 per cent. of the non-aggressives, were native-born. Of the non-aggressive total, 26 per cent. were Negroes, deriving in great part from Southern rural communities. The contrast between 71 per cent. and 42 per cent. for the incidence of foreign and native origins becomes more impressive when one examines Table V.

Here we discover that 92 per cent. of the native-born aggressives, as contrasted with 42 per cent. of the native-born non-aggressives, came from urban areas. Fifty-eight per cent. of the aggressives, as opposed to 18 per cent. of the non-aggressives, were born in metropolitan industrial areas. These figures document the hypotheses.

TABLE V—URBAN-RURAL ORIGINS (MOBILITY)

	Percentage.	
	Aggressives base 71.	Non-Aggressives base 42.
Metropolitan areas . .	58	18
Mid-west urban . .	20	6
Mid-west rural . . .	5	9
West urban . . .	1	0
West rural . . .	0	0
East urban . . .	0	0
East rural . . .	0	0
Southern Negro urban .	8	18
Southern Negro rural .	1	45
South-west white urban .	5	0
South-west white rural .	2	4

Twenty-three per cent. of the non-aggressives and 9 per cent. of the aggressives owned real property. The figures represent the purchase of small homes, heavily encumbered and constantly threatened with foreclosure. This application of the peasant-rural pattern in a new social context reveals an immigrant, peasant, non-aggressive trait; the trait of seeking orientation in the soil of the relatively unstable, urban, industrial environment. The claims of the non-aggressive would seem to be timid, or minimal, as contrasted with those of the aggressive.

TABLE VI—CITIZENSHIP

	Percentage.	
	Aggressives.	Non-Aggressives.
By birth . . .	71	42
Naturalization . .	22	41
First papers . .	6	4
No attempt . .	1	13

In Table VI, the figures on citizenship are recorded. Citizenship here is interpreted, firstly, as a skill in orienting one's self in a new social context; secondly, as a contact with government; and lastly, as an index to relative attachment to old loyalties. The most significant figures are those listed under " no attempt ", where the proportion of 13 per cent. to 1 per cent. in favour of the non-aggressives, despite the greater proportion of foreign-born in this category, indicates the relative reluctance of the non-aggressives to make new formal allegiances and their relative unfamiliarity with a new social context.

Having endured danger is important in predisposing an individual to cope vigorously with danger and uncertainty. Sixteen per cent. of the aggressives in the relief situation, compared with 5 per cent. of the non-aggressives, had worked in occupations considered as " dangerous ", judged by the high insurance rates.

A tabulation of occupational mobility revealed that 28 per cent. of the aggressives, as opposed to 13 per cent. of the non-aggressives, had three or four shifts in occupation. Greater mobility in these cases signified relatively more skills, wider social affiliations, and higher claims upon values.

Six per cent. of the aggressives, as compared with none among the non-aggressives, had been characterized in the case-records as neurotics. Ten per cent. of the aggressives, as compared with 6 per cent. of the non-aggressives, suffered from some permanent physical impairment.

The technique of field observation by participant-observers coming into frequent but casual contact with the persons studied is capable of being widely adapted and extended. The findings of this particular research make more definite the characteristics of those who are active in relation to the social environment when deprivations (in this case, withdrawal of income) are inflicted upon them. Aggressiveness was found to be most frequent among those who were familiar with this particular type of situation, and with government. Aggressiveness was also frequent among those whose careers showed the greatest deviations from conventional behaviour, and who were most experienced in managing a personal environment. Aggressiveness was frequent also among those who in the past had made relatively large and successful claims on the world for the available values (such as income), and whose deprivations were both large and recent. This should be qualified by saying that the persons studied were not recruited from those who in prosperous times were in the upper income brackets of the community ; but within the lower income layers, the relationship between substantial income and assertiveness in deprivation is clear.

More intensive case-studies will disclose more minute circum-stances which generate aggressiveness ; more extensive observa-tion of collective behaviour will keep these intensive researches in sound relation to the distribution of typical incidents along the career lines of those who live in a given culture at a given period.[3]

[3] Acknowledgment for co-operation which made the completion of this study possible is due primarily to Miss Sonya Forthal, of the University of Chicago, who contributed both to the formulation of problems and to the readings of case-records. Thanks are due also to Mrs. J. D. Twitchell and Miss Margaret Diers, both super-visors of the Halsted district of the Unemployment Relief Service during the progress of this investigation ; to Mr. Joseph L. Moss and Mrs. Edward J. Lewis, director and assistant director, respectively, of the Cook County Bureau of Public Welfare, who permitted the investigators to read the case-records ; and to the complaint aides who consented to make the ratings over the six-month period.

CHAPTER II

SELF-OBSERVATION : RECORDING THE FOCUS OF ATTENTION *

How can a busy man keep useful records ? Time, or rather, the lack of it, is the enemy—a deadlier enemy than lack of objectivity.

The inventive ability of man has not yet been adequately applied to the task of recording his own experience. There is, of course, the diary and the journal. However much we welcome the invaluable jottings of a Gideon Welles, we are always left thirsting for more. Besides, the essay-diary is highly selective and yet it chooses on the basis of no explicit principle. When we leaf through an essay-diary we learn that our diarist saw the head of a manufacturing corporation, who came to protest that he had been passed over in the awarding of government contracts. How many other manufacturers succeeded in reaching the secretary for the personal presentation of such a complaint ? We scan through the diary, and sure enough we find another instance, and then a second or a third. Are these all the manufacturers who got through to him during his years in office ? Or is the complaint so frequent that the secretary makes a note of it only on rare occasions ?

It is the problem of representativeness that plagues anyone who relies on the essay-diary. What is the typical, not the special, appointment pattern of a given official ? How much time is taken up in contact with members of the department, of other government agencies, with private persons ? Among the private persons, how many are seeking favours—appointments, revisions of contract, news of government decisions ? How many requests are acceded to and how many are postponed or rejected outright ?

A high degree of disciplined interest in human affairs is enough to keep some busy policy-makers busy on elaborate records. We cannot, however, assume this disciplined interest on the part of all " practical " men. We do not imply that the task of obtaining better sources for political science and history must be postponed to a future in which policy is in the hands

* Especially written for the present publication.

of conscientious and skilful historians and political scientists. Many active executives can be brought to understand how the keeping of certain records will yield facts that bear directly on their own efficiency.

If more "practical" men are to make better records, two requirements must be met. First, a question must be asked that seems to them worth answering. Second, a procedure must be available that does not interfere with their work.

One bureau chief in the federal government was having "budget trouble". A veteran of the public service in Washington, he commanded the destinies of a bureau devoted to the collecting, reporting and scientific processing of certain data. For several years his appropriation had remained stable, though the relative trend was downward. Although somewhat concerned about the failure of his operation to expand, he had done very little about it. We had occasion to ask him if he had ever looked objectively at his own methods of administrative management in search of a clue to the static position of his bureau.

We outlined to this bureau chief a simple method of keeping a record of his contacts. The purpose was to take note of every person who came to his focus of attention in the course of the day. He provided himself with a packet of slips (four inches by six, fitting snugly into the inner pocket of his coat). Only a slip a day was used. At the top he wrote the date. In the upper left-hand corner he wrote the letters " In ", and halfway down " Ex ". By the symbol " In " was meant " internal " ; by " Ex ", " external ". The words referred to persons inside or outside his bureau. Each time the chief had a face-to-face contact, he entered a tally opposite " In " or " Ex ".

The results of this extremely simple procedure were somewhat revealing to the administrator. Well over nine in every ten contacts were with members of his own bureau—this included all waking hours of the day. This bureau head was a bachelor who was interested in the scientific phases of his work and practically submerged himself among his immediate colleagues. The test period of record-making brought sharply to his focus of attention some of the facts about his ordinary focus of attention. The effect was to underline some of the factors explaining the static position of his bureau. He, as the representative of the collective life of this organization, was not impressing himself or the enterprise upon the environment upon which it depended for survival. The degree to which the chief had " internalized " his contacts was given even greater emphasis when he noted among the " Ex " entries whether the person, though outside his bureau, was inside his department, or whether he was in another executive agency, in Congress, or in private life. During the trial month the record showed not a single legislative contact and less than 10 per cent. of total contacts outside his department.

The executive secretary of a trade association, who used the same procedure for a test period, was also surprised to see how exclusively his focus of attention was controlled by members of the association. Well over nine in ten contacts were intra-organizational. Although nominally serving the membership as an intermediary with the external environment, he was actually doing a different job. He decided to alter his tactics and to extend the scope of his effective impact on the environment beyond the association.

A very different pattern was revealed by a college president, who made use of the recording system. Living in a large metropolitan area, constantly drawn into civic and other activities, the president realized—when the question was raised—that he had cut down his faculty-student associations. But he was shocked to see how far this process had gone. The test run showed that over half of his contacts were external, that is, with other than faculty, students, employees, board of trustees, parents of students. Of the internal contacts, more than half were with members of the board of trustees and with one dean. Sensing the degree of alienation that had grown up between him and the campus, the president deliberately modified his pattern of contact in order to multiply his direct associations with faculty and students.

Even such a simple " home-made " procedure as the record slip calls for the solution of many small technical problems. The basic idea is so flexible that any number of adaptations can be made. Suppose two people are interviewed at the same time ; a small circle can be added at the top of the tally to indicate the extra person. Suppose one person is an insider, the other an outsider ; the tally can be under " In " and the small circle blacked in. If the contact is by telephone, a small circle may be drawn at the bottom of the tally. Contacts outside the office can be shown by a dotted line.

Beginning with this humble device, a never-ending set of complications can be added in order to answer questions that

arise out of the material.   An administrator may want to know
in detail which persons or groups inside or outside of his organization occupy his attention.   The superintendent of a hospital
may examine his relations with trustees, medical staff, nurses,
administrative and technical employees, patients and families of
patients.   All these constitute the "internal" environment.   In
addition, he may want to distinguish certain groups in the
external environment—physicians, press, clergy, teachers, politicians, business men.   The persons or groups selected may be
shown by letters (A, B, C, . . .) put by the side of each tally
mark.

The basic procedure can be extended to characterize the
significance of each contact.   To what extent does the administrator play an indulgent rôle by granting requests and distributing rewards ?   To what extent does he play a deprivational rôle
by turning down requests and applying disciplinary measures ?
Every administrator is necessarily a source of both indulgence
and deprivation ;   however, it is possible for him to exercise
some measure of control over the balance.   The objective situation may justify tipping the balance one way or the other, but
even under adverse conditions, such as retrenchment, the administrator can often find ways of diluting his negative function.
Occasions may be created to justify a distribution of praise and
the giving of tangible reward.

With regard to technique, the administrator who gives the
indulgence may enter a plus at the top of the tally ;   a deprivation can be registered as minus (other contacts are assumed to
be zero).   If in the same relationship the interviewer is simultaneously plus and minus, overlap can be shown by circling the
signs.

The executive is himself a target of a stream of indulgences
and deprivations from his environment.   He may be the object
of praise or criticism, of promotion or reprimand.   If he cares
to describe the impact of life on his own experience, the administrator may modify the recording procedure in order to make
the appropriate entries.   One convenient expedient is to put
the plus and minus signs that refer to acts by the administrator
above the tally and to put signs referring to acts toward the
administrator below the tally.   If desired, entries can be very
detailed in regard to the nature of indulgence or deprivation.
In the interest of reliability, the record-maker may lay down
a series of instructions for his own guidance.   Plus 1 or minus 1

may be defined to mean indulgence or deprivation in accordance with Standard 1, power. Standard 2 may be income. Subdivisions of these and other standards may be carried out indefinitely. The power relation, for example, may be broken down into many categories. Plus 1A may be defined to mean acceptance of proposals by others ; such a notation would be used when another person accepts a suggestion. Minus 1A would mean a rejection. Plus 1B may mean approval of a past official act ; minus 1B disapproval.

The simple framework of the procedure can be adapted to more and more precise observations. Each contact may be timed approximately by dividing the slip horizontally according to hours or minutes. Slips may be filled out for each half-day or hour. With slight adaptation, the basic procedure can be applied to collective situations like committee meetings. On a diagram, movements can be assigned to individual participants according to the position they occupy. A tally can be made when anyone participates. New tallies can be entered for each successive five minutes occupied by an individual in continuous participation. (Purely formal remarks, such as unsuccessful efforts to address the chair, may be omitted.) The diagram (see p. 284) shows a record-sheet for two hours of the deliberations of a certain committee. The chairman was Number One, although it is plain that the weight of participation was borne by one, five, nine, thirteen, fifteen and eleven. Eight of the sixteen members did not speak. This was an evenly divided committee of experts and laymen. Number Five was an expert who was examined chiefly by layman nine. On this occasion, most of the experts were silent.

Even these rudimentary committee records are informative about individuals and groups. Number Fifteen is reputed to be a silent man, yet his record of committee participation, taken over a test period, showed that he was among the upper third in loquacity. When the order of participation was indicated on the slip (5—13—5—13—15, etc.), it was obvious that the participation pattern of Number Fifteen brought him in late in the discussion. Number Eleven was an " early talker " but had little to say when the " heavy talking " was done close to a vote. There was apparently a tendency for the experts to take part most actively when they sat next to or opposite a layman rather than another expert. The laymen, it appears, were somewhat inhibited under these circumstances.

```
                              ////  //
                              ////  ////
  ////        8    7    6    5    4    3    2        ////
  ////   9   ————————————————————————————————  1   ////
             10   11   12   13   14   15   16
              //   ////       //// /       ////
```

A record was kept of those who said " Yes " or " Yes, but "
to someone else, and those who said " No " or " No, but ".
The check at the top of a tally meant the former ; a cross meant
the latter.   A record of the person who approved or disapproved
was kept by marking his number on the slip in parentheses by
the side of a speaker's number.   Certain persons stood out as
" Yes " or " No " sayers ; the ordinary pattern was mixed.

These recording methods may be used by an individual to
discover many perhaps unanticipated characteristics.   Categories
may be used to describe the approach of the other person (or of
the self) much after the pattern described in the study of the
relief-client relationship.[1]   The type of aggressive or passive
approach may be assigned code numbers and added to the tally
of a given contact.

The basic procedure can be adapted to the recording of
what is said by the parties to a given contact relationship.   An
administrator may want a record of the frequency with which
he hears criticisms of himself, his organization, his policies, or
his ideas.   Every symbol (key word or phrase) can be assigned
a code number, to be recorded on a slip each time it occurs.
These methods of content analysis are more fully described in
connection with a study of what appears in the mass channels
of communication.[2]

These record-making devices are not only contributory to
personal insight ; from a scientific point of view they improve
the source materials of history and therefore of science.   These
methods are especially valuable in improving our knowledge of
the focus of attention, the long-neglected dimension of personal
and social reality.   To account for what people do it is necessary to describe their environment in two ways : as surroundings
and as milieu.   By surroundings we mean what the outside observer
sees regardless of whether the people who are there see it.   The
surroundings of a great power include all the people and resources

[1] See the preceding chapter.
[2] Cf. Lasswell, Harold D., and Associates, " The Politically Significant Content
of the Press : Coding Procedures ", Journalism Quarterly (March, 1942).

of all other powers in the world. The *milieu*, on the other hand, is what comes to the focus of attention of the members of a great power. The same surroundings do not always evoke the same milieu.

Since it is comparatively easy to find reliable ways to describe surroundings, the data available to political science is comparatively ample with respect to population, material resources, technical equipment, output, resource consumption and depletion. For a century the Marxist theory of social change has emphasized the formative significance of material resources and the instrumentalities of production upon society. To trace the sequence through from technology : new processes of production determine a new division of labour ; the new division of labour determines differences in social ideology and institution. It is emphasized that speculative ideas about science are socially insignificant until they modify technology, and speculative ideas about social norms have no weight unless they serve the needs of those who benefit from or are threatened by a new division of labour.

Historical and comparative research has often demonstrated high degrees of causal connection between changes in the environment and changes in institution and ideology. There is, for instance, no doubt of the broad correlation between life in a factory and the institutional and ideological pattern represented by trade unions.

Despite these successes, the conception of a close tie between technology and ideology has been a treacherous guide. We find, for example, prodigious time-gaps between exposure to a factory and trade union activity. Moreover, there are erratic time-gaps between form of trade union activity in one work situation and another. It is customary to minimize these gaps by calling them survivals of an earlier ideology or by speaking of lags. More refined methods of analysis and description will enable us to interpose two series of data between environment, in the sense of surroundings, and ideological and institutional effects of a " final " sort (e.g. trade union activity). The milieu of one group of workers may include clarifying explanations of why adjustments in wages and working conditions may be necessary to maintain the firm in production, while the milieu of a similarly situated group of workers in another plant may contain no such clarifying explanations. Unless our methods of data-gathering provide us with this type of material, we are at very least prone to underestimate the time relations between the " final effect " and the environmental (surroundings) change. Moreover, it is by no means demonstrated without these data that the choice of " final " effect is justified.

Some of the procedures outlined here are capable of providing many of the facts needed about the focus of attention of those who occupy known positions in the social process.   The ideal is to obtain more satisfactory records of the typical foci of attention (milieux) of policy-makers, advisers and members of the rank and file.

In this discussion, emphasis has been put upon self-observation as a means of describing those with whom one comes in contact and the content of what they say.   This is only part of the process of self-observation.   We may, in addition, take note of what we ourselves feel about the people with whom we are in contact.   We may take note of our expectations about the way in which the situation will develop.   In this is included our conceptions of goal and procedure for getting what we want (when the relationship is one in which objectives are consciously defined).   As a means of exploring the structure of expectation, demand and identification with which we enter any given series of contacts, we may make use of the technique of free fantasy (developed by Sigmund Freud for clinical purposes, though applicable to non-clinical situations).   Records of this type do not relate to the focus of attention (milieu) of the individual but to his predispositions and response.   It is important to keep these distinctions clear on both the conceptual and observational levels.   Unclarity in this zone has handicapped both the writing of history and the advance of political science.   Among political scientists, A. Lawrence Lowell and Graham Wallas have made the most valuable exploratory analysis of the function of attention in politics.   It has been impossible to implement their insights, however, in the absence of more adequate methods of recording empirical data.   Lowell's most significant suggestions are in *Public Opinion in War and Peace* (Cambridge, Mass., 1926). Nearly all of Wallas's remarkable essays are in point.

CHAPTER III

THE PROLONGED INSIGHT INTERVIEW OF FREUD *

The most abiding contribution of Sigmund Freud to the psychological and social sciences is his special standpoint for the observation of interpersonal events. Some of his own tentative applications of psychoanalysis to society have already been superseded, notably the formulations put forth in *Totem and Tabu.*[1] His distinctive terminology is in process of liquidation as his work merges with the broad stream of scientific development. But his observational standpoint remains ever fruitful for the investigation of interpersonal relationships ; it is capable of providing data which disconfirm, as well as confirm, his early hypotheses.[2]

What are the significant characteristics of the standpoint taken up by Freud ? The first mark of interest to us is intensiveness rather than extensiveness. It is prolonged and complex. Also, the psychoanalytic standpoint is scientific and therapeutic. It is used to obtain data which are relevant to the confirmation or the disconfirmation of a body of explanatory propositions, and it is used to heal disease. The mere fact that intimate data are assembled by psychoanalysts does not distinguish them from many other specialists. Intimate details have been collected for a great variety of non-scientific and non-therapeutic purposes in the history of culture. Political élites have been particularly active in obtaining intimate knowledge to further the survival of the politician rather than to contribute to science or health.[3]

The élites of ceremony, both magical and sacerdotal, have been active in procuring intimate data. In many primitive societies the confession of any violation of a rule is itself sup-

---

* From *The American Journal of Sociology*, 1939.
[1] A convenient statement of the objections to " the crime that began culture " is by Opler, M. E., " The Psychoanalytic Treatment of Culture ", *Psychoanalytic Review*, vol. 22 (1935).
[2] Freud's most extended direct contributions to social science are *Group Psychology and the Analysis of the Ego* (London, 1922) ; *The Future of Illusion* (London, 1928) ; and *Civilization and Its Discontents* (London, 1930).
[3] An Indian classic of political science, the *Arthasāstra of Kautilya*, dating perhaps from 300 B.C., furnishes an elaborate set of instructions for the spies who study the reliability of officials. The royal household, and many other groups within and without the kingdom, are objects of special surveillance (see Ch. XI in Book I, and other sections of the treatise).

posed to save the individual or the group from the deleterious consequences of the violation.[4]   The sacred élites were probably the first to use the study of the self as a means of improving the efficiency (and " morality ") of individuals.   The confession partly served this purpose.   It also supplied valuable information to the members of the group, and bound the confessing person by strong emotional ties to the symbols of the group as a whole. Secret societies have often copied for secular purposes the practices of sacred orders.[5]

The use by Freud of intimate data supplied by the subject as a means of healing is consonant with a long medical tradition.[6]   But it is evident that many therapeutic relationships which involve intimacy are not based upon science.   Sufferers may be exhorted to take a more optimistic view of life in order to rid them of suicidal thoughts.   This is not science until it is associated with a. naturalistic theory of how persons come to entertain such thoughts, and under what conditions admonitions by authoritative persons may diminish their occurrence.   Such scientific theories are formulated by Freud to account for both disease and recovery.   Thus the psychoanalytic standpoint may be said to be scientific in two different meanings : it is instrumental for science in so far as it is used to obtain data which confirm or disconfirm explanations and it is applied science in so far as psychoanalysts claim to base whatever methods of healing they employ upon such explanations as, it is alleged, have already been confirmed to a certain extent.[7]

[4] Secular élites have fostered the confession as a means of expediting legal administration.   Confession leads to alleviation of sanction in nearly every code.
[5] Thus Adam Weishaupt was deeply influenced by the model of the Society of Jesus when he founded the Illuminati in Bavaria in the eighteenth century for the purpose of spreading the new secular knowledge.   A novice was required to draw up a detailed report for the archives of the order containing complete information about his family and his own life.   He was to list the titles of all the books he possessed, the names of his personal enemies and the occasion of their enmity, his own strong and weak points of character, the dominant traits and interests of his parents, their acquaintances and friends, and many other items.   Monthly reports on his conduct were required, supplemented by special reports from time to time. The " Illuminated Minervals " were to become expert psychologists, especially by studying the behaviour of the little group of minervals who were placed under their direction.   It was hoped that the study of man would be so complete that two results would follow : the reformation of the world and adequate self-knowledge (Stauffer, Vernon, New England and the Bavarian Illuminati, New York, 1918).
[6] See Janet, Pierre, Psychological Healing (London, 1925).
[7] Secular élites other than those mentioned utilize personal history data on a large scale.   Specialists on the poor, the delinquent, and the immature have recently displayed a great expansion of interest in this direction.   A convenient guide to this literature is Young, Pauline V., Interviewing in Social Work (New York, 1935). The modern profit-seeking élite has made use of personal data for purposes which range all the way from espionage to the understanding of the relationship of business

A third characteristic of the psychoanalytic standpoint is that it is an interview.

Even within the psychoanalytical interview situation, there may be great differences. Sándor Ferenczi experimented with active therapeutic methods in which the rôle of the analyst as the source of prohibitions and prescriptions is exceptionally prominent.[8] The orthodox procedure is more passive ; but, although it is true that the free-association procedure puts initiative in the hands of the subject, the psychoanalytical interviewer is far from mute, as is implied in what Karen Horney called the " myth of the silent analyst ".

In the numerous modifications which have been made by psychiatrists in the orthodox interview of Freud, the rôle of the guiding hand of the interviewer has been both minimized and exaggerated. The group analysis of Trigant Burrow is supposed to take the leader off his authoritative pedestal and to add the analysis of himself to the material furnished by the group.[9] The modifications introduced by Alfred Adler and Carl Jung gave prominence to the part played by the physician, decreasing the scope of the subject.[10]

A fourth characteristic of the psychoanalytic standpoint is that it is a special kind of interview—the insight interview. The intention of the interviewer is to increase the skill of the subject in self-analysis. That this aim is not the exclusive property of psychoanalysts is evident from the allusion which has already been made to one of the purposes of the Illuminati. In that society, however, the transmission of skill was associated with indoctrination. The outstanding characteristic of the psychoanalytic procedure developed by Freud is the concentration upon skill without indoctrination. The interviewer offers interpretations to the subject which are intended to assist him in recognizing and avowing with serenity those aspects of himself which

to the total cultural environment. The psychoanalytic standpoint may be taken up as " instrumental for science " in business situations. But science is the proximate goal under these circumstances of an activity whose ultimate goal is some other value. An account of the experiments at the Western Electric Company's plant at Hawthorne is found in Mayo, Elton, *The Human Problems of an Industrial Civilization* (New York, 1933), and in the publications of T. N. Whitehead and other collaborators.

[8] Cf. the papers on " Technique " in *Further Contributions to the Theory and Technique of Psychoanalysis* (London, 1926).

[9] Consult Galt, William, *Phyloanalysis : A Study in the Group or Phyletic Method of Behaviour-Analysis* (London, 1933).

[10] For a mature and stimulating statement of the physician-patient relationship read Carl Jung's essays on " Problems of Modern Psychotherapy " and " The Aims of Psychotherapy " in his *Modern Man in Search of a Soul* (London, 1933).

are concealed from full waking awareness, or which are recognized, if at all, with great perturbation of affect.

The distinction between the insight interview and the indoctrination interview may be understood by contrasting psychoanalysis with the confession conducted by the élite of any ecclesiastical organization. There are certain similarities : in both the subject may relate anecdotes from his past and avow many impulses in his present life. But the differences are more profound than these comparatively superficial likenesses. The confessor classifies the incidents and the intentions communicated to him according to a preconceived set of normative standards. They are sins or not ; and, if sins, there are prearranged penances and indulgences. He makes use of the affects which are liberated in the confession to strengthen the sentiments toward the symbols affirmed by the church. Positive affects are directed toward the church ; negative affects are turned against non-conforming aspects of the self and others.

The psychoanalyst does not categorize the incidents and intentions which are told him into preferential categories, nor does he deal in penance and indulgences, nor does he focus loyalties upon symbols. He insists that the subject persevere in his quest for, and his skill in, self-analysis. He stimulates the subject to consider different propositions (interpretations) which relate his acts (including self-styled transgressions) to the rest of his personality. This includes the study of the part of the personality which regards the rest of it as transgressing (namely, the conscience, or super-ego). The subject discovers his own preferences in the act of subjecting them to such naturalistic analysis. Some remain ; others dissolve. The conscience itself is subject to profound modification.[11]

The interviewer systematically challenges the interpretation accepted by the subject (especially if these stem from the analyst). The interviewer knows that subjects are disposed to acquiesce in interpretations as a means of appeasing the anxieties of the moment ; yet this may stand in the way of deeper insight.

It should be recognized that insight is a limit which is approached and not reached. There are cases in which the existing neurosis is comparatively mild, in which the self-analytical goal and skill of the subject are low, when psychoanalysis is a long-drawn-out and relatively useless outlay of

[11] Some of the implications for ethical theory have been stated in Smith, T. V., *Beyond Conscience* (New York, 1934).

energy. There are cases in which neurosis may pass into psychosis if the anxiety level of the subject is increased. Indeed, one of the practical problems of psychoanalysts is precisely when not to analyse.[12]

In addition to such gross considerations as these, psychoanalysts are affected by a host of factors. At the beginning they were physicians with little understanding of the cultural context in which they and their patients were living. Some of them were not far removed from the traditional bias that diseases are processes which are destructive of the integration of the tissue bundle which comprises the individual. The use of the psychoanalytical method itself led to the discovery of the relevancy of cultural configurations. Gradually they reached out for a new whole whose integration-disintegration enters into the definition of health and disease. Increasingly health is defined as productive interpersonal relationships. But does every definition of productive not contain particular preferences of a particular culture?

Psychoanalysts, made more sensitive to cultural relativity than other psychopathologists, contribute to those who do not choose to include cultural adjustment in the definition of health, and search for a definition of this term which admits the possibility that healthy persons may be comparatively unsuccessful (maladjusted) in relation to prevailing preferences. Indeed, the definition sought is such that the acceptance of the norms of a given culture may be a case of disease. This might be true, for example, in the case of compulsive conformity as a means of escaping from the anxieties generated in the course of growing up within the culture.

By defining health as freedom from anxiety, the rejection of local norms is consonant with health when it is non-compulsive. An anxiety-free individual may recognize that he wants to perform acts which are viewed with hostility by the carriers of the culture which constitutes his environment. He may know that exposure will be followed, with a certain probability, by a change in the environment which constitutes a deprivation of a certain magnitude. He may perform the acts anyhow with a full view

[12] In semi-technical terms it may be said that the psychoanalyst tries to keep the anxiety level of the subject within the range of progressive adjustment. He wants to avoid such extreme concentrations of anxiety that the subject seeks to escape from the interview situation itself, or resorts to psychosis or conversion into somatic difficulties. The treatises by Otto Fenichel and Hermann Nunberg may be consulted in connection with the clinical aspects of psychoanalysis.

of this.   It must, of course, be said that, according to the definition of health accepted by most physicians, an individual who
rejects, that is, deliberately acts counter to, all survival opportunities offered by the environment, would not be called healthy.
Yet there are cases of suicide in which the critical physician is not
willing to make an off-hand diagnosis of neurosis or psychosis.[13]

Psychoanalysts become increasingly aware of the numerous
and subtle ways in which their own preferences diminish the
extent to which they approach the naturalistic ideal in their
relationships to the patient.   Intonations of voice may convey
approval or disapproval of professional or sexual attitudes of
the subject.

Some psychoanalysts discover that their own psychoanalysis
did not free them from compulsive acceptance of many of the
symbols and practices of the culture in which they happened to
be reared.

This insight gives rise to the suspicion that psychoanalysts,
in common with other psychopathologists, may obtain mitigation
of some of the neurotic symptoms of their patients by permitting
them to be displaced from primary to secondary symbols which
they leave unanalysed.   A stout affirmation of hostility to the
New Deal, to take a banal instance, may be passed without
challenge, and the hostilities of the subject may be displaced
more and more from symbols of reference to his wife or himself
to symbols of reference to political policies and groups.   If the
analyst is a political radical, he may find himself on the alert
against thoughtless repetitions of preferences for the *status quo*,
though he remains deaf to the voice of protest.   Strictly speaking, loyalties to secondary symbols of the environment are no
more exempt from the austere requirements of insight analysis
than loyalty to primary symbols.

It has been a sociologist with psychoanalytical training who
has coped most boldly with the problem of putting the psychoanalytical procedure itself in explicit relationship to the cultural-
historical setting in which it originates and survives.   Erich

[13] Among those who have struggled most strenuously to emancipate themselves
from the entangling tentacles of a particular culture—and of any culture—is Trigant
Burrow.   See his *The Biology of Human Conflict: An Anatomy of Behaviour, Individual
and Social* (New York, 1937).   A complementary process to separating health from
adjustment to a particular culture is the characterizing of some cultures or culture
patterns as themselves diseased.   An exhaustive and critical bibliography of the
application by psychiatrists of concepts of the pathological to society is Schneersohn,
F., " Zur Grundlegung einer Völker- und Massenpsychopathologie (Sozio-psycho-
pathologie) ", *Ethos*, vol. I (1925–6).

Fromm has characterized the conscious attitude of Freud toward his patients as one of tolerance, based upon relativism toward all preferences, and has posed the question of the nature of the unconscious attitude which supports it.   Fromm undertakes to demonstrate that this conscious liberalism of outlook is associated with an unconscious negative preference for those impulses which are tabooed by bourgeois society.   Hence Freud is said to stand as the representative of an order of society which demands obedience to certain specific prohibitions and prescriptions. This attitude is alleged to augment the anxiety level of the patient and thereby to diminish the probability that his resistances will be overcome and therapy will be successful.[14]

It is not within the scope of this paper to evaluate the foregoing affirmations but to indicate the profound problems which have received a rich, new context as psychoanalytic experience has advanced.   More and more psychoanalysts are discovering culture.   And, what is even more to the point, they are discovering culture as it operates within their own personalities during the prolonged intimacy of the psychoanalytical situation. They have a technique which they can incessantly use upon themselves in discerning the resistances within themselves which are attributable to the previously unsuspected incorporation of patterns of their own culture.   This tool for the awareness of culture can be employed by social scientists for the sake of insight into themselves in relation to the personality-culture manifold in which they are imbedded.   Skill in prolonged free fantasy, which is skill in self-analysis, becomes one of the indispensable tools of whatever social scientist is concerned with the fundamental problems of personality and culture.

The acquisition of skill in self-analysis by the routs of psychoanalysis is becoming more common among social scientists. Training in psychoanalysis which is undertaken less for therapeutic than for scientific purposes is called didactic analysis. Psychoanalytical training institutes are often willing to give special encouragement to the qualified social scientist who desires to enlarge his repertory of skills by means of psychoanalysis.

Those who acquire psychoanalytic technique, or who become familiar with the kinds of data which are revealed in the psychoanalytic interview situation, usually refine their own methods of observation in standpoints which are less intensive than the

[14] " Die gesellschaftliche Bedingtheit der psychoanalytischen Therapie ", *Zeitschrift für Sozialforschung*, vol. IV (1935).

psychoanalytic. It is safe to say that more care is now being given by social scientists to the recording of dreams, slips of the tongue, random movements, and possible somatic conversions than ever before.[15] Neurotic and psychotic personalities are sought after in different cultures for the sake of discovering the depth to which selected culture patterns are integrated in personality structure.[16]

The propositions which have been stated by psychoanalysis have been tremendously stimulating, even to those who were without the special training necessary to understand them fully. Among social anthropologists of standing who have been explicitly affected by psychoanalytical hypotheses, Bronislaw Malinowski and Margaret Mead have been particularly prominent.[17] Among sociologists, Erich Fromm [18] and John Dollard [19] are conspicuous examples. In the field of political sociology and psychology, the study of the genesis of attitudes toward authority has been given a new impetus.[20] The theory of law has not been unaffected, notably by way of Hans Kelsen.[21]

The result of inaugurating the study of the personality-culture manifold by the intensive method of Freud has been to make imperative the formulation of more serviceable concepts and to concentrate attention upon the observer's relationship to his field of reference. The Social Science Research Council's Committee on Personality and Culture has stimulated discussion and publication in the general field of methodology.[22]

[15] See, for an extreme example, Krout, Maurice, *Autistic Gestures : An Experimental Study in Symbolic Movement, Psychological Monographs*, No. 208 (1935).

[16] Bingham Dai, a sociologist with psychoanalytical training, has been engaged in such research at the Peking Union Medical College, Peking, China.

[17] An early book which reflects this interest in Malinowski is *Sex and Repression in Savage Society* (London, 1927) ; an early book by Margaret Mead is *Coming of Age in Samoa* (London, 1944).

[18] See his articles in the *Zeitschrift für Sozialforschung*.

[19] Notably in *Caste and Class in a Southern Town* (New Haven, 1937).

[20] See *Studien über Authorität und Familie*, ed. Max Horkheimer, Paris, 1936, especially the theoretical discussion by Erich Fromm. Allusion may also be made to Lasswell, *World Politics and Personal Insecurity* (New York, 1935) ; and Lin, Mou-sheng, " On Anti-statism " (University of Chicago dissertation, Chicago, 1937).

[21] A critical statement of Kelsen's position is in Cohen, Hyman E., *Recent Theories of Sovereignty* (Chicago, 1937), Chap. V. In America, Jerome Frank and Thurman Arnold have been appreciably influenced by psychoanalytical findings.

[22] Consult Dollard, John, *Criteria for the Life History* (New Haven, 1935) ; Mead, Margaret (ed.), *Co-operation and Competition Among Primitive People* (New York, 1936). Statements by Edward Sapir, Ruth Benedict, and L. K. Frank have been particularly stimulating. For a suggested method of mediating between the difficulties of the horizontal and the cross-sectional modes of studying personality and culture, see Lasswell, Harold D., " The Method of Interlapping Observation in the Study of Personality and Culture ", *Journal of Abnormal and Social Psychology*, vol. XXXII (1937), pp. 240-3. The *rapprochement* has been stimulated by the activities and the

A growing necessity of scientific work, made even more pressing by the emergence of psychoanalysis, is the calibrating of observations made from standpoints of varying degrees of intensiveness. Suppose we are told by one who has elicited a life-history document from Mr. A. that Mr. A. is a self-centred person who blames his environment for his difficulties, and that this trait has been stable in his personality for many years. Terms like self-centred and blame may be defined so that they refer to a very frequent use of complimentary expressions in alluding to the self, and of adverse references to the environment (pro-self, anti-other references).[23] The evidence for the stability of the trait is the lack of contradictory reminiscences about the early life of the subject.

How are such observations to be related to observations made from an intensive standpoint, such as psychoanalysis? If groups of persons who fitted the foregoing description from an extensive standpoint (S') were psychoanalysed, we might find that a certain proportion, say 70 per cent., would be described in a certain way by the psychoanalyst. The intensive observer (standpoint S'') might say that 70 per cent. were overcompensated persons, who were projecting certain accusations directed against themselves against the environment; and locate at a certain year the time when this trait was stabilized.

It seems safe to conclude this general statement of the influence of psychoanalysis on social science by the remark that we are on the threshold of rapid advance throughout the entire range of social scientific research, and that this advance will be enormously facilitated in the future, as in the past, by the work of Freud, and particularly by the insight interview which he invented.[24]

writings of specialists who are primarily physicians, notably Franz Alexander, Edward Glover, Karen Horney, James S. Plant, Theodor Reik, Harry Stack Sullivan, Robert Wälder, William A. White, and Gregory Zilboorg. Articles of general interest often appear in Imago, the Psychoanalytic Review, and Psychiatry (published by the William Alanson White Psychiatric Foundation, Washington, D.C.).

[23] For categories, see my " Provisional Classification of Symbol Data ", Psychiatry, vol. 1, No. 2 (1938).

[24] See also my " Verbal References and Psychological Changes during the Psychoanalytical Interview : A Preliminary Communication ", Psychoanalytic Review, vol. 22 (1935) ; " Objectifying the Psychoanalytic Interview (II) ", Psychoanalytic Review, vol. 23 (1936) ; and " Objectifying the Psychoanalytic Interview (III) ", Imago, vol. 23 (Vienna, 1937).

CHAPTER IV

THE WORLD ATTENTION SURVEY *

We gain insight into the lives of others when we know what they read, see and hear. This is one of the chief purposes to be served by any systematic survey of public attention. One general, though far from universal, human attribute is the tendency to overestimate the amount of attention given to the self by other persons. Everything concerning the precious ego is so intimate and immediate that it is difficult to accept a realistic

WORLD ATTENTION SURVEY

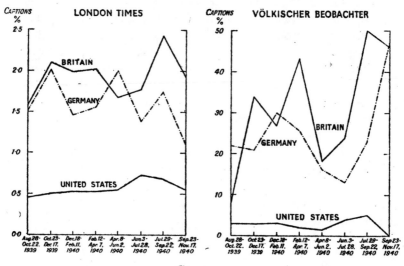

CHART I.

picture of what other people are thinking and feeling about us. We know this is true in our person-to-person relationships. It is equally true when we think of ourselves as Americans in contrast to Germans, British, or Russians. How much attention, for example, is being given to the United States by newspapers abroad, and what do the facts signify?

By means of a World Attention Survey it is possible to correct any tendency to overestimate the amount of attention given to the United States. Chart I reveals the comparatively modest

* From *Public Opinion Quarterly*, No. 3, 1941.

number of references to the United States appearing in two of the most influential newspapers in the world. Whether we speak of potential enemies, like Germany, or close friends, like Britain, we discover the comparatively small amount of attention paid to the United States during the early months of the current war.

Chart 2 is useful in correcting any false ideas about the extent to which the self is favourably or unfavourably presented to foreign peoples. The *Excelsior*, an important paper in Mexico

WORLD ATTENTION SURVEY

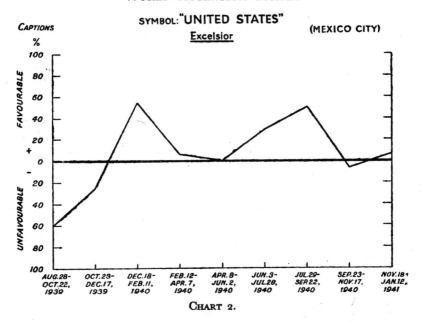

CHART 2.

City, was publishing news relatively unfavourable to the United States in the autumn of 1939. Since that time, the presentation of this country has been more favourable, or more balanced.

PUBLIC ATTENTION

The stream of public attention is related to policy. This is particularly true in totalitarian countries, where the Press and other agencies of mass communication are under strict discipline. Chart 3 shows something about totalitarian press strategy. The summer of 1939 was a period of active negotiation between Germany and the Soviet Union. The amount of attention paid to Germany in the influential Russian newspaper *Pravda* remained

WORLD ATTENTION SURVEY

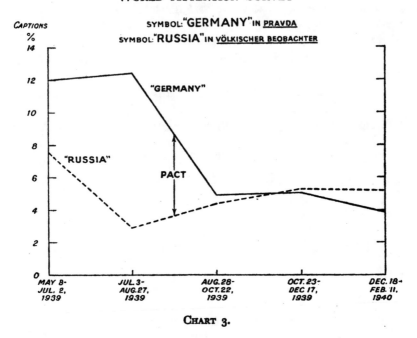

CHART 3.

WORLD ATTENTION SURVEY

ITALY

IL GIORNALE D'ITALIA

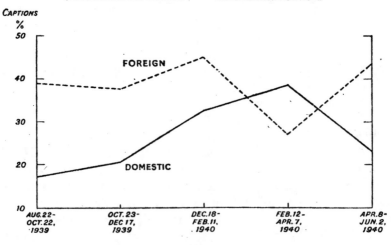

CHART 4.

steady during the summer. Not so the references to Russia in the *Völkischer Beobachter*. Here we see less and less attention paid to the Soviet Union, previously a target of bitter hostility. This indicated that Germany was clearing the path for a sudden change in diplomatic orientation, as was learned when the pact was announced.

Chart 4 exhibits totalitarian press strategy in another set of circumstances. As Italy moved toward the brink of war the amount of attention paid to foreign and domestic politics steadily rose ; but there came a time, as the crisis deepened, when the focus of attention was turned inward upon news of Italian politics. This was the phase, graphically shown in the chart, when attention to foreign political news dipped sharply. Shortly thereafter, attention flowed once more outward to the surrounding world.

Bridging Opinion and Action

The survey of world attention is able to supply us with data about many of the missing links in the process of political and social development. For a great many years scientific students of politics have been concerned about the connection between " material " and " ideological " factors. The propagandists of Marxism have contended for the primacy of the material over the ideological. Many anti-Marxists have indignantly rejected the primacy of the material and asserted the power of ideas in shaping society. It has been difficult to discuss these questions objectively for lack of data about ideological changes through time. Part of the deficiency is to be attributed to inadequate technique ; but this limitation is in process of being superseded. The symbols that come to the focus of attention can be objectively described, and their changes can be presented in convenient graphical form.

The attention survey is needed to supplement our knowledge of opinion and of material shifts in the environment. Between " opinion " and " material " change lie important intermediate events ; namely, the focusing of public attention. People cannot respond to an environment that is not brought to their notice. Hence we must describe the fluctuating focus of collective attention if we are to trace the connection between environment and response.[1]

---

[1] See Lasswell, *World Politics and Personal Insecurity* (New York and London, 1935), for a statement of the scientific importance of the focus of attention.

SCOPE AND TECHNIQUE

It is impossible to rely upon any single channel of communication if we are concerned with the total focus of attention. The charts in this article depict certain changes in the Press. A total survey would supplement them with data about other publications and about the contents of radio, newsreel and other agencies of mass communication. It should not be forgotten that the mass agencies themselves account for but a fraction of the daily span of attention. After all, most of the hours of the day are given over to other activities than reading newspapers, listening to broadcasts, or looking at motion pictures.

TECHNIQUE OF ANALYSIS

Something may be said about the technique of analysis applied to the contents of agencies of mass communication in this survey of attention.[2]   The general purpose of the technique is to describe the field of attention, to show the relative prominence of selected symbols, like the names of leaders, nations, policies, institutions. One index of prominence is appearance in a news caption ; the charts show the percentage of total captions (words) containing significant symbols. Where captions are missing, or de-emphasized (as on the editorial page), the number of inches (words) is taken.

In the interest of objectivity papers are described according to a code that is applied by workers who have learned how to use it. Coders are given regular tests to verify the comparability of their results. When the problem is to count the frequency of occurrence of explicit unit symbols—like " Germany " —the reliability is, of course, very high (99 per cent. agreement).

VALUE OF SYMBOLS

Since we are not only interested in the frequency of occurrence of specific symbols, but in the plus or minus character of the presentation, additional rules are laid down for coders. A *plus* presentation of a symbol puts it in a favourable light (an " indulgence ") ; a *minus* presentation puts it in an unfavourable setting (a " deprivation "). A symbol is presented favourably when shown as strong, or in conformity with a normative standard (of morality, legality, or divinity, for example). Properly applied, the reliability of plus and minus coding is high.

[2] See also Lasswell and Associates, " The Politically Significant Content of the Press : Coding Procedures ", in *Journalism Quarterly*, March, 1942.

It may be of general interest to publish some of the distinctions that have proved of value in content analysis. The following kinds of "indulgence" and "deprivation" may be distinguished :

1. INDULGENCE.

2. POSITIVE INDULGENCE REALIZED.

The gain is realized when the environment has already treated the object of reference indulgently ; BRITISH WIN BATTLE.

3. NEGATIVE INDULGENCE REALIZED.

Sometimes the gain is in the form of avoided loss ; BRITISH EVACUATE DUNKIRK SUCCESSFULLY.

4. POSITIVE INDULGENCE PROMISED.

Gains may be promised for the future, or presented as bound to occur in the future ; BRITISH VICTORY SURE.

5. NEGATIVE INDULGENCE PROMISED.

Avoided losses may be promised for the future, or shown as certain ; BRITISH SQUADRON WILL ESCAPE DESTRUCTION.

6. DEPRIVATION.

7. POSITIVE DEPRIVATION REALIZED.

Losses may already be sustained by an object of reference ; LONDON BOMBED SEVERELY.

8. NEGATIVE DEPRIVATION REALIZED.

Gains may have been blocked in the past ; BRITISH PLANS THWARTED.

9. POSITIVE DEPRIVATION THREATENED.

The losses may be referred to the future ; BRITAIN WILL LOSE.

10. NEGATIVE DEPRIVATION THREATENED.

Also blocked gains may be deferred to the future ; BRITISH ADVANCE WILL BE BLOCKED.

A representative—certainly not an exhaustive—list of standards is the following :

1. *Expediency (Strength)* describes the position of the object of reference in regard to such values as safety, power, goods, respect.

1*a. Safety.* Refers to physical integrity of persons, groups or things. BRITISH LIVES LOST ; BRITISH PILOTS RESCUED ; KING ESCAPES BOMBS ; AIR MINISTER DIES IN PLANE COLLISION.

1*ab. Efficiency.* Efficiency refers to level of performance of a function. HEALTH OF EVACUATED CHILDREN IMPROVES (biological efficiency) ; RESISTANCE TO DIPHTHERIA IN DEEP BOMB SHELTERS DECREASES.

1*b. Power.* In the most general sense, power is control over important decisions. It is measured according to the means of decision-making—fighting, diplomacy, voting, for example. GERMANS BREAK THROUGH AT SEDAN ; GERMAN PEACE OFFER REBUFFED ; LABOUR GAINS IN BY-ELECTION ; COURT REVOKES LICENCE OF COMMUNIST PERIODICAL.

1*bb*. *Efficiency*. SUPERIORITY OF NEW ANTI-AIRCRAFT DEVICES ; CLEVER AXIS DIPLOMACY WINS AGAIN ; PRIME MINISTER SPLITS OPPONENTS AND WINS VOTE OF CONFIDENCE.

1*c*. *Goods*. This term refers to volume and distribution of goods and services. FOOD RESERVES DOUBLED ; SOUTH AMERICAN MARKET PRESERVED.

1*cb*. *Efficiency*. WAR PLANTS 80 PER CENT. EFFICIENT ; HIGHLY SKILLED GERMAN OPTICIANS.

1*d*. *Respect*. BRITISH PRESTIGE SUFFERS ; BRITISH RESPECT GERMAN AIRMEN ; CAROL BOOED AS HE LEAVES ROUMANIA ; SPEAKS CONTEMPTUOUSLY OF ITALIAN ARMY.

1*db*. *Efficiency*. RIBBENTROP RECEIVED WITH GREAT POMP ; EXQUISITE COURTESY OF CHINESE DIPLOMATS EXTOLLED.

2. *Morality*.

2*a*. *Truth-Falsehood*. GERMAN LIES ARE BOLDER utilizes a moral standard, the obligation to refrain from the deliberate dissemination of falsehood. B.B.C. STICKS TO THE TRUTH.

2*b*. *Mercy-Atrocity*. GERMAN ATROCITIES MULTIPLY—the term " atrocity " makes use of a moral standard to justify acts, the obligation to refrain from inflicting unnecessary cruelty in the conduct of war. GERMANS RESCUE BRITISH SAILORS.

2*c*. *Heroism-Cowardice*. The obligation to act courageously ; RISKS LIFE TO RESCUE COMRADE ; SOLDIER DESERTS WOUNDED COMRADE.

2*d*. *Loyalty-Disloyalty*. The obligation to serve a common purpose ; ALL SECTIONS OF POPULATION PATRIOTIC ; FIFTH COLUMN ACTIVE IN NORWAY.

3. *Propriety*. The obligation to learn a conventional code ; GERMANS ARE A CRUDE AND BARBAROUS PEOPLE ; HIS MANNERS ARE PERFECT. If a code is deliberately violated, we have an example of disrespect (1).

4. *Divinity*. The standard is an obligation to abide by the Will of God ; GOD IS ON OUR SIDE ; GOD WILL PUNISH OUR ENEMIES.

5. *Legality*. The standard is the obligation to abide by law ; JAPANESE GOVERNMENT VIOLATES INTERNATIONAL LAW ; COURT UPHOLDS INTERNATIONAL LAW.

6. *Beauty*. The standard is æsthetic ; BEAUTIFUL EQUIPMENT

DESIGNED BY UNITED STATES OF AMERICA ; HIDEOUS GERMAN ART ON DISPLAY.

7. *Consistency.* The standards are logical relationships among propositions ; HITLER CONTRADICTS SELF ; CHURCHILL STATES LOGICAL CASE.

8. *Probability.* Probability of a statement with no imputation of deliberate falsification (2) ; EINSTEIN'S THEORY CONFIRMED.

9. *Euphoria-Dysphoria.* The standard is agreeable or disagreeable subjective states ; TERROR GRIPS BRUSSELS (terror is dysphoric) ; FESTIVE SPIRIT IN ROME (festive spirit is euphoric). " Hate " is dysphoric unless explicitly qualified ; GLORIOUS HATE SUNG BY POET.

10. *Omnibus.* Statements fusing many standards ; THE UNSPEAKABLE HUN.

INDEX OF NAMES

INDEX OF SUBJECTS